Encyclopedia of
Mythological Objects

T0055176

Encyclopedia of Mythological Objects

THERESA BANE

McFarland & Company, Inc., Publishers
Jefferson, North Carolina

LIBRARY OF CONGRESS CATALOGUING-IN-PUBLICATION DATA

Names: Bane, Theresa, 1969– author.
Title: Encyclopedia of mythological objects / Theresa Bane.
Description: Jefferson, North Carolina : McFarland & Company, Inc.,
Publishers, 2020. | Includes bibliographical references and index.
Identifiers: LCCN 2020018826 | ISBN 9781476676883 (paperback : acid free paper) ∞
ISBN 9781476639208 (ebook)
Subjects: LCSH: Mythology—Encyclopedias. | Folklore—Encyclopedias. |
Legends—Encyclopedias. | Religion—Encyclopedias.
Classification: LCC BL312 .B36 2020 | DDC 201/.303—dc23
LC record available at https://lccn.loc.gov/2020018826

BRITISH LIBRARY CATALOGUING DATA ARE AVAILABLE

ISBN (print) 978-1-4766-7688-3
ISBN (ebook) 978-1-4766-3920-8

Front cover image © 2020 Svetlana Turchenick/Shutterstock

Printed in the United States of America

*McFarland & Company, Inc., Publishers
Box 611, Jefferson, North Carolina 28640
www.mcfarlandpub.com*

For Frank J. Merriam.
Thank you for a lifetime of friendship.

Table of Contents

Preface

This encyclopedia of mythical items may well be the first of its kind, a volume dedicated wholly to naming and describing in as much detail as provided in the original source material the magical abilities of the possessions and weapons of folkloric heroes and gods. To maintain this book's integrity as a useful tool for academics and researchers, I did not include any items from fiction (popular or otherwise), save for those items originating from traditional fairy tales.

As there are no other books of this specific subject matter on the market to compare against, every precaution was taken to ensure that the items chosen for inclusion would prove useful not only to readers and researchers of today but also those of tomorrow and for years to come. For this reason, items that are modern literary and intellectual creations were not included. For instance, as a fan of the popular television show *Vampire Diaries*, set in the fictional town of Mystic Falls, Virginia (which, according to a map shown in one episode, is set about 12 miles southeast of my own home), I am aware that on the show there is an item said to be difficult to obtain: a daylight ring. This item, according to the lore of the show, when worn by a vampire, allows the creature to walk unharmed and unhindered in daylight. This bit of magic, being original to the mythology of *Vampire Diaries* and its spinoff companion shows, *Originals* and *Legacies*, will not appear in this book.

Items included are those mentioned (if not specifically by name, then at least by excellent description) as the amazing and powerful items utilized by the gods of the world's various religions. Of these, the ones that most immediately spring to mind, I suspect, would be those from the old Norse religion, most notably Mjolnir, the named hammer of the god of thunder, Thor. Due to Thor's popularity in recent times, thanks to modern comics and movie franchises, I imagine that many people are familiar with this weapon, though blissfully unaware of the amount of artistic license that has been taken with it for the sake of contemporary storytelling. Modern moviegoers are likely unaware that, according to the original mythology, Thor needed to wear his iron gloves (Jarngreipr) to wield the hammer in order to compensate for its short shaft.

Furthermore, I have also included the items named in the various folklore traditions from around the world, such as the stories of Reynard the Fox and the numerous works devoted to the lore of King Arthur. I did this not because they were works of popular fiction in their day, or because they are still being told centuries later, but because their message is timeless and as relevant to modern readers as it was to the first audience who heard these stories. Society chooses to keep these stories alive and, I imagine, will continue to do so for centuries to come.

Preface

As with my previous works—encyclopedic tomes on vampires, demons, fairies, monsters, spirits, giants, and mythic locations—I consulted and utilized every viable reference source that cataloged folklore, legends, mythologies, and world religions. In addition to art reference books, history books, and works of anthropology and sociology, most of my material came directly from the scriptures of our numerous religions.

Often I had to sit back and make hard decisions regarding what items would be included and which would not. There are few people who would rationally argue that BIRGA (the magical spear of Fionn mac Cumhaill), the ENDLESS BAG OF RICE (popular in Japanese lore), or the LASSO OF SIXTY LOOPS (from the Persian epic poem *Shahnameh*) actually exist. I feel it is safe to say that archaeologists are not holding their breath each time they put a spade into the earth in the hopes that this will be the time they unearth one of these items. However, the gopher-wood ark of Noah is a more complicated matter.

Was the world thrown into watery chaos to literally wipe the slate clean? Many of the world religions have such a tale, and in some of these stories a man built a box-like sailing vessel, collected up two of every animal (as well as his extended family), and survived the global natural disaster. Legend says the ark eventually ran aground in the mountains as the waters receded. It is not the most far-fetched story that comes to us from an ancient religion. In fact, the Old Testament book of Genesis gives fairly precise directions as to how such a vessel should be constructed. Biblical archaeologists have sought to discover this lost ark. Money is spent on expeditions to find it; sane, rational, scientific-minded people believe it is real and is just waiting to be discovered. For me, Noah's ark is less a mythological item and more akin to a crypto-archaeological artifact. As with the King Cheetah or Bigfoot—crypto-zoological animals sighted but yet to be proven to exist by science—I chose to err on the side of restraint and withhold its entry. Many other items are not included in this book based on this line of reasoning.

As a professional vampirologist—a mythologist who specializes in cross-cultural vampire studies—I work on several books at one time: aside from my primary focus, there are always multiple other books stewing on my mental back burner. As I do my research, I catalog every tidbit of information I can: typing out names and including descriptions, adding a source and page number in case I need to revisit the original material at a future date, and then electronically filing the information away under a broad heading, such as "demon," "fairy," "vampire" or (as in this case) "item." Eventually, I amass enough information to write my next book, an undertaking that takes about a year to complete once I sit down and set my mind to it.

From the beginning, I knew there would be enough material to warrant a book on the subject of mythological items, but I was concerned that it would be heavy with objects from Arthurian lore and Norse mythology. This worry reminded me to be more mindful of other cultures and seek out what would not be easy to find. A bit tricky, as I was not sure what I was looking for, precisely, but I was confident that I would recognize it when I found it.

In my reference library, I am partial to Phyllis Ann Karr's book on Arthurian mythology, *The Arthurian Companion*. Although this source contains her personal opinions and summations, it is well cited and lists various items not covered in other books.

A "must-have" book that I recommend everyone own a copy of is Heilan Yvette Grimes's *The Norse Myths*. Its only potential rival is, perhaps, H.A. Guerber's *Myths of the Norsemen*. Both of these books are rich enough to give readers a solid working knowledge of the subject.

As is my usual practice, I have made use of older books that claim to be the written transcriptions of the original oral folklore and tales traditionally told by the people of various nations. For me, the older the copyright, the better. In truth, I am partial to long, compound-complex sentences that are not afraid to embrace a semicolon. For my money, it matters not if the language and spelling is antiquated. Some of my best research material has a publication date from the mid- to late 1700s and 1800s. The language is richer, more verbose. These earlier editions best reflect the authors' original intent; it was a time when a researcher could speak the undiluted truth without fear of ridicule or having to water down ideas to comply with the mainstream thinking of the times. It's simply more pure.

After selecting which entries will make it into the book, I write each one out, mindful to include only the information cited in the source material; whenever possible, I like to use at least three sources per entry. I use fewer only when the source is highly reputable. I condense the entry to just the facts as they are presented and collate them. I do not elaborate or speculate. I include only information gleaned from reliable source material. My goal now, as it has been since my first encyclopedic work, is to offer brief, information-rich descriptions for each entry without adding my own commentary.

I would like to express my deep appreciation to my devoted and supportive husband, T. Glenn Bane, whose favorite question to me is "What letter are you on now?" Without him, this book would not have been possible.

Introduction

Once upon a time, about two and a half million years ago, ancient man picked up a stone, admired some quality of it, and fashioned it into the very first tool. It was this act that gave us an edge over the other primates. Tools and weapons made up for our lack of claws, teeth, and natural armor. Over the eons, our tool usage (combined with an ability to adapt to change) allowed us to capture the dominant position on the food chain, becoming not only an apex predator but also the dominant creature on the planet.

As with everything else under the sun, there were some ancient humans who were better at tool making than the other members of their tribes. This natural talent would give those individuals certain advantages, if not perks, among their people. As time wore on and humankind evolved, so, too, did that particular talent for constructing tools. Those who could do it well, who could construct a tool worth keeping and possibly even passing down to future generations, must have been held in high esteem. And their tools, with their superior craftsmanship coveted by others, well, they must have seemed downright magical.

Fire is a terrifying force of nature—it kills indiscriminately, damaging (if not destroying) everything it encounters. What- or whoever survives an encounter with fire suffers the painful wounds it leaves in its wake. Fire is so dangerous and deadly a force that nearly all living creatures are hardwired to fear it. With this in mind, can you imagine what it must have been like when the first person presented to his tribe his intentional creation of fire? It would have been an awe-inspiring and remarkable moment. It is no wonder that, thousands of years later, magical weapons from every culture on the planet would include, among their many other qualities, the ability to spew fire.

At some point, between 30,000 and 50,000 years ago, the hands of a sentient being put an intentional edge to a bit of flint, shaped it to their liking, and used it to skin an animal with ease. I wonder how wide those first set of eyes became when a laborious task was suddenly made easy. When a sharpened stone was tied to the end of a stick—a process that anthropologists call *hafting*—and used as a spear, that moment must have seemed inspired. I suspect that very first unnamed spear, the original one with the new and innovative advancement of being weaponized with a bit of flint secured to the end, became a prized possession. This proto-spear possessed the ability to kill a target faster and neater, not to mention with far less danger to its wielder. But its most remarkable feature was that it "worked" no matter who used it. Anyone could pick it up and kill with relative ease, skin their prize, and cook it with fire, preserving the food they did not immediately eat.

What strange and interesting times our primordial ancestors lived in.

I speak of these innovations—the use of stone-cutting tools, spears, and the willful cre-

Introduction

ation of fire—because these items were at one point in our time line the most important objects a person could have. With them, life was possible, even if not easy. Without them, death was imminent. Because these items were so important to the development of early human culture, society, and ultimately civilization as we know it, these possessions would take on a life of their own. A particular spear well crafted by a person of skill may have been given its own name and regarded as more than special because of its vital importance among the people who used it. It stands to reason that if a warrior could become renowned for his combat prowess and hunting capability, then his weapon (an extension of himself) might also be assumed to be "more than" another weapon. Only a warrior of particular skill could handle such a weapon, and therefore the weapon itself took on an identity and had its own story to tell. King Arthur is associated with Excalibur, but many knights used it; only Thor could wield Mjolnir.

It is no wonder that there are so many magical swords in our collective fairy tales, folklore, mythologies, and religions. Swords are widely symbolic. They represent authority, justice, power, protection, and righteousness, as well as the qualities we want our heroes and kings to have: courage, honor, strength, and truthfulness. To have a sword was literally to hold the power to change the course of history in the palm of your hand.

Certainly a skilled warrior with a sword made by a fine swordsmith would make for a good story character, but not a relatable one. It took time and resources to develop the specialized skills required to utilize a sword in such a way as to alter history. Normal folks are often the real heroes of some of our best and oldest tales. These are the people who sweat and toil for a meager existence and cannot afford to devote their energy to dreams of changing their stars, let alone actually doing it—unless, of course, they happen upon a magical sword. In these instances, possession of such a weapon is more than enough for the poorest and most downtrodden (though otherwise brave and good) farmhand to slay the dragon, rescue the princess, and win a kingdom of his very own where everyone lives happily ever after.

In the tales of King Arthur's court, all the knights of the Round Table had to prove themselves brave and noble warriors of great renown just to audition for a chance to be included in the outer circle. It then took quite the epic quest (literally) to join Arthur's innermost cadre. However, his most humble and devoted knights have the most impressive victories and heartfelt stories. Lancelot may have the eye of the queen and the ladies of the court, in addition to being a warrior supreme, but it is Sir Galahad who ultimately finds the Holy Grail.

When I began the enterprise of writing this volume, I wanted it to be more than the next encyclopedia in the line of encyclopedic tomes I have written. I wanted this one to enhance the other books, to add on to the story the other volumes told. When reading about Fenriswulf (Fenerriswulf/Fenrissulfrin) and his part in the Norse mythology, the fetters that bound him—Dromi, Gleipnir, and Laedingr—had a story of their own. Admittedly, theirs was not as grand or as in depth as the story of who they bound, but it was a tale that needed to be told. Not because I said so, but because the people who created the myth deemed it to be so when they named the items and told their tales.

When the time came to actually begin, I searched the Internet for a preexisting book covering the same subject matter. When I found none, I wondered why no one else had attempted this task. I already knew from personal experience that there are several role-playing game books from numerous companies that have supplemental volumes covering the subject I was tackling, but as both a game designer and a die-hard gamer, I already knew these books would not be helpful. To begin with, the objects would be described in the context of each game's system, and if the world that the item was to be used in had a preexisting backstory (and nearly all of them do), the item's description could not be trusted, as it would be altered to fit into the fictional world.

I was in uncharted waters, again, writing the book I wanted in my own library. And although any mythological book worth its cover price would contain some artifacts, I was not willing to settle for just the mainstream and most popular items from the most common folklores and mythologies. It was going to take untold hours of research to write the book I would want to buy for myself at any price.

This work contains the largest bibliography among my books for a reason: I was always looking for just one more entry to include. There were many items I did not include because they ultimately turned out to be real (such as elf arrows and Admiral Horatio Nelson's Chelengk) or at one time existed but have since been destroyed or lost (as is the case for the Scepter of Dagobert). Other items not included were artifacts claiming to be real (such as Confederate gold and the many small slivers of wood said to be taken from the cross upon which Christ was crucified). Additionally, I did not include the Veil of Veronica or the Shroud of Turin. Frauds or divine miracles? It is irrelevant for the purposes of this book. They each exist and thus can been examined, seen, and touched. Thousands of pages of research have been documented and published about these items. I'd say that they are about as real as it gets.

One of the first decisions I made was to exclude all spells or colleges of magic. I did not want to create a grimoire of any sort. Magical spells are uncountable, and if a researcher were ever to attempt to cover this subject, the effort would no doubt be limited to a single culture or type of magic. And even then, the variations of any given spell would be too broad to cover with any amount of confidence.

Also not included were the many amulets (used for protection against someone or something) and the talismans (used to attract or bring something to you) existing in various cultures, subcultures, and regional beliefs. Whether "real" or sympatric magic matters not—these charms are real; they can be purchased and directions for customizing and making your own from scratch can be read online. This is a topic worthy of its own book, but outside my range of expertise. However, if such a book ever does come on the market, I will most assuredly purchase two copies: one for reading and one for writing notes in the margins.

Each time I had to exclude a potential entry, I challenged myself to replace it. There were many items from ancient Celtic, Greek, Japanese, and Norse sources that were easy to find and that I had already included. I mined those myths more deeply, finding lesser-known magical accoutrements, gems, and weapons. I then turned my attention to lore and legends often overlooked in the West, such as those from ancient India, ancient Egypt, North and South American Indian tribes, Muslim lore, and Russia folktales, to name but a few.

Knowing that I would want my faith properly represented when written about by someone who does not share my beliefs I have attempted to maintain accuracy, neutrality and respect regarding all religions about which I write. I would hope that those who read this book will be seeking knowledge for the sake of better understanding of another culture or people and discovering why a particular item is so important in a specific mythos. I will never know

Introduction

what questions a person brings to one of my books, but I hope that within its pages I have supplied readers with enough information to find the answers they seek.

This book was written with the intent of being an all-inclusive encyclopedia of the many folkloric, legendary, and mythological items used by common folks, heroes, and the gods themselves. Each entry includes (whenever possible) the name of the original source material, as full a description of the item as the source materials provided, the magical abilities or innate power the item possessed, how it came into existence, and who owned or wielded it. Words and names presented in SMALL CAPS are cross references to their own entries elsewhere in the book, allowing the reader to follow the flow of information from one entry to another, linking together all the related knowledge of a single item.

Because information, language, and meaning change over time, some items' names have multiple spellings. Also, an item can have different names depending on which culture is telling its story. Something in Chinese folklore will not have the same name that it does in Korean or Japanese stories even though it is, for all intents and purposes, the same item in essentially the same tale. Because there are some items with many alternate names, I selected not the name I preferred, but rather the name that was most commonly used in all the works cited.

In such cases when an item has multiple names or variations on how its name is spelled, all alternates are listed directly under the main entry under the heading of "Variations." All alternative names are presented alphabetically and are also listed independently in the index.

THE ENCYCLOPEDIA

Abadi

In Roman mythology, Abadi was the stone that the god Saturn was given to eat by his wife, Ops; he believed it to be his newborn son, Jupiter.

In Phoenician mythology, Abadir was the name given to stones shaped like a cone; these were the oldest symbols of the Phoenician gods.

Sources: McClintock and Strong, *Cyclopedia of Biblical, Theological, and Ecclesiastical Literature: Supplement*, Volume 1, 4; Smedley, *Encyclopædia Metropolitana*, Volume 14, 13

Abyla

Variation: Pillars of Heracles

Abyla was one of the two pillars that the demigod and legendary hero Heracles toppled in classical Greek mythology, CALPE being the other. These pillars marked the end of the known world. Most versions of this story say Heracles traveled through many countries, and when he reached the frontiers of Europe and Libya, he constructed two pillars and placed one on each side of the Straits of Gibraltar. Collectively, the two pillars were known as the Pillars of Heracles. However, in one telling of the tale, originally a mountain stood in that place, but Heracles tore it asunder, separating it into two, allowing the sea to freely pass between the passageway he created.

Sources: Morris, *New Universal Graphic Dictionary of the English Language*, 1020; Smith, *A Classical Dictionary of Greek and Roman Biography, Mythology and Geography*, 398; Trumbull, *The Threshold Covenant, or The Beginning of Religious Rites*, 100

Acadine

In Sicilian folklore, the Acadine was said to be a magical fountain with the ability to reveal whether a document was truthful. According to legend, any document that contained falsehoods, when placed into the fountain, would immediately sink to the bottom, whereas truthful and sincere items would remain afloat. The fountain was also used, according to the lore, to test the fidelity, promises, and oaths people made; it was said that any who had broken their promises or otherwise proved to be false could not drink its water.

Sources: Brewer, *Dictionary of Phrase and Fable* 1900, 8; de Genlis, *Tales of the Castle*, Volume 3, 12

Acherontian Books, the

Originating in Etruscan mythology, the Acherontian Books were once said to be the most celebrated books of augury (meaning the interpretation of omens) in the known world. These books, which explained how to sacrifice animals to the gods so as to reveal aspects of the future through the release of their souls, supposedly came from the god Jupiter and were given to his grandson, a demigod named Tages.

Sources: Brewer, *Dictionary of Phrase and Fable* 1900, 8; Winning, "On the Aegypto-Tuscan 'Daemonology,'" 649

acqua della concordia

Variation: acqua della discordia

Said to be a magical potion used by Neapolitan witches, acqua della concordia was believed to be able to restore the love between children and their parents as well as the love between husbands and wives.

Sources: Andrews, "Neapolitan Witchcraft," 4

adamantine

A mythological substance, adamantine ("unconquerable" or "untamable") was noted for its ability to affect the gods. In classical Greek mythology, adamantine was the metal created by Gaea and used to make the grey-colored HARPE (or sickle—sources conflict) that her son Cronus ("Time"; Chronos/Cronos/Kronos/Saturn), a Titan and the god of time, used to castrate his father, Uranus ("Heaven"; Ouranos). This substance appears to be a key element in many Greek myths: An adamantine sword (also known as HARPE) was given to the demigod and hero Perseus by Hermes (Roman god Mercury), the god of animal husbandry, commerce, eloquence, fertility, language, looters, luck, sleep, thieves, trade, travel, and wealth, so Perseus would be able to decapitate the Gorgon Medusa. An adamantine sickle (or the sword HARPE—sources conflict) was used by Zeus (Roman god Jupiter), the god of fate, kings, lightning, sky, and thunder, to battle the Titan known as Typhon (Typhoes/Typhaon/Typhos). The wall of Tartarus had an adamantine gate guarded by the Fury Tisiphone, and the helmet of demigod and legendary hero Heracles was also said to be made of adamantine. Another Greek myth claims that the maiden Asteria, in order to escape the sexual advances of Zeus, transformed herself into a boulder and sank to the bottom of the sea; Zeus then caused the stone to rise to the surface and secured it to the bottom of the sea with an adamantine chain, thereby creating the island Asteria. In Norse mythology, adamantine chains were used to bind the god Loki to his underground prison (although other versions of the myth claim that it was the intestines of his own son).

Throughout ancient history, the words *adamantine* and *adamant* were used to refer to any extremely hard substance; by the Middle Ages, the word referred to diamonds.

Sources: Hansen, *Classical Mythology*, 96, 137–38; Hesiod, *Hesiod's Theogony*, 37–38; Smith, *Smaller Classical Mythology*, 6, 41, 59; West, *Hesiod: Theology*, 215

adaro

According to Melanesian folklore, adaro (loosely, "the shadow of fire") is the bad part of a soul's substance that lingers near a body after a person dies; this substance may develop into a ghost. If the adaro becomes a ghost, wizards can use these spirits to harm others; the cost of this hire is usually a pig. To protect against this danger, another wizard must be hired to have another adaro act in defense. The battle between these two spirits is said to happen with spears, invisibly, over the afflicted person. Occasionally, the ghost will manifest as a gar or flying fish and bite its prey—fatally.

Sources: Codrington, *The Melanesians*, 196; Mackenzie, *Myths from Melanesia and Indonesia*, 177–78, 206

adder stone

Variations: adder-bead, adder's gem, Adderstanes, aggri, Aggry, druidical bead, druid's stone, Glain Neidr, Gloine nan Druidh ("Druids' glass"), hag stones, Milpreve, serpent stone, serpent's eggs, snake's eggs, witch stones

Popular in ancient British folklore, the adder stone is described as round, perforated, and possessed of the ability to cure the poisonous bite of an adder. Often worn as a charm, these stones also provided many other services to those who wore them, such as curing whooping cough, warding off evil charms, preventing nightmares, protecting against eye diseases, and seeing through fairy and witchcraft glamours.

There are two different stories as to how an adder stone is created. The first claims the stone is actually the hardened saliva of a large clutch of serpents; the holes are made by the tips of the creatures' tongues. The second story of their origin claims the stones are in the heads of the adders and must be manually removed. In either case, it is said that a true adder stone will float when dropped in water.

Sources: Campbell, *Witchcraft & Second Sight in the Highlands & Islands of Scotland*, 84; Daniels and Stevens, *Encyclopedia of Superstitions, Folklore, and the Occult Sciences of the World*, Volume 2, 757; Grimassi, *Encyclopedia of Wicca & Witchcraft*, 201

Adhab, al

According to Islamic mythology, the prophet Muhammad owned a collection of nine different swords at the time of his death: al Adhab, al-Battar (see BATTER), Dhu'l Fakar (see DHUAL-FIRQAR), al Hatf (see HATEL), al KADIB, KOLAITE, MABUR, al MEHDHAM, and al ROFUB. Beyond its name, nothing else is known of the sword al Adhab.

Sources: Sale et al., *An Universal History, Part 2*, Volume 1, 184

Adylok

Variations: Adolake, Adyloke, Hatheloke

According to Continental Germanic mythology, Adylok was the good and swift sword forged by the legendary master blacksmith, Wayland (Gofannon/Volund/Weiland/Weyland) the Smith; it belonged to Torrent of Portyngale (Portugal).

Sources: Carlyon-Brotton et al., *British Numismatic Journal*, Volume 1, 14; Halliwell-Phillipps, *Torrent of Portugal*, 34

Aegis, the

Variations: **Aegis of Zeus**, SHIELD OF PERSEUS

In classical Greek mythology, the Aegis ("Violent Windstorm") was the breastplate, buckler, or shield belonging to Zeus (Roman god Jupiter), the god of fate, kings, lightning, sky, and thunder; it was adorned with golden tassels and bore the image of a *gorgoneion* (a Gorgon's head). When shaken, Mount Ida would shake; thunder would roll throughout the sky, sounding like the roar of a thousand dragons; and fear would fill the hearts of men. The Aegis was symbolic of storm clouds. Although it is not certain what the Aegis actually was (breastplate or shield), the magical nature of the item protected the bearer from any blow or spear attack.

Throughout the mythology, the shield was often loaned to Zeus's daughter Athena (Roman goddess Minerva), the goddess of crafts, military victories, war, and wisdom; rarely offered to his son Apollo ("to destroy" or "to drive away"), the god of archery, art, healing, hunting, knowledge, medicine, music, oracles, plague, prophecy, sun and light, truth, and young unmarried men; and, on at least one occasion, used by the hero Perseus.

Although it is typically said to have been created Hephaistos (Hephaestus; Roman god Vulcan), the god of bindings, the art of sculpture, fire, forges, metalworking, stonemasonry, and talismans, there are many stories about the origin of the Aegis: Euripides claimed that the original owner of the shield was a Gorgon and that it was made of goatskin (the image of the creature later added by Perseus to show his thanks). Another myth claims the Aegis is not a shield, but rather a cuirass (a piece of armor made of a breastplate and backplate hinged or otherwise fastened together) created by Athena from the skin she flayed off of the fire-breathing Chimera. A third story claims the Aegis is the tanned skin of the monstrous giant Pallas, also killed by Athena. A later myth says that Zeus skinned the goat Amalthea, who had nurtured him as an infant, in order to make the shield to do battle against the Titans.

Sources: : Berens, *Myths and Legends of Ancient Greece and Rome*, 106; Graves, *The Greek Myths*, 21–23; Kerenyi, *The Gods of the Greeks*, 50; Smith, *A Classical Dictionary of Greek and Roman Biography, Mythology and Geography*, 90, 139–40, 365, 369, 644, 1016

aegis of Athena, the

Variations: Aegis, Athena's aegis, shield of Athena

According to classical Greek mythology, the aegis of Athena (Roman goddess Minerva), the goddess of crafts, military victories, war, and wisdom, was a breastplate trimmed with tassels and emblazoned with the image of a gorgoneion so as to incite panic on the battlefield. As described by Hesiod, this item of awesome power was created by the smith of Olympus, Hephaistos (Hephaestus; Roman god Vulcan), the god of bindings, the art of sculpture, fire, forges, metalworking, stonemasonry, and talismans; it was he who embedded the head of the Gorgon Medusa into the aegis. Because the face of Medusa was so horrific to behold, it could literally turn a man into stone; in this way, the aegis was able to paralyze with fear any enemy who gazed upon it.

Sources: Roberts, *Encyclopedia of Comparative Iconography*, n.p.; Sears, *Mythology 101*, n.p.

aegis of Fafnir, the

Variations: aegis helm, dread helm ("aegishjalmr"), Frightener's helm, galea terrifica

In Norse mythology, the dragon god Fafnir (Fafner) wore a helmet named Aegis ("Helmet of Dread"). Originally owned by his father, Hreidmar, when Fafnir wore this helmet, it struck terror into the heart of any who saw it.

Sources: Coulter and Turner, *Encyclopedia of Ancient Deities*, 177; Morris and Magnusson, *The Saga Library*, Volume 2, 492; Pickering, *Beowulf*, xxxix

Sources

Aegishjalmr (AIG-is-hyalm-r)

In Norse mythology, Aegishjalmr ("Helm of Awe"/"Helm of Terror"/"Terror Helm") is the dark and terrifying helmet of Aegir, the god of the sea, probably created by Ivaldi's sons as part of the Hodd Niflunga. When the helmet is donned, the already frightening appearance of the god is intensified to such a degree as to fill a mortal with intense fear.

In Wagnerian mythology, in the *Volsunga Saga*, the Aegishjalmr is one of the items taken from the hoard of the dragon god Fafnir (Fafner) by Sigurd (Siegfried/Sigmund). Although it does not reappear again in this telling, the *Lay of Fafnir* and the *Lay of Reign* both say the helm has fear-inducing abilities; however, neither credits it with having any shape-shifting ability.

Sources: Dasent, *Jest and Earnest*, Volume 2, 88–89; Grimes, *The Norse Myths*, 254; McConnell et al., *The Nibelungen Tradition*, 162; Norroena Society, *Asatru Edda*, 333

aglaophotis

Variations: cynospastos, kynospastos ("dog-dragged")

A magical herb mentioned throughout books of magic and occultism, aglaophotis ("bright shining") was the name often used interchangeably with the peony in the ancient world. The second-century Roman author Aelian said that by night the plant shone brightly, like the twinkling of a star, but by day it was indistinguishable from similar-looking plants. According to Aelian, the only safe way to harvest the plant was by use of a dog. First, the animal must not be fed for several days; then a strong cord was tied around the base of the plant and looped over a tree branch, with the other end tied to the dog. Moving as far from the plant as possible, the dog was then offered savory food in the hope that it would uproot the plant. This method needed to be employed because it was believed that if a person removed the aglaophotis from the ground, they would be stricken with an illness such as blindness or perhaps, in extreme cases, die. With the rising of the sun, the dog would perish; the harvester would then bury the animal in the spot where the plant was extracted to appease the dog's soul. Only after a proper burial was given to the dog could the plant be safe to use to make cures for blindness and epilepsy.

The philosopher Theophrastus (371 BCE–287 BCE) warned that this plant could only be harvested during the night because if the woodpecker (a diurnal bird) were to see it happen, the person cutting the roots of the plant would lose their eyesight.

Aglaophotis was more thoroughly described by the Greek author, botanist, pharmacologist, and physician Dioscorides (40 CE–90 CE); he placed it in the peony family and, in his five-volume work titled *De Materia Medica*, determined it to be useful in warding off demons and the effects of witchcraft in addition to reducing fever.

Sources: Frazer, *Folk-lore in the Old Testament*, Volume 2, 388–89; Gerald, *The Herball or Generall Historie of Plantes*, 832; Salverte, *The Occult Sciences*, Volume 1, 32

agneyastra

Variations: agney astra, agniastra, agni-astra, agniratha, agni-ratha, fiery javelin of Brahma

Divine weapons (ASTRA) of fire described in the ancient Sanskrit epics (*Mahabharata* and the *Ramayana*) from ancient India, agneyastra are arrows, javelins, or some sort of non-edged projectile, like a rocket, imbued with tremendous power. This weapon plays an important part in each of the major Sanskrit epics. Each time the weapon is fired, it unleashes the firepower of a hundred flaming arrows (and thus it is commonly

used against an entire legion of men). It also is said to belch forth up to five fiery black meteors, trailing thick black smoke in its wake, filling the air with the scent of burning flesh.

Created from seven elements, agneyastra are difficult for scholars to describe physically, as the item also seems to manifest as a personal ability wielded by the user; additionally, the *Mahabharata* says the agneyastra can paralyze a person, "locking their senses fast in sleep," and can cause a great storm capable of bringing forth either fire or water from the heavens.

Those who utilize this weapon are known as Sastra-devatas ("gods of divine weapons"). Most commonly, the agneyastra is translated by scholars as "the fiery javelin of Brahma."

Sources: Balfour, *Cyclopædia of India and of Eastern and Southern Asia*, Volume 3, 44; Blavatsky, *Anthropogenesis*, 629–30; Dowson, *Classical Dictionary of Hindu Mythology and Religion*, 33, 271; Menon, *The Mahabharata*, Volume 2, 274, 355

Aindrastra

In Hindu mythology, an ASTRA is a supernatural weapon created or gifted by the gods to someone who then presides over the weapon. The wielder of an ASTRA is known as an astradhari.

Aindrastra was a divine weapon sent to Arjuna ("Spotless and Shining like Silver"), the heroic archer and main character in the Sanskrit epic *Mahabharata*. He used it to destroy a large portion of the Kaurava army, including the rakshasa Alambusa. However, Aindrastra was not as powerful an ASTRA as BHARGAVASTRA.

Sources: Menon, *The Mahabharata* Volume 1, 382; Subramaniam, *Mahabharata for Children*, 175, 179

Ajagav

Variations: Ajagava, PINAKA ("bow")

In the mythology of ancient India, Ajagav was the name of several bows, including the primitive bow of the god Shiva; it was said to have fallen from Heaven at the birth of the rishi Prithu, was made from the horns of a cow and a goat, and had all the colors of the rainbow. In earlier texts, the bow Ajagav is called PINAKA ("bow"). Two other owners of a bow with this name were the heroic archer and main character in the *Mahabharata*, Arjuna ("Spotless and Shining like Silver"), and Mandhatr. Because of its divine origins, Ajagav is considered an ASTRA.

Sources: Garg, *Encyclopaedia of the Hindu World*, Volume 1, 264; Kramrisch, *The Presence of Siva*, 92, 469; Sorensen, *An Index to the Names in the Mahabharata*, 27

akasha

In Sanskrit, the word *akasha* ("sky" or "space") refers to the base material found in all things; it is used in Buddhism, Hinduism, and Tibetan Bon to describe the experience of creative energy. It has no form and cannot be seen, tasted, or touched; the only characteristic it can manifest is sound or vibrations. Akasha is one of the five elements.

In more modern times, the idea of akasha has developed into a sort of comprehensible world memory—a vast, ethereal tablet of sorts—which contains all the knowledge of the world, the universe, and life itself. It is believed that this information may be accessed through a variety of methods, such as astral projection, conversing with spirit guides, and meditation (to name but a few). This concept is more commonly known as the Akasha Halls or the Akashic Records.

Sources: Dalal, *Hinduism*, 17; Hammer and Rothstein, *Handbook of the Theosophical Current*, 122

Akshaya Patra

In Hindu mythology, Akshaya Patra ("inexhaustible vessel") was a golden receptacle; the god of the sun, Surya, gave it to Yudishtira so he could feed the people who followed him into the Dwaita forest for his 12-year banishment. Each day the receptacle would be full of food, and it would remain so until Draupadi, the daughter of King Drupada of Panchal and mother of the Upapandavashad eaten from it; after that, it would not produce any more food until the next day.

Sources: Satyamayananda, *Ancient Sages*, n.p.; Srivastava, *Decoding the Metaphor Mahabharata*, n.p.

Alatyr

Variations: Ala'tyr, Father of all Stones, Latyr (see LATYR STONE), Latygor ("Stone"), Ldtyr, Vsem Kamnjam Kamen ("The All Stone")

In Russian folklore, Alatyr is a magical stone with the ability to heal; it was placed in the center of Booyan Island upon the World Tree and is guarded by two monsters. The first monster is a gigantic bird named Gagana, armed with copper claws and an iron beak; the second is an enormous snake named Garafena who lies in wait atop a bed of gold. Beneath the World Tree, there is a river whose water carries some healing properties (thanks to Alatyr's effect on the water).

Alatyr is invoked in many magical spells and incantations; it is believed that if it is not called upon, the spell will fail.

Sources: Bailey, *An Anthology of Russian Folk Epics*, 398; Dole, *Young Folks History of Russia*, 51; Jakobson, *Word and Language*, 624; Ralston, *Songs of the Russian People*, 375

albadara

Variations: LUZ, Os sacrum

In Arabic folklore, the albadara is a bone in the human body that defies destruction. According to the lore, at the time of resurrection, this bone—the sesamoide ("seed"; the bone of the first joint of the big toe)—will be the seed of a new body to be created.

Sources: Brewer, *Dictionary of Phrase and Fable* 1900, 57; Quincy, *Lexicon Physico-medicum*, 39

Ale of Immortality

Variation: Goibniu's ale (Gobanos)

In Celtic mythology, the Ale of Immortality was an intoxicant and a drink of the gods; it was first brewed to be consumed at the Feast of Ages hosted by Manannan mac Lir (Mannanan, Mannanos). When consumed by mortals, it causes elation and confers immortality by preserving them from old age, disease, and death, in addition to possessing various other desirable qualities. (For instance, after Angus Og drank the Ale of Immortality, four swans would fly over him as he traveled.)

In a tale from the *Book of Fermay*, Bodb Dearg gave the Ale of Immortality to his swine. Each day he would butcher and consume one, only to have it return to life, fit and healthy again, the following day.

Sources: Gray et al., *Mythology of All Races*, Volume 3, 51; Hastings et al., *Encyclopædia of Religion and Ethics: Picts–Sacraments*, 901; MacKillop, *Myths and Legends of the Celts*, n.p.

alectoria

Variation: alectorian stone

Common folklore tells us that the alectoria—a dark crystalline stone no larger than a bean, found in the intestines of capons who have lived for seven or more years—is imbued with magical properties. If a person carries the stone, they will be rendered invisible. However, if the stone is held in a person's mouth, it will grant a number of magical abilities, such as allaying thirst; bestowing honor (or preserving the honor of those who have already acquired it); ensuring the love of another; freeing those who are bewitched or otherwise under the influence of a magical spell; helping to regain a lost kingdom or gain a foreign one; making a wife agreeable to her husband; and rendering the user eloquent, constant, and amiable.

Sources: Daniels and Stevens, *Encyclopedia of Superstitions, Folklore, and the Occult Sciences*, Volume 2, 722, 752

Alfrothul

Variations: Alfqdul, Alfrodul, Alfrodull

In Norse mythology, Alfrothul ("blessed of the elfs" or "elf-beam") was the name of the sun prior to the great battle of Ragnarok; during the battle, it was consumed by the wolf Hati Hrodvitnirsson. Before Alfrothul was devoured, it gave birth to a daughter who became the new sun.

Sources: Crossley-Holland, *The Norse Myths*, 78; Grimes, *The Norse Myths*, 10, 254

alfskot (AHLV-skawt)

Variation: Elveskud

According to Norwegian folklore, when a person succumbs to a particular type of illness, they are said to have been hit with alfskot ("elf-shot")—that is, the arrows used by the Alfar, a race of elfs. Small, flint arrowheads (which are rare and seldom found) are said to be evidence and are worn as a powerful charm.

Sources: Salisbury and South Wales Museum, *Some Account of the Blackmore Museum*, 167; Wilson, *Prehistoric Annals of Scotland*, 180

alicorn

Variations: unihorn, unicorn horn

Present in many folklores and mythologies, an alicorn is the proper name for a unicorn's horn (the name originated with unicorn scholar Odell Shepard). The horn, once removed from the animal, is said to retain many of its magical properties, foremost of which is the ability to cure any disease. Additional abilities include being the antidote to any poison; curing colic, cough, cramps, epilepsy, gout, heart palpitations, melancholy, plague, pestilence, rabies, scurvy, and ulcers; serving as overall protection from evil when worn as a charm; acting as a powerful aphrodisiac; guarding against intestinal worms; removing sin from a person's soul; and whitening teeth. Drinking cups made from the horn were said to neutralize any poisoned beverage.

A more uncommon bit of folklore claims there is a mystic ruby (also known as a carbuncle or King of Gems) beneath the horn that is revealed once the horn is removed. This stone has its own mystical ability to banish evil, cure sadness, and counteract all poisons.

Numerous tests existed to determine whether an alicorn was genuine, such as adding powered alicorn to poison and having an assistant consume the beverage; covering a scorpion with alicorn powder to see whether the creature died; observing whether the horn would sweat in the presence of poison; making a circle around a spider with the horn, as an arachnid could not cross over a line made by an alicorn; and placing the horn in water, as a true alicorn would cause the water to bubble. In addition, poisonous creatures will die in the presence of an alicorn; poisonous plants will wither in its presence; poisoned food will form a dew over itself when close to an alicorn; when wrapped in silk and placed upon burning coals, the horn will not burn; and when burned, it will give off a sweet aroma.

Sources: Dudley, *Unicorns*, 61, 62, 67, 69; Ley, *Exotic Zoology*, 20–22; Shepard, *Lore of the Unicorn*, n.p.; Suckling, *The Book of the Unicorn*, n.p.

alkahest

Variations: alkahest, arcanum of fire, immortal solvent

In alchemic science, alkahest is a universal saline-based solvent capable of dissolving any material or substance, including gold. Highly valued for its medicinal properties, this red liquid is allegedly made of a careful base of mercury and unspecified salts; it can reduce anything to the "smallest atoms possible in nature." Alchemists sought to create this substance because, as put forth by Jan Baptist Van Helmont (a Flemish chemist, physiologist, and physician), water was the universal original substance, and alkahest could reduce other substances into their constitute or seminal principals.

Sources: Newman and Principe, *Alchemy Tried in the Fire*, 138, 249, 276, 292; Principe, *The Aspiring Adept*, 35

Almace

Variations: Almacia, Almice

In the French epic poem *Song of Roland* (*La Chanson de Roland*, circa 1040–1115), which retells the events of the Battle of Roncevaux Pass in 778 CE, Almace ("Alms" in Old Norse; possibly "The Cutter" in Arabic) was the sword of Turpin, the archbishop of Reims. Very little information is provided about Almace.

According to the Norse *Karlamagnus saga*,

three swords were made by the legendary blacksmith Wayland (Gofannon/Volund/Weiland/Weyland) the Smith and were presented to Charlemagne: Almace, Courtain and Durandal. When each was tested by striking a steel mound, Almace penetrated a hand's breadth into it without being damaged and was gifted to Bishop Turpin.

Sources: Pendergrass, *Mythological Swords* 4, 8, 9; Sayers, *The Song of Roland*, 38

alpleich

Variation: Elfenreigen

In German folklore, the alpleich is a piece of music that a person is said to hear before they die. According to a Brunswick tale, alpleich is described as similar to the song of a siren; it was the music the Ralzenfanger (also known as Bunting or Pied Piper) played to lure the rats into the Hamelin River (or Wesen River—sources vary) and subsequently the town's children into a cave at Koppenberg Mountain.

Sources: Brewer, *Dictionary of Phrase and Fable* 1900, 38; *Character Sketches of Romance, Fiction and the Drama*, Volume 2, 365; Mercer, *Light and Fire Making*, 38

Amanonuboko

Variations: Amano Nuboko, Ama-No-Uki-Hashi

In Japanese mythology, Amanonuboko ("Heavenly Halberd of the Marsh"/"Heavenly Jeweled Spear") was the jeweled spear given by the Lord of Heaven to the primal gods Izanagi and Izanami; they used it to stir up the primeval green sea and bring forth the eight islands of Japan.

Sources: Leviton, *The Gods in Their Cities*, n.p.; Satow, *Ancient Japanese Rituals*, 225

Ama-no-Saka-hoko

In ancient Shinto mythology, Ama-no-Saka-hoko ("Heavenly Hill Pillar"/"Heavenly Hill Pole"/"Heavenly Reversed Halberd"/"Heavenly Upside Down Spear") was the weapon of Ninigi-No-Mikoto, the grandson of the goddess of the sun, Amaterasu O Mi Kami; he was sent from the heavens to rule over Japan. According to legend, Ninigi-No-Mikoto landed upon the earth with Ama-no-Saka-hoko driven into the top of Takachilo in Hiuga.

However, according to *The Harima Fudoki*, when the legendary empress Jingo Kogo set out to conquer Korea, she set up sacred pillars on the fore and aft of her ship; doing so allowed her to safely travel across the sea. Upon her return to Japan, these pillars were erected on land and worshiped as gods.

Sources: Holtom, *The Political Philosophy of Modern Shinto*, 221; Waley, *The Secret History of the Mongols and Other Pieces*, 114

amarantha (ah-mar-AN-tha)

Variations: amarande, amarante

In classical Greek mythology, the amarantha ("beyond death"/"unfading flower") was said to be an eternally blooming species of flower.

Sources: Anderson, *Joyce's Finnegans Wake: The Curse of Kabbalah*, Volume 9, 93; Samuelson, *Baby Names for the New Century*, 15

amber tree

Once believed to be the source of amber, an amber tree was any species of tree growing in or near streams or coastal freshwater swamps where fish were seen and amber was found. Ancient naturalists were unsure whether amber—the yellowish or brownish product of the amber tree—was animal, mineral, or vegetable or if the would-be product of the amber tree was some sort of seed, the byproduct of the aptly named amberfish that lived near the amber tree, or perhaps even crystalized sea foam. It has been a common practice since ancient times to use amber in magical rituals and as a talisman in jewelry.

Sources: Hunger, *The Magic of Amber*, 18; Lehner, *Folklore and Symbolism of Flowers, Plants and Trees*, 85

ambrosia

Variations: amrta, mead, nectar, Soma

Historically considered the food of the gods, ambrosia ("undeath") is believed to convey longevity (if not outright immortality) to those who consume it; this substance has been described as both a beverage and a food and has been used as a perfume as well as a salve.

In classical Greek mythology, the gods and their horses consumed ambrosia; it was occasionally also given to their favorite mortals. When applied over a mortal's corpse, ambrosia prevented the body from decomposing. In one tale, Demeter (Roman goddess Ceres), the goddess of all useful fruits, grasses, and grains, covered the infant child of King Eleusis and Queen Metaneira with ambrosia and then placed the child in a hearth fire in order to burn away his mortal body.

Ancient Greek authors differ as to whether ambrosia grants immortality or simply prevents the gods from aging. Although ambrosia has been said to exude up from the earth, Zeus (Roman god Jupiter), the god of fate, kings, lightning, sky, and thunder, received ambrosia from doves who carried it to him from a place beyond the Clashing Rocks. Because the gods consume ambrosia almost exclusively, they do not have blood in their bodies, but rather a type of immortal fluid called ICHOR.

In Hindu mythology, ambrosia (more commonly known as SOMA) was obtained during the Samudra Manthan ("Churning of the Ocean"). At first, the gods were unified in their task, but order began to break down and chaos erupted; the neutral water was transformed into several elixirs, one of which was the divine ambrosia. The gods consumed ambrosia to gain immortality, but they could also use it to restore life to those who had been slain and to remove diseases from those afflicted. Any mortal who is given a drink of ambrosia will live the full course of their natural life and will die only from a natural death.

Sources: Hansen, *Classical Mythology*, 35, 101, 145; O'Flaherty, *Hindu Myths*, 35, 273

Amenonuhoko

Variations: Ame-no-nuboko ("Heavenly Swamp Spear"), TONBOGIRI (Japanese name)

In Shinto mythology, Amenonuhoko ("Heavenly Jeweled Spear") was the heavily bejeweled naginata (a long and wide blade on a wooden staff, similar to a halberd) used by the kami (gods) Izanagi ("Male Who Invites") and Izanami ("Female Who Invites"), who were instructed by the other kami to "make, consolidate, and give birth to the drifting land." Standing atop of the Drifting Bridge (also known as Amenoukibashi), they plunged the weapon into the turbulent ocean and began to stir. The frothy clumps of salt began to come together and eventually formed the first land mass, Onokoroshima.

Sources: Herbert, *Shinto*, 220; Pauley, *Pauley's Guide*, 4; Takahashi, *A Study of the Origin of the Japanese State*, 64

amortam

Variations: AMBROSIA, amrit ("deathless"), amrita ("without death"), amrta ("nectar"), dutsi (Tibetan), elixir of immortality, SOMA, Water of Immortality

A liquid much like milk in appearance, amortam of Hindu mythology is the beverage of the gods; it is said to grant them their immortality. It is described in Dharmic texts as a nectar with the ability to ease weariness and act as the antidote to all poisons. Supposedly, when the gods and demons called a truce to perform the Samudra Manthan ("Churning of the Ocean"), they used the body of the hydra Ananta as a rope and a great mountain as the stick for the churning process. The opposite of amortam is HALAHALA.

Sources: Balfour, *Cyclopædia of India and of Eastern and Southern Asia*, Volume 3 , 96; Dalal, *Hinduism*, 24, 240; Dekirk, *Dragonlore*, 32; Orme, *Historical Fragments of the Mogul Empire*, 357; Southey, *Southey's Common-place Book*, Volume 4, 253

ananaithidus

According to Camillus Leonardus, a sixteenth-century Italian astronomer, mineralogist, and physician, an ananaithidus is a stone used by necromancers to invoke demons.

Sources: Leonardus, *The Mirror of Stones*, n.p.

Ancile of Ares, the

Variation: Ares's Ancile

In classical Greek mythology, the Ancile of Ares (Roman god Mars) was the brass buckler or shield belonging to the god of war; on its face was the image of an apple surmounted by Victory with wings spread. It was described as cut away on all sides so that it had no angles. According to the myth, the ancile was thrown from the heavens to Prince Numa Pompilius; he was told that as long as the ancile was in his safekeeping, "Rome would be the Mistress to the world." To ensure its protection, Numa ordered eleven copies of the ancile made and entrusted their care to an order of priests known as the Salii. The ancile, along with its priests, resided in the Temple of Ares.

Sources: Bell, *Bell's New Pantheon*, Volume 2, 60; Grant and Hazel, *Who's Who in Classical Mythology*, n.p.

Andaokut

From the Tsimshian, a people who live along the Pacific Northwest coast of Alaska and British Columbia, comes the story of Andaokut ("mucus boy"), a HOMUNCULUS-like being created from the acumination of mucus a woman produced while mourning the loss of her child, who was stolen by the Great Woman of the Wood, Malahas. This witch was well known for abducting children and smoking them alive over a fire pit so she could eat them at her leisure. Andaokut grew very fast and soon asked its new parents for a bow and an arrow. After discovering why his foster mother cried so often, Andaokut set out to find Malahas. Through a series of carefully played tricks, he managed to kill the old witch the only way she could be slain—

by finding where she had hidden her small black heart and piercing it with an arrow. Once Malahas was destroyed, Andaokut gathered up the bodies of the children, laid them out carefully on the ground, and urinated all over them; this act brought them back to life.

Sources: Boas and Tate, *Tsimshian Mythology*, 903–7

Andvaranaut (AND-var-a-nout-r)

Variations: Andvaranautr, Andvarenaut, Andvari, Andvarinaut

In Norse mythology, Andvaranaut ("Andvari's Gift"/"Andvari's Gem"/"Andvari's Loom") was the magical golden ring first owned by the dwarf Andvari; it had the ability to both find and generate gold. The ring was the dwarf's most beloved possession, so when the god Loki forced him to surrender it in order to pay off a debt, Andvari placed a curse upon the ring: it would bring damnation, destruction, and ruin to anyone who wore it. Loki gave Andvaranaut (as well as an incalculably large treasure horde) to Hreidmar, king of the dwarfs, as recompense for having killed his son, Ottar (Otter/Otr). Soon thereafter, Fafnir (Fafner), the king's other son, murdered his father and then transformed himself into a dragon so as to better guard the treasure horde and ring. The hero Sigurd (Siegfried/Sigmund) slew the dragon and gave Andvaranaut to Brynhildr (Brunnehilde). Grimhild, queen of the Nibelungs, then manipulated Sigurd and Brynhildr into marrying her children, carrying the curse of Andvaranaut with them and into her family line.

Sources: Daly, *Norse Mythology A to Z*, 4–5; Dodds, *The Poetic Edda*, 204; Illes, *Encyclopedia of Spirits*, 182

Andvare-Force

Variation: Andvarafors

In Norse mythology, Andvare-Force is the force created by the waterfall in which Andvari the dwarf is able to maintain the form of a pike, a type of fish.

Sources: Anderson, *Norse Mythology*, 440

Angurvadel

Variations: Angurva, sword of Frithiof

In Norse mythology, Angurvadel ("Stream of Anguish") was the magical falchion (sword) belonging to the Icelandic hero Frithiof (Frithjof) the Bold. The weapon was made by dwarfs; it had a golden hilt and was inscribed with magical runes. In times of war the blade shone brightly, but during times of peace it glowed with a dim glimmer. Angurvadel was one of the hero's three prized possessions, the dragon-ship ELLIDE and the GOLDEN ARM RING being the other two.

Sources: Brewer, *Dictionary of Phrase and Fable* 1900, 1197; Cox and Jones, *Tales of the Teutonic Lands*, 222; Evangelista, *The Encyclopedia of the Sword*, 576; Tegnér, *Frithiof's Saga*, 120

Anima Mundi

Variations: PHILOSOPHER'S STONE

In ancient alchemical mythology, Anima Mundi ("the source of life") was believed to be the oldest of all the PHILOSOPHER'S STONES. The classical Greek philosopher Plato (428–347 BCE) believed it to be the animating principle of life but inferior to pure spirits. To the Stoics (a school of Hellenistic philosophy popular until about the third century CE), Anima Mundi was the whole and vital force of the universe. Modern-day occultists consider the Anima Mundi to be the Collective Unconscious. Psychoidal alchemy teaches that the Anima Mundi is the PHILOSOPHER'S STONE, purified, intensified, and greatly multiplied in power.

Sources: Raff, *The Wedding of Sophia*, n.p.; Regardie, *Philosopher's Stone*, 69, 237, 440

Anjalika Astra

Variations: Anjalika Arrow

In Hindu mythology, an ASTRA is a supernatural weapon created or gifted by the gods to someone who then presides over the weapon. The wielder of an ASTRA is known as an astradhari.

Named in *The Mahabharata* (one of the two Sanskrit epics from ancient India), Anjalika Astra was the arrow used by the heroic archer Arjuna ("Spotless and Shining like Silver") to kill the undefended and unarmed Karna from behind.

Sources: Hiltebeitel, *Mythologies: From Gingee to Kuruketra*, 411; Thadani, *The Mystery of the Mahabharata*, Volume V, 689, 690

Answerer

Variations: FRAGARACH, The Retaliator

In Irish lore, Answerer was the magical sword belonging first to the god of the sea and guardian of the Underworld, Manannan mac Lir (Mannanan, Mannanos), and then to his foster son, Lugh Lamfada, who in turn gave it to Cuhullin (Cu Chulaind/Cu Chulainn/Cuchulainn), who passed it to Conn of the Hundred Battles. Answerer, forged by the gods, was said to have the ability to pierce any armor, shield, or wall. Additionally, when held to a person's throat, they would be unable to move and compelled to answer questions put to them—hence the weapon's name. Answerer's magic also placed the wind at its wielder's command and inflicted wounds that would never heal.

Sources: Pendergrass, *Mythological Swords*, 39; Rolleston, *Myths & Legends of the Celtic Race*, 113, 125

anting-anting (UN-ting-l'N-ting)

In Filipino folklore, an anting-anting is an amulet used to protect the wearer from bullets. The actual item called an anting-anting may be made of anything, be it a bone, a button, a coin, a slip of paper with magical symbols scribed on it, a bit of polished coconut shell, a white stone from the stomach of a crocodile, or even a shirt—anything of no true intrinsic value. The amulet might be a charm on a necklace or bracelet or even set into a ring. Each one is unique and said to be passed down within family lines. Folklore says the anting-anting is so powerful that the person wearing it often is filled with bravado and may brazenly walk right up to the barrel of a gun or rush a bayonet. Shamans say the first anting-anting was created in ancient times by use of dark magic.

Sources: Kayme, *Anting-Anting Stories*, vi; Tope and Nonan-Mercado, *Philippines*, 76–77

antler scraping of the wiwilemekw

According to Maliseet-Passamaquoddy folklore, the wiwilemekw is a crocodilian-like creature with a rack of deerlike antlers said to live in rushing waters, such as rapids, waterfalls, and whirlpools. In the legend, anyone brave enough to acquire a scraping of antler from a live wiwilemekw would gain power and strength.

Sources: Rose, *Giants, Monsters, and Dragons*, 397; Zell-Ravenheart and Dekirk, *Wizard's Bestiary*, 101

Apple of Discord, the

Variations: apple of Eris, Golden Apple of Discord, Twistappel ("Strife Apple"—Dutch)

According to classical Greek mythology, the goddess of discord and strife, Eris ("Strife"; Roman goddess Discordia), was not invited to the wedding feast of King Peleus of Phthia to Thetis, a sea goddess; they were the future parents of the hero Achilles. True to her name, Eris inscribed the words "to the fairest" upon a golden apple, which she then tossed into the middle of the wedding feast for all to see. This small action was catalyst for a vanity-driven dispute among the goddesses Aphrodite (Roman goddess Venus), Athena (Roman goddess Minerva), and Hera (Roman goddess

Juno), as each claimed the apple for herself. This feud between the three goddesses eventually led to the events causing the Trojan War.

Sources: Graves, *The Greek Myths*, 165; Palmatier, *Food: A Dictionary of Literal and Nonliteral Terms*, 9–10

Apple of Ennui

In the Middle English romance *Ogier the Dane*, a knight of King Arthur, Ogier, comes to live on the eternally peaceful island of Avalon at the request of Morgan La Fay, the queen of the fairies; there he is gifted with and wears the Crown of Forgetfulness and the Ring of the Fairy Queen. Upon the island grows a magical apple tree; its fruit is so powerful that it will cause the person who eats it to feel some of the pain and sorrow experienced by the mortals of the world, which were otherwise suppressed by the Crown of Forgetfulness. Each time a person would eat from the tree, a little bit of the virtue of the magical items they wore would disappear. The effect was most traumatic on the minstrels of Avalon.

Sources: Courthope, *The Marvellous History of King Arthur in Avalon*, 17, 31, 35, 48, 78

apples of Idunn, the

Variations: Apples of Youth, Ellilyf Asa

In Norse mythology, the apples of Idunn were the eleven golden-colored apples raised and harvested by Idunn, an *asynjr* (female Jotun, or giant) and goddess of rebirth and spring; she was the caretaker of Brunnakr Grove. When the fruit was given to the Aesir (the gods of Asgard), their wounds were healed and they regained their youth. Idunn kept the apples in an ashwood casket. Each year she held a banquet at which her annual harvest of apples was served to the gods.

Sources: Coulter and Turner, *Encyclopedia of Ancient Deities*, 462; Grimes, *The Norse Myths*, 255; Guerber, *Hammer of Thor*, 73; Janik, *Apple*, 39; Oehlenschläger, *Gods of the North*, xxxviii

apples of immortality, the

Variations: apples of the Hesperides

The idea of apples bequeathing immortality to an individual is a concept shared by both the ancient Greeks and the ancient Norse.

For the Greeks, golden apples grew on a tree in an orchard in a hidden location on the slopes of Mount Atlas. There it was originally protected by thee nymphs, the Hesperides (the collective name for the daughters of the god Atlas). The eleventh labor of the demigod and legendary hero Heracles was to procure an apple from the orchard, which at that time was no longer guarded by the Hesperides, as they had been caught stealing apples; rather, the grove was under the protection of the sleepless dragon Ladon, who lay coiled around the tree's base. Merely possessing one of these apples was enough to grant immortality; consumption was not necessary.

In Norse mythology, there was an ongoing battle between the Jotuns (giants) and the gods of Asgard ("Enclosure of the Aesir") over possession of the apples of immortality. Mortals would also try to steal the apples. Idunn, a goddess of rebirth and spring, was the keeper of the apples; each year she would serve her crop of eleven apples to the gods during an elaborate banquet.

In the folklore of ancient Briton, the apples of immortality grew on the isle of Avalon. In Arthurian lore, this is the location where King Arthur was taken after his final battle to recover from his wounds.

Sources: Browning, *Apples*, 69–72; Condos, *Star Myths of the Greeks and Romans*, 102–3; Graves, *The Greek Myths*, 133; Janik, *Apple*, 39; Palmatier, *Food: A Dictionary of Literal and Nonliteral Terms*, 9–10

apples of Sodom, the

Variation: Dead Sea fruit

In medieval folklore of Europe, there was said to be a gigantic tree growing in the wasteland that once was the location of the cities Gomorrah and Sodom. Travelers were warned that should they ever come upon this tree, they must not yield to temptation and pick one of its delicious-looking apples, for the moment the fruit was plucked, it would burst into smoke and crumble into dust in the person's hand. This action would displease God, as it would demonstrate how susceptible the traveler was to the physical pleasures of the world.

Sources: Jameson, *Edinburgh New Philosophical Journal*, Volume 32, 32–33; Meltzer, *The Thinker's Thesaurus*, n.p.

apples of the Hesperides, the

Variations: APPLES OF IMMORTALITY, Golden Apples of the Hesperides

In ancient Greek mythology, the eleventh labor of Hercules was procuring an apple from the hidden orchard on the slopes of Mount Atlas. Hera (Roman goddess Juno), the goddess of childbirth, family, marriage, and women, had planted the tree herself; it was a wedding gift from Gia, the goddess of the earth and life, to Zeus (Roman god Jupiter), the god of fate, kings, lightning, sky, and thunder, when he and Hera wed. Although the fruit of the tree was still called the apples of the Hesperides, they no longer acted as its guardians, as they had been caught stealing apples. Hera placed the grove under the protection of the sleepless dragon Ladon, who lay coiled around the tree's base. Gold (or at least golden in color), these apples granted immortality to whoever possessed them.

Sources: Condos, *Star Myths of the Greeks and Romans*, 102–3; Graves, *The Greek Myths*, 133

Aqrab-E Suleimani

According to the medieval Persian saga of Amir Hamza, Aqrab-E Suleimani was one of the four swords once held by King Suleiman, the others being QUMQAM, SAMSAM, and ZUL-HAJAM. Amir Hamza swore to Shahpal that he would rid the land of rebels and was allowed to pick one of the swords to accomplish this goal. It was foretold that the shining blade Aqrab-E Suleimani would sever the heads of the *dev* (the personification of evil). As proof of his worthiness, Amir had to cleave in two a poplar tree the height and width of the demon Ifrit, a task he easily accomplished. If anyone but Amir hefted the blade, it would transform into a scorpion.

Sources: Jah, *Hoshruba*, 44, 243, 245, 261, 271, 279, 292, 361, 443

Ara

Variation: Arae

In classical Greek mythology, Ara was the name of the first alter; it was constructed by the Cyclopes during the time when Zeus (Roman god Jupiter), the god of fate, kings, lightning, sky, and thunder, was engaged in his ten-year war for ascendancy over his father, the Titan Cronus (a struggle known as the Titanomachy). The alter was described as having a cover over the flames so as to hide Zeus's lightning bolts from the Titans. After the Olympian gods won the war, they all swore their allegiance to Zeus upon Ara. Once order was restored, Zeus introduced the concept of an alter to mortals so that whenever they wanted to swear allegiance to one another, they would have a place to make a sacrifice. When men wanted to make a sacred pledge, they would lay their right hand upon the alter.

Sources: Condos, *Star Myths of the Greeks and Romans*, 37; See, *The Greek Myths*, 17

A'raf, al

Variations: Aaraaf, Araf, al Arat, Paradise of Fools

Arasteinn

In Islamic mythology, al A'raf ("the partition") is described in the Koran as the mystical Limbo-like domain and wall that separates and lies between Djanna (Paradise) and Jahannam (Hell). The occupants of this region are varied, consisting of angels in the form of men; the patriarchs and prophets; those individuals who in life were incapable of being morally good or evil, such as infants and the mentally challenged; those who went to war without their parents' leave and therein suffered martyrdom; and those whose good and evil works are so equal that they exactly counterbalance each other and therefore deserve neither reward nor punishment. The occupants, who will remain here for all eternity, have the ability to speak with the occupants in the adjoining domains. Interestingly, the souls in Heaven, when looking into the al A'raf, will only see Hell, and those damned souls in Hell who are looking back will only see the individuals who are in Heaven.

Sources: Hughes, *Dictionary of Islam*, 20–21; Smith, *Century Cyclopedia of Names*, Volume 6, 70; Stork, *A–Z Guide to the Qur'an*, 32; Van Scott, *Encyclopedia of Hell*, 10

Arasteinn

In Norse mythology, Arasteinn ("Eagle Stone") was the place where Korr rested after having done battle with the Sviar.

Sources: Norroena Society, *Asatru Edda*, 335

Areadbhair

Variation: Luin of Celtchar

One of the spears belonging to the Celtic god of the sun, Lugh ("Bright" or "Light") of the Long Arms (Artful Hands or Long Hands), Areadbhair ("Slaughterer") was said to be one of the treasures the Tuatha de Danann carried with them when they left their homeland, others being Gae Assail ("Spear of Assal"; see LUIN) and SLEA BUA ("Spear of Victory"). Areadbhair was said to have been created in the city of Gorias from yew; it was unbeatable in combat and needed to have its tip kept submerged in water, or else it would erupt into flames. (In other versions, the spear must be kept in a cauldron of boiling blood to prevent it from killing.) According to legend, the spear once belonged to King Pezar of Persia.

Areadbhair also appears in Arthurian Grail lore as the blood-letting spear that both wounds and heals (see BLEEDING LANCE).

Sources: Dudley, *The Egyptian Elements in the Legend of the Body and Soul*, 174; Ellis, *The Mammoth Book of Celtic Myths and Legends*, n.p.; Stirling, *The Grail*, n.p.

Argo, the

The epic poem *Argonautica*, written by Apollonius Rhodius in the third century BCE, tells the story of the hero Jason and his followers, the Argonauts ("Sailors of the *Argo*"), on their perilous journey to retrieve the GOLDEN FLEECE from the remote land of Colchis. The *Argo* was the ship in which they traveled. Constructed by the shipwright Argus from a design conceived by Athena (Roman goddess Minerva), the goddess of crafts, military victories, war, and wisdom, it was said that the prow of the ship was made from wood from the sacred forest of Dodona; this enabled the masthead to speak and prophesy.

Once the quest was successfully concluded, the *Argo* was consecrated to Poseidon (Roman god Neptune), the god of earthquakes, horses, and the seas, at which time the ship rose up, transformed, and became the constellation of Argo Navis.

Sources: Daly and Rengel, *Greek and Roman Mythology, A to Z*, 17; Stuttard, *Greek Mythology*, n.p.; Woodard, *The Cambridge Companion to Greek Mythology*, 168–69, 463

Ark of the Covenant, the

A sacred relic in Christian and Hebrew mythology, the Ark of the Covenant, first mentioned in the book of Exodus, is the vessel in which the *Shekinah* (the Divine Presence of the Lord) traveled with the Twelve Tribes of Israel while they wandered in the desert. It was also the container that held the two stone tablets inscribed with the Commandments that God had given to Moses.

God gave Moses explicit instructions as to how the vessel was to be constructed. It was a rectangle-shaped box constructed of acacia wood plated with gold inside and out, measuring two feet, three inches wide by three feet, nine inches long. A ring of gold was affixed to each of the top four corners so poles of acacia wood, also covered with pure gold, could slide through the rings in order to lift up and carry the vessel. The lid of the box was called the Mercy Seat; it, too, was made of the purest gold and was nine inches thick. On the top of the lid were two golden cherubim, facing one another, their wings outstretched making a protective covering over the lid. It was said that from the space between the lid and the cherubim, the Voice of God would speak to Moses, giving His orders to deliver to the Children of Israel. The Lord warned Moses that when a cloud appeared on the Mercy Seat between the wings of the cherubim, none should approach the Ark; any who did when the cloud was present would die.

The Ark also had the ability to levitate and move itself, and it would occasionally carry its pole bearers, the Kohathites (the sons of Kohath), with it. Sometimes jets of flame would shoot off of the Ark and kill one of the Kohathites. There are also a few mentions of times when the Ark would levitate people and toss them about.

As a weapon, the Ark was powerful. When it was taken into battle, the Israelites were unbeatable. First it made "a moaning sound"; then it would rise up into the air and rush forward into the enemy, slaying every man who stood against it. It was paraded around the Walls of Jericho and was given credit for their destruction.

When the Ark fell into the hands of the Philistines, it defaced the statue of their god, Dagon, and caused the people to develop painful and fatal tumors. The Ark was subsequently returned to the Israelites, but when the lid was lifted to see whether its contents were still within, seventy men fell dead. It moved about and eventually came to rest in the Temple of Solomon, where it sat in a room of solid gold known as the Holy of Holies, the most sacred part of the Temple.

On the first recorded occasion of the Ark having been placed in the Holy of Holies, priests who were privileged to have access to the area entered with incense burners and "offered strange fires which the Lord commanded they not." Consequently, fire shot out from the Ark and "devoured them as they died." In addition, voices were said to be heard conversing from behind the veil when no one was within the Holy of Holies. When the voice spoke, sparks or fire came off the cherubim, destroying nearby objects.

In 587 BCE, Jerusalem and the Temple of Solomon were destroyed by the Babylonians; there is no record of what became of the Ark, but it is assumed to either have been carried to safety (and thus is still in hiding) or was captured by the Babylonians and thereafter forever lost.

Christian and Hebrew tradition tells us that the Ark contained items other than the two stone tablets listing the Commandments, although there is debate over whether the items were *in*, *beside*, or *near* the Ark. These items include a *bolide* (meteor) that fell from heaven; the genealogy of the Jewish people; the ROD OF AARON, which magically flowered; the ROD OF MOSES (in Hebrew, *Shamir*); the SWORD OF METHUSE-LAH; the URIM AND THUMMIM; the VESTMENT OF ADAM; and other relics. Less frequently mentioned items in the Ark are the EMERALD TABLET; the HARP OF KING DAVID, which played music of its own accord; and the flute of King David.

Sources: *Book of the Covenant*, Volume 5, 27–28; Boren and Boren, *Following the Ark of the Covenant*, 2–13; *The Jewish Encyclopedia*, Volume 2, 105

armor of Achilles, the

Created by Hephaistos (Hephaestus; Roman god Vulcan), the god of bindings, the art of sculpture, fire, forges, metalworking, stonemasonry, and talismans, the armor of the demigod and hero Achilles was one of the famous warrior's most prized possessions, even beyond Xanthos, his immortal war horse gifted with human speech.

According to the *Iliad* (1260–1180 BCE), the ancient Greek epic attributed to Homer, Hephaistos made the armor out of gratitude for Thetis, the woman who raised him in his infancy, so she could give it as a gift to her son, Achilles. This armor was meant to replace the set that his comrade Patroclus had borrowed; unfortunately, when Patroclus died on the battlefield, his body was stripped and the equipment taken as spoils of war.

Publius Vergilius Maro (more commonly known as Virgil), a Roman poet from the Augustan period, wrote that Hephaistos made an entire set of armor for the hero; the panoply included a breastplate of bronze, a crested helmet, a spear, a sword, and a most exquisite shield (see SHIELD OF ACHILLES). According to Virgil, carved upon the front surface of the shield was the entire history of Rome. Homer describes the armor as being made of bright bronze and dappled with stars. There was said to be silver reinforcing the ankle areas. Achilles loans his armor out many times throughout the *Iliad*, and each of the heroes who wear it can feel its divine power when donned.

Sources: Homer, *The Iliad*, 349–53; Roman and Roman, *Encyclopedia of Greek and Roman Mythology*, 43, 200

armor of Karna, the

Variation: Kavacha ("Armor")

In Hindu mythology, Karna, the child of a virgin, was born with a golden breastplate and earrings that made him all but invincible, even to the weapons of heaven (see ASTRA). As long as Karna wore the armor, no ASTRA, nor arrow, nor sword, could break his skin. The earrings and armor were cut from his body and given to Indra, the god of the heavens, lightning, rains, river flows, storms, and *vajra* ("thunder"), in exchange for the ASTRA known as SAKTI.

Sources: Bryant, *Krishna*, 26–27, 33; Dalal, *Hinduism*, 108, 202.

armor of Thor, the

The armor of Thor is the collective name for the three prized possessions that Thor, the Norse god of thunder, habitually wore: JARNGREIPR, MEGINGJARDAR, and MJOLNIR.

Sources: Hall et al., *Saga Six Pack*, 103, 141; Norroena Society, *Satr Edda*, 374

Arondight (ah'ron-dit)

Variations: Ar'ondight, Arondite, Aroundight
Arthurian lore and medieval fiction claim that Arondight is the sword belonging to Sir Lancelot of the Lake, the bravest and strongest knight of the ROUND TABLE.

Sources: Brewer, *Dictionary of Phrase and Fable* 1900, 1197; Evangelista, *The Encyclopedia of the Sword*, 576; Frankel, *From Girl to Goddess*, 49; Jobes, *Dictionary of Mythology, Folklore, and Symbols*, Part 1, 422

arrow of Brahma, the

Variation: Brahmadanda ("Rod of Brahma")
In Hindu mythology, the arrow of Brahma is one of the weapons of the gods, an ASTRA; each time it is fired, it causes the destruction of an entire army. Once Brahma fired the arrow northward into Drumakulya; the place where the arrow landed became known as Desert Wilderness. Although the arrow dried up the water in the region, it left a single well filled with brackish water that came to be known as Vrana.

Sources: Dubois et al., *Hindu Manners, Customs, and Ceremonies*, 387; Hudson, *The Body of God*, 158

arrow of the serpent Capella, the

Variation: arrow of the Naga Capella
Few items in Hindu mythology compare to the power of the arrow of the serpent Capella. This arrow, an ASTRA, when launched into a massed army, would cause the fighters to fall to the ground in a state of lethargy, putting them all at the mercy of their approaching enemies.

Sources: Dubois et al., *Hindu Manners, Customs and Ceremonies*, 387

arrows of Cupid

In Roman mythology, the god of love, Cupid ("Desire"; Eros in classical Greek mythology), curious and impetuous by nature, had two sets of arrows he shot from his bow. The first group of arrows were dove fletched and caused the person struck with them to fall in love with the first person they saw; the second group of arrows were owl fletched and repelled love in whoever they struck. Cupid was often show blindfolded in art, as he was known to shoot his arrows off randomly.

Sources: Daly and Rengel, *Greek and Roman Mythology, A to Z*, 39, 52

Ascalon

In Christian folklore, the name of the spear (or sword—sources vary) wielded by Saint George when he killed the dragon was Ascalon. In medieval tales, the weapon is more often cited as a sword, and it made Saint George invincible in combat.

Sources: Auden, *Reading Albrecht Dürer's the Knight, Death, and the Devil Ab Ovum*, n.p.; Frankel, *From Girl to Goddess*, 49

Asgrindar (AHS-grind-ar)

Variation: Gates of Asgard
Asgrindar ("Gates of the Aesir") is the collective name for the gates that stand before Asgard ("Enclosure of the Aesir") in Norse mythology. Individually, each gate is called Asgrind. The specific names of each of the two gates are THRYMGJOLL and VALGRIND.

Sources: Grimes, *The Norse Myths*, 304; Norroena Society, *Asatru Edda*, 391

Asi

Variations: As, Khadga
The *Mahabharata*, one of the major epics of ancient India, tells the story of a war between two princes. In the "Shantiparva" section, the narrative describes how Brahma, the creator of the universe, produced the first sword, a weapon he named Asi. The sword has a long line of recorded possessors and wielders. Some translations of the text have the sword being a two-handed weapon, some six feet in length, and it is often referred to as *dirghasi* ("long sword"), mahasi, *nistringa* ("short sword"), and saber.

According to the legend, the devas (demigods) complained to Brahma about the evil and unjust rule of the danavas and asuras; in response, he collected sacrificial objects and performed a grand ceremony during which a horrific being, Asidevata, the god of swords, burst from the sacrificial fire. The monstrous Asidevata was described as exceedingly powerful and full of energy; it had a lean stomach, was overly tall, and had sharp teeth and a skinny frame. Upon seeing it, Brahma declared that Asidevata would be used to destroy the enemies of the gods and restore righteousness to the world. Asidevata immediately took the form of a sword, its edge sharp and glowing like fire. It was then gifted to Rudra so he might kill evildoers and restore order and the right way of living.

Rudra waged war against the danavas, daityas, and the enemies of the gods. When they were all slain, he assumed his natural form of Shiva and gave the now red-stained sword to Indra, the god of the heavens, lightning, rains, river flows, storms, and *vajra* ("thunder"), who passed it along to other gods.

Asi next went to Manu, the god of the human race, who was told to use the sword only to restore order and punish those who were major transgressors, never to kill anyone who committed a small sin. He heeded this advice and passed the weapon along to his son Kshupa and then to his other son, Ikshvaku.

From here Asi was handed down to a succession of people, beginning with Pururavas, who passed it to Ayu, who passed it to Nahusha, who passed it to Yayati, who passed it to Puru. Then Asi was stolen by Amurtarayas, who passed the sword to Bhumishaya, who passed it to Bharata Daushyanti, who passed it to Ailavila, who passed it to King Kuvalashva. Asi was subsequently taken from Kuvalashva by King Kamboja of Kambojas. Next Asi was passed to Muchukunda and then to Maruta. He passed it to Raivata, who passed it to Yuvanashva, who passed it to Raghu, who passed it to Harinashva. He passed the sword to Shunaka, who passed it to Ushinara. From him it went to the Bhojas and Yadavas, and from the Yadus it went to Shivi. He gave Asi to Partardanas of Kashi, but it was taken by Vishvamitras of the Ashtaka lineage, only to lose Asi to the Panchala Prishadashva. Then the sword came to be with the Brahmins of the Bharadvaja lineage; Drona, the last of his line, gave Asi to Kripacharya, who gave it to the Pandavas.

Sources: Burton, *The Book of the Sword*, 214; Hopkins, *The Social and Military Position of the Ruling Caste in Ancient India*, 285; Pendergrass. *Mythological Swords*, 10–11

astra

Variation: astrani

In Hindu mythology, an astra ("divine weapon") is a supernatural weapon created or gifted by the gods to someone who then presides over the weapon. The wielder of an astra is known as an astradhari. These weapons are often gifted to a person as a reward for some great feat of austerity or valor. The name of the weapon usually refers to its function or to the god who made a gift of it. The power level of the astra depends on the degree of austerity achieved by the person who won the astra; this decision is made by the presiding god.

Astras are frequently mentioned in the *Mahabharata* and the *Ramayana*, ancient Sanskrit epics, in which these weapons are used in many battles. Most often these astras are arrows and, naturally, utilized by archers.

There are many types of astras described in the *Mahabharata* and the *Ramayana*, such as Agney astra ("Weapon of fire"), which can produce an array of effects, including heat, flames, or pure energy.

In later times, the word *astra* came to signify any handheld weapon.

Sources: Edizioni, *Vimanas and the Wars of the Gods*, n.p.; Valmiki, *The Ramayana of Valmiki*, Volume 1, 339

Asurastra

In Hindu mythology, an ASTRA is a supernatural weapon created or gifted by the gods to someone who then presides over the weapon. The wielder of an ASTRA is known as an astradhari.

Asurastra was an ASTRA from the power-seeking asuras. Asurastra was said to be a metallic arrow belonging to Ravana; it had the ability to deploy what has been described as modern biological and bacteriological missiles.

Sources: Edizioni, *Vimanas and the Wars of the Gods*, n.p.; Sundaram, *Kamba Ramayana*, n.p.

atgeir of Gunnar, the

Described as a "spearlike spear," the magical atgeir of Gunnar was said to sing ("a ringing sound") in anticipation of the bloodshed it would cause in an upcoming battle; one of these spears was supposedly carried by the Islandic hero Gunnar Hamundarson.

An atgeir is a type of polearm, sometimes referred to as a "hewingspear" or "mailpiercer"; these weapons have both spear and swordlike characteristics and are used to slash and stab.

Sources: Classen, *Magic and Magicians in the Middle Ages and the Early Modern Time*, 124; Kane, *The Vikings*, n.p.

Atra, al

According to Islamic mythology, the prophet Muhammad owned at least three half-pikes at the time of his death; their names were al Atra, al HAFR, and al NAB'A. Atra was pretested for him by Zobeir Ebn Awan.

Sources: Osborne et al., *A Complete History of the Arabs*, Volume 1, 254; Sale et al., *An Universal History, Part 2*, Volume 1, 185

aurr

Variations: aur, hvitr aurr ("white clay")

In Norse mythology, aurr ("loose clay") was the fertilizer-like substance that staved off decay; the Norns collected it from Uppsah Spring to spread on the tree YGGDRASIL.

Sources: Anderson, *Norse Mythology*, 460; Grimes, *The Norse Myths*, 256

ausadhirdipyamanas

The handsome, twin gods of Hindu mythology known collectively as the Ashvins ("horsemen") were the dispensers of the ausadhirdipyamanas ("phosphorescent plants"/"resplendent plants"), magical herbs used for healing, rejuvenation after a battle, and restoring youth to the gods and select mortals. When these types of plants were sought, they had the ability to choose to become invisible.

Sources: Garrett, *A Classical Dictionary of India*, 241; Smith, *Hinduism*, 212; Storl, *Untold History of Healing*, 134

Auspicious Cloud

In the tale of Xuanzang, the monk who traveled from China to India to obtain Buddhist scriptures, the god figure Sun Wukong ("Monkey King") used a vehicle never described but only referred to as Auspicious Cloud as means of transportation. It was always nearby and seemed to have the ability to hover and fly.

Sources: Wu, *Journey to the West*, 1, 29, 145, 146, 184, 226

automatons

Variation: automotoi

In classical Greek mythology, automatons ("self-acting") were statues of animals, humans, and monsters that were then animated or otherwise brought to a kind of life by one of the gods; usually this was done by Hephaistos (Hephaestus; Roman god Vulcan), the god of bindings, the art of sculpture, fire, forges, metalworking, stonemasonry, and talismans. The list of automatons thus created includes the CAUCASIAN EAGLE, the GOLDEN MAIDENS, the GOLDEN TRIPODS, the KABEIRIAN HORSES, the KELEDONES, KHRYSEOS AND ARGYREOS, the KOLKHIS BULLS, and TALOS.

Sources: Bonnefoy, *Greek and Egyptian Mythologies*, 88–89; Westmoreland, *Ancient Greek Beliefs*, 54

Awadzamakat

In the regional folklore of the Caucasus mountains, and according to Abkhazian legends, Awadzamakat was the largest of all the earthenware pitchers that the Nart heroes used to contain their wine (NARTSANE). When a hero stood near the pitcher and spoke of his heroic deeds, the NARTSANE within would begin to boil and bubble. Awadzamakat, which was kept buried in the Klukhor Pass, never ran out of wine. It would also give those who drank from it strength in addition to prolonging their life.

Sources: Belyarova, *Abkhazia in Legends*, n.p.

axe of Perun, the

Variations: axe of Perunu, hammer of Perun

Perun ("God" and "thunderbolt"), the god of thunder and lightning in Slavic mythology, was said to be the king of the gods. His axe (battle-axe or hammer—translations vary), when thrown, would return to him. Although Perun is often compared to the Norse god of thunder, Thor, Perun's axe did not have its own name as Thor's hammer (MJOLNIR) did.

Sources: Hubbs, *Mother Russia*, 119; Sibley, *The Divine Thunderbolt*, 270

Ayamur

In Phoenician mythology, Ayamur ("Driver") and YAGRUSH ("Chaser") were the two clubs created and named by Kothar; the weapons were then given to Baal ("Rider of the Clouds"), a god of storms, in order to defeat Yam, god of the sea.

Sources: Gowan, *Theology in Exodus*, 135; Pritchard and Fleming, *The Ancient Near East*, 109, 112

ayudhapurusha

Variations: ayudha purusa, shastradevata ("dagger, knife, or any cutting instrument")

In Hindu art, an ayudhapurusha ("weapon person") is the anthropomorphic depiction of an ASTRA, a divine weapon; occasionally these weapons are considered the embodiment of the deity in solid form. In art, the weapon is depicted as a two-armed being wearing a crown, shown emerging from the weapon they embody or carrying it on their head or in their hands. Masculine weapons have the word *purusha* ("man") in their names, while feminine weapons have *devi* ("goddess") in theirs. Traditionally, *shakti* (spear) and *gada* (club) are considered feminine, while *chakra* (discus) is neutral, and *khadga* (sword) and TRISHUL (trident) are masculine.

Those who utilize such weapons are known as Sastra-devatas ("gods of divine weapons").

Sources: Dallapiccola, *Dictionary of Hindu Lore and Legend*, n.p.; Lochtefeld, *The Illustrated Encyclopedia of Hinduism: A–M*, 75

Az Isten Kardja

Variations: Isten Kardja ("Sword of God"), SWORD OF ATTILA, sword of God, sword of Mars

The legendary sword said to be carried by Attila the Hun was named Az Isten Kardja. According to legend, when Bleda, Attila's brother and tribal leader, died on a hunting trip, the elders called a council to decide who would be the new leader. When infighting broke out, a young man reported that a flaming sword had suddenly appeared in a nearby field; the elders followed the youth to the site. Upon arrival, the sword leaped into the air and flew into Attila's outstretched hand. The sword was made with such quality that it was decided the weapon had to be a divine gift and an omen as to who should be the next leader.

Sources: Pendergrass, *Mythological Swords*, 67; Roberts, *Leadership Secrets of Attila the Hun*, n.p.

azoth

Variations: Azoth of the Philosophers, Mercury of the Philosophers

According to alchemy and alchemic texts, azoth ("first matter") is considered a universal medicine or solvent. It is described as a second and living water or the soul of dissolved bodies.

Sources: Frankel, *From Girl to Goddess*, 49; Haeffner, *Dictionary of Alchemy*, 59–60; Hauck, *The Complete Idiot's Guide to Alchemy*, 229

Babr-e Bayan

Variations: Babr, Palangina

Babr-e Bayan ("Raging Tiger" or "tiger skin cuirass") was the coat worn by the legendary Persian hero Rostam (Rustam); this mythical garment was said to be fire- and waterproof as well as protection against all manner of weapons. Described as dark colored, this coat may have also been furred or hairy, as it was said that when Rostam donned it, it looked as if he had "sprouted feathers." Beneath Babr-e Bayan was a shirt of metal plates, and beneath that a tunic of lightweight chainmail.

Although the name of Babr-e Bayan does not translate easily, there are oral tales of Rostam, at the age of fourteen, slaying a sea dragon called Babr-e Bayan. After defeating the creature, he made himself a coat out of its hide.

Sources: Stronge and Victoria and Albert Museum, *Tipu's Tigers*, 36–37; Yarshater, *Encyclopædia Iranica*, Volume 13, 89

baetylus

Variations: bethel, betyl

Sacred stones in classical Greek mythology, the baetylus were believed to have been endowed with life, having fallen from the heavens. Likely meteorites, these objects were dedicated to the gods or, in some cases, revered as the living symbol of a god depending on their shape. For instance, a pyramid-shaped baetylus was associated with Zeus (Roman god Jupiter), the god of fate, kings, lightning, sky, and thunder, while more conical-shaped baetylus were associated with Apollo ("to destroy" or "to drive away"), the god of archery, art, healing, hunting, knowledge, medicine, music, oracles, plague, prophecy, sun and light, truth, and young unmarried men. The practice of worshiping these stones continues into modern times.

Sources: Doniger, *Merriam-Webster's Encyclopedia of World Religions*, 106; Palmer, *Rome and Carthage at Peace*, 99

bag of wind, the

In *The Odyssey*, the ancient Greek epic attributed to Homer, Aeolus, controller of the winds and the ruler of the Island of Aeolia, captured the gentle West Wind in a tightly sealed leather bag. This bag was then gifted to Odysseus so he could easily sail back to his home, Ithaca.

Sources: Homer, *The Odyssey*, 178–79; Smith, *The Hero Journey in Literature*, 41

baguette d'Armide, de

Variations: wand of Armida

In the Italian epic *Gerusalemme liberate*, by poet Torquato Tasso, the baguette d'Armide ("wand of Armida") was a golden, powerful, and sacred object; it had the ability to drive off and expel ghosts, phantoms, and spirits of every type, including those of the air, earth, and fire. The sight of the wand makes those who see it tremble in fear, as it can also cause ten thousand types of plague and break any magical enchantment.

Sources: Eccles, *Rinaldo and Armida*, 26, 59; Guerber, *The Book of the Epic*, 210–13

Bajura

According to Islamic mythology, Bajura was the standard of the prophet Muhammad.

Sources: Brewer, *The Dictionary of Phrase and Fable 1900*, 60

Balifarda

Variations: Balisarda, Balisardo

In the Italian epic poem *Orlando Furioso* (1516), written by Ludovico Ariosto, Balifarda was Orlando's sword, which was stolen by the cunning dwarf and thief, Brunello. The sword was then given to Rogero, the main character of the epic. Balifarda, forged by a sorceress, had the ability to cut through anything, including enchanted substances.

Sources: Ariosto, *Orlando Furioso*, Volume 1, 230

balm of Fierabras, the

Variation: balsamo de Fierabras

Originating in French chivalric legends but popularized in Italian chivalric literature, the balm of Fierabras (Fierbras) was a magical healing balm that contained the last of the fluid in which Christ was embalmed. This balm was stolen by the giant Saracen (Muslim) Fierabras when he sacked the city of Rome with his father, Balan. The balm had the miraculous ability to cure any wound. Ultimately, Fierabras was defeated by the hero Oliveros, who in turn gave the balm to Charlemagne so it could be returned to Rome.

Sources: Elliot, *Modern Language Notes*, 102–3; Mancing, *The Cervantes Encyclopedia: A–K*, 57

Balmung

Variations: Balmus, GRAM, NOTHUNG

The magical sword Balmung was said to have been forged by the legendary blacksmith, Mimer. The edge of the sword was so keen it was able to cut through a strand of wool floating on water.

In one Germanic story, Odin—the god of battle, death, frenzy, the gallows, healing, knowledge, poetry, royalty, the runic alphabet, sorcery, and wisdom—stabbed Balmung into the BRANSTOCK TREE and then proclaimed that whoever could pull the sword free was destined to win in battle. Nine of the Volsung princes attempted the feat, but it was the youngest, Sigurd (Siegfried/Sigmund), who was successful; he eventually used the sword to defeat both the Nibelungs and Fafnir (Fafner), the dwarf whose greed transformed him into a dragon. Hagen, half-brother of King Gunther, then killed Sigurd and stole Balmung. Kriemhild, the widow of Sigurd, used Balmung to behead Hagen for murdering her husband.

Sources: Evangelista, *The Encyclopedia of the Sword*, 576; Orchard, *Dictionary of Norse Myth and Legend*, 59; Pendergrass, *Mythological Swords*, 40–41

Bap

Variations: Abufihamet ("Father of Wisdom"), Baffometi, Bafometz, Baphomet, Baphometh, Bufihammet ("Source of Understanding")

The original name of the idol allegedly worshiped by the Knights Templar, Bap (the shortened form of the name Baphometh), was said to have been a corruption of the name Mahomet (Mohammed). Precisely what this idol was or what it looked like is unclear. Some sources say it was the severed head of John the Baptist, which had the ability to speak; other sources say it was a wooden carved post. The Templars themselves, when pressed to answer questions during interrogation, offered a wide array of descriptions of the idol, causing their captors to believe that the Bap had the ability to change shapes.

Sources: Davis, *Knights Templar*, 42–43; Napier, *Pocket A–Z of the Knights Templar*, n.p.; Roe et al., *The New American Encyclopedic Dictionary*, Volume 1, 378

Baptism

The celebrated swordsmith Ansias created three swords for the fictional giant Saracen (Muslim) knight Fierabras (Fierbras): Baptism, FLORENCE, and GRABAN. Each sword took three years to make. In *The Legend of Croquemitaine*, Baptism was hacked by a giant when testing the edge of another sword, GLORIOUS.

Sources: Brewer, *Dictionary of Phrase and Fable 1900*, 1197; L'Epine, *The Days of Chivalry*, n.p.; Numismatic and Antiquarian Society of Philadelphia, *Proceedings of the Numismatic and Antiquarian Society of Philadelphia for the Years 1899–1901*, 65

Barahoot

Variations: Bal'a'hoot, Borhut

In the Valley of Barahoot in the province of Hadramout, Yemen, there is said to be a well known only as Barahoot; its water is black and fetid. Each evening the souls of idolaters and infidels are taken to the well and made to drink from it. The valley is allegedly filled with owls and black serpents.

Sources: Lane, *Manners and Customs of the Modern Egyptians*, 531; Merrick and Majlisi, *Hayat al-qulub*, 165

barnacle tree

Variations: annes'de la mer, barchad, barnacha, barnacle goose, bernaca, bernekke, bernicle, bernicle goose, goose tree, tree goose

In the Middle Ages, it was believed that the barnacle goose (a bird smaller in size than a common wild goose, weighing only about five pounds) began its life as a crustacean, the barnacle, growing upon the barnacle tree. In 1187, the chronicler and clergyman Giraldus Cambrensis wrote that these geese grew from small *bernacae* attached to fir timber adrift at sea. As the *bernacae* developed, the growing creature could be seen within hanging downward from the wood by its bill. Upon reaching full development, the bird broke free and took to the sky. Cambrensis, having allegedly witnessed this phenomenon firsthand, also said the barnacle goose was the only bird in the world to be conceived without intercourse between the parents or development in a nest.

Sources: Ashton, *Curious Creatures in Zoology*, 104; *Chambers's Encyclopaedia*, Volume 1, 746; Isaacs, *Animals in Jewish Thought and Tradition*, 179; Zell-Ravenheart and Dekirk, *Wizard's Bestiary*, 21

batrachite

Variations: bufonite, TOADSTONE

Believed to be a mystical stone found in frogs, batrachite stones were allegedly used by ancient physicians and naturalists to counteract the effects of poisons and sorcery. According to medieval European folklore, the color of the batrachite was said to be the same color of the frog it was taken from.

Sources: Crump and Fenolio, *Eye of Newt and Toe of Frog*, 139; *Harvard Encyclopedia*, Volume 3, 196

Batter, al

Variation: al Battar ("the Cutting")

Al Batter ("the Striker" or "the Trenchant") was said to have been one of the three swords of the prophet Muhammad; the other two swords were HATEL and MEHDHAM. These swords, along with other treasures, came into his possession as wealth confiscated from the Jewish tribe Banu Kainoka prior to their banishment to Syria.

Other sources list al Batter as "al Battar" and as one of nine swords owned by the prophet: al ADHAB, al Battar, Dhu'l Fakar (see DHUAL-FIRQAR), al Hatf (see HATEL), al KADIB, KOLAITE, MABUR, al MEHDHAM, and al ROFUB.

Sources: Brewer and Harland, *Character Sketches of Romance, Fiction and the Drama*, Volume 4, 378; Irving, *Works of Washington Irving*, Volume 9, 132; Sale et al., *An Universal History, Part 2*, Volume 1, 184

battle-axe of Culhwch, the (KIL-hooch)

Variation: hatchet of Culhwch

Appearing in both Arthurian and Celtic lore, Culhwch is of royal blood and a cousin of King Arthur. Appearing in one of the many quest tales, he appears in Arthur's court under the pretense of getting his hair cut—a rite of passage—but also to ask for his cousin's assistance in searching for the woman he is to marry: the beautiful princess Olwen. Culhwch is described as radiantly attractive, fully armed and armored, outfitted with hunting hounds, and mounted upon a fine war horse. Among his possessions is a battle-axe "the forearm's length of a full grown man from ridge to ridge"; it was so sharp as to "make the air bleed" and could be swung more quickly than a dewdrop could fall to the ground.

Sources: Ashe, *The Discovery of King Arthur*, 160; Green, *Celtic Myths*, 35

Beagalltach

Variation: Begallta

Two swords were given to Diarmuid Ua Duibhne (Diarmid O'Dyna) by his father, Angus of the Brugs, in Celtic mythology: Beagalltach ("Little Fury") and MORALLTACH ("Great Fury"). Diarmuid carried each weapon for a different purpose; Beagalltach was taken on his small adventures when he did not foresee much danger, and MORALLTACH was taken on affairs he considered to be of life and death.

Sources: Joyce, *Old Celtic Romances*, 302

bed of Helius, the

In classical Greek mythology, Helius, one of the Titans, slept in a bed that was hollow and had wings. Like many of the gods' possessions, it was forged by Hephaistos (Hephaestus; Roman god Vulcan), the god of bindings, the art of sculpture, fire, forges, metalworking, stonemasonry, and talismans. While Helius slept, he was carried from the west to east.

Sources: Parada, *Genealogic Guide to Greek Mythology*, 192

bed trap of Hephaistos, the

In classical Greek mythology, Hephaistos (Hephaestus; Roman god Vulcan), the god of bindings, the art of sculpture, fire, forges, metalworking, stonemasonry, and talismans, was a brilliant inventor. Because he was so ugly, Zeus (Roman god Jupiter), the god of fate, kings, lightning, sky, and thunder, chose him to marry the beautiful goddess of love, Aphrodite (Roman goddess Venus). However, Aphrodite had many extramarital affairs. In one tale, Hephaistos discovered that his wife was entangled with Ares (Roman god Mars), the god of war. Enraged by the infidelity, he created many fine shackles, so delicately and skillfully crafted that even the eyes of the gods could not see them until it was too late. He draped the shackles over the bedpost and from the ceiling rafters. When the lovers lay together the next time, they were instantly ensnared and unable to break the bonds. Hephaistos then called the gods together to witness their shame and to demand back all the treasure he gave Aphrodite's father as her bride price.

Sources: Morford and Lenardon, *Classical Mythology*, 80–81

beer of oblivion

In Finnish mythology, the beer of oblivion was the drink given to those individuals who entered the underworld, Tuonela, first by swimming through icy rivers and then battling through a dense and thorny forest only to face the flesh-eating monster named Surma who guarded the Gates of Decay. Survivors of the ordeal gained entry and were given the beer of oblivion to drink in what would seem to be a reward. However, any who consumed the beverage immediately forgot about Earth and the world of mortals, thus giving them no reason to attempt to escape Tuonela.

Sources: Bartlett, *The Mythology Bible*, 139; Wilkinson, *Myths & Legends*, 103

Bele's Bane (Bay-leh)

Variations: Sumarbrandr ("Summer Sword"), Sword of Sharpness

In Norse mythology, Bele's Bane was one of the swords of the god Freyr (Frey/Yngvi), the god of fertility, peace, rain, and sunshine; it is described as only an *ell* (forty-five inches) long, with the ability to fight on its own against giants.

In other sources, such as the twelfth-century historical work *Islendingabok*, the name of Freyr's sword is given as Sumarbrandr ("Summer Sword").

Sources: Hodgetts, "On the Scandinavian Elements in the English Race," 141; Magnusen, "The Edda-Doctrine and Its Origin," 240; Rasums, *Norroena*, Volume 12, 73, 292; Titchenell, *The Masks of Odin*, 99

bell of the biloko, the

In the folklore of Democratic Republic of the Congo, there is a vampiric creature called a biloko ("food") said to live in the deepest sections of the rainforest within hollowed trees. Rather than hair growing on its body, the biloko is said to be covered with grass, using leaves as its clothing; it has long, sharp claws, piercing eyes, and a snoutlike nose. When the creature rings its magical bell, anyone who hears it will fall asleep. Then the biloko will pick up its prey and, opening up its mouth incredibly wide, swallow the person whole. Because of its magical bell, a biloko is often appointed as the guardian of a hidden treasure. Fortunately, amulets and fetishes can be made to protect the wearer from the bell's magic.

Sources: Chopra, *Academic Dictionary of Mythology*, 53; Knappert, *Bantu Myths and Other Tales*, 142; Knappert, *Myths and Legends of the Congo*, 130

belt of Aphrodite

Variations: Aphrodite's magic girdle, cestus of Aphrodite, love-belt of Aphrodite, girdle of Aphrodite

According to the *Iliad* (1260–1180 BCE), the ancient Greek epic attributed to Homer, Hera (Roman goddess Juno), the goddess of childbirth, family, marriage, and women, supported the Achaeans during the Trojan War. The goddess of love, Aphrodite (Roman goddess Venus), gave Hera her own belt to help Hera win back the love of her husband Zeus (Roman god Jupiter), the god of fate, kings, lightning, sky, and thunder, who had become indifferent and outwardly hostile to her. The magical belt was created to contain such allurements as beguilement, dalliance, desire, joy, love, the pains of love, and passion.

Sources: Parada, *Genealogic Guide to Greek Mythology*, 192; Whatham, "The Magical Girdle of Aphrodite," 336

belt of Goibniu

Goibniu (Gaibne/Gaibniu/Gobha/Goibhnionn/Goibnenn/Goibniu Sear), the Celtic god of blacksmithing, forged a magical belt that he gave to the mythic Irish hunter and warrior Fionn mac Cumhaill (Finn MacCool/Finn MacCumhail). It granted supernatural protection.

Sources: Mountain, *The Celtic Encyclopedia*, Volume 3, 715

belt of Hippolyte (Hip-POLLY-tee)

Variations: belt of Ares, belt of Hippolyta, girdle of Hippolyta, girdle of Hippolyte, Hippolyte's belt, Hippolyte's girdle, magical belt of Hippolyta, war belt of Hippolyte

The Greek demigod and legendary hero Heracles was ordered to serve King Eurystheus for twelve years in order to atone for his madness-driven murder spree in which he killed his wife, children, and two of his brother's children (in some accounts, Megera, his wife, survived). During this time of servitude, Heracles had to perform twelve impossible tasks, the ninth of which was retrieving the belt of Hippolyte, the queen of the Amazons. The belt was a gift to her from her father, Ares (Roman god Mars), the god of war. The belt was symbolic of Hippolyte's sovereignty and authority over the Amazons. In the myths, the *zoster* (a type of belt) is said to be magical, made of heavy leather, and worn more across Hippolyte's chest, enabling her to carry her spear and sword.

In most versions of the myth, she visited him on his ship and was so impressed with the demigod that she made him a gift of the girdle. However, Hera (Roman goddess Juno), the goddess of childbirth, family, marriage, and women, acting upon her vengeful inclinations against the illegitimate children of her husband Zeus (Roman god Jupiter), assumed the form of an Amazon and spread a rumor that Heracles had abducted their queen. The women warriors rallied together and attacked Heracles's ship. In the fray, Hippolyta was slain and Heracles made his escape with the girdle.

In an earlier version of the myth, Heracles sailed to the Amazonian capitol, Themiscyra, and demanded the girdle, which Hippolyta refused to surrender. A bloody battle ensued, killing all the Amazon champions: Aella ("Whirlwind"), Alcippe the Virgin, Asteria, Celaend, Deianera, Eriboia, Eurybia, Marpe, Peothoe, Philippis, Phoebe, and Tecmessa. Their race was nearly made extinct. A commander by the name of Melanippe finally offered to surrender, and Heracles declared he would allow her to live if she surrendered her girdle. Antiope, a princess among the Amazons, was given to Heracles's friend, the Athenian hero Theseus, for accompanying him on the adventure. The remaining Amazons regrouped, joined up with Scythian allies, and marched after Theseus to Athens to rescue their princess. Again, they were routed, and Antiope, who had since become Theseus's loyal wife and mother of their son, Hippolytus, died in the battle.

Sources: Hard, *The Routledge Handbook of Greek Mythology*, 263–64; Hreik, *Hercules*, 43–50; Huber, *Mythematics*, 89–90; Seigneuret, *Dictionary of Literary Themes and Motifs*, Volume 1, 44; Tatlock, *Greek and Roman Mythology*, 219–20; Wilde, *On the Trail of the Women Warriors*, 12–13

Benben

In the Heliopolitan tradition of Egyptian mythology, Benben was the mound that Atum, the god of creation, settled upon; the mound arose from Nu, the primordial water. The Benben is described as looking like a pyramid or stunted obelisk. It is from this stone that the first god appeared. The Benben is a symbol of the sun and believed to be a stargate. The Benu, a sacred and mythological bird perpetually in flight, saw the Benben rise up and landed upon it to take rest.

Sources: Crisologo and Davidson, *Egyptian Mythology*, 18–21; Remler, *Egyptian Mythology, A to Z*, 28–29

benevolent sword of Masamune, the

Variation: sword of Masamune

In Japanese folklore, the great swordsmith Masamune (circa late thirteenth century) was said to have created the greatest swords ever forged. Although Masamune was a real person, the story of his participation in a competition against another swordsmith by the name of Muramasa likely was not.

In the tale, the two men set out to determine who was the greater swordsmith; each of their completed swords was suspended over a stream. The sword of Muramasa cut everything that touched the blade, whether animals or floating leaves. The sword of Masamune, however, actually repelled animals, and at the last moment, floating leaves swerved out of the way. A traveling monk determined that Muramasa had created a bloodthirsty weapon of evil that would kill indiscriminately, whereas Masamune had made a blade that was innately benevolent and would only take a life with discretion, making it the superior weapon.

There are also tales in which Muramasa's swords were said to drive their owners to commit suicide and murder; those who owned one of his swords were only permitted to wear it into battle.

Sources: Blomburg, *The Heart of the Warrior*, 52; Winkler, *Samurai Road*, n.p.

Betra, al

According to Islamic mythology, the prophet Muhammad owned at least seven cuirasses (a piece of armor made of a breastplate and backplate hinged or otherwise fastened together) at the time of his death; their names were al Betra, DHAT AL FODHUL, DHAT AL HAWAFHI, DHAT AL WELHAL, al FADDO, al KHERNA, and al SA'ADIA. Beyond its name, nothing else is known of al Betra ("the Intersected").

Sources: Osborne et al., *A Complete History of the Arabs*, Volume 1, 254; Sale et al., *An Universal History, Part 2*, Volume 1, 185

Bhargavastra

Variation: Bhargav astra

In Hindu mythology, an ASTRA is a supernatural weapon created or gifted by the gods to someone who then presides over the weapon. The wielder of an ASTRA is known as an astradhari.

Bhargavastra was an ASTRA from Parashurama, an avatar of Vishnu, the god of preservation. Bhargavastra was said to have the ability to cause severe damage to an army in one blow. The damage also caused the surviving army to forget its military training, cut the opposing army's defenses, and damage (if not destroy) their remaining weapons. The weapon was fired up into the air, where it "hang[ed] fire in the sky" so that thousands of arrows would fall "screaming" to the earth; it destroyed all the arrows of Arjuna ("Spotless and Shining like Silver"), the heroic archer and main character in the Indian epic *Mahabharata*. The Bhargavastra was believed to be more powerful than the AINDRASTRA.

Sources: Edizioni, *Vimanas and the Wars of the Gods*, n.p.; Menon, *The Mahabharata* Volume 2, 382; Subramaniam, *Mahabharata for Children*, 28, 221

Bhaumastra

In Hindu mythology, an ASTRA is a supernatural weapon created or gifted by the gods to someone who then presides over the weapon. The wielder of an ASTRA is known as an astradhari.

Bhaumastra was an ASTRA from Bhoomi, the goddess of earth. It was said to have the ability to carve deep tunnels in the ground in order to collect or summon (translations conflict) gems. The noise made by this device was said to be deafening.

Sources: Edizioni, *Vimanas and the Wars of the Gods*, n.p.; Menon, *The Mahabharata*, Volume 1, 146, 147

bident of Hades, the

Variation: Hades's pitchfork

The bident (a two-pronged spear) was the traditional weapon of Hades (Roman god Dis/Pluto), the god of the Underworld, in classical Greek mythology; his black bident had the ability to create earthquakes and force lightning up from the earth. The bident of Hades is often confused with the TRIDENT OF POSEIDON (Roman god Neptune), the god of earthquakes, horses, and the seas.

Sources: Loh-Hagan, *Hades*, 68; Sibley, *The Divine Thunderbolt*, 91–92

Bifrost (BEE-frost)

Variations: Asa Bridge, Asabridge, Asbru ("bridge"), Bilrost, Bridge of the Gods ("Asbru"), the Rainbow Bridge, Vindhjalms Brii ("Vindhjalmr's Bridge")

The Rainbow Bridge of Norse mythology, Bifrost ("the trembling way") spans the sky connecting Midgard (Earth) to Asgard ("Enclosure of the Aesir"). According to the *Prose Edda*, written in the thirteenth century by Icelandic historian Snorri Sturluson, the bridge ends at the residence of the god Heimdallr (Heimdal) in Himinbjorg; it is he who guards it, preventing the Jotuns (giants) from crossing. Heimdallr was appointed watchman of the bridge due to his magnificent senses as well as his horn GJALLARHORN, which, when blown, will sound an alarm loud enough to be heard throughout the nine worlds.

Made of air, fire, and water, the bridge looks to be three fragile strands of matter, but, in truth, it is impossibly strong. It has been prophesied that Bifrost will be destroyed by the forces of Muspell. Until that time, each day the gods ride on horseback over the bridge to the URDARBRUNNR WELL, where they sit in judgment, except for Thor, who must go on foot, wading through the rivers Kormt and Ormt and the stream Kerlaug. As the god of thunder, Thor's passage would shatter Bifrost.

Sources: Anderson, *Norse Mythology*, 189; Daly, *Norse Mythology A to Z*, 12; Evans, *Dictionary of Mythology*, 44; Guerber, *Myths of the Norsemen*, 153; Norroena Society, *Asatru Edda*, 399

Big Twisted Flute

In Sioux folklore, Big Twisted Flute was a flute carved in the phallic shape of a twisted, headless horse; it was said to be made of cedar and had five finger holes. Possessed of magic, when played by a man, Big Twisted Flute would emit a haunting melody and create a powerful love spell to entice the woman of his choice as his mate.

Sources: Hassrick, *The Sioux*, 162–63; Monger, *Marriage Customs of the World*, 88, 201

Bilskirnir

Variations: Bilskirne, Bilskirner, Thudvangar, Thurdheimr

In Norse mythology, Bilskirnir ("Storm Serene"/ "Lightning") was the hall of the god of thunder, Thor. This home to fallen warriors was described as thatched with shields that glowed red. The gleaming purple interior had 540 rooms, making it equal in size to VALHALLA.

Sources: Grimes, *The Norse Myths*, 258

Birga

Variations: spear of Fiacha, spear of Fionn mac Cumhaill

In Irish lore, Fiacha was the son of Conga, a trusted warrior of the king of Ireland; his magical spear was gifted to the hero Fionn mac Cumhaill (Finn MacCool/Finn MacCumhail) so he would be able to guard the island of Tara and prevent it from being burned by Aillen, the son of Midgna. The spear was described as having a sharp, blue edge with a poisonous tip, a blue guard, and 30 rivets of Arabian gold; it was noted for being deadly, as it had never made a bad throw. When the spearhead is placed against a person's forehead, they are rendered immune to the effects of the dulcimer of Aillen, which has the ability to put anyone to sleep, no matter what they are doing.

Sources: Dooley and Roe, *Acallam Na Senorach*, 51–54; Gregory and MacCumhaill, *Gods and Fighting Men*, 166, 273

Black Pullet, the

Variation: Hen with the Golden Eggs

A French magical publication (or grimoire) known as *The Black Pullet* was published in 1740; this book revealed the secret formulas and methods by which a magician could create magical amulets, rings, and talismans, among other items. The title came from the book's most sought-after creation: a hen that could lay golden eggs, or (if the spell was not performed properly) at least a hen capable of detecting gold. A specific breed of chicken was used in the spell—a pullet—and, as expected, it needed to be completely black. Kept hooded so it never saw the light of day, the bird was made to lay and hatch a clutch of eggs, kept in a box lined with black materials, one of which would produce a golden-egg-laying black pullet.

Sources: Anonymous, *The Black Pullet*, 65–66, 74; Pickover, *The Book of Black*, 66

black stone of Thorston, the

In fairy lore, a local hero by the name of Thorston rescued the child of a dwarf who was taken by a dragon; the unnamed dwarf insisted on rewarding his savior and made him accept several gifts. One of these gifts was a black stone. According to the story, if the stone was placed in the palm of the user's hand and a fist made tight around it, he would become invisible.

Sources: Dunham, *The Cabinet Cyclopaedia*, Volume 26, 73; Keightley, *World Guide to Gnomes, Fairies, Elves, and Other Little People*, 71

bleeding lance, the

Variations: Avenging Lance, Lance of Longinus, Spear of Longinus

According to the Grail legend, the bleeding lance was the weapon that gave an infected wound to the Grail king; it was a cursed item, wielded by a heathen, and "the lance by which it is said that one day the Kingdom of Logres shall be destroyed." However, the lance also had the magical ability to heal any wound: when laid against the injury, it would draw out the infection and remove all pain. In one story, the blood is taken from the lance and carried to a wounded Arthur in order to heal him. In the story of Perceval, the lance is described as pure white and resting in a stand while a constant flow of blood from its iron tip falls into a silver pot, where the contents then flow through golden pipes into smaller silver pots. It is also said that the sight of the bleeding lance during the Grail Presentation causes all who see it to break out into loud lamentations.

With the introduction of Christianity, the bleeding lance was associated with the HOLY LANCE from Christian apocrypha. In 1098, it was widespread rumor that the spear which had pierced the body of Jesus by the Roman solider known as Longinus had been discovered in Antioch.

Volgate cycles claim that Joseph of Arimathea, an early follower of Christ, carried the lance to Briton, where it was kept hidden with the HOLY GRAIL. There, Balin the Savage used the lance to wound King Pelleham, but later Sir Galahad used it to restore the king to health.

The bleeding lance has also been likened to AREADBHAIR, a weapon from Celtic mythology.

Sources: Bruce, *The Arthurian Name Dictionary*, 73; Jung and von Franz, *The Grail Legend*, 71, 86, 87, 217

Blikjandabol (BLEEK-yand-a-buhl)

Variation: Blikianda Bol

In Norse mythology, Hel, the goddess of the underworld, has an enormous hall named ELJUD-NIR ("Preparer of Pain"/"Sprayed with Snowstorms"), which is fully decorated with many named items. The *arsal* (bed curtain) hangings around her bed are called Blikjandabol ("Gleaming Disaster"/"Glittering Evil"/"Splendid Misery").

Sources: Byock, *The Prose Edda*, 34; Norroena Society, *Satr Edda*, 339

Blodgang

Variation: Burtgang

In Continental Germanic mythology, Blodgang ("Combat to the First Blood") was the sword of Heime (Hama); it had the reputation of being one of the best weapons ever fashioned but was broken into pieces during a duel with Thidrek when it was struck against the helmet HILDIGRIM. The two men became friends, and Thidrek gave Heime the sword NAGELRING.

Sources: de Beaumont and Allinson, *The Sword and Womankind*, 8; McConnell et al., *The Nibelungen Tradition*, 84

blood of the hydra, the

The Greek demigod, legendary hero Heracles was ordered to serve King Eurystheus for twelve years in order to atone for his madness-driven murder spree in which he killed his wife, children, and two of his brother's children (in some accounts, Megera, his wife, survived). During this time of servitude, Heracles had to perform twelve impossible tasks, the second of which was slaying the multi-headed hydra ("water snake") living in the swamps of Lerno; although there is no traditional description of the creature, the number of heads ranges from two to hundreds in artistic renderings and stories. In the course of this battle, Heracles used the sword HARPE, which once belonged to his great-grandfather.

Once the hydra was slain, Heracles dipped the heads of his arrows into its highly poisonous blood (or gall—sources vary); even a slight scratch would prove fatal.

Sources: Hard, *The Routledge Handbook of Greek Mythology*, 258; Hreik, *Hercules*, 13–18; Huber, *Mythematics*, 14–19

Blue Cloud

In Chinese Buddhist mythology, there are four brothers known collectively as the Diamond Kings of Heaven (*Ssu Ta Chin-kang* or *T'ien-wang*); statues of them stand guard in pairs on the left and right sides of the entrances to Buddhist temples. The god and guardian of the east, Mo-Li Ch'ing ("Prue"), is the oldest of the brothers and carries a magical sword named Blue Cloud; upon its blade the words "Ti, Shui, Huo, Feng" ("Earth, Water, Fire, Wind") are inscribed. When drawn, the sword creates a black wind that in turn creates tens of thousands of spears, which will attack invaders with such ferocity that their bodies will turn into dust. Immediately following this attack, the air is filled with tens of thousands of spontaneously created golden serpents of fire. A thick smoke rises up from the ground, blinding and choking the remaining invaders so the fire serpents can ensure that no one will escape.

Sources: Buckhardt, *Chinese Creeds and Customs*, 163; Werner, *Myths and Legends of China*, 121

Blutgang

Dietrich of Bern (a popular character in German literature and legend) had an entourage of warriors, one of which was named Heime. The son Studas, a breeder of war hoses, Heime was unafraid of Prince Dietrich in spite of the young nobleman's fame. Heime was described as a bold knight, churlish, gloomy, and cruel of heart even when not warring; nevertheless, he had a heart full of valor, great daring and fierceness, and strength beyond his years. Heime arrived before the prince on a swift grey horse named Rispa and wielding a sword named Blutgang ("Blood-Fetcher").

Sources: Brewer, *Dictionary of Phrase and Fable* 1900, 1197; Mackenzie, *Teutonic Myth and Legend*, 424

bo shan

In Chinese folklore, only dragons with wings, known as *ying long*, have the natural ability to fly. Wingless dragons have a knot or lump on their forehead that allows flight; this feature is known as a *chi mu*. If male dragons who lack these physical traits wish to fly, they must carry a bo shan, a magical wand that grants them the gift of flight. Female dragons do not carry a bo shan but rather an umbrella in their tail.

Sources: Bates, *All about Chinese Dragons*, 23–24

boat of Manannan mac Lir, the

Manannan mac Lir (Mannanan, Mannanos), god of the sea and guardian of the Underworld in Celtic mythology, was a master of shape shifting and had many varied powers and magical items. One of his possessions was a self-propelling boat made of copper. It was also drawn by a horse named Enbharr ("Splendid Mane" or "Water Foam"). No one was ever slain while riding on her back, as she was said to be as swift as a cold spring wind.

Sources: Macbain, *Celtic Mythology and Religion*, 97; Monaghan, *Encyclopedia of Celtic Mythology and Folklore*, 311

Bodn

Variations: Boden, Bohn

In Norse mythology, Bodn ("Offering") was one the vessels that held a portion of the PRE-

32

cious Mead; the others were Odrerir and Son. In the "Skaldskaparmal" portion of the *Prose Edda*, Icelandic historian Snorri Sturluson explicitly states that Odrerir was a bronze kettle in which the blood of Kvasir was fermented, while Bodn and Son were barrels.

Sources: Grimes, *The Norse Myths*, 259; Hawthorne, *Vikings*, 17; Lindow, *Norse Mythology*, 252

Bohun Upas

Variations: Anitar, Poison Tree of Java, Upas-Tree

In the folklore of fifteenth-century Europe, tales of a fantastic and poisonous tree growing on the islands near Cathay (China) known as the Bohun Upas ("Tree Poison") were widespread among travelers; highly stylized pictures of it also appeared in books. Stories claimed the tree was so toxic that falling asleep in its shade would be fatal. Other stories said that the Malaysians executed their prisoners by forcing them to drink the tree's sap.

Sources: Booth, *An Analytical Dictionary of the English Language*, 357; *London and Edinburgh Philosophical Magazine and Journal of Science*, Volume V, 218

bone of Ullr ("ULL-er")

Variations: bone of Ollerus, bone of Ull, bone of Ullinn

Ullr ("Splendid"), the little-known god of winter from Norse mythology, was a skilled wizard and said to be an expert archer, hunter, runner with snowshoes, skater, and skier. One of Ullr's possessions was a magical bone onto which he carved magical runes that, when spoke aloud, allowed him to teleport. Other remarkable properties of the bone were that it could be transformed into ice-shoes and skies that allowed one to travel across both snow and water. With a different enchantment, the bone could be transformed into a ship. When the bone was not being used for travel, it could be transformed into a shield and used in combat; in this form, it was called *Ullr kjoll*. Other weapons of Ullr are mentioned, such as his bow (Ullr almsima) and swords (Ullr bramds, Ullr branda, and Ullr benloga), but no particular magical ability is ascribed to them.

Sources: Kauffmann, *Northern Mythology*, 69, 81–82; Rydberg, *Teutonic Mythology* volume 3, 628

Book of Fferyllt, the

In Arthurian and Celtic lore, Gwion Bach ap Gwreang was an enchantress and the wife of a nobleman; she performed divinations and practiced magic, and her tale is told in the Middle Welsh manuscript *Book of Taliesin*. In the story, Gwion Bach ("Bright and Small") used a tome called the *Book of Fferyllt* (*Book of Virgil*), which contained much of her knowledge of alchemy, druidic lore, herbology, and magical spells.

Sources: Fries, *Cauldron of the Gods*, 411–12; McColman, *The Complete Idiot's Guide to Celtic Wisdom*, 138

bow and arrows of Heracles

The bow and arrows of the legendary demigod and hero Heracles from classical Greek mythology do not have any innate magical abilities, but they are mentioned in many myths and played a significant role in the Trojan War.

After slaying the hydra, Heracles dipped his arrows in the creature's blood, envenoming them. While hunting, Heracles accidentally shot one of these poisoned arrows into the noble centaur Chiron, who was famed for educating many Greek heroes, including Achilles, Aeneas, Asclepius, Jason, Peleus, and Heracles himself.

On another occasion, Heracles shot the centaur Nesso (Nessus), who had attempted to rape his wife, Deianeira. As Nesso (Nessus) died, he convinced Deianeira to collect some of his blood and semen to create a love potion that would keep her husband faithful to her (see LOVE POTION OF DEIANEIRA). When Deianeira learned that her husband was bringing back the princess Iole, she covered his robe with the potion. However, the concoction burned into his flesh and down to his bones, driving him mad with pain and causing him to commit suicide. The man who lit the funeral pyre for Heracles, Philoctetes, was given the hero's bow and arrows.

En route to fight in the Trojan War, Philoctetes was bitten by a snake; when the wound could not be healed, he was left on the island of Lemnos. Philoctetes remained there, living off the birds he hunted with the bow and arrows, until a prophecy was revealed: the Trojan War would not be won by the Achaeans without the bow and arrows of Heracles. Diomedes and Odysseus (or Neoptolemus and Odysseus—sources conflict) retrieved the items, returned to the battlefield and used the weapons to kill Paris.

Sources: Hard, *The Routledge Handbook of Greek Mythology*, 258; Hreik, *Hercules*, 13–18; Warner et al., *Library of the World's Best Literature: A–Z*, 13, 671–13, 672

bow of Apollo, the

One of the most feared weapons in classical Greek mythology was the bow of Apollo, the god of archery, art, healing, hunting, knowledge, medicine, music, oracles, plague, prophecy, sun and light, truth, and young unmarried men. Apollo ("to destroy" or "to drive away") used his bow to shoot anyone who angered him. Made of two silver ram horns, the bow produced a blinding flash of light when the arrow was released; it had the ability to cause famine, pestilence, and plague or to grant health. People who died in their sleep or suddenly were said to have been shot by the bow of Apollo.

Sources: Hard, *The Routledge Handbook of Greek Mythology*, 142–43; Lang, *A Book of Myths*, n.p.

bow of Artemis, the

A symbol of the new moon, as it was crafted with silver and inlaid with gold by moonlight, the bow of Artemis (Roman goddess Diana), the goddess of children, hunting, virginity, unmarried girls, and wild animals, from classical Greek mythology was a powerful weapon. Like the bow of her brother, Apollo ("to destroy" or "to drive away"), Artemis's bow, created by the Cyclopes, had the ability to cause plagues and heal the sick. When a young girl or woman died suddenly, it was said that she had been shot by the bow of Artemis.

Sources: Callimachus, Hymn 3 to Artemis; Rigoglioso, *The Cult of Divine Birth in Ancient Greece*, 224

bow of Eurytus, the

Variations: bow of Odysseus, bow of Ulysses

In classical Greek mythology, Eurytus was an extremely skilled archer who was also proud and boastful; his ego was so great that he challenged Apollo ("to destroy" or "to drive away"), the god of archery, art, healing, hunting, knowledge, medicine, music, oracles, plague, prophecy, sun and light, truth, and young unmarried men, to a test of skills. After Apollo killed him for being so presumptuous, the powerful bow Eurytus had favored was passed down to his son Iphitus, who was also the brother of King Eurystheus of Mycenae. Iphitus traded the bow to Odysseus in exchange for his sword and spear. This was the bow Odysseus used to kill all the suitors who sought the hand of his wife, Penelope.

Sources: Daly and Rengel, *Greek and Roman Mythology, A to Z*, 18, 39, 55; Westmoreland, *Ancient Greek Beliefs*, 349

bow of Ilmarinen, the

Variations: the golden bow, golden bow of Ilmarinen

In a legend from Finland found in the epic poem *The Kalevala*, Ilmarinen, a god with remarkable smithing abilities, used the magical elements in his forge to create many remarkable items. One such item was a magical bow that glowed like the moon. Having a copper shaft tipped with silver, this bow was the most beautiful and perfect item Ilmarinen ever made; however, it was corrupted. The bow was not content unless it killed one warrior a day (two on holy feast days). Displeased, Ilmarinen broke it into pieces and threw it back into the magical heat of his forge.

Sources: Friberg et al., *The Kalevala*, 99; Mouse, *Ilmarinen Forges the Sampo*, 55

bow of Kaundinya, the

In Cambodian oral folklore, the Indian Brahman priest Kaundinya had a prophetic dream: he was to travel to the Great Lake and there find his riches. Upon waking, Kaundinya took up his magical bow and went to the Great Lake. He ventured onto the water, where he encountered the beautiful naga princess, Soma (*naga* are a race of demonic beings described as human with the lower body of a snake). Kaundinya used his magical bow and shot an arrow into her boat, which initially frightened her but later caused her to fall in love with Kaundinya. As a wedding dowry, her father, the Naga King, sucked up the water of his country and gave it to Kaundinya to rule; this land became known as Nokor Phnom.

All variations of this tale take the time to mention that Kaundinya's bow was magical; however, none of them say what magical properties the bow possessed or what the enchantment on the arrow he fired may have been (if any).

Sources: Fee and Webb, *American Myths, Legends, and Tall Tales*, Volume 1, 555–56; Lee and Nadeau, *Encyclopedia of Asian American Folklore and Folklife*, Volume 1, 1, 223; Monod, *Women's Wiles*, 86

box of Pandora, the

Variation: Pandora's box

The beautiful but inquisitive Pandora ("All-Gifted"/"All-Giving") from classical Greek mythology was used by Zeus (Roman god Jupiter), the god of fate, kings, lightning, sky, and thunder, to settle a score with the Titan Prometheus for giving the gift of fire to mankind. Pandora was herself a creation by Hephaistos (Hephaestus; Roman god Vulcan), the god of fire, forges, metalworking, sculpture, and stonemasonry. Once his commission was completed, Zeus gave Pandora to Prometheus's brother Epimetheus to be his wife, although Epimetheus had been warned by his brother not to accept any gifts from Zeus. As a wedding present, Pandora was given a divine box or jar to keep watch over, having been instructed to never open the lid or glance inside. Eventually curiosity got the better of her and she opened the box, releasing a host of horrors into the world—the many plagues of mankind that cause them grief, illness, and strain. Fortunately, she was able to keep one last element inside the box: hope.

Sources: Daly and Rengel, *Greek and Roman Mythology, A to Z*, 110, 123; Westmoreland, *Ancient Greek Beliefs*, 91–92

Brahmaastra

Variation: Brahma astra

In Hindu mythology, an ASTRA is a supernatural weapon created or gifted by the gods to someone who then presides over the weapon. The wielder of an ASTRA is known as an astradhari.

Brahmaastra was an ASTRA from the god Brahma, the Creator. Brahmaastra was said to have the ability to destroy an entire army with one blow. The weapon would manifest with its tip looking like the Brahma. This is the only ASTRA powerful enough to harm the Brahma; its power is said to have been comparable to a modern-day nuclear bomb. Brahmaastra also had the ability to counter the abilities and powers of the other ASTRAS.

Sources: Edizioni, *Vimanas and the Wars of the Gods*, n.p.; Rao, *Mahabharata*, 37–39

Brahmandastra

Variation: Brahmand astra

In Hindu mythology, an ASTRA is a supernatural weapon created or gifted by the gods to someone who then presides over the weapon. The wielder of an ASTRA is known as an astradhari.

Brahmandastra was designed to be a defensive weapon, wielded by Vashishta against Vishwamitra. The *Mahabharata*, one of the major epics of ancient India, described the staff as manifesting all five heads of the Brahma at its tip; this is significant, as he lost one of his heads fighting Siva. Brahmandastra is said to have the power and strength of the *Brahmand*, the entire solar system, all fourteen realms in the Hindu cosmology.

Sources: Agarwal, *Mahabharata Retold: Part 1*, 47

Brahmashira

Variation: Brahmashirsha astra

In Hindu mythology, an ASTRA is a supernatural weapon created or gifted by the gods to someone who then presides over the weapon. The wielder of an ASTRA is known as an astradhari.

Brahmashira was an ASTRA from Brahma, the Creator. It allegedly had the ability to destroy the devas (demigods). When this weapon manifested, it was said to have four heads of the Brahma on its tip; this description leads scholars to believe that Brahmashira was an evolution of BRAHMAASTRA and, therefore, four times as powerful.

The *Mahabharata* describes, quite clearly, the terrible force and power this weapon possessed. Once invoked, it blazed up with inferno-like flames and a gigantic sphere of fire; *vajra* ("thunder") rolled across the sky and "thousands of meteors fell," filling every living creature with horror as the whole earth shook. In the area where the weapon struck, there was total destruction; nothing in its radius survived. It took twelve years for even a single blade of grass to sprout, but even then the area remained poisoned.

Sources: Edizioni, *Vimanas and the Wars of the Gods*, n.p.; Subramaniam, *Ramayana*, 508

Branstock Tree

In German folklore, Volsung, the son of King Rerir, in his youth had built his hall around the Branstock Tree; its branches formed the roof of the house, and its trunk was the center of the great hall. Many tales say it is an oak tree, but the rest say it is an apple tree (referring to an earlier tale of the then childless King Rerir).

Volsung's hall was known as the Hall of the Branstock. One night in the main hall, while celebrating a less-than-desired wedding of his only daughter Signy to a less-than-desirable king, a stranger (Odin, the god of battle, death, frenzy, the gallows, healing, knowledge, poetry, royalty, the runic alphabet, sorcery, and wisdom) in a blue cape stormed in. After drinking a horn of mead, he drew a sword (BALMUNG) that shone brightly and stabbed it into the trunk of the Branstock Tree. The stranger proclaimed that whoever could pull the sword from the tree would be its wielder. All men present attempted to free the sword, but it was the youngest of the Volsung princes, Sigurd (Siegfried/Sigmund), who was successful.

Sources: Boult, *Asgard and the Norse Heroes*, 139; Colum, *The Children of Odin*, 236–37

Brattach

In the Irish epic *Tain Bo Cuailnge* (*The Cattle Raid of Cooley/The Tain*), Brattach was the sword of Menns; it is named as being among the many cups, drinking horns, goblets, javelins, shields, and swords kept in Tete Brec, one of the three households of the Ulster hero Cuhullin (Cu Chulaind/Cu Chulainn/Cuchulainn).

Sources: Kinsella and Le Brocquy, *The Tain*, 5; Mountain, *The Celtic Encyclopedia*, Volume 4, 861

brazen castanets of Heracles, the

The Greek demigod and legendary hero Heracles was ordered to serve King Eurystheus for twelve years in order to atone for his madness-driven murder spree in which he killed his wife, children, and two of his brother's children (in some accounts, Megera, his wife, survived). During this time of servitude, Heracles had to perform twelve impossible tasks, the traditional sixth (or fifth—sources conflict) of which was slaying the Stymphalian birds. Because these birds were incredibly predatory, violent, and present in large flocks in a dense woodland area, strategy was needed to hunt them. A few versions of the myth claim Heracles made the bronze castanets (or rattle) himself, but most versions state that Athena (Roman goddess Minerva), the goddess of crafts, military victories, war, and wisdom, gifted it to him. In either case, the noise created by the musical instrument frightened the birds into taking flight. While a few of them flew away, never to be seen again (or to the Isle of Ares, where the last of their kind tangled with Jason and the Argonauts), the rest were shot down by Heracles with his bow and arrow.

Sources: Hreik, *Hercules*, 34–36; Huber, *Mythematics*, 53–64; Murgatroyd, *Mythical Monsters in Classical Literature*, n.p.

brazen serpent

According to biblical lore, poisonous serpents were sent to punish the Israelites as they wandered in the desert after the exodus from Egypt, because they were losing faith in the Lord. Realizing their sin, they prayed and asked for forgiveness. God then spoke to Moses, commanding him to construct a serpent of brass and place it on a pole as a sign of His forgiveness and love. Anyone who was bitten by a snake had only to look upon the brazen serpent Moses had constructed, and they would be cured. The brazen serpent remained in the temple for five centuries, but it was eventually denounced by prophets as an item of idolatry.

Sources: Erskine, *The Brazen Serpent*, 11; Johnson, *Lady of the Beasts*, 182; Morris, *Moses: A Life in Pictures*, 26

breastplate of Manannan

Manannan mac Lir (Mannanan, Mannanos), god of the sea and guardian of the Underworld in Celtic mythology, was a master of shape shifting and had many varied powers and magical items. One of his possessions was a breastplate that no weapon could pierce.

Sources: Macbain, *Celtic Mythology and Religion*, 97

Breidablik (BRADE-a-blick)

Variations: Baldr's Brow, Breidablik, Breroablik

In Norse mythology, Breidablik ("Vast Splendor") is the home of the god Balder; nothing unclean can enter into its halls, and nothing unclean can be found there. It was constructed in the land of least evil in Asgard ("Enclosure of the Aesir"). Balder lives in Breidablik with his wife, the goddess Nanna Nepsdottr; their hall, FEIKSTAF, was made of shining gold and silver. Chamomile flowers grow here in such abundance that it is sometimes called Baldr's Brow because of its medicinal powers. Breidablik is considered *gridastadr* ("a sacred place").

Sources: Anderson, *Norse Mythology*, 186, 279; Daly, *Norse Mythology A to Z*, 13–14; Dunham, *History of Denmark, Sweden, and Norway*, Volume 2, 55; Grimes, *The Norse Myths*, 19, 200, 215; Sturluson, *Younger Edda*, 77, 84, 259

Brimir

Variation: Brimer

A mead hall in Norse mythology, Brimir ("Radiance")—named after Midvitnir ("Mead Wolf"/"Mid Wolf"/"Sea Wolf"), the Jotun who lived there—was located in OKOLNIR near Nidavellir. The mead served within was the PRECIOUS MEAD, which Midvitnir stole and stored in the SKULL OF HEIDRAUPNIR and HORN OF HODDROFNIR. Brimir was constructed after Ragnarok; here, the Aesir would meet at to talk about the old days, enjoy themselves, and relax, as the hall always had plenty of mead.

Sources: de Beaumont and Allinson, *The Sword and Womankind*, 8; Grimes, *The Norse Myths*, 58, 259

Brisingamen (BREES-ing-am-en)

Variations: Bringa-Men, Brising Belt, Brisinga Necklace, Brisingamen Necklace, Brisinga-Men, Brising's Necklace, Necklace of Freya

In Norse mythology, Brisingamen was a necklace of great beauty forged by the four dwarf brothers Alfrig, Berling, Dvalin, and Grer. Freyja ("Lady"), the goddess of beauty, death, fertility, gold, love, seidr (a type of sorcery), sex, and war, so deeply desired the necklace that she purchased it with the promise to sleep one night with each of the brothers. The god Loki stole the necklace from her, but it was eventually recovered and returned to her by Heimdallr (Heimdal). The discovery of how she came to own the jewelry caused her husband, Odr, to leave her. Freyja wandered throughout Midgard (Earth) in search of her husband, calling out his name and weeping bitter tears of gold.

Sources: Bellows, *The Poetic Edda*, 158; Grimes, *The Norse Myths*, 259–60; Hawthorne, *Vikings*, 17; Norroena Society, *Asatru Edda*, 340

Broken Sword, the

In French medieval Arthurian folklore, the Broken Sword refers to the weapon used to wound Joseph of Arimathea in the thighs. The son of King Pelles presented the weapon to three knights of the ROUND TABLE who happened upon his castle. They were told the sword would mend itself for the one who would achieve the "adventures of the Grail." Each tried to restore the weapon, but for Galahad the repair was so perfect that it was if the weapon was new again. They decided among themselves that Sir Bors should keep it, as he had exceptional virtue and worthiness.

Sources: Kibler and Palmer, *Medieval Arthurian Epic and Romance*, 264; Weston, *The Legend of Sir Lancelot Du Lac*, 139

bronze dome of the heavens, the

As one of the Titans who fought against the Olympian gods in the Titanomachy, Atlas was sentenced by Zeus (Roman god Jupiter), the god of fate, kings, lightning, sky, and thunder, to carry the bronze dome of the heavens (in which the starry constellations were fixed) on his shoulders. The vault had seven zones—one for the moon, one for the sun, and one for each of the known planets: Mercury, Venus, Mars, Jupiter, and Saturn, respectively. Atlas held the dome aloft beneath the axis of heaven and spun it, thereby causing the stars to seem to rise and set.

Sources: Hockney, *World, Underworld, Overworld, Dreamworld*, n.p.; Roman and Roman, *Encyclopedia of Greek and Roman Mythology*, 92

Brosinga mene

Variation: Brisinga men

In the Old English epic *Beowulf*, there is an allusion to the legendary tale of the hero Hama stealing the necklace of the Brosings: the Brosinga mene. The collar (or tork) was said to be one of the adornments of Freyja ("Lady"), the goddess of beauty, death, fertility, gold, love, seidr (a type of sorcery), sex, and war.

Sources: Lindow, *Norse Mythology*, 89; Room, *Who's Who in Classical Mythology*, 223; Wyatt and Chambers, *Beowulf*, 89

buckler of Jan ibn Jan, the

In Persian folklore, the great adventurer Kinf Tahmuras (Tahumers) possessed a potent buckler that once belonged to the king of the djinn, Jan Ibn Jan. Tahmuras wore this buckler on his arm when he rode the magical bird, Simurgh, to Jinnistan to face the Deevs.

Sources: Keightley, *The Fairy Mythology by Thomas Keightley*, 18

bull hide of King Hyrieus, the

According to classical Greek mythology, King Hyrieus of Thrace was childless; to rectify this problem, he was told by Zeus (Roman god Jupiter), the god of fate, kings, lightning, sky, and thunder, to urinate on a bull hide. Hyrieus obeyed, so Zeus had Hermes (Roman god Mercury), the god of animal husbandry, commerce, eloquence, fertility, language, looters, luck, sleep, thieves, trade, travel, and wealth, and Poseidon (Roman god Neptune), the god of earthquakes, horses, and the seas, bury it. Nine months later, a child was born from the bull hide; he was named Orion.

Sources: Room, *Who's Who in Classical Mythology*, 223

Byrgir (BERG-ir)

Variations: Brygi, Byrger, Byrgvi

In Norse mythology, Byrgir ("Hider of Something") was the well from which Bil and Hjuki drew water at the behest of the Jotun Vidfinnr. The water of Byrgir had the power to give the drinker youthfulness; it was used to make a batch of mead so delicious that it was hidden and stolen numerous times.

Sources: Grimes, *The Norse Myths*, 260; Norroena Society, *Satr Edda*, 25

caduceus of Asclepius (kuh-DEW-see-us)

Variations: Asclepius, Caduceus, caduceus of Aesculapius, rod of Aesculapius, rod of Asclepius, rod of Asklepios, staff of Hermes, staff of Tiresias

Caladbolg

Often confused with the ROD OF HERMES, the caduceus ("herald's staff") of Asclepius is a roughly hewn walking staff entwined by a single snake. In classical Greek mythology, Asclepius was a demigod of medicine and the son of Coronis and Apollo ("to destroy" or "to drive away"), the god of archery, art, healing, hunting, knowledge, medicine, music, oracles, plague, prophecy, sun and light, truth, and young unmarried men. Asclepius was renowned for his ability to heal the sick; he was so talented that he could even bring the dead back to life by using an unnamed magical herb shown to him by a snake. Hades (Roman god Dis/Pluto), the god of the Underworld, was displeased that the dead could be resurrected and brought his grievance to Zeus (Roman god Jupiter), the god of fate, kings, lightning, sky, and thunder. Fearing humans would be made immortal, Zeus threw his thunderbolt at Asclepius, killing him.

Sources: Cavanaugh, *Hippocrates' Oath and Asclepius' Snake*, n.p.; Graves, *The Greek Myths*, 49.; Layman, *Medical Terminology Demystified*, 8

Caladbolg

Variations: Calad Bolg ("Hard Lightning"), Caladcholf ("hard blade"), Caladcholg, Caledfwlch ("Hardnotch"), Caledvwlch, Calesvol, Calibor, Calibore, Caliburn, Caliburnus, Calwdvwlch, Escalibor, Escalibore, EXCALIBUR, Lightning Sword

A sword from Celtic, Irish, and Welsh mythology, Caladbolg ("Hard-belly" or "Hard-lightning") was said to have first belonged to the hero Lete before passing to his son, Fergus mac Leti, and then coming to the great and exiled Ulster hero, Fergus mac Roich of the Ulster Cycle. According to the cleric and historian Geoffrey of Monmouth (circa 1095–1155), the sword was forged on the Insula Avallonis (Isle of Avalon). In the Ulster Cycle, Fergus would chant an obscure verse over the sword and then, wielding it with both hands, cause tremendous devastation, as the blade would become as large as "a rainbow crossing the sky." In one story he cut through a hundred men; in another he lopped the tops off of three adjoining hills to defuse his battle rage (neither story is clear regarding whether this destruction occurred because of the size of the blade or due to its lightning-fast wielding capability).

In another tale, King Arthur names those of his possessions that a visiting kinsman, Culhwch, may not ask for—"RHONGOMIANT, my spear, WYNEBGWRTHUCHER my shield, CARNWENNAN my knife, and Gwenhwyfar, my wife"—as they are essential to his status and identity. Although the king does not use his sword in this tale, it is used by Llenlleawc Wybel to kill Diwrnach. As the king's sword, there are said to be two engraved snakes upon it; when pulled from its scabbard, their tongues emitted flames. The blade is also said to have a luminescent quality, as bright as the light of two burning torches.

Sources: Koch, *Celtic Culture: G–L*, 146, 328, 329; Pendergrass, *Mythological Swords*, 12; Puhvel, *Beowulf and the Celtic Tradition*, n.p.

Caleuche

The *Caleuche* is a ghost ship from the folklore of Chiloe Island, Chile; it sails at night just beneath the surface of the waters off the channel between the island and the mainland. According to the legend, the ship only manifests at night, making a dramatic appearance by suddenly bursting through a fog bank and surfacing to ride the waves, brightly lit up with lanterns. Commanded by el Millalobo, the master of the sea, the *Caleuche* punishes those who bring hardship to the creatures of the sea or the ocean waters. Those who catch sight of the *Caleuche* are said to have their head cocked or mouth twisted if they survive the sighting; otherwise the eyewitness will die.

The ghost ship is crewed entirely of shipwrecked sailors who died, as well as witches; they come and go from the ship by riding the great sea-horse, Caballo Marino. On calm nights there is great laughter and merriment, as well as music, to be heard from the *Caleuche*.

Sources: Bingham and Roberts, *South and Meso-American Mythology A to Z*, 46; Minnis, *Chile Insight Guide*, 274; Roland, *Frightful Ghost Ships*, 9–11

Calmali

Variations: Harzgfakadruma ("TREE OF THORNS"), Kantakadruma, Salmali, Salmalia Malabarz'ea, Tree of Hell, Tree of Yama

In Hindu mythology, Calmali is a tree associated with torture and said to grow in Hell. The tree has very large thorns that snag and entangle the dead as they pass by it. Yama, the god of this region, is said to live nearby Calmali. The *Mahabharata* describes the tree as having red flowers that can be seen at a great distance; it also states that no wind ever blows and disturbs Calmali's leaves.

Sources: Folkard, *Plant Lore, Legends, and Lyrics*, 189; Porteous, *The Forest in Folklore and Mythology*, 201–2

Calpe

Variations: Pillars of Heracles

Calpe was one of the two pillars that the demigod and legendary hero Heracles toppled in classical Greek mythology, ABYLA being the other. These pillars marked the end of the known world. Most versions of this story say Heracles traveled through many countries, and when he reached the frontiers of Europe and Libya, he constructed two pillars and placed one on each side of the Straits of Gibraltar. Collectively, the two pillars were known as the Pillars of Heracles. However, in one telling of the tale, originally a mountain stood in that place, but Heracles tore it asunder, separating it into two, allowing the sea to freely pass between the passageway he created.

Sources: Morris, *New Universal Graphic Dictionary of the English Language*, 1020; Smith, *A Classical Dictionary of Greek and Roman Biography, Mythology and Geography*, 398; Trumbull, *The Threshold Covenant, or The Beginning of Religious Rites*, 100

candlestick of the Fisher King

The French poet and troubadour Chretien de Troyes (1130–1191) is best known for his work on Arthurian lore and his creation of the character of Sir Lancelot. In his telling of the Grail Quest, de Troyes describes the candlestick of the Fisher King (Crippled King/Maimed King/Wounded King/Anfortas/Bron/Evelake/Parlan/Peliam/Pellam/Pelles). In the tale, Sir Perceval witnesses a ceremony that occurs before dinner in which the BLEEDING LANCE, the candlestick, and the Grail itself are paraded through the room. The candlestick is said to be golden, inlaid with black enamel, and large enough that two pages are needed to carry it, holding ten candles in its branched arms. The light of the candlestick is brilliant but, compared to the glowing radiance of the Grail, dim.

Sources: Greer, *Secret of the Temple*, n.p.; Karr, *Arthurian Companion*, 159

canoe of Gluskab, the

In Abenaki mythology, the mythic cultural hero and giant Gluskab (Glooscap) arrived in this country by means of his granite canoe. Having an affinity for stone (as his canoe proves), he taught the people how to make arrowheads, fire, fishing nets, and stoneware, along with the knowledge of good and evil and how to use tobacco.

Sources: Calloway and Porter, *The Abenaki*, 23; Malinowski, *Gale Encyclopedia of Native American Tribes: Northeast, Southeast, Caribbean*, Volume 1, 12

canoe of Maui, the

Variations: Pirita-o-te-rangi ("the vine or creeper of heaven"), Te Waka-a-Maui ("the Canoe of Maui")

In Maori mythology, the magical canoe of the cultural hero Maui allowed him to sail over the ocean more swiftly than any wind could blow.

Sources: Westervelt, *Legends of Ma-Ui*, 97; White, *Ancient History of the Maori*, 117

cap of invisibility

Variations: cap of Hades, concealing helmet, dogskin of Hades, Helm of Darkness, Helm of Hades, Helmet of Hades, Helmet of Invisibility, Helmet of Orcus, Helmet of Pluto

Created by the Cyclopes of classical Greek mythology for the god of the Underworld, Hades (Roman god Dis/Pluto), during the Titanomachy (the war against the Titans), the cap of invisibility would, when worn, make its wearer invisible even to supernatural beings and creatures, such as the gods themselves.

Those who have worn the cap in addition to Hades include Athena (Roman goddess Minerva), the goddess of crafts, military victories, war, and wisdom; Hermes (Roman god Mercury), the god of animal husbandry, commerce, eloquence, fertility, language, looters, luck, sleep, thieves, trade, travel, and wealth, in his battle against the giant Hippolytus; and Perseus, a hero, who was given the cap by Athena in order to help him defeat the Gorgon, Medusa.

The cap of invisibility is not unique to classical Greek mythology, as it appears in many different cultures. No matter how the item came to be, it always performs the same function—namely, making the wearer invisible. The cap of invisibility can easily be found in Chinese folktales, the folklore of India, the legends of the Omaha and Zuni Native American tribes, Norse mythology, and the folklore of Portugal, to name but a few. The cap of invisibility also appears frequently in fairy lore, which is prevalent all across Europe and exists in most regions of the world in one fashion or another.

Sources: Garry and El-Shammy, *Archetypes and Motifs in Folklore and Literature*, 162; Hastings et al., *Encyclopædia of Religion and Ethics: Hymns–Liberty*, 406; Martinez, *Lost History of the Little People*, n.p.

cap of oblivion

In British fairy lore, the cap of oblivion was a hat worn exclusively by a species of fairy known as an *ellyllon*. When this cap was worn by a mortal, it would make the person follow the ellyllon and join in his fairy dance. The cap also prevented the person from correctly remembering the events that took place.

Sources: Sikes, *British Goblins*, 69

carmot

A legendary stone from alchemic lore, carmot was believed to be a key element (and therefore a much-sought-after ingredient) needed to construct a PHILOSOPHER'S STONE. It was described as dark red in color. Carmot, as an element or compound, is only referenced in alchemic formulas and studies.

Sources: Hauck, *The Complete Idiot's Guide to Alchemy*, 105; Hunter, *The American Dictionary and Cyclopedia*, Volume 12, 581

Carnwennan

Variations: Carnwenhau ("White Hilt"), Cernwennan

In Welsh Arthurian lore, Carnwennan ("Little White-Hilt") was King Arthur's dagger; it appears only in the Welsh traditions and was thought to be among the triad of weapons given to Arthur by God (the other two being CALADBOLG and RHONGOMIANT). In some tales Carnwennan was said to have the magical ability to shroud its wielder in shadows. It was first named in *Culhwch and Olwen*, where Arthur used it cut the Very Black Witch in half.

When Arthur tells Culhwch that he may ask and receive anything of him, the king makes a short list of his prize possessions that are the seven exceptions to his offer: CALADBOLG, his sword; Carnwennan, his dagger; Gwenhwyfar, his wife; GWENN, his cloak; PRYDWEN, his ship; RHONGOMIANT, his spear; and WYNEBGWRTHUCHER, his shield. Carnwennan was named sixth.

Sources: Bromwich and Evans, *Culhwch and Olwen*, 64; Jones, *The Mabinogion*, 136

carving dish of the Fisher King, the

Variation: tailleor of the Fisher King

The French poet and troubadour Chretien de Troyes (1130–1191) is best known for his work on Arthurian lore and his creation of the character of Sir Lancelot. In his telling of the Grail Quest, there is a description of the carving dish of the Fisher King (Crippled King/Maimed King/Wounded King/Anfortas/Bron/Evelake/Parlan/Peliam/Pellam/Pelles). In the tale, Sir Perceval witnesses a ceremony that occurs before dinner in which the BLEEDING LANCE (among other items) is paraded through the room. The carving dish—small and made of pure silver—was carried by a single damsel, the daughter of Brom (or Gron), the king of the Waste Land, brother to the Fisher King.

Sources: Karr, *Arthurian Companion*, 159; Loomis, *The Grail*, 33, 37, 62, 82

Castaly

A fountain in classical Greek mythology, Castaly was said to pour forth water with the ability to give those who drank it the gift of poetry. Sacred to the Muses, the fountain was said to be located in Parnassus. The nymph of the fountain was named Castalia, a daughter of Achelous; the nymphs of the Castalian spring were known as the Castalides. Castaly is often confused with the WELL OF CASSOTIS.

Sources: Brewer, *Dictionary of Phrase and Fable* 1900, 220; Smith, *Dictionary of Greek and Roman Biography and Mythology: Abaeus–Dysponteus*, 627

Catum, al

Al Catum ("the Strong") was said to be a bow belonging to the prophet Muhammad. According to legend, the bow did not live up to its name, as it broke the first time it was used in combat. Al Catum, along with other treasures, came into Muhammad's possession as wealth confiscated from the Jewish tribe Banu Kainoka prior to their banishment to Syria.

Sources: Brewer and Harland, *Character Sketches of Romance, Fiction and the Drama*, Volume 4, 377; Irving, *Works of Washington Irving*, Volume 9, 132; Osborne et al., *A Complete History of the Arabs*, Volume 1, 254; Sale et al., *An Universal History, Part 2*, Volume 1, 185

Caucasian eagle, the

Variations: Aetos Kaukasios, Kaukasian eagle, Kaukasios eagle

In classical Greek mythology, AUTOMATONS ("self-acting") were statues of animals, humans, and monsters that were then animated or otherwise brought to a kind of life by one of the gods; usually this was done by Hephaistos (Hephaestus; Roman god Vulcan), the god of bindings, the art of sculpture, fire, forges, metalworking, stonemasonry, and talismans. Other AUTOMATONS were the GOLDEN MAIDENS, the GOLDEN TRIPODS, the KABEIRIAN HORSES, the KELEDONES, KHRYSEOS AND ARGYREOS, the KOLKHIS BULLS, and TALOS.

Although there is an alternative origin for the eagle—that of being one of the children of the

Titan Typhoon and his wife, the drakaina Echidna—the Caucasian eagle was in either case under the command of Zeus (Roman god Jupiter), the god of fate, kings, lightning, sky, and thunder. For his crime of gifting fire to mankind, Prometheus was rendered helpless and chained to a mountain. Zeus also ordered the Caucasian eagle to go to Prometheus daily and rip him apart, consuming his innards.

The Caucasian eagle was slain by the demigod and legendary hero Heracles in a volley of arrows so as to save Prometheus. Afterward, the arrows, eagle, and Prometheus all were taken into the night sky, thus creating the constellations Aquila the Kneeler and Saggita.

Sources: Bonnefoy, *Greek and Egyptian Mythologies*, 88–89; Ridpath, *Star Tales*, 12; Westmoreland, *Ancient Greek Beliefs*, 54

cauldron of Annwn, the

Variation: cauldron of Rebirth and Inspiration

From the Welsh poem *Preiddeu Annwn* (*The Spoils of Annwn*), the cauldron of Annwn ("Very Deep") appears in the Book of Taliesin; dating from between the ninth and twelfth centuries, it tells how King Arthur and his men traveled to the Land of the Dead (Annwn) by means of his favorite ship, PRYDWEN, to see the Lord of Death and obtain his cauldron. This object is described as enameled with flowers, studded with diamonds (or pearls), and cooled by the breath of the nine maidens who protect it.

The cauldron is said to have "many" magical abilities, one of which is the ability to never boil the food of a coward or a perjurer. Because the cauldron belongs to the Lord of Death and it was taken from the land of the dead, it is assumed that, like the CAULDRON OF BRAN THE BLESSED, it can also restore the dead to life.

Sources: Murphy-Hiscock, *The Way of the Hedge Witch*, 59; Zakroff, *The Witch's Cauldron*, n.p.

cauldron of Bran the Blessed, the

Variations: cauldron of Rebirth, Pair Dadeni ("The Cauldron of Rebirth")

In Welsh mythology, the cauldron of Bran the Blessed had the power to restore the dead back to life. The body of the deceased was to be placed in the cauldron, and the next day they would emerge not only alive but also in peak physical condition. Unfortunately, a side effect of the cauldron was that those who were resurrected by it lost the ability to speak.

Initially, Pair Dadeni was owned by the giant Llasar Llaes Gyfnewid and his wife Cymydei Cymeinfoll, who resided in Ireland. Although they had a place in the court of King Matholwch, they were not accepted and a serious attempt was made to burn them alive. They fled to the court of King Bendigeidfran and gave him Pair Dadeni to show their appreciation of his hospitality.

The cauldron was part of the dowry of the sister of Bran, Branwen, who married King Matholwch of Ireland. It was included in the dowry to compensate for the mutilation and slaughter of Matholwch's horses by Bran's half-brother, Efnisien. When the newly married couple returned to Ireland, they took the cauldron with them. However, the cauldron was used against Bran years later when he went to war against his brother-in-law, as the slain were continuously raised and put back in the ranks. Efnisien hid among the dead so he would be thrown in it; once inside, he sacrificed his life and destroyed the cauldron.

Sources: Murphy-Hiscock, *The Way of the Hedge Witch*, 59; Zakroff, *The Witch's Cauldron*, n.p.

cauldron of the Dagda, the

Variations: Ardagh Chalice, cauldron of Abundance, cauldron of Plenty, Dagda's Cauldron, Undry

According to Irish lore, when the Tuatha de Danann came to Ireland, they carried with them four magical treasures: the cauldron of the Dagda, CLAIDHEAMH SOLUIS, LIA FAIL, and LUIN; each of these magical items came from one of their cities—Falias, Findias, Gorias, and Murias—and each item was carried by a druid. The city of Murias was the place from which the druid Semias carried the cauldron of the Dagda.

The cauldron of the Dagda, the Celtic god of abundance, artistry, banquets, death, excess, inspiration, life, music, the sky, and war, had the magical ability to provide an endless supply and variety of food, which ensured that no one ever went hungry. As a result, the cauldron could never be emptied.

Sources: Adams Media, *The Book of Celtic Myths*, 76–77; Ellis, *Brief History of the Druids*, 73, 124; Zakroff, *The Witch's Cauldron*, n.p.

cauldron of Dyrnwch the Giant, the

Variation: pair Dyrnwch gawr

In British and Welsh folklore, there is a series of items (always thirteen in number) called the THIRTEEN TREASURES OF THE ISLAND OF BRIT-

AIN (in Welsh, they are called *Tri Thlws ar Ddeg Ynys Prydain*). Although in more modern times the items listed are different, the original thirteen items from the fifteenth century were the cauldron of Dyrnwch the Giant, CHARIOT OF MORGAN MWYNFAWR, CHESSBOARD OF GWENDDOLEU AP CEIDIO, COAT OF PADARN BEISRUDD, CROCK AND DISH OF RHYGENYDD YSGOLHAIG (two items), HALTER OF CLYDNO EIDDYN, HAMPER OF GWYDDNO GARANHIR, HORN OF BRAN GALED, KNIFE OF LLAWFRODEDD FARCHOF, MANTLE OF ARTHUR IN CORNWALL, sword of Rhydderch Hael (DYRNWYN), and WHETSTONE OF TUDWAL TUDGLYD.

Much like the CAULDRON OF ANNWN, the cauldron of Dyrnwch the Giant had the magical ability to discern between the food of a brave man (whose food would cook quickly) and that of a coward (whose food would never cook). In Arthurian lore, this item appears in a Middle Welsh tale titled *Culhwch and Olwen*; in it, King Arthur requests the use of the cauldron from its owner, King Odgar, but his steward, Diwrnach, refuses to lend out his prize possession. Arthur and a small entourage go to Ireland to ask directly for the use of the cauldron but are refused a second time. Arthur's champion, Bedwyr, then seizes the cauldron while Llenlleawg the Irishman uses his sword, Caledfwlch (see CALADBOLG), to kill Diwrnach and all his men with a single swing.

Sources: Patton, *The Poet's Ogam*, 510; Pendergrass, *Mythological Swords*, 24, 26; Zakroff, *The Witch's Cauldron*, n.p.

cauldron of Hymer, the

Variation: cauldron of Hymir

The Norse epic poem *Song of Hymir* tells of one of many deeds of the god of thunder, Thor. In this story, the Norse gods are invited to dine with the god of the sea, Aegir. To mark the occasion, Thor and the god of war, Tyr, travel to the Jotun (giant) Hymer to use his cauldron, which is a mile wide and deep (and thus likely the only cauldron large enough to make a single batch of mead for all the gods in one brewing). In the course of the poem, Thor kills Jormungandr (the Midgard serpent), Hymer, and all of the giants who try to stop the theft of the cauldron; he then returns with the cauldron, Aegir brews the mead, and a great feast is held.

Sources: Keyser, *The Religion of the Northmen*, 46; Zakroff, *The Witch's Cauldron*, n.p.

cauldron of inspiration, the

Variations: cauldron of Caridwen, cauldron of inspiration and science, cauldron of wisdom

Appearing only in the Middle Welsh manuscript *Book of Taliesin*, the cauldron of inspiration owned by Tegis Voel and used by his wife Caridwen to improve their ugly son, Morfran. The family lived in the middle of Lake Tegis, beneath the waves, making the cauldron an innately magical vessel. It is said that Caridwen boiled her brew nonstop for a year and a day until only three drops of concentrated inspiration remained. Morfran consumed the drops and became a highly skilled and famous bard. The overflow of the cauldron ran into a nearby stream and poisoned the horses of Gwyddno Garanhir, the legendary ruler of the sunken kingdom Cantre'r Gwaelod.

Sources: *Anniversary Papers by Colleagues and Pupils of George Lyman Kittredge*, 244; Zakroff, *The Witch's Cauldron*, n.p.

Ceard-nan Gallan

In Celtic lore and Irish mythology, Ceard-nan Gallan ("Smith of the Branches") was the sword of the great poet and bard Oisin, one of the Fianna and the narrator for much of the Fenian Cycle. The weapon was so named because it was exceptionally well suited to cutting down the strong and the young.

Ceard-nan Gallan was one of the six swords made by Lon Lonnrach the *beangruagach* ("giant woman"); the other swords were CHRUAIDH COSGARREACH, DRUIDHE LANNACH, FASDAIL, LIOBHANACH, and MAC AN LUINE.

Sources: Gregory and MacCumhaill, *Gods and Fighting Men*, 268; Leodhas, *By Loch and by Lin*, n.p.

Cedar of the End

Variation: Lote tree of Heaven

In Islamic mythology, the Cedar of the End is said to be a gigantic tree sitting beneath the Throne of God; it has billions of leaves upon it, some old and withered while others are young and green. Each leaf upon the tree represents the soul of a living person and has their name written on it. Whenever a leaf falls from the tree, the angel of death, Nduli Mtwaa roho (Azra'il), gathers it up, descends to the Earth, finds the person whose name is on the leaf, and then takes their soul back up to Heaven.

Sources: Cornell, *Voices of Islam*, 157; Knappert, *African Mythology*, 233

celtar

Variations: keltar, mantle of concealment

In Celtic mythology, druids would create a celtar (mantle) that had the power to make its wearer invisible. In some tales, these items were created by a fairy and given to a human as a gift or reward.

Sources: Joyce, *A Smaller Social History of Ancient Ireland*, 103

chain of Cilydd Canastyr, the

In the Welsh Arthurian legends, Cilydd Canastyr ("Hundred-Grips" or "Hundred Holds") was one of the warriors under the command of King Arthur; he owned the singular chain worthy of being matched with the COLLAR OF CANHASTYR CANLLAW. These items, along with the LEASH OF CORS CANT EWIN, would be used by the houndsman Mabon in order to handle the hound of Greid, Drudwyn. All of these items and the hound needed to be gathered together in order for Culhwch to hunt the boar Twrch Trwyth.

Sources: Bruce, *The Arthurian Name Dictionary*, 153; Ellis, *The Chronicles of the Celts*, 327; Mountain, *The Celtic Encyclopedia*, Volume 3, 764

chair of forgetfulness

Variations: chair of Lethe

Located in the Underworld of classical Greek mythology, the chair of forgetfulness is seldom referenced, even by the ancient writers. It was supposedly encountered when the hero and demigod Theseus and his companion Pirithous descended into the Underworld to abduct the goddess of vegetation, Persephone (Roman goddess Proserpine), wife of Hades (Roman god Dis/Pluto), the god of the Underworld.

In some versions of the tale, as they wandered through the Underworld, they rested upon some rock, which then grew into or all around them, trapping them in place, where they were subsequently tortured by the Erinyes, the three goddesses of vengeance. In another version, they were joyfully greeted by Hades, who bade them to sit and rest; when they did, they were bound to the chairs (or rocks—the story varies), where they were then tortured by the Erinyes.

Sources: Hansen, *Handbook of Classical Mythology*, 180, 260, 329; Pausanias, *Pausanias's Description of Greece*, Volume 5, 381

Chandrahas

Variations: Chandrahasa, Moon Blade

An ASTRA from Hindu lore, Chandrahas ("the laughter of the moon"—a reference to the crescent moon) was gifted to the rakshasa and king of Lanka, Raavan, by Shiva. This scimitar was indestructible, but if it was ever used for an unjust cause, Chandrahas would immediately return to Shiva.

Sources: Beer, *The Handbook of Tibetan Buddhist Symbols*, 124; Cakrabarti, *The Penguin Companion to the Ramayana*, 91

chariot of Baal

Variation: storm chariot of Baal

A deity worshiped throughout the ancient Middle East, especially in ancient Canaan and Phoenicia, Baal ("Lord"), a god of fertility, is described as driving his war chariot across the sky, bringing the rain with him. The chariot itself is described as a great cloud.

Sources: Smith, *The Ugaritic Baal Cycle*, 297; van der Toorn et al., *Dictionary of Deities and Demons in the Bible*, 704

chariot of Dionysus, the

In classical Greek mythology, Dionysus (Roman god Bacchus), the god of fertility, the grape harvest, religious ecstasy, ritual madness, theater, winemaking, and wine, had a chariot decked out with flowers, garlands, and wreaths. In art, it is sometimes shown as being pulled by centaurs, while in others it is pulled by elephants, leopards, panthers, or tigers (these animals were commonly used in Roman art for the god and were often used as symbols of victory).

Sources: Immerzeel and Kersten, *Coptic Studies on the Threshold of a New Millennium*, 1362; Stephenson, *Constantine: Roman Emperor, Christian Victor*, n.p.

chariot of Eos, the

In classical Greek and Roman mythology, the purple chariot of the goddess of the dawn, Eos, was pulled by Lampos and Phaeton, two *hippoi athanatoi* (immortal horses of the gods).

Sources: Bechtel, *Dictionary of Mythology*, 122, 171; Breese and D'Aoust, *God's Steed*, 92

chariot of fire, the

According to the Bible, a chariot of fire is the vehicle in which the prophet Elijah ascended into Heaven. In the book of 2 Kings 2:8–11 RSV, Elijah strikes the water, making it part; from the dry land rises up the chariot of fire and its flaming horses, creating a great whirlwind that lifts Elijah up into the air and then takes him up to Heaven.

Sources: Barnes, *Dictionary of the Bible*, 196, 311; Ryken et al., *Dictionary of Biblical Imagery*, 139, 569

chariot of Freyja, the

In Norse mythology, Freyja ("Lady"), the goddess of beauty, death, fertility, gold, love, seidr (a type of sorcery), sex, and war, has a chariot that is pulled by two *fress* ("tom-cats"), according to "Skaldskaparmal," the first part of the *Prose Edda*, written by the Icelandic historian Snorri Sturluson. However, in the "Gylfaginning" section, the chariot is said to be pulled by two *kottr* ("martens" or "weasels").

Sources: Grimes, *The Norse Myths*, 131, 263; Grimm, *Teutonic Mythology*, Volume 1, 306

chariot of Hades, the

In classical Greek mythology, the chariot of Hades (Roman god Dis/Pluto), the god of the Underworld, was pulled by four (or six—sources vary) black *hippoi athanatoi* (immortal horses of the gods). The chariot played an integral part in the abduction of Persephone (Roman goddess Proserpine), as Hades left the Underworld through a crack in the earth but returned with his captive in the golden chariot. This is also the vehicle Hades employs when he returns Persephone to her mother; even Hermes (Roman god Mercury), the god of animal husbandry, commerce, eloquence, fertility, language, looters, luck, sleep, thieves, trade, travel, and wealth, uses the chariot to leave the Underworld, flying in it over the earth. Antiquity names four of Hades's *hippoi athanatoi*: Abaster ("Away from the Stars"), Abatos ("Inaccessible"), Aeton ("Swift as an Eagle"), and Nomos.

Sources: Konstantinou, *Female Mobility and Gendered Space in Ancient Greek Myth*, 50–60; Leeming and Page, *Goddess: Myths of the Female Divine*, 69–70

chariot of Helios, the

Variations: CHARIOT OF SOL, chariot of Sun, Helios's chariot, Sol's chariot, Sol Invictus's chariot

In classical Greek mythology, Helios (Sol), the personification of the sun and one of the Titans, had a *quadriga* (a chariot drawn by four horses abreast) that he drove across the sky on a daily basis. The chariot was pulled by four *hippoi athanatoi* (immortal horses of the gods). All of the horses were said to have flaring nostrils that breathed forth flame. Different sources give the horses different names: Abraxas (Therbeeo), Aeos, Aethiops ("Like a Flame"), Aethon ("Blazing," "Burning" "Fiery Red" or "Shining"), Astrope, Bronte, Chronos, Eous, Lampoon, Lampos ("Glitter" or "Shine"), Phaethon ("Sheen-Mane," "Shining-Mane," "Shining One"), Phlegon ("Flaming"), Purocis ("Fiery Hot"), Puroeis, and Pyrois.

Sources: Apollodorus and Hyginus, *Apollodorus' Library and Hyginus' Fabulae*, 158; Breese and D'Aoust, *God's Steed*, 86; Brewer, *Dictionary of Phrase and Fable* 1900, 565; Guirand, *Larousse Encyclopedia of Mythology*, 160; Parada, *Genealogical Guide to Greek Mythology*, 35; Rose, *Giants, Monsters, and Dragons*, 178

chariot of Medea, the

Variations: dragon-chariot of Medea

According to classical Greek mythology, Medea was the daughter of King Aeetes of Colchis, niece of Circe, priestess of the goddess Hecate, and a sorceress. She murdered King Creon and his daughter, Princess Glauce, because Glauce was the lover of her husband, the Argonaut Jason. Then, in a final act of rage, Medea killed her two children fathered by Jason. With her vengeance complete, Medea fled Corinth in her chariot, a vehicle pulled through the sky by a pair of flying serpents. The chariot was given to her by her grandfather, Helios (Sol).

Sources: Clauss and Johnston, *Medea*, 67, 142, 312; Morse, *The Medieval Medea*, 29

chariot of Morgan Mwynfawr, the

Variations: Car Morgan Mwynfawr, chariot of Arianrhod, chariot of Morgan the Wealthy, Kar Morgan Mwynfawr ("chariot of Morgan the Wealthy")

In British and Welsh folklore, there is a series of items (always thirteen in number) called the THIRTEEN TREASURES OF THE ISLAND OF BRITAIN (in Welsh, they are called *Tri Thlws ar Ddeg Ynys Prydain*). Although in more modern times the items listed are different, the original thirteen items from the fifteenth century were the CAULDRON OF DYRNWCH THE GIANT, chariot of Morgan Mwynfawr, CHESSBOARD OF GWENDDOLEU AP CEIDIO, COAT OF PADARN BEISRUDD, CROCK AND DISH OF RHYGENYDD YSGOLHAIG (two items), HALTER OF CLYDNO EIDDYN, HAMPER OF GWYDDNO GARANHIR, HORN OF BRAN GALED, KNIFE OF LLAWFRODEDD FARCHOF, MANTLE OF ARTHUR IN CORNWALL, sword of Rhydderch Hael (DYRNWYN), and WHETSTONE OF TUDWAL TUDGLYD.

Typically cited as the fourth item, the chariot of the king of Morgannwg, Morgan Mwynfawr (the Wealthy), son of Athruys, was said to be able to quickly transport a man to any destination he wished.

Sources: Dom, *King Arthur and the Gods of the Round Table*, 106; Pendergrass, *Mythological Swords*, 25; Stirling, *King Arthur Conspiracy*, n.p.

chariot of Pelops, the

In classical Greek mythology, Pelops was the owner of a golden chariot drawn by a pair of tireless, winged horses. According to the legend, he was the son of King Tantalus, ruler of the lands around Mount Sipylos. Tantalus had the boy killed, chopped up and made into a stew to be served to the gods so as to test their omniscience; however, the gods restored the child to life. Pelops was so beautiful that Poseidon (Roman god Neptune), the god of earthquakes, horses, and the seas, abducted the youth and took him to Mount Olympus, where he kept him as a lover for many years. When Pelops was returned to earth and sought a wife, he fell in love with Hippodameia, the only daughter of King Oenomaus. It had been decreed that only the man who defeated the king in a chariot race would wed his daughter; the heads of those who had tried and failed were nailed to the castle gates. Pelops went to the ocean and prayed to his old lover, asking for assistance in winning Hippodameia's hand. Poseidon gave him the chariot and two *hippoi athanatoi* (immortal horses of the gods).

Sources: March, *Dictionary of Classical Mythology*, 380; See, *The Greek Myths*, n.p.

chariot of Poseidon, the

Variations: chariot of Neptune (Roman), chariot of the Sea

Poseidon (Roman god Neptune), the Greek god of earthquakes, horses, and the seas, had a chariot that was drawn by a pair of *hippocamps* (fish-tailed horses); on some occasions, it was depicted as being drawn by dolphins.

This was the chariot Poseidon used to travel back and forth between his watery kingdom and Mount Olympus. It was also the chariot he used when he abducted Pelops, the young man he had fallen in love with.

Homer, the legendary author of the *Iliad* and the *Odyssey*, described the chariot as pulled by a pair of bronze-shod horses with long, streaming manes of gold. Poseidon, clothed in gold, used a golden whip to spur the horses on; they were so fleet of foot that they could run across the waves without ever getting the bronze axle of the chariot wet.

Sources: Keightley, *The Mythology of Ancient Greece and Italy*, 78; March, *Dictionary of Classical Mythology*, 380

chariot of Selene, the

Variation: Selene's chariot

In ancient Greek mythology, the chariot of the Titan Selene, goddess of the moon, was pulled across the night sky by a pair of oxen or winged white horses, although she was occasionally depicted as riding side-saddle on a bull, mule, or ram. In ancient Roman mythology, Selene was known as Diana or Luna.

Sources: Daly and Rengel, *Greek and Roman Mythology, A to Z*, 131–32; Littleton, *Gods, Goddesses, and Mythology*, Volume 4, 374–75; Varadpande, *Ancient Indian and Indo-Greek Theatre*, 108

chariot of Sol, the

Variation: Sol's chariot

The chariot of the Norse goddess of the sun, Sol, was pulled across the sky by a pair of horses named Aarvak ("Early Awake" or "Early Waker") and Alsvin ("Fleet One"); they were born in Muspellsheimr, the divine realm of warmth and brightness. Collectively, the team represented the dawn. Magical runes were carved on Aarvak's ears. As the horses pulled the god's chariot, the shield SVALIN protected them from the harmful rays of the sun.

Sources: Coulter and Turner, *Encyclopedia of Ancient Deities*, 5; Grimes, *The Norse Myths*, 255; Norroena Society, *Asatru Edda*, 25; Rose, *Giants, Monsters, and Dragons*, 178

chariot of Surya, the

Variations: Aditya's chariot, chariot of Aditya, chariot of Surya, Surya's chariot

In Hindu mythology, the god of the sun, Surya, had a huge chariot usually pulled by seven green horses named Anushtup, Brihattee, Gaayatree, Jagatee, Pankti, Trishtup, and Unshnik. On occasion, the vehicle is depicted as being pulled by seven red mares or one white mare with seven heads.

The chariot is set upon a single gigantic wheel that is attached to the Pole Star (Dhruva); galloping incredibly fast, it takes the team of horses an entire year to complete one lap of the wheel. As Surya makes his journey, each month of the year a different group of seven celestial beings accompanies him: Aadityas (gods), Apsara (celestial female cloud spirits), Gandharvas (male nature spirits), Raakshasas (demons), Rishis (hermits), Sarpas (nagas), and Yakshas (nature spirits). Each of the celestial beings has a role to fulfill: The Apsara dance while the Gandharvas sing. Rishis

chariot of Thor

offer up their worship. The Raakshasas walk behind the chariot, acting as its rear guard. The Sarpas harness the horses to the chariot while the Yakshas hold their bridles. Additionally, the Baalkhilyas (sages) surround the chariot on all sides, assisting it as it moves from the moment of sunrise to the moment of sunset.

Sources: Charak, *Surya*, 52, 62; Coulter and Turner, *Encyclopedia of Ancient Deities*, 444

chariot of Thor, the

Variations: chariot of Thunder, Thor's chariot

Tanngnjostr ("Tooth Cracker"/"Tooth Gnasher") and Tanngrisnir ("Gap Tooth") were the two male goats who pulled the chariot of the god of thunder, Thor, according to Norse mythology. The goats were bridled with silver reins. If either of these goats were ever killed, they could be resurrected once their bones were reconstructed.

Sources: Grimes, *The Norse Myths*, 301; Jennbert, *Animals and Humans*, 49; Norroena Society, *Asatru Edda*, 390; Rydberg, *Teutonic Mythology*, Volume 1 of 3, 853

chariot of Triptolemus, the

Variations: chariot of Triptolemos, dragon chariot of Triptolemus, serpent chariot of Triptolemus

In the Eleusinian mysteries, Triptolemus ("He Who Pounds the Husks") was a demigod, hero, and prince of Eleusis; he presided over the milling of wheat and the sowing of grain. According to the myth, when Demeter (Roman goddess Ceres), the goddess of all useful fruits, grasses, and grains, was grieving over the abduction of her daughter Persephone (Roman goddess Proserpine), Triptolemus welcomed her warmly and bestowed upon her all of his hospitality. After Persephone was returned to her mother, the goddess repaid Triptolemus's kindness by showing him the art of agriculture. Additionally, she gifted him with a magnificent chariot pulled by two dragons (or a winged chariot drawn by serpents—translations vary) in which he flew across the sky, spreading seeds of wheat wherever he traveled. The serpents are depicted in art as being next to the wheels of the chariot and not in the traditional fashion, drawing it from the front.

Sources: Ogden, *Drakon*, 200; Roman and Roman, *Encyclopedia of Greek and Roman Mythology*, 133, 501

Chastiefol

Variation: sword of Arthur

In the Arthurian French romance tale from the late fourteenth (or early fifteenth) century *Le Chevalier du Papegau* ("The Knight of the Parrot"), a young King Arthur is armed with the sword Chastiefol, not EXCALIBUR.

Sources: Bruce, *The Arthurian Name Dictionary*, 115; Vesce, *The Knight of the Parrot*, 41, 102

cherubim chariot

Variations: chariot of God, the throne chariot

There are a number of occasions in the Bible when cherubim (a type of angel) are described as the means by which the chariot of God is made mobile, such as in Chronicles, Ezekiel, Kings, and the Book of Enoch. Depending on the translation of the biblical text, God is usually said to be upon his throne chariot, which is pulled by the cherubim, but more traditional translations and those done by modern biblical scholars describe God as riding upon the cherubim themselves. The chariot is described as a "shining brilliance," made of a crystal-like substance with wheels of fire.

Typically the cherubim are described as winged, and they serve God as His attendants, offering Him their worship. In ancient Middle Eastern art, cherubim are depicted as creatures, typically winged bulls or lions with human faces; however, in Christian depictions, cherubim have the face of a child and a set of small wings.

Sources: van der Toorn et al., *Dictionary of Deities and Demons in the Bible*, 191–92, 349; Wood, *Of Wings and Wheels*, 44–48

chessboard of Gwenddoleu ap Ceidio, the

In British and Welsh folklore, there is a series of items (always thirteen in number) called the THIRTEEN TREASURES OF THE ISLAND OF BRITAIN (in Welsh, they are called *Tri Thlws ar Ddeg Ynys Prydain*). Although in more modern times the items listed are different, the original thirteen items from the fifteenth century were the CAULDRON OF DYRNWCH THE GIANT, CHARIOT OF MORGAN MWYNFAWR, chessboard of Gwenddoleu ap Ceidio, COAT OF PADARN BEISRUDD, CROCK AND DISH OF RHYGENYDD YSGOLHAIG (two items), HALTER OF CLYDNO EIDDYN, HAMPER OF GWYDDNO GARANHIR, HORN OF BRAN GALED, KNIFE OF LLAWFRODEDD FARCHOF, MANTLE OF ARTHUR IN CORNWALL, sword of Rhydderch Hael (DYRNWYN), and WHETSTONE OF TUDWAL TUDGLYD.

Gwenddoleu ap Ceidio was a historical Brythonic king and said to be the owner of a remarkable chessboard. The oversized board was made of gold and the large pieces were silver; when set up to play, the pieces would move themselves. In Continental versions of the Grail myth, the chessboard appears with one of Arthur's own knights playing against it, trying to develop his strategy and tactical skills. In the French Arthurian tales, when the chessboard appears, it only plays itself.

Sources: Bromwich, *Trioedd Ynys Prydein*, n.p.; Patton, *The Poet's Ogam*, 510; Pendergrass, *Mythological Swords*, 24–25

chessboard shield and ivory pieces of Sir Gawain, the

In Chretien de Troyes's *Perceval*, Sir Gawain (Gawaine) is trapped in a tower at Escavalon without a shield. In making his escape, he comes upon a chess set, scaled up to be ten times larger than the usual size. In a show of his great strength, Gawain topples over the pieces and takes up the chessboard to use as his shield. The king of Escavalon's sister aids his escape by using the ivory chessmen as missiles, hurling them down on the attacking mob.

Sources: Guerin, *The Fall of Kings and Princes*, 179–80; Karr, *Arthurian Companion*, 192

chintamani stone

Variations: Chintaman stone, Chinta-mani, Cintamani Stone, Divya-ratna, Norbu Rinpoch, Stone of Heaven

In Hindu and Buddhist traditions, the chintamani ("treasure of the world") stone is said to have come to earth from either Heaven or a planet in orbit around the Syrian star; the stone was a gift to the king of Shambhala, ruler of the land of the immortals. According to this tradition, a chest containing four items fell from the sky in 331 CE; many years later, five travelers arrived to explain the contents of the box.

This green-colored stone is a powerful item; its presence can make a person ageless and immortal. It also had the ability to transform any substance into gold and allow a person to see into the past as well as the future. The chintamani stone is said to be carried on the back of a horse known as Lung-ta, and it allows kings and sages to travel great distances at a high speed.

Sources: Baker, *The Enigmas of History*, n.p.; Lanfranchi, *Chintamani or Moldavite*, n.p.

Chinwat Bridge

Variations: Bridge of the Judge, Bridge of the Mason, Bridge of the Requiter, Bridge of the Sep-

arator, Cinnuuato Peretush ("Account-keeper's Bridge"), Cinvat Bridge, Cinvato Paratu, al Serat, al SIRAT

In ancient Persian mythology, on the fourth day after a person's death, their *urvan* ("soul") will travel to the Chinwat Bridge accompanied by one of two types of divine beings. The first is a *daena*, a beautiful maiden who greets the righteous soul; the other is a demon known as a vizaresha, who meets the infidels and the sinners.

The Chinwat Bridge is described as thinner than a hair, yet sharper than the blade of a sword. It crosses a great chasm filled with monsters and the gate to Hell; on the far side of the bridge is the entrance to Paradise. Demons stand at the foot of the bridge and argue for the soul to be turned over to them. A soul heavy with evil will fall into the pit and forever remain trapped, tortured by demons and ghouls, whereas a good soul is light and will be able to cross the bridge easily.

Sources: Segal, *Life After Death*, 85–87; Van Scott, *The Encyclopedia of Hell*, n.p.

Chruaidh Cosgarreach

In Celtic lore and Irish mythology, Chruaidh Cosgarreach ("Hardy Slayer") was the sword of Coilte, a Fianna in the Fenian Cycle. Chruaidh Cosgarreach was one of the six swords made by Lon Lonnrach the *beangruagach* ("giant woman"); the other swords were CEARD-NAN GALLAN, DRUIDHE LANNACH, FASDAIL, LIOBHANACH, and MAC AN LUINE.

Sources: Gregory and MacCumhaill, *Gods and Fighting Men*, 268; Leodhas, *By Loch and by Lin*, n.p.

Chrysaor

In Edmund Spenser's epic poem *The Faerie Queene* (1590), Chrysaor ("He who has a Golden Sword") is the golden sword and the personal weapon of Sir Artegal, the Knight of Justice. Chrysaor, "tempered with Adamant," had once been used in battle by Zeus (Roman god Jupiter), the god of fate, kings, lightning, sky, and thunder, when he fought the Titans; it was able to cut through anything. The sword then passed into the safe keeping of Astrea, who held on to it until passing it to Sir Artegal.

Sources: Brewer, *Dictionary of Phrase and Fable* 1900, 1197; Pendergrass, *Mythological Swords*, 4

claidheamh anam

Variations: claudheamh anam

In Celtic folklore, a claidheamh anam is the

Claidheamh Soluis

soul-sword of a kelpie; it is a weapon capable of cutting the hardest heart and penetrating into the deepest soul without spilling a single drop of blood.

Sources: Ellis, *The Mammoth Book of Celtic Myths and Legends*, n.p.; Ellis, *The Chronicles of the Celts*, 257

Claidheamh Soluis

Variations: Claiomh Solais, Cruaidin Catutch-enn, Laidheamh Soluis, Sword of King Nuadd

According to Irish lore, when the Tuatha de Danann came to Ireland, they carried with them four magical treasures: the CAULDRON OF THE DAGDA, Claidheamh Soluis, LIA FAIL, and LUIN; each of these magical items came from one of their cities—Falias, Findias, Gorias, and Murias—and each item was carried by a druid. Claidheamh Soluis was forged in the city of Findias ("Blessed" or "Bright") and then carried to Ireland by the druid Uscias (Uiscias).

A claidheamh soluis ("sword of light" or "shining sword") is a type of sword appearing in Irish and Scottish Gaelic traditions. Typically these swords have brilliantly shining blades and are wielded by a hero who must complete three tasks with his companions, one of which may be an animal or a female servant. Often these tales are about acquiring a bride or proving one's worthiness to be a husband. The adversary is more often than not a giant who can only be defeated by a secret means, the secret revealed by the females in the story with the claidheamh soluis playing an important role. Examples of a claidheamh soluis would be CRUAIDIN, the sword of Cuhullin (Cu Chulaind/Cu Chulainn/Cuchulainn); Claidheamh Soluis, one of the FOUR TREASURES OF THE TUATHA DE DANANN and the sword of Nuada Airgeadlamh; and EXCALIBUR, the sword of Arthur.

As Laidheamh Soluis, the unstoppable sword of the mythic Irish hero Nuada Airgetlam (Nuada of the Silver Arm), it was considered a "righteous" blade, meaning that if the sword was fighting for a cause, the cause was just.

Sources: Ellis, *Brief History of the Druids*, 73, 124; Pendergrass, *Mythological Swords*, 13, 15

Clarent

In the Middle English poem *Alliterative Morte Arthure* (circa 1400), Clarent was named as one of the swords of King Arthur; it was a ceremonial blade, a sword of peace used in knighting ceremonies. The sword was kept in a vault in Walling-ford Castle and, other than the king himself, only his queen, Guenevere (Guinevere), knew of its location. When Arthur saw Mordred carrying the weapon in battle, he knew instantly that Guenevere had betrayed him. Most stories say this was the sword Mordred used to kill Arthur.

Sources: Bruce, *The Arthurian Name Dictionary*, 120; Goller, *The Alliterative Morte Arthure*, 18–19; Warren, *History on the Edge*, 212

Clinschor's pillar

Variations: Clinschor's magic pillar, magic mirror of Clinschor, mirror of Clinschor, Virgil's mirror

In *Parzival*, a thirteenth-century German romance written by Wolfram von Eschenbach, there is a character named Clinschor, a duke, castrated sorcerer, and nephew to the Roman poet Virgil, who is encountered by Sir Gawain (Gawaine), one of the knights of King Arthur. The palace of Clinschor, Schastel Marveile, was constructed with many automated defenses, free-roaming lions, and a host of magical enchantments. It was built upon a shining pavement as smooth as glass. Within its walls, Gawain sees a large pillar, similar to a gigantic mirror. Looking into it, one can see everything in a six-mile radius by day or by night. The pillar is solid, and neither "hammer nor smith" can destroy it. Lady Orgeluse tells Gawain that she believes the pillar was stolen in Tabronit from Queen Seaundille.

Clinschor learned his magic and the creation of his pillar in the land of Persida, an Oriental city and the birthplace of magic, located in "the East"; it is the Arabic homeland of Feirefiz, Parzifal's Muslim half-brother.

Sources: Churton, *Gnostic Philosophy*, n.p.; Classen, *Magic and Magicians in the Middle Ages and the Early Modern Time*, 105, 308, 311

cloak of darkness

Irish folktales tell of an item called the cloak of darkness. Similar to a CLOAK OF INVISIBILITY, a cloak of darkness will ensure that no living creature, man, or woman of the natural world will be able to see the person wearing the cloak, and it will also allow them to travel to any place they can picture in their mind "quicker than the wind can carry."

In one story, the cloak of darkness has the ability to summon people who can only be imagined. In "The Three Daughters of King O'Hare," the oldest princess wanted to be married, so she borrowed her father's magical cloak and, wearing it, wished for the most handsome man under the sun to be her husband. Not a breath later, a four-horse golden coach pulled up to the home and the most attractive man she had ever seen stepped forth.

Sources: Curtin, *Myths and Folk-lore of Ireland*, 50; Haase, *The Greenwood Encyclopedia of Folktales and Fairy Tales*, 217

cloak of invisibility

Variations: coat of invisibility, mantle of invisibility

Cloaks of invisibility appear in the fairy tales, folklore, legends, and myths of numerous cultures and religions throughout history. The cloak of invisibility most commonly appears in tales from China, England, Germany, Ireland, Japan, Philippines, and the United States of America. Typically, these stories include an archetypical trickster character using the cloak. Possession of such a powerful magical item like this or a TARNKAPPE is always coveted by others and prized by the owner.

Operation of a cloak of invisibility is traditionally simple, as in nearly all cases donning the garment is enough; on the few occasions when it requires activation, saying a few magical words will suffice.

Sources: Garry and El-Shammy, *Archetypes and Motifs in Folklore and Literature*, 161–63; Haase, *The Greenwood Encyclopedia of Folktales and Fairy Tales*, 217; Seigneuret, *Dictionary of Literary Themes and Motifs*, Volume 1, 416

cloak of Manannan mac Lir

Variation: cloak of forgetfulness

Manannan mac Lir (Mannanan,Mannanos), god of the sea and guardian of the Underworld in Celtic mythology, was a master of shape shifting and had many varied powers and magical items. One of his possessions was a cloak that, when he took it off and shook it out, would cause forgetfulness of the present as well as the past.

Sources: Macbain, *Celtic Mythology and Religion*, 97; Monaghan, *Encyclopedia of Celtic Mythology and Folklore*, 311

cloth of plenty

Irish folktales tell of an item called a cloth of plenty. Similar to a CORNUCOPIA, it will ensure that the user will never be hungry or thirsty again. All one must do is spread the cloth out and ask for whatever food and beverage is desired; in the blinking of an eye, the wish will be granted.

Sources: Curtin, *Myths and Folk-lore of Ireland*, 69–70

Cloud Tree

Variations: Ambrosia Tree, Kalpadruma, TREE OF KNOWLEDGE, Tree of the Buddha, Tree of Wisdom

In Buddhist mythology, the Cloud Tree is a tree so divine that it literally glows; the blossoms that fall from its branches glisten. It is described in shape as similar to a palm tree and is surrounded by beautiful flowers and musical streams. The branches, leaves, roots, and trunk are made of the most glorious gems. Even the soil the tree grows in is pure; the grass beneath is more beautiful than the "tints of a peacock's neck." The Cloud Tree is said to be able to fulfill all desires, give knowledge and wisdom, and bestow inconceivable bliss. It was while sitting beneath this tree that the Buddha gained enlightenment.

Sources: Altman, *Sacred Trees*, 39; Folkard, *Plant Lore, Legends and Lyrics*, 4; Porteous, *The Forest in Folklore and Mythology*, 197

club of the Dagda

Variation: fork of the Dagda

The Celtic god of abundance, artistry, banquets, death, excess, inspiration, life, music, the sky, and war, the Dagda wielded a club so large and powerful that it took eight strong men to carry it; the club was also moved on wheels because of its extreme weight. When using the club, the Dagda would use the head of the weapon to strike his enemies dead with a single blow; however, if he so chose, he would use the other end of the weapon and strike them a second time, restoring them to life. Symbolic of lightning, the club of the Dagda was used to furrow deep trenches in the earth that were then used as boundary lines between provinces; these ditches were known as "the mark of the Dagda." Boundary stones further highlighted the terrain; tampering with the stones or the ditches would anger the god.

Infrequently, the Dagda is said to carry a fork; it has all the same abilities and properties as the club but appears in stories where feasting is predominant.

Sources: Davidson, *Myths and Symbols in Pagan Europe*, 204, 207; Koch, *Celtic Culture: A–Celti*, 553–54, 1632

club of iron of the giant of Saint Michael's Mount, the

According to the folklore of Cornwall, England, after King Arthur slew Cormeilian (also known as Corineus, Cormilan, Cormorant, and Gourmaillon), the giant of Saint Michael's Mount, he kept the giant's iron club and kirtle (cloak) as trophies.

Sources: Karr, *Arthurian Companion*, 115; Malory and Caxton, *Le Morte Darthur*, 96; Rose, *Giants, Monsters, and Dragons*, 87

clue of Ariadne

In classical Greek mythology, Ariadne was the beautiful daughter of King Minos of Crete. Minos had an elaborate and gigantic enclosed labyrinth constructed to hold Asterion, better known as the Minotaur ("bull of Minos"), the illegitimate child born of Queen Pasiphae and a divine bull. Asterion was a fed a diet of youths and maidens, individuals supplied by the city of Athens as tribute for the death of Crete's Prince Androgeos. When Theseus, son of King Aegeus of Athens, was sent as part of the tribute, he convinced Ariadne that he would marry her if she helped him escape the labyrinth. She supplied him with her clue of string, which he used to literally thread his way through the labyrinth. After dispatching the Minotaur, Theseus was able to backtrack by following the thread and made good his escape with Ariadne, although he later abandoned her.

Sources: Lucian, *The Works of Lucian*, Volume 2, 197; Stevens, *Ariadne's Clue*, 3

coat of Padarn Beisrudd

Variations: Pais Padarn Beisrydd ("red coat of Padarn Beisrydd"), tunic of Padarn Beisrudd

In British and Welsh folklore, there is a series of items (always thirteen in number) called the THIRTEEN TREASURES OF THE ISLAND OF BRITAIN (in Welsh, they are called *Tri Thlws ar Ddeg Ynys Prydain*). Although in more modern times the items listed are different, the original thirteen items from the fifteenth century were the CAULDRON OF DYRNWCH THE GIANT, CHARIOT OF MORGAN MWYNFAWR, CHESSBOARD OF GWENDDOLEU AP CEIDIO, coat of Padarn Beisrudd, CROCK AND DISH OF RHYGENYDD YSGOLHAIG (two items), HALTER OF CLYDNO EIDDYN, HAMPER OF GWYDDNO GARANHIR, HORN OF BRAN GALED, KNIFE OF LLAWFRODEDD FARCHOF, MANTLE OF ARTHUR IN CORNWALL, sword of Rhydderch Hael (DYRNWYN), and WHETSTONE OF TUDWAL TUDGLYD.

The coat of Padarn Beisrudd is described as crimson in color and of exceedingly expert craftsmanship. There are two stories about this item. In the first version, the coat would fit no one but Padarn Beisrudd himself. In the other, the coat would magically fit any true nobleman but would

be unwearable by anyone of a base character or of the lower class.

Sources: Patton, *The Poet's Ogam*, 510; Pendergrass, *Mythological Swords*, 26; Williams, *A Biographical Dictionary of Eminent Welshmen*, 338

cohuleen driuth

Variation: cochallin draiochta ("little magic hood")

In Irish folklore, a cohuleen driuth is a magical cap or hat belonging to a merrow (a species of merfolk similar to a mermaid). According to the lore, the female of the species can, while wearing her cap, leave her home in the ocean and venture onto the land. On occasion, merrow females have even taken mortal men as husbands. If ever the cohuleen driuth is lost or stolen, this fairy creature cannot return back to the ocean's depths without drowning. If the merrow should marry, the cap must be kept from her; if ever she finds it, she will take it and instantly return to the ocean.

The male merrow is as ugly as the female is beautiful. Although there are stories of the males loaning their own or an extra cohuleen driuth to a mortal, there are no tales of them taking humans as wives.

Sources: Eason, *Fabulous Creatures, Mythical Monsters, and Animal Power Symbols*, 151; Froud and Lee, *Faeries*, 121; Keightley, *Fairy Mythology*, 152; Spence, *Minor Traditions of British Mythology*, 50–52; Wallace, *Folk-lore of Ireland*, 90

Colada

One of the two swords of Rodrigo Diaz de Vivar (circa 1043–1099), better known as El Cid Campeador ("the Champion"), Colada was said to have been won in combat from the Count of Barcelona and, along with El Cid's other sword TIZONA, passed on to his sons-in-law. After discovering that the men beat his daughters and abandoned them on a roadside, he asked for the swords to be returned. Colada was later gifted to Sir Matyin Antolines, one of El Cid's knights.

Appearing in the epic poem *Cantar de mio Cid*, Colada has the ability to frighten off the unworthy, but only when it is being wielded by a brave warrior.

Sources: Brewer, *Dictionary of Phrase and Fable* 1900, 1197; Evangelista, *The Encyclopedia of the Sword*, 576; Pendergrass, *Mythological Swords*, 17

collar of Canhastyr Canllaw, the

In the Welsh Arthurian legends, Canhastyr Canllaw owned the singular collar worthy of being matched with the CHAIN OF CILYDD CANA-

STYR. These items, along with the LEASH OF CORS CANT EWIN, would be used by the houndsman Mabon in order to handle the hound of Greid, Drudwyn. All of these items and the hound needed to be gathered together in order for Culhwch to hunt the boar Twrch Trwyth.

Sources: Bruce, *The Arthurian Name Dictionary*, 101; Ellis, *The Chronicles of the Celts*, 327; Mountain, *The Celtic Encyclopedia*, Volume 3, 764

comb of Guenevere

The French poet and troubadour Chretien de Troyes (1130–1191) is best known for his work on Arthurian lore and his creation of the character of Sir Lancelot. In one story, when Guenevere (Guinevere) was captured by Meliagrant, an evil and proud man who thought himself to be Lancelot's equal, she left her ivory gilded comb upon a stone in the middle of a meadow so her rescuers would be better able to find her. To ensure that whoever found it would know it belonged to her, she left several strands of her beautiful golden hair in it.

Sources: Karr, *Arthurian Companion*, 219; Morewedge, *The Role of Woman in Middle Ages*, 52–55

conch shell of Triton, the

Triton, the son of Poseidon (Roman god Neptune), the god of earthquakes, horses, and the seas, and Amphitrite, lives with his parents in their beautiful palace at the bottom of the sea, according to ancient Greek mythology. Triton had a conch shell he carried; when he blew into it, the conch could either raise up a violent storm at sea or calm the waves to perfect sailing conditions.

Sources: Littleton, *Gods, Goddesses, and Mythology*, Volume 8, 1144

copper ship for Ilmarinen, the

In a legend from Finland, Ilmarinen, a god with remarkable smithing abilities, used the magical elements in his forge to create many items; unfortunately, he was very unlucky in love. After creating the SAMPO for the witch Louhi as a gift in exchange for permission to marry her daughter, he was rejected by his beloved. Heartbroken and wanting to return home, Louhi created a red copper ship in which to leave.

Sources: Friberg et al., *The Kalevala*, 99; Jennings, *Pagan Portals*, n.p.; Mouse, *Ilmarinen Forges the Sampo*, 58

Coreuseuse

Variations: Corchense, Coreiseuse, Coreuseus ("Fury"), Corroceuse, Courechrouse, Couresceuse, Corsheuse

The sword of King Ban of Benoic, Coreuseuse ("Wrathful") was passed down to his son, Sir Lancelot, according to the Vulgate. With this sword, Ban would always charge the first opponent he saw and, with a single blow, cut him in half, even if the opponent was mounted on horseback.

Sources: Bruce, *The Arthurian Name Dictionary*, 130; Karr, *Arthurian Companion*, 118, 150; Lacy, *Lancelot-Grail*, 157

cornucopia

Variations: Horn of Amalthea, Horn of Plenty

The sacred goat from classical Greek mythology, Amalthea ("Tender Goddess"), suckled the infant god of fate, kings, lightning, sky, and thunder, Zeus (Roman god Jupiter), while he lived on the island of Crete, where he was raised by the Melissae. Zeus broke off one of Amalthea's horns and, in doing so, created the cornucopia, a horn with the magical ability of filling with anything the user desired. Hades (Roman god Dis/Pluto), the god of plenty as well as the Underworld, is often depicted carrying the cornucopia as he abducts the goddess of vegetation, Persephone (Roman goddess Proserpine), as well as when he is following the winged chariot of the demigod Triptolemus, master of the milling of wheat and the sowing of grain.

Sources: Berens, *Myths and Legends of Ancient Greece and Rome*, 16; Illes, *Encyclopedia of Spirits*, 119–20; Loomis, *Celtic Myth and Arthurian Romance*, 230

Corrougue

Otuel, an arrogant and brash pagan knight who eventually converted to Christianity and joined the court of Charlemagne, once bragged that he would cut any man who challenged him in two. No sooner had he spoken these words than an unnamed French knight accepted the dare. In a breath Otuel drew his sword, Corrougue, and killed the knight just as he claimed he could.

Sources: Brewer, *Dictionary of Phrase and Fable* 1900, 1196; Ellis, *Specimens of Early English Metrical Romances*, 328–29

Coscrach

In the Irish epic *Tain Bo Cuailnge* (*The Cattle Raid of Cooley/The Tain*), Coscrach was the sword of Cuscraid; it is named as being among the many cups, drinking horns, goblets, javelins, shields, and swords kept in Tete Brec, one of the three households of the Ulster hero Cuhullin (Cu Chulaind/Cu Chulainn/Cuchulainn). Coscrach is described only as "triumphant."

Cosgarach Mhor

Sources: Kinsella and Le Brocquy, *The Tain*, 5; Mountain, *The Celtic Encyclopedia*, Volume 2, 521

Cosgarach Mhor

Variation: the Great Triumphant One

A sword from Celtic mythology, Cosgarach Mhor was wielded by Osgar, one of the Fianna, a warrior who followed Fionn mac Cumhaill (Finn MacCool/Finn MacCumhail) in the Irish Fenian Cycle stories.

Sources: Gregory and MacCumhaill, *Gods and Fighting Men*, 268

Courser, the

In the American tradition of tall tales, the *Courser* was said to be a sailing vessel; the master of the *Courser* was literally a giant by the name of Captain Alfred Bulltop Stormalong. According to the tales, there was always plenty to eat on the ship and the crew was content; the crew rode on horseback to move around because the vessel was too large to traverse on foot. It was said that the masts of the ship were hinged so as to sail beneath the moon and sun safely; its sails were stitched together in the Sahara Desert because that was the only place empty and vast enough to hold them. When Captain Stormalong was not manning the wheel himself, thirty-two men were needed to steer the *Courser*.

Sources: Fee and Webb, *American Myths, Legends, and Tall Tales*, Volume 1, 193; Kingshill, *The Fabled Coast*, n.p.

Courtain (KOOR-tan)

Variations: Cortana, Curtana, Kurt

In the French epic poem *Song of Roland* (*La Chanson de Roland*, circa 1040–1115), which retells the events of the Battle of Roncevaux Pass in 778 CE, Courtain was the sword of Ogier the Dane. The sword was believed to be magical in at least its creation, for it is said that the fairy Morgana had the ability to morph objects. She created a sword to be gifted to Ogier rather than the one Charlemagne intended to give him. Upon the blade of the sword she created were engraved the words "My name is Cortana, of the same steel and temper as JOYEUSE and DURANDAL." Another legend, however, states that the legendary blacksmith Wayland (Gofannon/Volund/Weiland/Weyland) the Smith forged the sword, along with ALMACE and DURANDAL.

In *The Legend of Croquemitaine*, the celebrated swordsmith Munifican created three swords: COURTAIN, DURANDAL, and SAUVAGINE. Each

sword took three years to make, and each was eventually used to test the edge of the sword GLORIOUS, which managed to hack into each of them.

Sources: Brewer, *Dictionary of Phrase and Fable* 1900, 1197; Evangelista, *The Encyclopedia of the Sword*, 576; L'Epine, *The Days of Chivalry*, n.p.; Pendergrass, *Mythological Swords*, 19; Sayers, *The Song of Roland*, 38

crane bag

One of the possessions of Manannan mac Lir (Mannanan, Mannanos), the Celtic god of the sea and guardian of the Underworld, the crane bag was made from the hide of a magical crane who was at one time Aoife, the beloved of Ilbrec (the son of Manamman). In this bag, Manannan kept the belt and smith hook of Goibniu (Gaibne/Gaibniu/Gobha/Goibhnionn/Goibnenn/Goibniu Sear), the god of blacksmithing (see also BELT OF GOIBNIU; SMITH HOOK OF GOIBNIU), as well as the bones of Asail's pig, the helmet of the king of Lochlann (Norway), the shears of the king of Alba (Scotland), and his own home. When it was high tide, all of these items were in the bag and accessible to Manannan; however, when it was low tide, the bag was empty.

Sources: Greer, *The Druid Magic Handbook*, n.p.; Gregory and MacCumhaill, *Gods and Fighting Men*, 202; Mountain, *The Celtic Encyclopedia*, Volume 3, 715

Crann Buidhe

Variations: the crann buidhe of Manannan, Gae Buide ("Yellow Spear"), the spear of Manannan, Yellow Spear of Diarmuidh O'Duibhne

In Celtic mythology, Diarmuid Ua Duibhne (Diarmid O'Dyna) wielded a magical spear by the name of Crann Buidhe ("Yellow Branch"). Although it could inflict a wound no one could recover from, this yellow-shafted spear was not as powerful as the red-shafted GAE DEARG. Crann Buidhe was the weapon Diarmuid took with him when he went adventuring and did not feel a need to carry his more powerful weapon. Sadly, Crann Buidhe failed him when Diarmuid, who was under a *geasa* (magically imposed condition or promise) never to hunt boar, was attacked and killed by one.

Sources: Joyce, *Old Celtic Romances*, 302; Leviton, *The Gods in Their Cities*, 236; MacCulloch et al., *Celtic Mythology*, Volume 3, 66

crimson copper pan, the

In Japanese lore, there is a tale of man-eating centipede living in the mountains near Lake Biwa; the cultural hero and famed monster-slayer Hidesato was asked by the Dragon King to destroy the creature. Hidesato coated one of his arrowheads in his own saliva, as it was widely believed that human saliva was poisonous to such creatures. He then shot the arrow into the head of the centipede, piercing its brain and killing it instantly. The hero was rewarded with three magical items, one of which was a crimson copper pan (see also ENDLESS BAG OF RICE and SILK ROLL OF HIDESATO). Similar to the CROCK AND DISH OF RHYGENYDD YSGOLHAIG of British and Welsh folklore, this magical pan would instantly fill itself up with whatever food Hidesato wished.

Sources: Kimbrough and Shirane, *Monsters, Animals, and Other Worlds*, n.p.; Roberts, *Japanese Mythology A to Z*, 22

Crocea Mors

Variations: Agheu Glas ("Grey Death"), Angau Coch ("Red Death")

According to the British cleric who played a major role in the development of the tale of King Arthur, Geoffrey of Monmouth (circa 1095–1155), Crocea Mors ("Yellow Death") was the sword of Julius Caesar. It shone brightly in the sun and always managed to kill anyone it struck. The sword was originally a gift from Venus (Greek goddess Aphrodite), the Roman goddess of beauty, fertility, love, prostitution, sex and victory, to the Trojan prince Aeneas. Later Vulcan (Greek god Hephaistos), the Roman god of fire, the forge, and volcanoes, gifted the sword to Caesar, who used it during his conquest of Britain.

When the British prince Nennius engaged in single combat with Caesar, Crocea Mors became stuck in Nennius's shield, allowing him to defeat Caesar. Nennius used the sword for the rest of his life—fifteen days—before he finally succumbed to the head wound Caesar had inflicted on him with the sword. Crocea Mors was said to have been buried with Nennius.

Sources: Brewer, *Dictionary of Phrase and Fable* 1900, 1197; Pendergrass, *Mythological Swords*, 18

crock and dish of Rhygenydd Ysgolhaig, the

Variations: crock and dish of Rhygenydd the Cleric (Gren a desgyl Rhygenydd Ysgolhaig), dish of Rhygenydd

In British and Welsh folklore, there is a series of items (always thirteen in number) called the THIRTEEN TREASURES OF THE ISLAND OF BRITAIN (in Welsh, they are called *Tri Thlws ar Ddeg Ynys Prydain*). Although in more modern times the items listed are different, the original thirteen items from the fifteenth century were the CAULDRON OF DYRNWCH THE GIANT, CHARIOT OF MORGAN MWYNFAWR, CHESSBOARD OF GWENDDOLEU AP CEIDIO, COAT OF PADARN BEISRUDD, crock and dish of Rhygenydd Ysgolhaig (two items), HALTER OF CLYDNO EIDDYN, HAMPER OF GWYDDNO GARANHIR, HORN OF BRAN GALED, KNIFE OF LLAWFRODEDD FARCHOF, MANTLE OF ARTHUR IN CORNWALL, sword of Rhydderch Hael (DYRNWYN), and WHETSTONE OF TUDWAL TUDGLYD.

According to the lore, whatever food was wished to be in the crock and dish of Rhygenydd Ysgolhaig would magically appear.

Sources: Bruce, *The Arthurian Name Dictionary*, 464; Pendergrass, *Mythological Swords*, 24, 26

Croda

In the Irish epic *Tain Bo Cuailnge* (*The Cattle Raid of Cooley/The Tain*), Croda was the sword of Cormac; it is named as being among the many cups, drinking horns, goblets, javelins, shields, and swords kept in Tete Brec, one of the three households of the Ulster hero Cuhullin (Cu Chulaind/Cu Chulainn/Cuchulainn). Croda is described only as "bloody."

Sources: Kinsella and Le Brocquy, *The Tain*, 5; Mountain, *The Celtic Encyclopedia*, Volume 2, 485

Crown of Forgetfulness, the

In the story of Ogier the Dane, a Middle English romance, Ogier is compelled to travel to Morgan La Fay, the queen of fairies. In her eternally perfect spring-day garden, she asks him to live there with her forever. She places upon his finger the RING OF THE FAIRY QUEEN and upon his head the Crown of Forgetfulness, a priceless crown of gold myrtle leaves and laurel branches, more costly than any mortal treasury could purchase. The crown removed all of Ogier's past worries and fears; nothing troubled him, and a living love stirred up from within. He was then able to live in the fairy dream of love and pleasure for about 200 years.

Sources: Courthope, *The Marvellous History of King Arthur in Avalon*, 17, 31, 35, 48, 78; Cox, *Popular Romances of the Middle Ages*, 362

Cruadh Chosgarach

A sword from Celtic mythology, Cruadh Chosgarach ("Hard Destroying One") was the sword of Cafite mac Ronain, one of the Fianna, a warrior who followed Fionn mac Cumhaill (Finn MacCool/Finn MacCumhail) in the Irish Fenian Cycle stories.

Sources: Gregory and MacCumhaill, *Gods and Fighting Men*, 268

Cruaidin

Variations: Cruaidin Cailidcheann ("Hard, Hard Headed"), Cruaidin Cotatcenn

In the stories of the Ulster Cycle, and in Manx and Scottish folklore, the Irish mythological hero Cuhullin (Cu Chulaind/Cu Chulainn/Cuchulainn) wielded a sword named Cruaidin. The weapon is described as having a hilt of gold with silver ornamentation. The blade was flexible; if its tip was bent back to the hilt, it would snap back into place as straight as it ever was. The blade was also incredibly sharp, keen enough to cut a hair on water and able to cleave a man in two without him realizing it until some time had passed.

Sources: Gregory, *Cuchulain of Muirthemne*, 45; Pendergrass, *Mythological Swords*, 13

cup of Djermscheed

A popular subject in the myths and poetry of ancient Persia, the cup of Djermscheed was a magical cup filled with the DRAFT OF IMMORTALITY and used for divination; by looking into it, everything in the world, all the good and evil, could be seen.

Sources: Nye, *Encyclopedia of Ancient and Forbidden Secrets*, 45

cup of Goibniu

The Celtic god of blacksmithing, Goibniu (Gaibne/Gaibniu/Gobha/Goibhnionn/Goibnenn/Goibniu Sear) possessed a magical cup; it never ran out of immortal ale and made all those who drank from it immortal.

Sources: MacCulloch, *Celtic Mythology*, 31; Smyth, *A Guide to Irish Mythology*, 69

cup of Jamshid

Variations: Grail of Jamshid, Jaam-e Jam, Jami-Jarnshid

In Persian mythology, the cup of Jamshid was a turquoise vessel of divination owned by the rulers of ancient Persia; the entirety of the world was reflected in this magical seven-ringed cup, and staring into it would grant visions. The cup was said to have been filled with the DRAFT OF IMMORTALITY. In addition to revealing the future, it could transform a king into a god. According to the myth, King Jamshid, who discovered the

cup while excavating the city of Istaker, is said to have ruled 20,000 years ago, making the cup at least that old.

Sources: Bennett, *Liber 420*, n.p.; Pinkham, *Guardians of the Holy Grail*, 32

cup of Llwyr

Retrieving the magical cup of Llwyr was one of the thirteen conditions set before Culhwch that had to be completed before the giant Ysbaddaden would allow Culhwch to marry his daughter, Olwen. According to Welsh mythology and the story *Culhwch and Olwen*, Culhwch was a cousin of King Arthur. The collection of the cup of Llwyr was important because it was the only cup able to hold a drink as strong as a *bragget* (a type of beer and mead concoction), which was made from honey nine times sweeter than the first swarm.

Sources: Fee, *Gods, Heroes, & Kings*, 187; Lacy and Wilhelm, *The Romance of Arthur*, 45

cup of penance

In Norse mythology, the cup of penance was the drinking vessel of Thor, the god of thunder; one end of it extended into the ocean of Midgard (Earth). Thor drank so heavily from the cup that the level of the ocean dropped, thus causing the ebb and neap of the tide.

Sources: Grimes, *The Norse Myths*, 260

Cura Si Manjakini

A fabulous sword said to have belonged to Sang Sapurba, the legendary ancestor of Malay kings; this weapon was the symbol of power and rightful sovereignty.

Sources: Samad, *Sulalatus Salatin*, 28

Cyriac's well

In some parts of Germany, it was believed that when a child did not thrive, it was a *changeling* (a fairy being left by a fairy when it steals a human child). The creature was then taken to Cyriac's Mead, a place near Neuhausen, and was forced to drink from Cyriac's well. Then the being was left there unattended for nine days, at the end of which it would either die from exposure or recover. Jacob and Wilhelm Grimm (noted German academics, authors, cultural researchers, and linguists who collected folklore) recorded a story of how a woman suspected that her child had been swapped out with a changeling. She was advised to brew beer in an acorn where the creature could watch. The changeling was so amazed at the spectacle that it exclaimed, "I am as old as any oak in the wood, but never have I seen beer brewed in an acorn," and then disappeared.

Sources: Keightley, *World Guide to Gnomes, Fairies, Elves, and Other Little People*, 227

Dainsleif

Variations: Daiinsleif, Dansleif

A sword from Norse mythology, Dainsleif ("Dain's Heirloom") was made by the dwarf Dain, according to Icelandic historian Snorri Sturluson. Similar to the sword TIRFING, this weapon was said to be cursed because once it was drawn from its scabbard, it could not be sheathed until it had killed a man. In addition, once Dainsleif struck a target, it either killed the person or left a wound that would never heal. According to legend, King Hogni drew Dainsleif when rescuing his daughter, Hild, when she was abducted by Hedin Hjarrandason.

Sources: Brodeur, *Snorri Sturluson: The Prose Edda*, 50; Daly, *Norse Mythology A to Z*, 15; Grimes, *The Norse Myths*, 261; Hawthorne, *Vikings*, 18; Pendergrass, *Mythological Swords*, 3

Dancing Hut

Variations: Baba Yaga's Hut, Dancing Hut of Babba Yaga

According to Hungarian folklore, Baba Yaga ("old woman Yaga" or "old woman Jadwiga") was originally a benevolent and kind fairy; over time, however, her stories changed, and she became a cannibalistic old crone or witch, small and ugly. In some stories, Baba Yaga was a race of evil fay and not an individual. The name and character of Baba Yaga appeared in a number of eastern European and Slavic myths.

Baba Yaga dwelled in a living hut surrounded by a picket fence, the top of which was decorated with the skulls of her victims. The hut itself, windowless and with a false door, had proportionally large chicken legs which it rested upon. When she wished to enter her home, Baba Yaga had to enact a magical spell that would compel the hut to lower itself to ground level. Anyone who tried to pick the lock to her home would be surprised to discover that the keyhole was nothing more than a mouth full of sharp teeth. The hut was filled with scores of invisible servants who protected and served Baba Yaga.

In some tales, Baba Yaga's hut was connected with three mysterious riders. The first dressed in black and rode upon a black horse decked out in black barding and tack; he was the personification of the night. The second rider, dressed in red upon a red horse, was the personification of the sun, and the third rider, dressed in white upon a white horse, personified the day. If a visitor asked about the riders, Baba Yaga would explain what they were, but if she was ever asked about her invisible house servants, she would try to kill the questioner.

It has been theorized that the concept of Baba Yaga's hut was not so farfetched. The nomadic tribal hunters of Serbia would build log cabins upon the tall stumps of two or three trees, the roots of which looked just like chicken feet. These huts would have a trapdoor built into the floor that could only be reached by ladder (while a bear was not only strong enough to break in a sturdy door but also stubborn enough to keep at it until the door broke, no bear, regardless of its size or strength, can climb a ladder). Small shrines containing clay figurines have also been found with this same sort of construction. Russian archaeologists Yefimenko and Tretyakov discovered in 1948 some small huts fitting the description of Baba Yaga's hut; circular fences surrounded the huts, and inside they also found traces of corpse cremation.

Sources: Johns, *Baba Yaga*, 141–42, 146; Rose, *Spirits, Fairies, Leprechauns, and Goblins*, 29; Rosen, *Mythical Creatures Bible*, 234; Wikimedia Foundation, *Slavic Mythology*, 117

Dancing Water

Variations: Aab-i-Hayat, amrita, Chasma-i-Kausar, elixir of life, Maha Ras, Mansarover, Milk of the Gods, Pool of Nectar, SOMA, Soma Ras, WATER OF LIFE AND DEATH

In nearly every culture there are stories of heroes and kings seeking out a magical formula that will grant them immortality, or at least rejuvenate their bodies to a youthful appearance and vigor. In many French fairy tales, and in some Arabic, Chinese, Egyptian, Enochian, Gnostic, Greek, and Sumerian texts, this magical potion is called Dancing Water.

Equated with the alchemist's PHILOSOPHER'S STONE, when a person quaffs a vial of Dancing Water, the drink is described as "white droplets" of "liquid gold." The beverage always works quickly, in most cases instantly restoring the person to peak physical perfection, healthy and youthful once more. More often than not, when this occurs, the person is also granted immortality, now eternally fit and in their prime.

Dart-that-flew-Straight

Sources: Coulter-Harris, *Chasing Immortality in World Religions*, n.p.; Lightman, *The Accidental Universe*, 35

Dart-that-flew-Straight

In ancient Greek mythology, Procris was one of the three daughters of Erechtheus, the king of Athens, and his wife Praxithea; she married Cephalus, the son of Deioneus. Soon after the marriage, Cephalus was abducted by Eos, goddess of the dawn, who kept him in her company for eight years. When he desired to go home to his wife, the goddess convinced him that Procris could be easily seduced by a stranger and challenged Cephalus to prove her wrong by disguising him and sending him home. Unfortunately, he succeeded and shamed his wife for being unfaithful, sending her away. Procris traveled to Crete and came into the court of King Minos, famous for his affairs; his wife, Queen Pasiphae, had cast a spell on her husband so that whenever he ejaculated he would emit millipedes, scorpions, and snakes—a condition that deprived him of heirs. Procris promised the king that she could secure a method for him to father children; she achieved this goal by inserting the bladder of a goat into the queen's genitalia, allowing her to conceive. The king was so pleased that he bestowed two gifts on Procris: Laelaps the hound (which was capable of catching any prey it was sent after) and the Dart-that-flew-Straight. Procris returned to her husband and, with the assistance of Artemis (Roman goddess Diana), the goddess of children, hunting, virginity, unmarried girls, and wild animals, disguised herself as a young man and tricked Cephalus into entering a hunting competition. When she won, she revealed herself; her husband, ashamed and now understanding how easily one can be tricked, accepted his wife's return. Once reunited, Procris presented her husband with the hound and the Dart-that-flew-Straight. Not long after the joyful reunion, Cephalus, while hunting, accidently threw the Dart-that-flew-Straight at some rustling bushes. Sadly, it was Procris and not game whom he struck, killing her.

Sources: Parada, *Genealogic Guide to Greek Mythology*, 156; See, *The Greek Myths*, 83–84

deaf coach

Variation: Coiste Boahar

In the folklore of Galway County, Ireland, it is said that when someone is about to die, the deaf coach is seen racing down a very specific set of roads: it heads south from Faughart Church to Beronan Bridge, crossing Forkill Road onto O'Hagan's crossroads and then, by way of Kilcurry, heading back to the church. The black coach is pulled by four headless horses and steered by a headless driver. The coach is *deaf* (meaning "muffled" or "rumbling") and said to be as silent "as a bicycle." Seeing the deaf coach is uncommon and startling, but not a sign of misfortune.

Sources: Evan-Wentz, *Fairy Faith in Celtic Countries*, 29–30; Jacobs et al., *Folk Lore*, Volume 10, 119, 122

Del Chliss

In Manx and Scottish folklore, the mythological hero Cuhullin (Cu Chulaind/Cu Chulainn/Cuchulainn) wielded a spear named Del Chliss ("the Dart of Feats"). He used Del Chliss to slay the three brothers Fannall ("Swallow"), Foill, and Tuachell ("Cunning"); he then decapitated each and laid claim to their gear. In the *Tain Bo Cuailnge* section of the Ulster Cycle, Del Chliss is described as a "wily weapon" and is used by Cuhullin both thrown and as a handheld weapon. He may have also used it to remove the brothers' heads.

Sources: Kinsella and Le Brocquy, *The Tain*, 89, 263; Woodard, *Myth, Ritual, and the Warrior in Roman and Indo-European Antiquity*, 123

Devadatta

Variation: Devadettam

In Hindu mythology, Devadatta ("God-Given") is the conch belonging to heroic archer Arjuna ("Spotless and Shining like Silver"), the main character of the Indian epic *Mahabharata*. Devadatta was used as a war trumpet; the sound it created would instill fear into the heart of the enemy. It would also avert natural disasters, banish evil spirits, and frighten away harmful creatures.

Sources: Beer, *The Handbook of Tibetan Buddhist Symbols*, 10; Marballi, *Journey through the Bhagavad Gita*, 14

devastra

In Hindu mythology, an ASTRA is a supernatural weapon created or gifted by the gods to someone who then presides over the weapon. The wielder of an ASTRA is known as an astradhari.

Devastras are described as something very much like a modern-day missile. A devastra is an ASTRA from the gods in general; if one is requested or summoned frivolously, it will consume the summoner.

Sources: Edizioni, *Vimanas and the Wars of the Gods*, n.p.; Menon, *The Mahabharata* volume 2, 513

dewcup charms

In the folklore of the Iroquois people of North America, there are said to be three types of mountain-dwelling nymph or *jogah* ("dwarf people"): the Gandayah, the Gahonga and the Ohdows.

Gandayah are the nature spirits of the earth's fertility; they create little magical items called dewcup charms, which attract fruits and grains and cause them to bloom and sprout. These spirits will also release fish that are caught in fishermen's traps.

Sources: Chopra, *Academic Dictionary of Mythology*, 114

Dhadu Monara

Variations: Dhadu Monara Yantra ("Great Peacock Machine"), PUSHPAKA VIMANA (Hindu)

Sinhala Buddhist legend claims that Dhadu Monara ("Wooden Peacock") was the flying aircraft used by King Ravana of Sri Lanka; it appears in *Ramayana* (*Rama's Journey*), an ancient Indian epic poem dating between 500 and 100 BCE, making it possibly the first literary reference to a flying vehicle. The king would use this vehicle (often described as a flying chariot) to travel to each of his ten kingdoms. Of note, there are two cities in Sri Lanka called Wariyapola ("aircraft place"), and each is said to have been a site where King Ravana would land Dhadu Monara. These ancient airports, located in dense jungles, still have plainly marked clearings that resemble runways.

Sources: Mason, *Rasa Shastra*, 470, 478; Rough Guides, *The Rough Guide to Sri Lanka*, n.p.

Dhat al Fodhul

According to Islamic mythology, the prophet Muhammad owned at least seven cuirasses (a piece of armor made of a breastplate and backplate hinged or otherwise fastened together) at the time of his death; their names were al BETRA, Dhat al Fodhul, DHAT AL HAWAFHI, DHAT AL WELHAL, al FADDO, al KHERNA, and al SA'ADIA. Beyond its name, nothing else is known of Dhat al Fodhul ("the Excellent" or "Full of Excellence").

Sources: Osborne et al., *A Complete History of the Arabs*, Volume 1, 254; Sale et al., *An Universal History, Part 2*, Volume 1, 185

Dhat al Hawafhi

According to Islamic mythology, the prophet Muhammad owned at least seven cuirasses (a piece of armor made of a breastplate and backplate hinged or otherwise fastened together) at the time of his death; their names were al BETRA, DHAT AL FODHUL, Dhat al Hawafhi, DHAT AL WELHAL, al FADDO, al KHERNA, and al SA'ADIA. Beyond its name, nothing else is known of Dhat al Hawafhi ("Adorned with a Border and Fringe").

Sources: Osborne et al., *A Complete History of the Arabs*, Volume 1, 254; Sale et al., *An Universal History, Part 2*, Volume 1, 185

Dhat al Welhal

According to Islamic mythology, the prophet Muhammad owned at least seven cuirasses (a piece of armor made of a breastplate and backplate hinged or otherwise fastened together) at the time of his death; their names were al BETRA, DHAT AL FODHUL, DHAT AL HAWAFHI, Dhat al Welhal, al FADDO, al KHERNA, and al SA'ADIA. Beyond its name, nothing else is known of Dhat al Welhal ("Fortified with a Leather Belt").

Sources: Osborne et al., *A Complete History of the Arabs*, Volume 1, 254; Sale et al., *An Universal History, Part 2*, Volume 1, 185

Dhual-firqar

Variation: Dhu'l Fakar

According to Islamic doctrine, Ali ibn Abi Talib, the cousin and son-in-law of the prophet Muhammad, owned a wonderful sword named Dhual-firqar ("the Trenchant").

Other sources list the sword as Dhu'l Fakar as being one of the nine swords owned by the prophet at the time of his death, the other swords being al ADHAB, al Battar (see BATTER), al Hatf (see HATEL), al KADIB, KOLAITE, MABUR, al MEHDHAM, and al ROFUB. As Dhu'l Fakar, the sword originally belonged to Monba Edn al Hahaj, who was slain in the Battle of Bedr; it was then presented to Muhammad. After Muhammad's death, Dhu'l Fakar passed to Ali.

Sources: Boren and Boren, *Following the Ark of the Covenant*, 13; Brewer and Harland, *Character Sketches of Romance, Fiction and the Drama*, Volume 4, 378; Sale et al., *An Universal History, Part 2*, Volume 1, 184

Divine Throne

In the non-canonical Book of the Watchers, Enoch (who ascended into Heaven to play an intercessory role for the Watchers then pleading their case) described the divine throne of God in great detail, as well as the room in which it was located. According to this account, the throne sat in the innermost part of the celestial sanctuary. "As for its floor, it was of fire and above it was lightning and the path of the stars; and as for the ceiling, it was flaming fire. And I observed and saw inside it a lofty throne—its appearance was like crystal and its wheels like shining sun; and I heard the voice of the cherubim and from beneath the throne were issuing streams of flaming fire. It was difficult to look at."

Sources: Gallusz, *The Throne Motif in the Book of Revelation*, 53–54

Door of Battle

Variation: Coma Catha

In the Irish epic *Tain Bo Cuailnge* (*The Cattle Raid of Cooley/The Tain*), the Door of Battle was the shield of Celtchar; it is named as being among the many cups, drinking horns, goblets, javelins, shields, and swords kept in Tete Brec, one of the three households of the Ulster hero Cuhullin (Cu Chulaind/Cu Chulainn/Cuchulainn). Door of Battle is described only as brown in color.

Sources: Kinsella and Le Brocquy, *The Tain*, 5; Mountain, *The Celtic Encyclopedia*, Volume 2, 431

Doors of Ebony and Ivory, the

The Doors of Ebony and Ivory were located in the castle of Queen Igraine of Arthurian lore; one door was made of the finest ebony, and the other was constructed from the best ivory. Both were beautifully carved and trimmed with gold and magical precious gems. Hung with golden hinges, the doors also had golden latches. The floor beneath the doors was made of highly polished black, blue, red, white, and violet stones. These doors opened into the chamber of the WONDROUS BED.

Sources: Karr, *Arthurian Companion*, 130; Kibler and Palmer, *Medieval Arthurian Epic and Romance*, 178

dracontias

Variations: dragon stone, dtacontias

According to medieval European legends and travelers' tales, the dragons of Ethiopia were very large (some 35 feet in length) and had either one or two sets of wings. Preying on elephants along the arid coast, these dragons were sought after for the precious stone (called dracontias) set within their brains, which allowed them to see in the dark. Dracontias was much sought after by alchemists, but in order for the stone to be effective for alchemic purposes, it needed to be removed while the dragon was still alive.

The dracontias is said to be as about the size of an olive and most beautifully colored. When placed in water that was then boiled, the brew became a powerful remedy for any disease, most effective against diarrhea, dysentery, nosebleeds,

and plague; it was also an antidote to any poison, guaranteeing complete recovery.

Sources: Conway, *Dancing with Dragons*, 29–30; Rose, *Giants, Monsters, and Dragons*, 103

Draft of Immortality, the

An elixir from Zoroastrian mythology, the Draft of Immortality is created by mixing the fat of the primordial ox Hadhayosh (Hadhayaosh/Sarsaok) with white herbs. This drink will then be given to righteous people for their resurrection.

Sources: Boyce, *A History of Zoroastrianism*, 89; Rose, *Giants, Monsters, and Dragons*, 165

Dragon Banner, the

According to Arthurian lore, Merlin (Merddyn/Myrddin) gave King Arthur this banner for his battle against the rebel kings. It was sometimes carried by Sir Kay and sometimes by Merlin himself. On at least one occasion when the banner was being carried by Merlin, the dragon upon the banner spat fire from its mouth.

Sources: Karr, *Arthurian Companion*, 131; Lacy et al., *The New Arthurian Encyclopedia*, 14, 230

dragon fat candles

According to Chinese folklore, candles made of dragon fat are especially bright, able to light up the countryside for 100 miles; however, they must have a wick of "fire-washed cloth" (asbestos).

Sources: Bates, *All about Chinese Dragons*, 23; de Visser, *The Dragon in China and Japan*, 96

dragon teeth

Dragons are present in the folklore and mythology of nearly every culture. In ancient Greek mythology, when Cadmus slew the dragon of Ares (Roman god Mars), the god of war, he extracted the creature's teeth, planted them in the soil and, nearly in an instant, grew an army of soldiers. He then tossed a gem among them, which the soldiers fought and killed over. When only five remained, the battle was halted and the survivors went on to found the city of Thebes under Cadmus's leadership.

In European folklore, it was believed that carrying dragon teeth wrapped in deerskin would win the favor of a prince.

Sources: Gribble, "The Alpine Dragon," 570; Sample, *The Dragon's Teeth*, 15

Dragvandil

In the Icelandic epic *Egil's Saga*, Egill Skallagrimsson (Egil Skallagrimsson) had two swords: one was called Nadder, and the other, given to him by

Arinbiorn, was known as Dragvandil. Dragvandil (Egill's preferred weapon) was the sword he used in the battle against Atli the Short. Although Egill hacked apart Atli's shield, enabling him to land many blows to his opponent's body, Dragvandil's blade was unable to cut into Atli's flesh.

Sources: Eddison, *Egil's Saga*, 281; Keyser, *The Religion of the Northmen*, 247

draught of Thor, the

In Norse mythology, King Loke ruled the land of Utgard, where no one was tolerated unless they distinguished themselves in some way. As Thor and his servants traveled through this territory, they came upon the king, who sought to test the god of thunder. Presented with a long drinking horn, Thor was tasked with drinking the contents in no more than three draughts. He was unable to do so, but this was because the drinking horn was magically connected to the sea. When Thor drank, he reduced the level of the water and created the ebb of the ocean.

Sources: Anderson, *Norse Mythology*, 318–21; Sturluson, *The Prose Edda*, n.p.

Draupnir (DROUP-nir)

Variations: Draupne, Draupner, Drippe, Ring of Power

In Norse mythology, Draupnir ("the Dropping"/"Dropper") was an arm-ring made of red gold and shaped as an *ouroboros* (a snake holding its own tail in its mouth—the symbol of eternal renewal). Every nine days the ring would produce nine more identical rings of equal beauty and value, if not ability.

Draupnir, along with the spear GULLINBURSTI and the hammer MJOLNIR, was part of a set of three gifts forged by the dwarf brothers Brokkr and Eitri to win a wager against the god, Loki, who bet they could not craft anything finer than the gifts made for the Aesir by the Sons of Ivaldi. The victor would win Loki's head. In the end, it was the hammer MJOLNIR that won the contest for the brothers; however, Loki was able to use a loophole in the rules to avoid a beheading.

When Odin's son Balder died, Draupnir was placed on his funeral pyre; it was retrieved by Hermodr and given as a gift by Skirnir, the servant of the god of fertility, peace, rain, and sunshine, Freyr (Frey/Yngvi), to woo Gerdr.

Sources: Grimes, *The Norse Myths*, 263; Norroena Society, *Satr Edda*, 341; Orchard, *Dictionary of Norse Myth and Legend*, 102

drinking horn of Mimir (MEEM-ir)

Mimir is the Jotun from Norse mythology who keeps guard over MIMIRSBRUNNR WELL, a well of knowledge and memory; it is located at the Jotunheimr root of YGGDRASIL ("memory" and "wise"). Although he drank from the well daily, Mimir would not allow others to do the same unless they paid a dear price; Odin, the god of battle, death, frenzy, the gallows, healing, knowledge, poetry, royalty, the runic alphabet, sorcery, and wisdom, sacrificed one of his eyes for foresight and wisdom.

At dawn, the sunlight would change the water of the well into a golden-brown mead; only then would Mimir, using his golden drinking horn, take a single draught (more than that would destroy him with too much knowledge). When Odin sacrificed his eye for a single sip of the mead, he broke his bargain, nearly draining the horn dry. Mimir then threw Odin's eye into the well. Over time, Mimir used the eye as a vessel to carry the well's water to water the roots of YGGDRASIL. Other times, it became the cup he would use for his morning sip of mead.

Sources: Daly, *Norse Mythology A to Z*, 69; Grimes, *The Norse Myths*, 287; Norroena Society, *Asatru Edda*, 335, 336, 351, 354, 357, 361, 371, 374, 375, 376, 377

Dromi (DROHM-i)

Variations: Droma, Drome, Drone

In Norse mythology, Dromi ("Fetter") was the second chain forged in Asgard ("Enclosure of the Aesir") by the god of thunder, Thor, in an attempt to bind the son of the god Loki known as Fenriswulf (Fenerriswulf/Fenrissulfrin); it was said to be twice as strong as the first chain Thor had forged, LAEDINGR, which also failed.

Sources: Grimes, *The Norse Myths*, 263; Hawthorne, *Vikings*, 18; Norroena Society, *Satr Edda*, 341

Druidhe Lannach

In Celtic lore and Irish mythology, Druidhe Lannach ("Magic Blade") was the sword of Osgar ("Deer Friend"), a popular character in the Fenian Cycle and one of the Fianna. Druidhe Lannach was one of the six swords made by Lon Lonnrach the *beangruagach* ("giant woman"); the other swords were CEARD-NAN GALLAN, CHRUAIDH COSGARREACH, FASDAIL, LIOBHANACH, and MAC AN LUINE.

Osgar was a popular character in English ballads, but the occasional Gaelic words would slip in, leading to statements such as "the sword was

Duban

at his side that gave no second wound." The inference here is that Druidhe Lannach had the ability to kill a man with the landing of a single stroke.

Sources: Gregory and MacCumhaill, *Gods and Fighting Men*, 268; Leodhas, *By Loch and by Lin*, n.p.

Duban

According to Irish legend, the shield of Cuhullin (Cu Chulaind/Cu Chulainn/Cuchulainn), known as Duban ("Black"), was designed by the supernatural Dubdethba; it is the shield the hero carries in *The Tain* (also known as *Tain Bo Cuailnge* or *The Cattle Raid of Cooley*). In this epic, the shield is described as dark red with five circles of gold and trimmed in *findruine* (a type of white bronze) or silver.

Sources: Kinsella and Le Brocquy, *The Tain*, 5; Sims-Williams, *Irish Influence on Medieval Welsh Literature*, 303

Durandal

Variations: Durandarte, Durendal, Durlindana, "The terror of all wrong-doers"

In the French epic poem *Song of Roland* (*La Chanson de Roland*, circa 1040–1115), which retells the events of the Battle of Roncevaux Pass in 778 CE, the indestructible Durandal ("To Endure") was originally the sword of Charlemagne but was later gifted to Roland. With Durandal in hand, Roland held off a hundred thousand Muslims while Charlemagne and his army retreated to France.

There are varying accounts for the origin of the sword, the most popular of which is that it was forged by the legendary blacksmith Wayland (Gofannon/Volund/Weiland/Weyland) the Smith along with two other swords (COURTAIN and ALMACE). However, it is also said to have been given to Charlemagne by an angel; another story claims Durandal was the very sword once wielded by the ancient hero Hector of Troy. In *The Legend of Croquemitaine*, it was forged by Munifican for Roland but was later destroyed by the sword GLORIOUS to test the edge of the blade.

Durandal is described as both indestructible and the sharpest sword in existence. Additionally, it is said to have had a golden hilt containing the blood of Saint Basil, some hair of Saint Denis, a piece of raiment (formal clothing) of the Blessed Virgin Mary, and a tooth of Saint Peter.

Sources: Brault, *The Song of Roland*, 36, 251, 252, 443; Brewer, *Dictionary of Phrase and Fable* 1900, 1197; Caro, *The Road from the Past*, 21, 106–7; Evangelista, *The Encyclopedia of the Sword*, 577; Pendergrass, *Mythological Swords*, 4, 9, 22, 48; Sayers, *The Song of Roland*, 38

dyrar veigar (DEER-ar VAYG-ar)

In Norse mythology, dyrar veigar ("precious liquids") is a potion of bliss made from the blended meads of the Underworld fountains; it was given to Ottar (Otter/Otr) by the goddess of beauty, death, fertility, gold, love, seidr (a type of sorcery), sex, and war, Freyja ("Lady"), to drink.

Sources: Norroena Society, *Satr Edda*, 342; Rydberg et al., *Teutonic Mythology*, Volume 2, 526

Dyrnwyn

Variations: Dyrnwyn Gleddyf Rhydderch Hael ("White Hilt Sword of Rhydderch Hael")

In British and Welsh folklore, there is a series of items (always thirteen in number) called the THIRTEEN TREASURES OF THE ISLAND OF BRITAIN (in Welsh, they are called *Tri Thlws ar Ddeg Ynys Prydain*). Although in more modern times the items listed are different, the original thirteen items from the fifteenth century were the CAULDRON OF DYRNWCH THE GIANT, CHARIOT OF MORGAN MWYNFAWR, CHESSBOARD OF GWENDDOLEU AP CEIDIO, COAT OF PADARN BEISRUDD, CROCK AND DISH OF RHYGENYDD YSGOLHAIG (two items), HALTER OF CLYDNO EIDDYN, HAMPER OF GWYDDNO GARANHIR, HORN OF BRAN GALED, KNIFE OF LLAWFRODEDD FARCHOF, MANTLE OF ARTHUR IN CORNWALL, sword of Rhydderch Hael (Dyrnwyn), and WHETSTONE OF TUDWAL TUDGLYD.

A sword from Anglo Saxon mythology, Dyrnwyn ("White Hilt") belonged to Rhydderch Hael. It was said that Dyrnwyn would burst into flames when drawn by a man of noble spirit; if an unworthy person attempted to use the sword, the fire would consume them. Rhydderch was quick to lend his sword to whoever would ask, earning him the nickname *Hael* ("Generous"); however, as soon as the person was cautioned as to the weapon's magical ability, it was quickly returned unused.

Sources: Indick, *Ancient Symbology in Fantasy Literature*, 138; Patton, *The Poet's Ogam*, 510; Pendergrass, *Mythological Swords*, 24–25

Ear of Beauty

In the Irish epic *Tain Bo Cuailnge* (*The Cattle Raid of Cooley/The Tain*), Ear of Beauty was the shield of Conchobor; it is named as being among the many cups, drinking horns, goblets, javelins, shields, and swords kept in Tete Brec, one of the three households of the Ulster hero Cuhullin (Cu Chulaind/Cu Chulainn/Cuchulainn). Ear of Beauty is described as having four golden borders.

Sources: Kinsella and Le Brocquy, *The Tain*, 5; Mountain, *The Celtic Encyclopedia*, Volume 2, 471

earrings of Karna

Variation: kundala ("earrings")

In Hindu mythology, Karna, the child of a virgin, was born with a natural breastplate (see ARMOR OF KARNA) and golden earrings that made him all but invincible, even to the weapons of heaven (see ASTRA). The earrings were said to be as radiant as the sun, and as long as Karna wore them, no one was able to harm him. The earrings and armor were cut from his body and given to Indra, the god of the heavens, lightning, rains, river flows, storms, and *vajra* ("thunder"), in exchange for the ASTRA known as SAKTI.

Sources: Bryant, *Krishna*, 26–27; Dalal, *Hinduism*, 197

Echtach

In the Irish epic *Tain Bo Cuailnge* (*The Cattle Raid of Cooley/The Tain*), Echtach was presumably the sword of Amargin, as it is described only as a "death-eater." Echtach is named as being among the many cups, drinking horns, goblets, javelins, shields, and swords kept in Tete Brec, one of the three households of the Ulster hero Cuhullin (Cu Chulaind/Cu Chulainn/Cuchulainn).

Sources: Kinsella and Le Brocquy, *The Tain*, 5; Mountain, *The Celtic Encyclopedia*, Volume 2, 307

Eckesax

Variations: Ecke-sax, Ekkisax

According to German mythology, the good and great sword Eckesax belonged to the giant Ecke until he was defeated by Falke, the faithful steed of the young and heroic Prince Dietrich von Bern. According to the *Eckenlied*, Ecke had captured the widowed Lady of Drachenfels and her nine daughters. Dietrich sought out the giant to rescue the women, but he confronted the giant at night, a time when he was not at his fighting best. Just as the young hero was about to fall victim to the giant, the prince's steed sensed what was about to occur and entered into the fray, rearing up and stomping the giant to death.

Sources: Guerber, *Legends of the Middle Ages*, 116; Jobes, *Dictionary of Mythology, Folklore, and Symbols*, Part 1, 423; Macdowall, *Epics and Romances of the Middle Ages*, 164, 168

Egeking

Variations: Edgeking ("King of Swords"), Erkyin

In the medieval poem *Greysteil*, Sir Graham (Grime) acquires the magical sword Egeking from Lady Loosepine (Loospaine) so he may confront Lord Greysteil (Greysteel) and kill him, thereby avenging the death of her previous husband, Lord Egek. The poem tells us that the sword came from "beyond the Greek sea" and is referred to as a "treasure of great price."

Sources: Gray, *Later Medieval English Literature*, 526; Pendergrass, *Mythological Swords*, 4; Rickert, *Early English Romances in Verse*, 183

Egishjalmr (AIG-is-hyalm-r)

Variations: Aegishjalmr, Aegishjalmur, Helm of Dread

In the *Volsunga Saga*, the hero Sigurd (Siegfried/Sigmund) slew the dragon god Fafnir (Fafner) to gain his treasure hoard; one of the items in the hoard was a helmet named Egishjalmr ("Helm of Awe" or "Terror-Helm"). When worn, the helm cast a mesmerizing and terrifying aura around the person wearing it.

Sources: Byock, *The Saga of the Volsungs*, 66; Morris, *The Story of Sigurd the Volsung and the Fall of the Niblungs*, 192

eitr (AYT-r)

The mythical substance from which all life originates in Norse mythology, eitr is said to be highly poisonous in its raw form. Some serpents, including Jormungandr (the Midgard serpent), are capable of producing eitr. Ymir ("Groaner"; Aurgelmir), the first giant, was made of eitr.

Sources: Norroena Society, *Satr Edda*, 343; Rydberg, *Teutonic Mythology* Volume 2, 359, 371, 375; Sherman, *Storytelling*, 517

Ekkisax

Variation: Eckesachs

The dwarf king, magician, and master-forger Alberich, from the thirteenth-century epic poem *Thidrekssaga*, created the pattern-welded sword Ekkisax ("No Knife"); it is described as well polished, marked with gold, and *wyrmfah* (or having serpentine characteristics). When held with the point down toward the earth, the markings on the blade not only resembled a snake but also seemed to be moving downward into the ground. Likewise, when the sword was held so that its tip pointed to the sky, it appeared as if a snake was racing from the hilt down the side of the sword and out into the sky.

Sources: Classen, *Magic and Magicians in the Middle Ages and the Early Modern Time*, 122; Davidson, *The Sword in Anglo-Saxon England*, 162, 166

Eldhrimnir (EHLD-reem-nir)

Variation: Eidhrimner

In Norse mythology, Eldhrimnir ("Fire-Rime"/ "Soot Blackened"/"Sooth with Fire") is the cauldron of Odin, the god of battle, death, frenzy, the gallows, healing, knowledge, poetry, royalty, the runic alphabet, sorcery, and wisdom. The cauldron resides in his great hall. Each day the chef, Adhrimnir, boils Saehrimnir (the magical boar) in order to feed the *einherjar* ("lone fighters"—the spirits of brave warriors who died in battle) who live in VALHALLA.

Sources: Daly, *Norse Mythology A to Z*, 24; Grimes, *The Norse Myths*, 263; Hawthorne, *Vikings*, 18; Orchard, *Dictionary of Norse Myth and Legend*, 37; Norroena Society, *Satr Edda*, 343

Elf-King's Tune, the

Although traditional Norwegian fiddlers claim to know this song, they will never play the Elf-King's Tune, claiming that as soon as they begin, not only will young and old people alike leap to their feet to dance, but they will also be joined by the surrounding inanimate objects. Another reason musicians will offer up to explain why they do not play the tune is because once they begin, they will be unable to stop on their own; someone will have to sneak up behind them and cut the strings of their instrument. Some lore claims that if the fiddler has the presence of mind to play the song backward, he will then be able to play the melody back to the beginning, at which point he will be able to stop.

Sources: Dudley, *Poetry and Philosophy of Goethe*, 290–91; Keightley, *World Guide to Gnomes, Fairies, Elves, and Other Little People*, 79

Eljudnir

Variation: Elvidnir ("Damp with Sleet")

In Norse mythology, Hel, the goddess of the underworld, has an enormous hall named Eljudnir ("Preparer of Pain"/"Sprayed with Snowstorms"), which is fully decorated with many named items. The hall has high walls, banisters, and a huge gate. The goddess's bed curtains are named BLIKJANDABOL, the bed is named KOR, her dish is referred to as HUNGR, the knife she uses is called FAMINE, the threshold to her home is a pitfall called FALLANDAFORAD, her male slave is Ganglati ("Lazy"), and her woman servant is named Ganglot ("Slothful").

Sources: Daly, *Norse Mythology A to Z*, 21; Norroena Society, *Satr Edda*, 339

Ellide

Variations: the dragon-ship *Ellide*, *Ellida*, *Fllida*

Frithiof (Frithjof) the Bold, a hero of Icelandic legend, was said to have a magical ship named *Ellide*. It was originally a gift from the god of the sea, Aegir, to one of the hero's ancestors as a reward for his kindness. *Ellide* was one of Frithiof's three prized possessions, ANGURVADEL and the GOLDEN ARM RING being the other two.

The bow of *Ellide* sported the head of a dragon with its mouth wide open and was fashioned from gold. The stern of the ship had a long and twisted tail, and its underside was painted in blue and golden scales. The ship's planks were not assembled by a shipwright; rather, they had grown together. The sails were said to be black and trimmed in red; these sails were often referred to as *Ellide's* wings, for when they were let down, the ship could sail faster than any vessel, as if flying over the surface of the water, even in the most treacherous weather.

Ellide responded to the voice of its captain. In one tale, Frithiof was being beaten up by the sea witches Ham and Heyd, who had conjured up a storm and a whale to sink the ship, thus taking down the hero as well. However, Frithiof called out to the *Ellide* for help; it answered by stretching out its wings, racing across the raging ocean as if it were smooth, and ramming the whale head on, killing it instantly.

Sources: Cox and Jones, *Tales of the Teutonic Lands*, 222, 230; Nye, *Encyclopedia of Ancient and Forbidden Secrets*, 49; Sladen, *Frithjof and Ingebjorg*, 11, 18, 24, 47

Ellilyf Asa (EHL-i-leev AHS-a)

Variations: APPLES OF IDUNN, Epli Elliyf ("Apples Against Old Age"/"Apples of Old Age Medicine"), Eppli Ellifo

In Norse mythology, the Ellilyf Asa ("The Gods' Remedy Against Old Age") were the golden apples that grew on the tree YGGDRASIL; they were the fruit that granted eternal youth to the gods. The guardian of the apples was a golden-haired goddess of rebirth and spring named Idunn; she alone had the ability to bless and sanctify the apples and bring forth their magical ability. Eating an apple she had not consecrated would yield no miraculous benefits. The collective name for the Ellilyf Asa was Epli Ellifu ("eleven apples").

Sources: Daly, *Norse Mythology A to Z*, 45; Grimes, *The Norse Myths*, 264; Norroena Society, *Satr Edda*, 343; Rydberg, *Teutonic Mythology* Volume 3, 645

Emerald Tablet, the

In Cabalistic traditions, the ARK OF THE COV-
ENANT contained more than the stones on which
the Ten Commandments were written; it also
held other fabulous and mysterious relics, one of
which was the Emerald Tablet. This item was a
translucent emerald crystal that contained all of
the mysteries of the universe. One of the secrets
the Emerald Table kept was the name of God, the
mere utterance of which could unravel all of Creation. Because this item had the potential to be so
dangerous, the tablet was placed within the ARK
OF THE COVENANT for safekeeping.

One remarkable feature of the Emerald Tablet
was its ability to change the text on its surface as
was necessary. When this shift would occur, the
item would groan, vibrate, and on occasion emit
a powerful light.

Traditional lore says the Emerald Table was
acquired by Enoch either as a relic passed down
from Adam or during one of Enoch's many trips
to serve in the celestial realm. Eventually, he
placed the tablet in the great pyramids of Egypt
to protect them from the upcoming flood Ultimately, these items were removed by Moses and
placed in the ARK OF THE COVENANT.

Sources: Boren and Boren, *Following the Ark of the Covenant*, 15–16; Hauck, *The Emerald Tablet*, n.p.

endless bag of rice, the

In Japanese lore, there is a tale of man-eating
centipede living in the mountains near Lake Biwa;
the cultural hero and famed monster-slayer Hidesato was asked by the Dragon King to destroy the
creature. Hidesato coated one of his arrowheads
in his own saliva, as it was widely believed that
human saliva was poisonous to such creatures.
He then shot the arrow into the head of the centipede, piercing its brain and killing it instantly.
The hero was rewarded with three magical items,
one of which was a straw tawara rice bag (see
also CRIMSON COPPER PAN and SILK ROLL OF
HIDESATO). No matter how much rice Hidesato
scooped out of it, the bag never emptied; according to the legend, it fed his family for centuries.

Sources: Kimbrough and Shirane, *Monsters, Animals,
and Other Worlds*, n.p.; Roberts, *Japanese Mythology A to
Z*, 22

ephemeral fruits

In ancient Greek mythology, the gigantic, monstrous, and serpentine Typhon (Typhoes/Typhaon/
Typhos) was a storm giant and the personification
of volcanic forces. An enemy to Zeus (Roman god
Jupiter), the god of fate, kings, lightning, sky, and
thunder, whom Typhon had already once rendered
helpless by removing the sinew from his legs, the
giant was convinced by the Fates to eat the ephem-
eral fruits, promising him that doing so would
make him grow stronger. Typhon, having no reason to doubt their word, did as they suggested, but
the fruits had the opposite effect—the more he
consumed, the weaker he became.

Sources: Hard, *The Routledge Handbook of Greek
Mythology*, 85; Parada, *Genealogic Guide to Greek Mythology*, 193

Excalibur

Variations: Calabrum (*Historia Regum Bri-
tanniae*), Calabrun (*Historia Regum Britanniae*),
Calad Bolg ("Hard Lightning"), CALADBOLG
(Irish, "Hard Cleft"), Caladcolc, Caladcolg, Caled-
fwlch (Welsh), Caledvwlch, Calesvol (Cornish),
Calibor, Caliborc, Calibore (*Historia Regum Bri-
tanniae*), Caliborne (*Historia Regum Britan-
niae*), Calibourch, Calibourne, Caliburc (Geoffrey
Gaimar), Caliburn, Caliburnu, Caliburnus (Latin),
Callibor (*Historia Regum Britanniae*), Calliborc
(*Historia Regum Britanniae*), Callibourc (*Historia
Regum Britanniae*), Caluburn, Chalabrum (*Histo-
ria Regum Britanniae*), Chaliburn, Claiomh Solais
("Sword of Light"), Escalibor (Old French), Esca-
liborc (*Historia Regum Britanniae*), Escalibor'p,
Excalibor (Old French), Kaledvoulc'h (Breton),
SWORD IN THE STONE

Perhaps one of the best-known swords in history, the legendary blade Excalibur ("To Liberate
from the Stone") is often misunderstood, as many
authors over the years have told the tale of its primary wielder, the legendary hero King Arthur of
Camelot, in their own way. There are many versions of the history of the once and future king,
his knights, their adventures, and the mythical
sword.

The confusion surrounding Excalibur begins
with its origin story. It is generally agreed that the
sword was forged in another world and came to
ours by means of the magic of Merlin (Merddyn/
Myrddin) or as a gift from the Lady of the Lake.
It is a popular misconception that Arthur pulled
Excalibur from the famous stone, thereby proving
his divine right to the throne (see SWORD IN THE
STONE). Arthur did pull a sword from a stone, as
the story has it, but it was not Excalibur. Arthur
carried that first sword into battle until it broke.

Faddo, al

It was only then that Merlin said he knew where Arthur could acquire a sword worthy of a king: enter Excalibur.

Whoever forged the weapon, whether an elf of Avalon or the legendary master blacksmith, Wayland (Gofannon/Volund/Weiland/Weyland) the Smith, they made the sword magically sharp; its edge was supernaturally keen, making it invaluable in battle. It could cut through a bar of iron or a feather with equal ease. Excalibur's blade was so bright that it was like looking at a bolt of lightning; it shone like a flame in the heat of battle. Many legends also speak of an inscription on the blade, such as "Excalibur Always for God and King" or something akin to "Take me up" on one side and "Cast me away" on the other.

Excalibur aided in establishing the validity of Arthur as the rightful king, as it all but ensured his victory in battle; in fact, the sword became the symbol of his kingship, rather than his crown. However, it is interesting to note that the sword was not as powerful as the scabbard that held it. According to Merlin himself, the SCABBARD OF EXCALIBUR was "ten times" more powerful than the blade.

In the Battle of Camlann, Arthur was mortally wounded; afterward, he told one of his knights (typically Bedivere or Girflet) to throw Excalibur into a particular lake. It was a common Celtic practice to dispose of the personal arms and armor of great warriors in such a fashion. Although the knight (whose identity varies) did not do as asked right away, ultimately Excalibur was thrown into the water, returned from whence it came, and once again in the possession of the Lady of the Lake.

Sources: Evangelista, *The Encyclopedia of the Sword*, 577; MacKillop, *Dictionary of Celtic Mythology*, 64–65, 174; Peterson and Dunworth, *Mythology in Our Midst*, 52–54; Pyle, *The Story of King Arthur and His Knights*, 92–93

Faddo, al

According to Islamic mythology, the prophet Muhammad owned at least seven cuirasses (a piece of armor made of a breastplate and backplate hinged or otherwise fastened together) at the time of his death; their names were al BETRA, DHAT AL FODHUL, DHAT AL HAWAFHI, DHAT AL WELHAL, al Faddo, al KHERNA, and al SA'ADIA. Beyond its name and the fact that it was taken from the Jewish tribe Banu Kainoka prior to their banishment to Syria, nothing else is known of al Faddo ("the Silver" or "Washed with Silver").

Sources: Osborne et al., *A Complete History of the Arabs*, Volume 1, 254; Sale et al., *An Universal History, Part 2*, Volume 1, 185

Fadha, al

Al Fadha was said to have been one of the cutlasses of the prophet Muhammad. This silver sword, along with other treasures (such as the sword al SA'ADIA), came into his possession as wealth confiscated from the Jewish tribe Banu Kainoka prior to their banishment to Syria.

Sources: Brewer and Harland, *Character Sketches of Romance, Fiction and the Drama*, Volume 2, 378; Irving, *Works of Washington Irving*, Volume 9, 132

Fail Not

According to Arthurian legend, Fail Not was the bow Tristan created for himself while he lived in hiding in the woods. This mechanical bow was set to release its arrow whenever a deer crossed its path; it never missed its mark.

Sources: Barlow, *William Rufus*, 123; Fedrick, *The Romance of Tristan*, 87

Fair Banquet

Fairy lore tells us there is a magical green table with golden feet called Fair Banquet; when sighted, it is straddling a small stream and covered with the finest breads and rich wines.

Sources: Keightley, *World Guide to Gnomes, Fairies, Elves, and Other Little People*, 352

fairy food

Traditional fairy lore describes the taste of fairy food as akin to wheaten bread mixed with honey and wine; it also warns that whoever consumes so much as a single bite of fairy food while in the fairy realm will be trapped there forever, as they are actually transformed in some small way, becoming a part of the fairy realm. Naturally, fairy food also smells delicious and is very appealing to the eye, but typically this appearance is just a facade. If the food is not an illusion, it may be a spell cast over some leaves or pebbles or other items offering no nutritional value whatsoever. It is also possible for fairies to steal away the nutrients and sustenance of human food; thus, when it is consumed, the person will remain hungry and unsatisfied.

Sources: Keightley, *World Guide to Gnomes, Fairies, Elves, and Other Little People*, 354; Moorey, *The Fairy Bible*, 54

fairy loaf

Variation: pharisee loaf

A fairy loaf is, according to legend, a loaf of

bread that a fairy gives to a mortal out of charity; the loaf will always remain fresh and never diminish in size as long as some condition is met, such as never revealing the source of the loaf or ensuring that one's children always eat a slice.

Fossilized sea urchins are called fairy loafs, and there is a saying in Norfolk that claims, "If you keep a fairy loaf, you will never want bread." Interestingly, the word "urchins" is also a euphemism for "fairies."

Sources: McNamara, *Star-Crossed Stone*, 119, 128; Spence, *Legends and Romances of Brittany*, 53; Wright, *Rustic Speech and Folk-Lore*, 208

falcon cloak, the

Variations: falcon garb, falcon plumes, falcon skin, feather cloak ("kahu huruhuru")

Owned by Freyja ("Lady"), the goddess of beauty, death, fertility, gold, love, seidr (a type of sorcery), sex, and war, as well as being the leader of the Valkyries in Norse mythology, the falcon cloak was one of her two prized possessions (the other being BRISINGAMEN). The cloak would grant its wielder the magical ability to transform into a falcon and take flight.

Sources: Conway, *Maiden, Mother, Crone*, 69–70; Guerber, *Myths of the Norsemen*, 135; Roberts, *Norse Gods and Heroes*, 66–67

Fallandaforad (FAL-and-a-vawr-ath)

Variations: Fallanda Foral ("Periolus Precice"), Fallende Gefahr, Stumbling-block

In Norse mythology, Hel, the goddess of the underworld, has an enormous hall named ELJUD-NIR ("Preparer of Pain"/"Sprayed with Snowstorms"), which is fully decorated with many named items. One item of note in her hall is the threshold, Fallandaforad ("Falling to Peril"), a literal pitfall that must be crossed to gain entry.

Sources: Daly, *Norse Mythology A to Z*, 21; Norroena Society, *Satr Edda*, 345; Thorpe, *Northern Mythology*, 50

Famine

In Norse mythology, Hel, the goddess of the underworld, has an enormous hall named ELJUD-NIR ("Preparer of Pain"/"Sprayed with Snowstorms"), which is fully decorated with many named items. Famine is the name of her knife.

Sources: Daly, *Norse Mythology A to Z*, 21; Norroena Society, *Satr Edda*, 345

Farsha

In Indian mythology, Farsha ("Battle-Axe") was the preferred weapon of the hand-to-hand combat master (and ill-tempered disciple to Shiva) Parshuram. Farsha is described as having four cutting edges—one on each end of the blade and one on each end of the weapon's shaft.

Sources: Kumar, *An Incredible War*, n.p.

Fasdail

In Celtic lore and Irish mythology, Fasdail ("Make Sure") was the sword of Goll Mac Morna, a Fianna in the Fenian Cycle. Fasdail was one of the six swords made by Lon Lonnrach the *bean-gruagach* ("giant woman"); the other swords were CEARD-NAN GALLAN, CHRUAIDH COSGAR-REACH, DRUIDHE LANNACH, LIOBHANACH, and MAC AN LUINE.

Sources: Gregory and MacCumhaill, *Gods and Fighting Men*, 268; Leodhas, *By Loch and by Lin*, n.p.

Fatuk, al

According to Islamic mythology, the prophet Muhammad owned at least three shields at the time of his death; their names were al Fatuk ("the brilliant"), al RAZIN, and al ZALUK. Beyond its name, nothing else is known of al Fatuk ("the Brilliant").

Sources: Osborne et al., *A Complete History of the Arabs*, Volume 1, 254; Sale et al., *An Universal History, Part 2*, Volume 1, 185

fear gorta (plural: fir gorta)

Variations: far gorta, gorta man

In Irish folklore, the fear gorta ("hungry man") is traditionally regarded as a fairy spirit, possibly the ghost of someone who died of hunger. Standing by the roadside, the spirit begs for food; anyone who gives it an offering is blessed with good fortune. However, there is a belief in Slieve-an-irain that a fear gorta is a stone that, if trod upon, causes an overwhelming fit of hunger to overtake the person who disturbed it.

Sources: Jacobs et al., *Folk Lore*, Volume 4, 183; Monaghan, *Encyclopedia of Celtic Mythology and Folklore*, 180; Yeats, *Fairy and Folk Tales of the Irish Peasantry*, 81

fear gortagh (fear gor-ta)

Variations: fair-gortha, fairy grass, fear gortach, fod gortach, foidin mearuil ("stray sod"), grave grass

In Ireland there are patches of earth that have vampiric tendencies. Known as fear gortagh ("hungry grass"), these are places where people have died from starvation. Looking like the grass all around it, there is nothing to give such a place away for what it is until you happen to walk upon it—then suddenly you'll become very hungry. Retreating from the spot will not reverse the effects, as the fear gortagh has already begun the process of eating away at your life energy. In order to save yourself, you must quickly eat and drink something, or you will succumb to hunger pangs and die.

Sources: Jones, *New Comparative Method*, 70, 73; Kinahan, *Yeats, Folklore, and Occultism*, 73; Royal Society of Antiquaries, *Journal of the Royal Society*, Volumes 72–73, 107; Wilde, *Ancient Legends, Mystic Charms, and Superstitions of Ireland*, 183, 226

fe-fiada mantle

Variation: ceo druidechta

In Celtic mythology, druids have the ability to create a CELTAR (mantle), which has the magical power to make its wearer invisible. Druids can also raise a fe-fiada, which not only will make a person invisible but also is a symbol of protection. In some stories a fe-fiada is a fog or mist used to obscure a well or castle; other times it is used to cover a battlefield to give one side a distinct advantage over the other. Fairy places are encircled with a fe-fiada to keep mortals from seeing them. In Irish Christian legend, Saint Patrick and his followers would sing a fe-fiada as they traveled, making them appear as a herd of deer to their enemies.

There are also tales of fe-fiada mantles, cloaks that would make the wearer invisible. In one story, the banshee Eevin gave such a cloak to the Dalcassiah hero Dunlang O'Hartigan, who was invisible and protected from harm so long as he wore the mantle. However, as soon as he removed it, he was slain.

Sources: Ellis, *The Druids*, 249; Joyce, *A Smaller Social History of Ancient Ireland*, 103

Feikstaf

Variation: Feiknastafr

In Norse mythology, Feikstaf was the hall of the god Balder and his wife Nanna Nepsdottr; it was located on his estate BREIDABLIK and had a shining gold roof and silver pillars, allowing it to be seen from afar. Evil was not allowed within its walls, and chamomile flowers grew in abundance all around the hall.

Sources: Grimes, *The Norse Myths*, 19, 265

Fensalir

Variations: Fensal, Fensala, Fensalar

In Norse mythology, Fensalir ("Bog Hall"/"Water Hall") was the oceanside hall of the goddess Frigg ("Beloved"); it was made of gold and silver and completely encrusted with pearls. It was said that sometimes, when a person drowned, Fensalir was the hall their spirit would go to. Fensalir was also where the god Loki, disguised as an old woman, was able to win Frigg's confidence and learn of Balder's vulnerability.

Sources: Grimes, *The Norse Myths*, 265; Lindow, *Norse Mythology*, 114

fern flower

Variation: fire flower

A magical plant said to blossom for a brief period of time on the eve of the summer solstice, the fern flower appears in the folklore of Estonia, Finland, Germany, Lithuania, Wales, and Southern Europe. The fern flower will give the ability to speak with and understand animals, good fortune, good luck, and wealth to any who can obtain it. However, the flower is closely guarded by evil spirits, dragons, snakes, storms, and wood trolls that must be overcome before the flower can be plucked. Once the guardians are defeated and the flower retrieved, its possessor will also be magically protected from future encounters with the same creatures. The flower is described as a white blossom "smelling like corruption" and will emit a bolt of flame when plucked; sometimes a thunderstorm will break out as well.

Sources: Arrowsmith, *Essential Herbal Wisdom*, n.p.; Froude, "Mystic Trees and Flowers," 608

Finnsleif

Variation: Finn's Legacy

The mail shirt of King Adils of Sweden, Finnsleif ("Finn's Legacy") was likely made by the dwarfs and was one of the king's prized possessions, as weapons were unable to penetrate it. According to the story, King Adils enlisted the assistance of his stepson, King Hrolf Kraki, to defeat King Ali of Norway; he promised to pay his stepson's entire army in addition to giving Hrolf any three Swedish treasures. Hrolf accepted and sent his twelve best berserkers. Adils defeated Ali and on the battlefield claimed his opponent's helmet, HILDIGOLT, and his warhorse, Raven. When the time for payment came, the berserkers asked for three pounds of gold each for themselves and the treasures Finnsleif, HILDIGOLT, and SVIAGRIS for their king.

Sources: Anderson, *The Younger Edda*, 215, 278; Byock, *The Prose Edda*, 59

fire stone of Thorston, the

In fairy lore, a local hero by the name of Thorston rescued the child of a dwarf who was taken by a dragon; the unnamed dwarf insisted on rewarding his savior and made him accept several gifts. One of these gifts was a unique stone. According to the story, it was a triangular stone with a steel point, red on one side, white on the other, with a yellow border all around. If the stone was pricked with the tip on the white side, a hailstorm would suddenly occur, so violent and thick that no one would be able to see through it. To stop the storm, all one needed to do was prick the yellow edge, as this action would cause the sun to come out and melt away the hail. When the red side was pricked, it created sparks and flames so great they were painful to look upon. Lastly, the stone and its gifts would return back to the owner whenever he desired them to do so.

Sources: Dunham, *The Cabinet Cyclopaedia*, Volume 26, 73; Keightley, *World Guide to Gnomes, Fairies, Elves, and Other Little People*, 72

firebird plumage

The firebird (zhar-ptitsa), a creature from Slavic myth, is described as a beautiful bird whose feathers glow, emitting orange, red, and yellow light as bright as a bonfire. It is said that even if a father is taken from the firebird, its plum will still glow brightly enough to light up a room.

Sources: Dixon-Kennedy, *Encyclopedia of Russian & Slavic Myth and Legend*, 86; Gohdes, *American Literature*, Volume 13, 319; Nigg, *A Guide to the Imaginary Birds of the World*, 89–90

fishhook of Maui, the

Variations: fishhook of Eden, fishhook of Tarauga, Manaia, Tawakea ("Put a Patch On"), Tu-whawhakia-te-rangi ("Taking Hold of the Sky")

In Polynesian mythology, the cultural hero Maui, both a deity and a human, brought fire from the underworld to mankind and invented the barb on fishhooks, which he named Muri-ranga-whenua. With his fishhook and the assistance of his brothers—Maui Mua ("Maui Who Was"), Maui Roto ("Maui Who Is Within"), Maui tiki tiki o te Rangi ("Maui Who Is from Heaven"), and Maui Waho ("Maui Who Is Without")—he was able to pull up the island of New Zealand. The ear of the youngest brother, Maui tiki tiki o te Rangi, was used as bait.

Sources: Best, "Notes on the Art of War as Conducted by the Maori of New Zealand," 78; Dieffenbach, *Travels in New Zealand*, Volume 2, 88, 89; White, *Ancient History of the Maori*, 117

five-colored jewel, the

A Japanese folktale from the Heinan period tells the story of a wealthy bamboo cutter's daughter by the name of Nayotake no Kaguya-hime ("Shining Princess of the Supple Bamboo") who wishes to marry only a man who truly loves her. She manages to whittle down her suitors to five and states that she will marry the one who is able to show her something special she wishes to see. The suitor named Dainagon Otomo no Marotari, the middle counselor, is given the task of bringing her a five-colored jewel, a precious gem that can only be found in the neck of a dragon and has the brilliant glow of five different colors.

Sources: Rimer, *Modern Japanese Fiction and Its Traditions*, 288; Shirane, *Traditional Japanese Literature*, 115

Flamberge

Variations: Floberge ("Flame Cutter"), Froberge, Plamberge

Although now the word *flamberge* is used to specify a specific type of sword, the name can be traced back to Flamberge, the sword of the legendary hero Renaud de Montauban, a knight of Charlemagne and one of the four sons of Aymon. Flamberge is said to have been made by legendary master blacksmith Wayland (Gofannon/Volund/Weiland/Weyland) the Smith and was originally owned by Maugis (Malagigi), who then made a gift of it to his cousin, Renaud.

In *The Legend of Croquemitaine*, the celebrated swordsmith Galas created three swords: Flamberge, HALTECLERE and JOYEUSE. Each sword took three years to make, and each was eventually used to test the edge of the sword GLORIOUS, which managed to hack into each of them.

Sources: Brewer, *Dictionary of Phrase and Fable* 1900, 1197; Evangelista, *The Encyclopedia of the Sword*, 577; Frankel, *From Girl to Goddess*, 49; Keightley, *World Guide to Gnomes, Fairies, Elves, and Other Little People*, 33; L'Epine, *The Days of Chivalry*, n.p.

flaming sword

The idea of a flaming sword is a common theme in various folklores, myths, and legends. These weapons are described as items of divine, magical, or supernatural power, emitting flames and burning more brightly than the sun. They are a classic symbol of power, strength, and vitality.

The Sumerian god Marduk used a flaming sword that also utilized lightning bolts in his battle against Baal and the dragon Tiamat.

The Book of Genesis (3:24) says God placed a

cherubim at the Gates of Paradise, armed with a flaming sword that revolved, turned, and moved in every direction, after He banished Adam and Eve from the Garden of Eden. Eastern Orthodox Christian tradition says after the birth of Jesus, the sword was removed, thus allowing humanity to reenter.

Norse mythology has the Jotun Surtr wielding an unnamed flaming sword as he defends the borders of the first world, Muspellsheimr (see FLAMING SWORD OF SURTR).

One of the THIRTEEN TREASURES OF THE ISLAND OF BRITAIN was Rhydderch Hael's flaming sword DYRNWYN. Attila the Hun was likewise said to wield the flaming sword AZ ISTEN KARDJA.

Sources: George and George, *The Mythology of Eden*, 173, 174; Pendergrass, *Mythological Swords*, 24–25, 33

flaming sword of Surtr, the

The Jotun Surtr ("Black"/"Swarthy One") of Norse mythology is stationed at the border of the first world, Muspellsheimr, to defend it; at the end of days, he will use his flaming sword to attack the gods and burn the world (see MED SVIGA LAEVI). The sword of Surtr is described as "very fine" and shining more brightly than the sun.

Sources: Colum, *Nordic Gods and Heroes*, n.p.; Loptson, *Playing with Fire*, n.p.

Florence

The celebrated swordsmith Ansias created three swords for the fictional giant Saracen (Muslim) knight Fierabras (Fierbras): BAPTISM, Florence, and GRABAN. Each sword took three years to make. In *The Legend of Croquemitaine*, the sword was made for Strong-in-the-Arms and was hacked by a giant when testing the edge of another sword, GLORIOUS.

Sources: Brewer, *Dictionary of Phrase and Fable* 1900, 1197; L'Epine, *The Days of Chivalry*, n.p.; Numismatic and Antiquarian Society of Philadelphia, *Proceedings of the Numismatic and Antiquarian Society of Philadelphia for the Years 1899–1901*, 65

flying carpet

Variations: magic carpet, magic carpet of Tangu, Prince Housain's carpet

A common trope and a traditional fantasy symbol, the flying carpet is used to transport riders to the destination of their choice. Most often this effect is achieved by the carpet rising into the air and literally flying its passenger, although on a few occasions the carpet transports the person instantly.

The earliest recorded use of a flying carpet was by King Solomon; the carpet was described as sixty miles long and wide, made of green silk, with a golden weft. When he sat upon it, Solomon controlled the wind and was able to fly through the air quickly; birds would soar overhead and act as a canopy, giving him shade.

In the Middle Eastern story *Tales of Sheherazade, or A Thousand and One Nights*, the carpet used by Prince Husain does not fly through the air so much as it magically transports a person "in the twinkling of an eye" to any destination they choose.

Sources: Brewer, *Dictionary of Phrase and Fable*, Volume 1, 217–18; Ish-Kishor, *The Carpet of Solomon*, n.p.

Flying Dutchman, the

Perhaps the most famous ghost ship of nautical folklore, the *Flying Dutchman* (*De Vliegende Hollander*) is cursed to never make port, endlessly sailing the seas, particularly around the Cape of Good Hope, Western Cape province, South Africa. Sailors say the vessel is usually (but not always) the harbinger of death; seeing it may cause the witness to be stricken with blindness or be the victim of a shipwreck.

In some versions of the tale, the *Flying Dutchman* has the ability to change its appearance. This odd feature for a phantom ship fits in nicely with another aspect of the story: The *Flying Dutchman* may attempt to come alongside another vessel in an attempt to deliver a shipment of mail. If the shipment is accepted, every soul on board will die before their ship can make port.

According to the legend, the captain—usually called Vanderdecker, Van Demien, Van Straaten, or some similar Dutch-sounding name—was at sea and heading to port when he did something to incur the wrath of God; some versions of the tale say he insisted on sailing on a Sunday, bragging that not even God could keep him from making port, or killed his brother and his brother's new wife in a fit of jealous rage. Whatever the reason, the ship was cursed to sail the sea for eternity.

The ship itself is typically described as a class of old sailing ship; it almost always has a high poop deck and an eerie phosphorescent light, and even in a storm, it can sail against the tide and wind. The crew, like the riggings and sails, are described as ragged and worn.

Sources: Barrington, *Voyage to Botany Bay*, 30; Brunvand, *American Folklore*, 459; Goss, *Lost at Sea*, 34–35, 42

flying throne of Kay Kavus, the

A mythological shah of Iran from Persian lore, Kay ("King") Kavus was described as not only having a mean streak but also being ambitious, depraved, petulant, and unpredictable. In many of his ill-advised forays into adventure, he was rescued by the celebrated hero Rostam (Rustam). In one such adventure, Kay Kavus constructed for himself a flying throne. In *Shahnameh* (*Shahnama*), an epic poem written by Ferdowsi (circa 977 CE), it is described as a throne made of gold and wood attached vertically to four long poles. Specially trained eagles were chained to the bottom of the throne, while bits of meat were hung from the tops of the poles; this arrangement enticed the ravenous raptors to fly up toward the food, lifting the throne with them.

Sources: Ferdowsi, *Shahnameh*, n.p.; Shirazi, *A Concise History of Iran*, 36; Stoneman et al., *The Alexander Romance in Persia and the East*, xiii, 16; Yarshater, *The Cambridge History of Iran*, Volume 3, Issue 1, 374

Folkvangar

Variations: Folkvanger, Folkvangr

In Norse mythology, Folkvangar ("Folk Fields"/ "Field of Warriors") was the field where SESS-RYMNIR the estate of the goddess of beauty, death, fertility, gold, love, seidr (a type of sorcery), sex, and war, Freyja ("Lady")was located. This is where she received a chosen portion of those known as *einherjar* ("lone fighters"—the spirits of brave warriors who died in battle); the rest of the einherjar moved on to VALHALLA.

Sources: Grimes, *The Norse Myths*, 265; Norroena Society, *Asatru Edda*, 347

Fountain of Youth

Supposedly a spring with the magical ability to restore the health and youth of anyone who bathes in or drinks from it, the Fountain of Youth has been referenced in tales and legends dating back as far as the fifth century BCE. Among other accounts, Herodotus mentions a fountain in Macrobia (ancient Libya) with water that increased the life span of its residents.

The quest for eternal youth is a common theme in myths and legends, as demonstrated by the stories of the APPLES OF IDUNN, the water of the well BYRGIR, DANCING WATER, elixir of life, the PHILOSOPHER'S STONE, and SOMA, to name but a few.

The legendary search for and so-called discovery of the Fountain of Youth by Spanish explorer Juan Ponce de Leon was not associated with the explorer until after his death. Nevertheless, the story that he went looking for the fountain and its restorative waters to cure himself of old age (and, in the process, discovered what would become the American state of Florida) remains popular.

Sources: Heinrichs, *Juan Ponce de Leon Searches for the Fountain of Youth*, 32; Herodotus, *The Histories Book 3*, 114; Morison, *The European Discovery of America*, 504

four-string guitar of Mo-li, the

In Chinese Buddhist mythology, there are four brothers known collectively as the Diamond Kings of Heaven (*Ssu Ta Chin-kang* or *T'ien-wang*); statues of them stand guard in pairs on the left and right sides of the entrances to Buddhist temples. The god and guardian of the west is Mo Li Hai (known in Sanskrit as Virupakshu, or "Far Gazer"); he carries a magical four-string guitar. When this instrument is played, the men of the enemy camp become so enthralled with the music that they do not notice their camp has caught fire and is blazing all around them.

Sources: Buckhardt, *Chinese Creeds and Customs*, 163; Werner, *Myths and Legends of China*, 122

four treasures of the Tuatha de Danann, the

Variations: the four jewels of the Tuatha de Danann, the Hallows of Ireland

According to Irish lore, when the Tuatha de Danann came to Ireland, they carried with them four magical treasures: the CAULDRON OF THE DAGDA, CLAIDHEAMH SOLUIS, LIA FAIL, and LUIN; each of these magical items came from one of their cities—Falias, Findias, Gorias, and Murias—and each item was carried by a druid.

Sources: Ellis, *Brief History of the Druids*, 73, 124; Loomis, *Celtic Myth and Arthurian Romance*, 237

Fragarach

Variations: The ANSWERER, Freagarthach, the Retaliator, Sword of Air, sword of Gorias

In Irish mythology, the sword Fragarach was said to have been forged by the gods; it was wielded first by the god of the sea and guardian of the Underworld, Manannan mac Lir (Mannanan,Mannanos), and then by his foster son, Lugh Lamfada. This magical blade had the ability to penetrate any type of armor, deliver a wound no one could survive, and give its wielder the power to control the wind.

Sources: Pendergrass, *Mythological Swords*, 39; Rolleston, *Myths & Legends of the Celtic Race*, 113, 121

Frodi

Frodi, Mill of (fro'de)

Variation: GROTTI

In Norse mythology, the Mill of Frodi was said to have belonged to Peace Frodi, a king who ruled Denmark when there was believed to be peace throughout the world; it was given to him by Hengikiaptr ("Hanging Jaw"). This enchanted mill could easily grind up anything Frodi wished, including gold, peace, and prosperity.

Sources: Guerber, *Myths of the Norsemen*, 128; Thorpe, *Northern Mythology*, 207

Fulminen

In Norse mythology, Fulminen was the name given to the thunder and lightning that shot forth from MJOLNIR, the hammer of Thor.

Sources: Grimes, *The Norse Myths*, 288

Fusberta

Fusberta was the sword of Rinaldo in *Orlando Furioso*; it and his steed were found by the wizard knight Malagigi in a dragon's hoard.

Sources: Ariosto, *Orlando Furioso*, Volume 1, 35; Brewer, *Dictionary of Phrase and Fable*, Volume 1, 494

Gada, the

Variation: Gedak

In Hindu mythology, an ASTRA is a supernatural weapon created or gifted by the gods to someone who then presides over the weapon. The wielder of an ASTRA is known as an astradhari.

The primary weapon of the avatar of Shiva and the Hindu god of strength, Hanuman, is a blunt-headed mace known as the Gada ("Mace"); it has come to symbolize a destroyer of evil. Because a gada, in general, is a heavy weapon (usually made of wood or iron, weighted with rings and stones), it is also a symbol of great strength. Traditionally, Hanuman is shown holding his weapon in his right hand.

Sources: Kaur, *The Regime of Maharaja Ranjit Singh*, 15; Lutgendorf, *Hanuman's Tale*, 41, 258

Gae Bolg

Variations: Death Spear, Gae Bolga ("Spear of Lightning"), Gae Bulg, Gae Bulga, Gai Bulga, Spear of Mortal Pain, spear of Cuchulain

In Irish mythology, Gae Bolg ("Barbed Spear"/ "Bellows Dart"/"Belly Dart"/"Belly Spear"/"Gapped Spear") is a javelin (or spear) sharp enough to pierce stone and wrought iron alike. The shaft of the weapon was covered with barbs, and when it entered an enemy's body, the barbs would open up, thereby making it impossible to remove without killing its victim. Gae Bolg belonging to the hero Cuhullin (Cu Chulaind/Cu Chulainn/Cuchulainn).

According to the legend, a hero by the name of MacBuain, while walking along the shore, found the remains of the sea monster known as the Curruid (Coinchenn), which had died fighting another sea monster. From the remains, MacBuain used one of its bones to construct a javelin he called Gae Bolg. In some versions of the tale, the weapon had seven different heads, each with seven barbs of its own.

Eventually MacBuain passed the weapon to MacInbar, who in turn passed it to his friend Lena, who gave it Dermeil, who gave it to the woman warrior and teacher at the war college of Alba (Scotland), Scathach. She gave the weapon to her daughter Aife, who was at the time the mistress of the hero Cuhullin as well as the mother of his only son, Connla. Aife subsequently made a gift of Gae Bolg to Cuhullin.

Scathach had a special martial style she created specifically to use Gae Bolg, and she only taught the technique to Cuhullin. One of the ways in which the weapon was utilized was by placing it near the ground, between one's toes, and then (likely) kicking it upward into one's opponent, slipping past their defenses. It was with this weapon and fighting style that, on separate occasions, Cuhullin killed his foster brother, Ferdiad, and his own son, Connla.

Similar to the spear LUIN, when thrown, Gae Bolg never missed its mark and landed with deadly accuracy.

Sources: Gregory, *Cuchulain of Muirthemne*, 45; Leviton, *The Gods in Their Cities*, 236; O'Reilly, *Ethics of Boxing and Manly Sport*, 220, 222, 234

Gae Dearg

Variations: Crann-derg ("Red Javelin"), Ga-der, Gai Dearg

Two spears were given to Diarmuid Ua Duibhne (Diarmid O'Dyna) by Manannan mac Lir in Celtic mythology: the invincible Gae Dearg ("Red Spear") and CRANN BUIDHE ("Yellow Branch"). Diarmuid carried each weapon for a different purpose: CRANN BUIDHE was taken on his small adventures when he did not foresee much danger, and Gae Dearg was taken on affairs he considered to be of life and death.

Sources: Joyce, *Old Celtic Romances*, 302; MacCulloch et al., *Celtic Mythology*, Volume 3, 66

Galatine

According to Arthurian lore from medieval romances, the sword of Sir Gawain (Gawaine), Galatine, was given to him by the Lady of the Lake; however, some sources claim it was forged by the legendary master blacksmith, Wayland (Gofannon/Volund/Weiland/Weyland) the Smith.

Sources: Karr, *Arthurian Companion*, 168; Malory, *La Mort D'Arthure*, Volume 1, 180; Sherman, *Storytelling*, 441

Galetea

Variation: Glathea

The Roman poet Ovid (Publius Ovidius Naso; 43 BCE–18 CE) originated the tale of the mythical artist Pygmalion of Cyprus, who created a statue in the image of Venus (Greek goddess Aphrodite), the goddess of love, so realistic that it came to life; however, in that story, the statue was not named. Ovid wrote two other stories with characters named Pygmalion. In one of these stories, Pygmalion was disgusted with the immorality of the women of Amathus and eventually fell in love with the ivory statue of the sea nymph Galetea ("Milky White"), who was loved by Polyphemus the Cyclops. Because of Pygmalion's devoted petitions to Venus, the statue came to life and Pygmalion was able to marry her; together they had a son named Paphos.

In the thirteenth century, there was a tale from the Lancelot-Grail Cycle called "Estoire-del Sait Grall" that told the story of a Saracen (Muslim) king named Mordrain who fell in love with a life-sized wooden female doll that he kept finely adorned in lavish outfits.

Sources: Bulfinch, *Bulfinch's Greek and Roman Mythology*, 168–69; Clark, *Aphrodite and Venus in Myth and Mimesis*, 91, 99

Galoshes of Fortune, the

Variation: Lykkens Kalosker (Danish)

Appearing in the literary fairy tale of the same name, the Galoshes of Fortune were a pair of time-traveling boots written about by Hans Christian Andersen; he was inspired by a folkloric item called SEVEN-LEAGUE BOOTS. In the story, the boots are delivered by two fairies to a group of guests at a dinner party; when worn, they will instantly transport the person to any condition in life, time, and place of their choosing. For instance, a person might wish to go to another period in history or to have a high-ranking position in their own time. The person will remain where they were sent until they come to realize that they were better off where they were. Removal of the boots will transport the person back to their own place and time.

Sources: Anderson, *The Fairy Tales and Stories of Hans Christian Andersen*, 53–81; Rossel, *Hans Christian Andersen*, 24

Gambanteinn (GAM-ban-tayn)

Variations: Gambantein, Laevateinn, sword of Freyr, TAMSVONDR

In Norse mythology, Gambanteinn ("Wand of Revenge"), which appears twice in the *Poetic Edda*, was the magical sword of Freyr (Frey/Yngvi), the god of fertility, peace, rain, and sunshine; it gave off sunbeams, had the ability to fight of its own accord, was forged by Volundr, and was considered the best sword in Norse legend. The name of this weapon was changed to TAMSVONDR after Skirnir carved runes upon it three times and used it to threaten Gerdr.

Freyr gave Gambanteinn to the giants Gymir and Aurboda as the bride price for their daughter, Gerdr ; he knew when making this transaction that it would cause his death at the time of Ragnarok. In fact, this sword was the very weapon Surtr ultimately used to slay Freyr. It was placed in the Ironwood forest and guarded by Angerboda's shepherd Eggber ("Sword Watcher") until the time that Surtr's son, Fjalar, retrieved it for his father.

Sources: Grimes, *The Norse Myths*, 268; Norroena Society, *Asatru Edda*, 348; Rydberg, *Teutonic Mythology*, Volume 2, 154, 155, 449, 476, 477

Gambantrim

Variation: Gambatrin

In Norse mythology, Gambantrim was the runic staff of Odin, the god of battle, death, frenzy, the gallows, healing, knowledge, poetry, royalty, the runic alphabet, sorcery, and wisdom; he loaned the staff to Hermodr to use against Hrossthjofi.

Sources: Blavatsky, *The Theosophical Glossary*, 124; Grimes, *The Norse Myths*, 268

Gan Jiang

Variation: Ganjiang

According to Chinese legend, Gan Jiang and MO YE were a pair of twin swords named after their creators, a husband-and-wife swordsmith duo. Legend says that all blacksmiths can distinguish the sex of metal when objects are commissioned to be made in pairs; in these cases, the Genie of the Bellows operates the bellows, the *jiao* dragon heats up the furnace, the Master of the Rain washes down and sweeps, and the Red Sovereign loads the furnace with charcoal.

The story goes that the king of Chu commissioned twin swords from the husband, Gan Jiang, who collected iron from five mountains and gold from the ten directions. The wife, Mo Ye, sacrificed her hair and nails to the fire, which had 300 boys and girls working the bellows. As the three-year process drew to an end, and after giving birth to Chibi, their son, Mo Ye leaped into the furnace, as a human sacrifice was required to make the different metals meld together. The male (yang) sword is described as having a tortoiseshell pattern.

Sources: Bonnefoy, *Asian Mythologies*, 258; Wagner, *Iron and Steel in Ancient China*, 113–14

Gandiva

Variation: Gdndlva

In Hindu mythology, an ASTRA is a supernatural weapon created or gifted by the gods to someone who then presides over the weapon. The wielder of an ASTRA is known as an astradhari.

Gandiva is a divine bow, and although sources vary regarding who possessed the bow, for how long they kept it, and who they passed it to, it retained its magical ability to punish evil and wicked people in addition to enabling its wielder to fight one *lakh* (100,000 warriors).

The bow was said to have originally been created by the god and creator of the universe, Brahma, from the gandi plant; it remained in his possession for 1,000 years. It then passed to Prajapati ("Grandfather") for another 1,000 years until it was given to Indra, the god of the heavens, lightning, rains, river flows, storms, and *vajra* ("thunder"), who held it for 3,585 years. Next Gandiva went to Candra ("Moon") for 503 years. Shakra then used it for 85 years, and Soma used it for 4,500 years. Varuna, the god of justice, sky, truth, and water, held it for 100 years before he passed it, along with a quiver of inexhaustible arrows, to Arjuna ("Spotless and Shining like Silver"), the heroic archer and main character in the Indian epic *Mahabharata*, who kept it for 65 years. When Arjuna no longer needed the bow, he returned it and the quiver to Varuna.

Gandiva is described as an exceedingly heavy, indestructible bow with 100 strings; when fired, it made a sound like thunder. The bow was decorated with hundreds of gold bosses, and its tips were radiant. It has been worshiped by demons and humans alike.

Sources: Debroy, *The Mahabharata*, Volume 5, n.p.; Walker, *Hindu World*, Volume 1, 56; Williams, *Handbook of Hindu Mythology*, 132

gandr (GAND-r)

Variations: gand, gandur

In Norse mythology, originally *gandr* ("magic device"/"wand") was a word used to describe anything magical (such as saying the hammer of Thor, MJOLNIR, is gandr). However, gandr eventually came to refer specifically to a staff or wand used for ceremonial purposes.

Sources: Norroena Society, *Asatru Edda*, 348

Garment of Light

Variations: Garment of Radiance, Wreath of Radiance

In Jewish mythology, it is said that on the first day of Creation, God created the heavens by wrapping Himself in a *tallit* (prayer shawl) of white fire; the light that shone from it diffused through the world. This item is said to be covered with letters of the Hebrew alphabet written in black fire. This garment is not always worn by the deity; however, it is as radiant as His own form, which is almost never described in any detail. On occasion, authors will try to further describe the Garment of Light by saying it "glistens like gold" and is covered with a list of precious gems.

Sources: Barasch, *The Language of Art*, 48, 49; Schwartz, *Tree of Souls*, 82, 83

Garudastra, the

In Hindu mythology, an ASTRA is a supernatural weapon created or gifted by the gods to someone who then presides over the weapon. The wielder of an ASTRA is known as an astradhari.

In the *Ramayana* (*Rama's Journey*), an ancient Indian epic poem dating between 500 and 100 BCE, Lord Rama "strung his bow" with Garudastra ("Garuda Missile"), which released thousands of birds of prey into the air, attacking the NAGAASTRA sent by Ravana during their epic battle. In some interpretations of this passage, the Garudastra is written to be more clearly defined as an arrow shot from Rama's bow that flies apart into many Garuda (the legendary king of birds) to attack the demonic naga on the ground (*naga* are a race of demonic beings described as human with the lower body of a snake).

Sources: Menon, *The Ramayana*, 104; Tapovanam, *Souvenir, Spiritual Refresher Course*, 40

Gastrofnir (GAST-rawp-nir)

Variation: Gastropnir

In Norse mythology, Gastrofnir ("Guest Refuser") is the gate in LERBRIMR, the wall that surrounds Asgard ("Enclosure of the Aesir"); it was created by the sons of Solblindi. The gate, which operates by means of a series of chains used to lower and raise it, will deny passage to any uninvited guest. It was also designed to kill or trap anyone who attempts to tamper with its mechanism, entwining them in chains. In addition, Gastrofnir is protected by two *garms* (wolf-dogs), Geri and Gifr, who will act as its guardians until the end of the world (Ragnarok).

Sources: Grimes, *The Norse Myths*, 268; Rydberg, *Norroena*, Volume 3, 754; Rydberg, *Teutonic Mythology* volume 2, 512

Gates of Sleep, the

It was a folkloric belief among the citizens of ancient Rome that dreams were sent to people by shades (spirits) and passed through one of two gates. The first gate, made of horn, would show the dreamer visions of truth and foretell future events. The other gate was made of polished ivory and would send dreams filled with empty promises and false visions. The legendary author Homer also mentions this belief, writing of the Gates of Sleep in the nineteenth book of *The Odyssey*, the ancient Greek epic poem.

Sources: Bandera, *Sacred Game*, 145–46; Granger, *The Worship of the Romans*, 45–46

Gelgja (GEHLG-ya)

The Icelandic historian Snorri Sturluson gave the name Gelgja ("Links") to the strong chain that was used to bind Fenriswulf (Fenerriswulf/Fenrissulfrin), the monstrous son of the god Loki, to the boulder GJOLL, where it was intended that he would be held captive forever. Gelgja was said to have been forged from magical materials.

Sources: Daly, *Norse Mythology A to Z*, 37; Garmonsway, *An Early Norse Reader*, 123; Norroena Society, *Asatru Edda*, 349

Gimle (GIM-lee)

Variations: Gimil, Gimill, Gimli, Gimlir

In Norse mythology, Gimle ("Fire Shelter"/ "Gem Roof"/"Heaven") was a hall located in the southern part of Asgard ("Enclosure of the Aesir") near Brunnakr Grove and Urdarbrunnr; it was described as the most beautiful place in all of Asgard. Originally, gold-roofed Gimle was where only the most righteous people dwelled; after the Battle of Ragnarok, it will be these people who will populate the world.

Sources: Grimes, *The Norse Myths*, 270; Norroena Society, *Asatru Edda*, 351

girdle of Laurin

In German folklore, the dwarf king Laurin owned many magical items; one item of these was a magical girdle that gave him the strength of twenty-four men.

Sources: Jiriczek, *Northern Hero Legends*, 83; Keightley, *World Guide to Gnomes, Fairies, Elves, and Other Little People*, 207

Gjallarbru (GYAL-ar-broo)

Variations: Giallar Bridge, Giallarbu, Gjallar Bridge, Gjallarrbridge, Gjallarbro, Gjoll Bridge

In Norse mythology, Gjallarbru ("Echoing Bridge"/"Gjoll Bridge") was the golden-roofed bridge spanning the subterranean river Gjoll, which connected the land of the living with the land of the dead; it was held in place by a single strand of hair. Any who wished to cross the bridge needed to pay a toll in blood to the bridge's guardian, the skeleton maiden Modgudr; she would cut them and let them bleed out into the river, as only ghosts are light enough to cross Gjallarbru.

Sources: Daly, *Norse Mythology A to Z*, 39; Grimes, *The Norse Myths*, 73, 210, 270; Hawthorne, *Vikings*, 18; Norroena Society, *Asatru Edda*, 351

Gjallarhorn (GYAL-ar-hawrn)

Variations: Argjoll ("Early-Resounding"), Giallar Horn, Gillar-Horn, Gillarhorn, Gjall, Gjallar-Horn

In Norse mythology, Gjallarhorn ("Loud Sounding Horn," "Resounding Horn," "Ringing Horn," "Yelling Horn") was the crescent-shaped horn that, when blown, would summon the Aesir to Ragnarok; until the time it was needed, the horn was kept hidden in MIMIRSBRUNNR WELL next to Odin's eye. Odin is the god of battle, death, frenzy, the gallows, healing, knowledge, poetry, royalty, the runic alphabet, sorcery, and wisdom.

It is possible the horn itself came from the remains of the slain Audhumla.

Sources: Grimes, *The Norse Myths*, 270; Norroena Society, *Asatru Edda*, 350; Norroena Society, *Satr Edda*, 25

Gjoll

Variations: Gioll

In Norse mythology, Gjoll ("Resounding") was the boulder to which Fenriswulf (Fenerriswulf/Fenrissulfrin), the monstrous son of

Gladsheim

the god Loki, was bound with the chain GEL-
GJA. It was intended that Fenriswulf would
remain bound to the boulder forever, but prophecy foretold that he would escape at the time
of Ragnarok and join in the battle between the
giants and the gods.

Sources: Daly, *Norse Mythology A to Z*, 39; Grimes, *The
Norse Myths*, 73, 80; Hawthorne, *Vikings*, 19

Gladsheim (GLATHS-haym)

Variations: Gladasheim, Glad-heim, Gladsheim, Glathsheim

In Norse mythology, Gladsheim ("Home of
Brightness"/"Home of Gladness"/"Home of Joy")
was the very first building constructed in Asgard
("Enclosure of the Aesir"); made of gold, inside
and out, it contained twelve thrones, one of which
was taller than the others—HLIDSKJALF, reserved
for Odin, the god of battle, death, frenzy, the gallows, healing, knowledge, poetry, royalty, the
runic alphabet, sorcery, and wisdom. Gladsheim
was used to hold council and conduct general
meetings.

Sources: Grimes, *The Norse Myths*, 270; Norroena Society, *Asatru Edda*, 352

glass of Reynard the Fox, the

Written of in the fifteenth century by Hermann
Barkhusan of Rostock, Reynard the Fox possessed
a glass globe (telescope) set in the most remarkable wood. The glass was crafted so perfectly that
one could see things as far off as a mile as if the
events were happening just a few feet away. The
wood casing, decorated with gold and precious
gems, was impervious to the effects of age, damp,
dust, and worms.

Sources: Day, *The Rare Romance of Reynard the Fox*,
124

Gleipnir (GLAYP-nir)

A magical chain made by the dwarfs of Norse
mythology, Gleipnir ("Fetter") was created to
bind Fenriswulf (Fenerriswulf/Fenrissulfrin), the
monstrous son of the god Loki, to the boulder GJOLL. According to the Icelandic historian
Snorri Sturluson, the chain was made from the
beard of a woman, the breath of a fish, the noise of
a cat's footfall, the roots of a mountain, the sinews
of a bear, and the spittle of a bird. It was said to be
as light as silk, as smooth as ribbon, and impossibly strong. Once Gleipnir held Fenriswulf, it was
tied to the chain GELGJA, which bound him to
GJOLL.

Gleipnir was the third such item created to
bind Fenriswulf; the first two, DROMI and LAE-
DINGR, were made by the god of thunder, Thor,
and failed.

Sources: Daly, *Norse Mythology A to Z*, 40; Grimes, *The
Norse Myths*, 271; Hawthorne, *Vikings*, 19; Norroena Society, *Asatru Edda*, 351

Glitner

Variations: Castle of Peace, Glitnir

In Norse mythology, Glitner ("Glittering") was
the hall of Forseti (Forsete; "President"), the god
of justice and the son of Balder and Nanna; it was
built with golden pillars that supported a silver
dome, as all matters of law are handled in the light
of day and in the open.

Sources: Anderson, *Norse Mythology*, 296, 297;
Grimes, *The Norse Myths*, 271; Tegnér, *Frithiof's Saga*,
66, 68, 292

Glorious

The sword of Oliver, Glorious, was made,
according to *The Legend of Croquemitaine*, collectively by the three swordsmith brothers: Ansias,
Galas, and Munifican; each of them spent two years
on its construction. Then each of the swordsmiths
made three other swords: Ansias made BAPTISM,
FLORENCE, and GRABAN; Galas made FLAMBERGE,
HALTECLERE, and JOYEUSE; and Munifican made
COURTAIN, DURANDAL, and SAUVAGINE. When
all ten swords were completed, the three brothers
called upon a giant to take Glorious and strike each
of the other swords on its edge about a foot from
the pommel. Glorious passed its trial unscathed.

Although Oliver used Glorious in his battle
against Angoulaffre (a direct descendent of Goliath, the governor of Jerusalem, and the traveling
companion of Murad Henakyeh Meimomovassi,
prince of Castile, Leon, Portugal, and Valentia),
he was still defeated.

Sources: Brewer, *Dictionary of Phrase and Fable* 1900,
1197; Evangelista, *The Encyclopedia of the Sword*, 577;
L'Epine, *The Days of Chivalry*, n.p.

Gnita

Variations: Gnita-heath ("Glittering Heath"),
Gnitaheid, Gnitaheidr, Gnitaheior

In Norse mythology, Gnita ("Glittering") is the
home of Fafnir (Fafner) in his monstrous dragon
form; it is where he kept the treasure known as
ANDVARANAUT.

Sources: Anderson, *Norse Mythology*, 377, 447; Bennett,
Gods and Religions of Ancient and Modern Times, Volume
1, 388

Gnod (NAWTH)

A legendary vessel, the *Gnod* (*Rumbling*) was commissioned by the ruler of Halogaland, Asmund (Asmundr).

When his first wife, Brynhild, died, Asmund sought to remarry, this time to the daughter of a sultan. Knowing there was a trap being laid out to kill him, he commissioned a special ship, which he named *Gnod*; he planned to sail it to the wedding. *Gnod* was said to be the largest ship north of the Aegean Sea and earned him the nickname Gnod-Asmund. According to legend, the *Gnod* sank, along with a cargo of treasure, into the sea, and neither the ship nor the treasure were ever recovered.

Sources: Norroena Society, *Asatru Edda*, 353; Palsson and Edwards, *Seven Viking Romances*, n.p.

gold ring of Thorston, the

In fairy lore, a local hero by the name of Thorston rescued the child of a dwarf who was taken by a dragon; the unnamed dwarf insisted on rewarding his savior and made him accept several gifts. One of these gifts was a gold ring. According to the story, as long as Thorston wore this ring, he would never be in want of money.

Sources: Dunham, *The Cabinet Cyclopaedia*, Volume 26, 73; Keightley, *World Guide to Gnomes, Fairies, Elves, and Other Little People*, 72

golden apples of Aphrodite, the

Variation: apples of Aphrodite

In classical Greek mythology, Atalanta, a princess of Arcadia and an adopted child of Artemis (Roman goddess Diana), the goddess of children, hunting, virginity, and wild animals, had taken a vow never to marry. After returning from a boar hunt with the Argonauts, she was ordered by her father, the king, to wed. Atalanta agreed only on the condition that her potential groom had to defeat her in a footrace. If he did not, she then won the right to kill him. Many princes died trying to win her hand. One suitor, Prince Melanion (Hippomanes), prayed and made sacrifices to the goddess of love, Aphrodite (Roman goddess Venus), for assistance. Aphrodite loaned him three of her golden apples; they had been taken from the Garden of Hesperides by the demigod and legendary hero Heracles and given to Eurystheus, who in turn gave them to the goddess. Aphrodite knew apples were sacred to Artemis, so she told Melanion to drop them as he ran, one at a time; this would cause Atalanta to pause and pick them up. The tactic worked, giving Melanion enough time to pull ahead, maintain a lead, and eventually win the race and the hand of Atalanta.

Sources: Crowther, *Sport in Ancient Times*, 146; Graves, *Greek Gods and Heroes*, n.p.

golden arm ring, the

Variation: Frithiof's arm-ring

Frithiof (Frithjof) the Bold, a hero from of Icelandic legend, was said to have three magical and prized possessions: the sword ANGURVADEL, the ship ELLIDE, and a golden arm band.

The arm band is described as having the images of the gods and a calendar etched onto it, with a glittering ruby embedded into its middle. The armlet was made by legendary master blacksmith Wayland (Gofannon/Volund/Weiland/Weyland) the Smith for Thorsten, but it was stolen by Sote, who fled across the sea to Britain with it. Thorsten, accompanied by King Bele, gave chance and, upon their landing, came upon a cave and tomb; within was Sote's black ship, shimmering like a flame. Upon the mast was the skeletal ghost of Sote in a flame robe; Thorsten alone entered the cave and confronted the ghost. Eventually, he won the combat but would never speak of it, saying only "Would rather I had died than bought the ring so dear."

Sources: Cox, *Popular Romances of the Middle Ages*, 381; Cox and Jones, *Tales of the Teutonic Lands*, 221

golden bough, the

The demigod and hero Aeneas of classical Greek and Roman mythology was born of the union of Prince Anchises of Troy and the goddess of beauty, fertility, love, prostitution, sex and victory Venus (Greek goddess Aphrodite). Aeneas had been told by the Sibyl that if he wanted to gain safe passage into and through the Underworld, he needed to travel to the forest around Lake Avernus; a special sign would be given by the gods to reveal its location. In the case of Aeneas, it was two white doves, the sacred birds of Venus. Then the golden bough had to be presented as an offering to Proserpine (Greek goddess Persephone). The branch is described as golden in both leaf and stem and will quickly regrow after it is cut, but only those who have been blessed by Fate may do so. The ferryman of the river Styx will respect anyone who boards his vessel carrying the golden bough.

Sources: Murray, *Classical Manual*, 442; Virgil, *Aeneid* 6, 17, 34, 38

golden calf, the

Variation: egel masseka ("calf of fusion"/"calf of molten metal")

The story of the golden calf is in the biblical book of Exodus, chapter 32. As the story goes, Moses had ascended the mountain to commune with the Lord, leaving Aaron in charge. The people became increasingly nervous with each passing day of Moses's absence. After 40 days, they approached Aaron and asked him to make them "gods" (the plural is used in the original text, although he only created one idol). Aaron had the people gather up their gold jewelry and used it to cast a calf-shaped statue. Unnamed in the text, the idol was worshiped as their new god and the people made sacrifices to it. The Lord knew what had happened and told Moses, in His anger, that He was going to destroy them; Moses interceded on their behalf and returned to his people, carrying with him the stone tablets on which the Ten Commandments were written. When he arrived in the camp, he, too, was angry and broke the tablets in his rage; then he called those loyal to him and the Lord to his side. He bade the faithful to kill the most devout followers of the golden calf—about three thousand people. Moses then took up the golden calf, burned it in the fire, put its ashes in water, and forced the survivors of the massacre to drink the water. Afterward, the Lord told Moses to lead the people to the Promised Land, but He assured him that, when the time was right, He would punish the people for their sin.

Sources: Garbini, *Myth and History in the Bible*, 91–99; Johnson, *Lady of the Beasts*, 182

golden crown and white gown of Glauce, the

In Greek mythology, the daughter of King Aeetes of Colchis, Medea, is perhaps best known for being the niece of Circe and a priestess of the goddess Hecate, as well as a sorceress. Medea assisted the hero Jason in stealing the GOLDEN FLEECE; they were later married and had between one and fourteen children (depending on the source).

Sources vary as to what happened next in the story, but according to Euripides, one of the three best-known ancient Greek tragedians, Jason abandoned Medea for a new bride: Glauce the Theban. Medea sought her revenge by first sending her would-be replacement a wedding gift—a beautiful white gauze gown and a golden crown, each one coated with a special type of poison called NAPHTHA. Then she murdered her own children where her husband could find their bodies before leaving in a chariot pulled by flying serpents.

After Glauce donned the items from Medea, she screamed out suddenly in excruciating pain, frothing at the mouth, eyes rolling up into her head. The crown smoldered at first and then burst into flames with a supernatural strength that could not be extinguished. The more Glauce struggled to free herself from the poisoned gown and flaming, golden crown, the hotter the flames became. Eventually, she succumbed and died, her features burned away and her body blistered, boiled, and stripped of flesh.

Sources: Graves, *The Greek Myths*, 160-161.; Smith, *A Classical Dictionary of Greek and Roman Biography, Mythology and Geography*, 1004; Stuttard, *Looking at Medea*, 196–97

Golden Fleece, the

The Golden Fleece was a much sought-after item in ancient Greek mythology, as it wove itself into many different adventures.

The king of Thessaly, Athamas, married the goddess of clouds, Nephele; they had two children: a son named Phrixus and a daughter called Helle. When the king took a second wife named Ino, his queen left him, causing drought to befall the land. Ino took her anger out on the stepchildren and convinced her husband that the only way to end the drought was to kill his son. Nephele sent a golden, flying ram to rescue her children; it carried them away, across the sea, but Helle looked down, swooned from the dizzying height, and fell to her death. Phrixus safely reached Colchis, where he was welcomed into the house of Aeete. There he sacrificed the ram and hung its fleece in a grove dedicated to Ares (Roman god Mars), the god of war, where it was guarded by a dragon that never slept.

When Jason sought to reclaim the throne of Iolcus from his murderous uncle, Pelias, he was challenged to return with the Golden Fleece as proof of his right to rule. Jason gathered a group of companions to go with him, departed on the ARGO, and, over the course of several years filled with adventures and trials, finally arrived on the distant island of Colchis. However, King Aeetes wanted to kill Jason, so he set before the hero three tasks that needed to be achieved before he could claim the Golden Fleece. Jason was disheartened at the thought of fulfilling more quests. Hera, the goddess of childbirth, family, marriage, and women, intervened and caused Aeetes's daughter Medea, a powerful sorceress, to fall in love with Jason so she would assist him. By use of her magic and treachery, they completed the tasks, escaped with the fleece, and set sail for Jason's home port of Iolcus. The return voyage was also filled with numerous adventures, trials, and tribulations.

In one version of the tale of the Golden Fleece, Hermes (Roman god Mercury), the god of animal husbandry, commerce, eloquence, fertility, language, looters, luck, sleep, thieves, trade, travel, and wealth, gave a lamb with golden fleece to the two sons of Pelops and Hillodameia, Atreus and Thyestes. Atreus, now king, sacrificed the lamb to the gods but kept its fleece for himself; it became a symbol of authority and kingship.

Sources: Coolidge, *Greek Myths*, 172–82; Daly and Rengel, *Greek and Roman Mythology, A to Z*, 17, 23, 80; Eddy and Hamilton, *Understand Greek Mythology*, n.p.

golden goblet of Heracles, the

In ancient Greek mythology, the tenth labor of demigod and legendary hero Hercules was to return with the herd of beautiful red cattle from the island of Erytheia without asking for or purchasing them. These cattle belonged to Geryon, reported to be the strongest man alive; the son of Chrysaor and Callirrhoe, he had three giant-sized bodies joined at the waist. The cattle were guarded by the herdsman Eurythion and his two-headed dog, Orthrus.

Hercules battled his way across what would become Europe with the sun blazing down upon him every step of the way. No longer wishing to struggle in the heat, he nocked an arrow in his bow (see BOW AND ARROWS OF HERACLES), but just as he was about to shoot the sun, Helios (Sol), the personification of the sun, intervened. The Titan offered the demigod use of his golden goblet, explaining that it was shaped like a water lily and would prove to be more reliable than any boat Heracles could acquire to move the red cattle across the ocean. Heracles agreed and set sail in it, using his lion pelt as a sail.

Sources: Graves, *The Greek Myths*, 287.; Westmoreland, *Ancient Greek Beliefs*, 131

Golden Maidens, the

Variation: Kourai Khryseai

In ancient Greek mythology, AUTOMATONS ("self-acting") were statues of animals, humans,

and monsters that were then animated or otherwise brought to a kind of life by one of the gods; usually this was done by Hephaistos (Hephaestus; Roman god Vulcan), the god of bindings, the art of sculpture, fire, forges, metalworking, stonemasonry, and talismans. Other AUTOMATONS were the CAUCASIAN EAGLE, the GOLDEN TRIPODS, the KABEIRIAN HORSES, the KELEDONES, KHRYSEOS AND ARGYREOS, the KOLKHIS BULLS, and TALOS.

Forged out of pure gold by Hephaistos, the Golden Maidens (as the two were collectively known) were created to be the personal female servants in his palace of brass on Mount Olympus. These AUTOMATONS appeared to be human, as they were fully articulated, could speak, and were even created with the gift of intelligence. According to the legendary author Homer, not only did the maidens tend to his home, but Hephaistos would also lean upon them as he walked.

Sources: Bonnefoy, *Greek and Egyptian Mythologies*, 88–89; Seyffert, *A Dictionary of Classical Antiquities, Mythology, Religion, Literature and Art*, 277; Westmoreland, *Ancient Greek Beliefs*, 54

golden throne, the

In classical Greek mythology, Hephaistos (Hephaestus; Roman god Vulcan), the god of bindings, the art of sculpture, fire, forges, metalworking, stonemasonry, and talismans, was the son of Zeus (Roman god Jupiter), the god of fate, kings, lightning, sky, and thunder, and Hera (Roman goddess Juno), the goddess of childbirth, family, marriage, and women, but because he was born not only ugly but also with deformed feet, he was cast by his mother out of Olympus and into the ocean. Rescued and raised by Eurynome and Thetis, Hephaistos created many wonderful items. One such invention was a beautiful golden throne with invisible chains; it was designed to imprison anyone who sat upon it. Hephaistos made a gift of the throne to Hera, who fell into the trap and remained imprisoned until her discarded son was recalled to Olympus.

Sources: Anthon, *A Classical Dictionary*, 1394; Seyffert, *A Dictionary of Classical Antiquities, Mythology, Religion, Literature and Art*, 277

golden tripods, the

Variation: tripodes khryseoi

In ancient Greek mythology, AUTOMATONS ("self-acting") were statues of animals, humans, and monsters that were then animated or otherwise brought to a kind of life by one of the gods;

Gordian knot

usually this was done by Hephaistos (Hephaestus; Roman god Vulcan), the god of bindings, the art of sculpture, fire, forges, metalworking, stonemasonry, and talismans. Other AUTOMATONS were the CAUCASIAN EAGLE, the GOLDEN MAIDENS, the KABEIRIAN HORSES, the KELEDONES, KHRYSEOS AND ARGYREOS, the KOLKHIS BULLS, and TALOS.

The golden tripods were a creation of Hephaistos; these items were described as a set of twenty wheeled, three-legged tables made of gold. They were gifted with intelligence and would of their own accord roll themselves around Olympus to serve the gods as needed; when their task was completed, they would then roll back to the home of Hephaistos. It is also said of these AUTOMATONS that the gods would eat their meals off them; when finished, the tripods would roll away.

Sources: Bonnefoy, *Greek and Egyptian Mythologies*, 88–89; Nosselt, *Mythology Greek and Roman*, 113–14; Westmoreland, *Ancient Greek Beliefs*, 54

Gordian knot, the

A legend associated with Alexander the Great, the Gordian knot has become a metaphor for solving a difficult problem by using "out of the box" thinking.

According to legend, the kingdom of Phrygia was without a king; the oracle of Telmissus, the Phrygian capital, decreed that the next man to enter the city by means of an ox cart would become the king. When a poor farmer named Gordias came into the city via ox cart with his wife and son, Midas, he was named king. Gordias left his cart and tied his ox to a post using a knot so intricate that no one was unable to untie it. Afterward, it was said that whoever could untie the knot would be the next king of Phrygia. When Alexander the Great heard the prophecy, he tried his hand at undoing the knot but was unable to do so after many attempts. In a flash of anger and brilliance, he drew his sword, cut the knot in two, and declared that he had defeated the Gordian knot with what has come to be called an "Alexandrian solution."

Sources: Fox, *Alexander the Great*, 149; Graves, *The Greek Myths*, 168-169.; Westmoreland, *Ancient Greek Beliefs*, 189, 735

Gorm Glas

In Celtic mythology, Gorm Glas ("Blue Green") was the sword of Conchobar; it was used in tandem with the shield OCHAIN. Conchobar loaned Gorm Glas as well as OCHAIN and two spears to Fiacra the Fair so that he might go and "do bravery and great deeds."

Sources: Gregory, *Cuchulain of Muirthemne*, 130; O'Sheridan, *Gaelic Folk Tales*, 148

Goswhit

The helmet of King Arthur, Goswhit ("Goose White") was passed down to him from King Uther Pendragon. Arthurian lore describes it as a steel helmet with many jewels set in gold as well as the painted image of a dragon.

Sources: Dixon, *The Glory of Arthur*, 116; Harlow, *An Introduction to Early English Literature*, 34–35; Lambdin and Lambdin, *Arthurian Writers*, 54

Graban

The celebrated swordsmith Ansias created three swords for the fictional giant and Saracen (Muslim) knight, Fierabras (Fierbras): BAPTISM, FLORENCE, and Graban. Each sword took three years to make. In *The Legend of Croquemitaine*, the sword was made for Strong-in-the-Arms and was hacked by a giant when testing the edge of another sword, GLORIOUS.

Sources: Brewer, *Dictionary of Phrase and Fable* 1900, 1197; L'Epine, *The Days of Chivalry*, n.p.; Numismatic and Antiquarian Society of Philadelphia, *Proceedings of the Numismatic and Antiquarian Society of Philadelphia for the Years 1899–1901*, 65

Grail Sword

Variation: the Broken Sword

A legendary sword from Arthurian lore, the Grail Sword is one of several items associated with the Fisher King (Crippled King/Maimed King/Wounded King/Anfortas/Bron/Evelake/Parlan/Peliam/Pellam/Pelles). In Chretien de Troyes's *Perceval*, the sword was forged by the smith Trabuchet and given to Sir Perceval by the Fisher King; it is described as a magnificent blade with a ruby hilt. However, the knight is cautioned that the blade will shatter should it ever be used in battle; if that were to happen, it could only be repaired by Trabuchet in Coyatre.

In the medieval romance *Parzival*, written by the knight and poet Wolfram von Eschenbach, Perceval is told the sword is good for only one blow, as it will shatter with a second. The only way in which it can be repaired in this version is by submerging it in a spring named Lac.

In the various continuations of Troyes's *Perceval*, Sir Gawain (Gawaine) learns that the sword was broken when Sir Partinal used it to kill Goondesert and that a perfect Grail Knight would be able to repair the sword. Although Gawain manages to mend the weapon, a hairline fracture is still present, representing his near perfection. By the end of the tale, Gawain restores the Grail Sword to perfection.

In yet another of the many tales of the Grail Sword, the blade was said to have once belonged to King David, who left it to Solomon with the task of recasting the pommel. The sword was then placed in a luxuriously furnished ship commissioned by Solomon's queen (likely the one referred to as "Pharaoh's daughter"). The ship, and consequently the sword, was eventually discovered by the Knights of the Quest; Sir Galahad took the blade up and wore it.

Sources: Bruce, *The Arthurian Name Dictionary*, 234; Patrick, *Chamber's Encyclopædia*, Volume 10, 136; Spence, *A Dictionary of Medieval Romance and Romance Writers*, 145

Gram

Variations: Balmung, Gramr, Nothung

In Norse mythology, Gram ("Anguish"/"Grief"/ "Wrath") was forged by legendary master blacksmith Wayland (Gofannon/Volund/Weiland/ Weyland) the Smith but belonged to his father, the giant Wade. Sigurd (Siegfried/Sigmund) came into possession of the sword when he retrieved it from the Branstock Tree in the hall of the Volsung, where Odin—the god of battle, death, frenzy, the gallows, healing, knowledge, poetry, royalty, the runic alphabet, sorcery, and wisdom—had thrust it. This was the weapon Sigurd then used to slay the dragon god Fafnir (Fafner). In a slight variation of the story, Gram was broken and reforged, after which it was sharp enough to cut an anvil in two.

Sources: de Beaumont and Allinson, *The Sword and Womankind*, 8; Evangelista, *The Encyclopedia of the Sword*, 576; Orchard, *Dictionary of Norse Myths and Legends*, 59–60; Pendergrass, *Mythological Swords*, 13

Graysteel

Variations: Greysteel, Greysteil

In Icelandic lore, the famous sword Graysteel (said to have been forged by dwarfs) was magically enchanted to never have a dull edge and to always cut deeply into whatever it struck, be it flesh or iron, even if it was a glancing blow. Originally the weapon belonged to Kol, the captive and thrall of Ingibjorga's foster son. Kol loaned the weapon to Gisli the Soursop to use in his duel against Bjorn as long as he promised to return the weapon when asked. Having won the duel, Gisli retained the sword. When the day came that Kol asked for its return, Gisli tried to purchase it many times, but Kol would not sell for any price. They ultimately came to blows. Kol cleaved his ax into Gisli's skull at the same time that Gisli managed to crash Graysteel into Kol's head, shattering both his skull and the sword; however, Kol managed to prophesy an ill-fated future for the sword before his death.

Thorgrim, a priest of Freyr (Frey/Yngvi), the god of fertility, peace, rain, and sunshine, gathered the pieces of Graysteel and reforged the weapon into a barbed spear with runs upon the head; the spearhead was mounted upon a haft a span long.

Many years later, Graysteel the spear was used in the Battle of Breidabolstad by Gunnlaug to kill Bjorn Thorvalddson. It was also used in the Battle of Orlygstad by Sturla Sighvatson, who slew many enemies with it, but the tip of the spear would bend, forcing him to pause on the field of combat to stomp it flat. This misfortune caused Sturla, a descendent of Gisli, to be taken captive by his enemies and brutally slain.

Sources: Brewer, *Dictionary of Phrase and Fable* 1900, 1197; Dasent, *The Story of Gisli the Outlaw*, vvvii, 4–7; Eddison, *Egil's Saga*, 281; Pendergrass, *Mythological Swords*, 4

Green Armor, the

A suit of armor from Arthurian legend, the Green Armor was said to magically protect its wearer from all physical injuries, leaving them completely unaffected by such assaults. The Green Armor was owned and worn by Sir Engamore of Malverat, also known as the Knight of the Green Sleeves; he was the champion of Lady Ettard of Grantmesnel.

Arthurian legend also tells of a second suit of green armor, this one worn by the Green Knight, a man of green complexion also armed with a green helm and shield and mounted upon a green horse. In the story, he rides into Arthur's court and offers a challenge: he will allow himself to be decapitated if in one year's time the knight who does so surrenders to the same fate. Sir Gawain (Gawaine) accepts the challenge and beheads the knight; the Green Knight then picks up his head and tells Gawain where to go in a year's time to fulfill his side of the bargain. The rest of the tale is about Gawain's integrity and loyalty. Here, the Green Knight is symbolic of the regenerative powers of nature.

Sources: Metzner, *Green Psychology*, n.p.; Pyle, *The Story of King Arthur and His Knights*, 229

Green Dragon Crescent Blade

A legendary Chinese weapon wielded by the equally legendary experienced, diplomatic, and gigantic General Guan Yu, the Green Dragon Crescent Blade was a *yanyuedao* (a type of pole arm) with the chopping power of a sword but the length of a spear; sources vary as to its weight, ranging from as little as 18 pounds to as much as 100 pounds. After his death, Guan Yu was deified as a god of war, and his weapon became symbolic of his soldierly potency.

It should be noted that although yanyuedao weapons do exist, archaeological studies have shown that they appeared in the Northern Song Dynasty (960–1127), some 800 years after Guan Yu was said to have lived.

Sources: Dong, *Asian American Culture*, 330; O'Bryan, *A History of Weapons*, 79

green sash, the

Variations: girdle of Gawain (Gawaine), the green girdle

In Arthurian lore, Sir Gawain (Gawaine) comes to stay at the castle of Bercilak while questing for the Green Chapel, the place where he will surrender his head to the Green Knight. During his stay (the period between Christmas Day and New Year's Day), he complies with a local custom that requires him to give his daily winnings to the lord of the castle. Each day the wife of Lord Bercilak (Lord Bernlak de Hautdesert), the servant of Morgan La Fay, attempts to seduce him, but he remains steadfast. One day she offers him a green sash, claiming it is magical and will protect its wearer from any physical blow. He accepts the sash as a gift rather than an item won at tournament and therefore neglects to surrender it to Bercilak, who (it is later revealed) is the Green Knight.

Sources: Hanson, *Stories of the Days of King Arthur*, 126–28; Knight, *The Secret Tradition in Arthurian Legend*, 64; Lacy et al., *The Arthurian Handbook*, 196–97

Gridarvolr (GREETH-ar-vuhl-r)

Variations: Gridarvol, Gridarvold, iron rod of Grid, rod of Grid

In Norse mythology, Gridarvolr ("Gridr's Wand"/"Safety Staff") was the magical staff of Gridr ("greed, impetuosity, vehemence, violence"), an *asynjr* (female Jotun, or giant), which she loaned to the god of thunder, Thor. She also made him a gift of her belt of strength, MEGINGJARDAR, and her iron gloves, JARNGREIPR, so as to assist him in thwarting the murderous plot

of Geirrod. Typically Gridarvolr is described as made of rowan wood, but occasionally it is said to be made of iron.

Sources: Grimes, *The Norse Myths*, 272; Norroena Society, *Asatru Edda*, 353; Norroena Society, *Satr Edda*, 25; Orchard, *Dictionary of Norse Myth and Legend*, 10

Grjotanagardr

Variations: Griottunagardr, Grjollon, Grjottungard

In Norse mythology, Grjotanagardr ("Stone Fence House") was the mountain home of Hrungnir; it was there that the clay giant Grjottungard was created.

Sources: Anderson, *The Younger Edda*, 170, 171, 174; Grimes, *The Norse Myths*, 272

Grotti (GRAWT-i)

Variations: Cosmic Mill, Eyliidr ("The Island Mill"), Eyluthr, Grotti Mill, Grottimill, Heavenly Mill, Luthr, Mill of Skerries, Mill of the Storms, Skerja Grotta, Skerry-Grotti, World Mill

Grotti ("Grinder") is the World Mill that turns the sky, grinding the limbs of Jotuns (giants) to create soil for Midgard (Earth); it also creates maelstroms and moves the starry vault of the night sky. Nine *asynjr* (female Jotuns) turn the millstone, which has the ability to grind out whatever the grinder wishes, be it grain, happiness, riches, or salt. Originally the asynjr ground out artistry, gold, luck, peace, plenty, and wisdom. A Jotun by the name of Lodurr (Gevarr, the ward of the atmosphere) oversees the daily operations of the mill.

Although the nine asynjr are responsible for keeping the millstones turning, others have happily assisted in turning the wheels; names given as one of the nine mothers of Heimdallr (Heimdal) or those who spent time turning the millstones are Angeyja ("She Who Makes the Island Closer"), Atla ("The Awful-Grim Maiden"), Beyla ("Milkmaid"), Byggvir ("Grain Spirit"), Eyrgjafa ("She Who Creates Sand Banks"), Fenja, Gjalp ("Roarer"), Greip ("Grasping"), Imdr ("Ember"), Jarnsaxa ("Iron Chopper"/"She Who Crushes the Iron"), Menja ("Jewel Maiden"), Ulfrinna ("She Wolf"), and Ulfrun ("Wolf-Runner").

Sources: Norroena Society, *Asatru Edda*, 12–13, 354

Guingelot

Variation: *Wingelock*

Wade, a folkloric hero of England during the Middle Ages, was once a popular character, but over the course of time, his tales and exploits have been lost. What is known of Wade is that he had a magical boat named *Guingelot* (*Going Slowly*) that would travel to any location in a matter of minutes. This knowledge comes to us from a note made by Thomas Speght, an editor of Geoffrey Chaucer who made a passing remark about the folk hero in his notes. Apparently the adventures and exploits of Wade and *Guingelot* were lengthy and strange, but common enough that Speght did not feel the need to go into any detail; in his own words, "Concerning Wade and his bote called Guingelot, and also his strange exploits in the same, because the matter is long and fabulous, I pass it over."

Sources: Allard and North, *Beowulf and Other Stories*, 59; Wade, *The Wade Genealogy*, 13, 26–27

Gullinbursti

Variations: boar with bristles of gold, Frey's boar, golden boar of the sun, Slidrugtanni ("Dangerous Tooth") the boar

In both "Gylfaginning" and "Skaldskaparmal," the first and second parts of the *Prose Edda*, written in the thirteenth century by Snorri Sturluson, Gullinbursti ("Gold Bristle") was a boar made of living gold. Gullinbursti was created by the dwarfs Brokkr and Eitri for a bet they had with the god Loki at the same time that they created the ring DRAUPNIR and Thor's hammer MJOLNIR. The boar had the magical ability to run through the air and water by day and night, faster and more surefooted than any horse. There was also never a night so dark that Gullinbursti could not light the way with his golden bristles.

Sources: Keightley, *World Guide to Gnomes, Fairies, Elves, and Other Little People*, 68; Lindow, *Norse Mythology*, 90, 153, 277

Gullinn Hjalti

Variations: Fetill Hjalti, Gullinhjalti

Gullinn Hjalti ("Golden Hilt"), the sword of King Hrolf Kraki in old Norse tales, also becomes the sword of hero Hjalti. In *Hrolf's Saga*, the sword is used to prop up a dragon that has been slain. The cowardly Hott is told by the king that only a man who is brave and daring may wield this weapon. Hott retrieves the sword and, in doing so, either is transformed into such a man or proves he is no longer a coward. Pleased with the transformation, the king renames Hott as Hjalti ("Hilt"). Typically, however, Hrolf Kraki wielded the sword SKOFNUNG.

In the Old English epic *Beowulf*, the titular hero discovers a sword in the underwater cave of Grendel's mother; that weapon is called *gylden hilt* (though this may not be the weapon's proper name). Most likely the sword in *Beowulf* is not connected to the sword to of King Hrolf Kraki. The similarity between the two names was first pointed out by Friedrich Kluge in 1896; after this time, the name of the sword in *Beowulf* was usually printed as "Gyldenhilt."

Of note, the old Norse word for "hilt" refers to the guard piece between the blade and the hilt, not the part of the sword that one would grasp, as it does in Old English.

Sources: Byock, *Saga of King Hrolf Kraki*, n.p.; Chambers, *Beowulf*, 475; Olson, "The Relation of the Hrolfs Saga Fraka and the Bjarkarimur to Beowulf," 11–12, 39–40, 59

Gungnir (GUNG-nir)

Variations: Gugner, Gungne, Gungner

In Norse mythology, Gungnir ("Swaying One") was the spear forged by the Sons of Ivaldi from the sacred ash tree YGGDRASIL. This weapon belonged to Odin, the god of battle, death, frenzy, the gallows, healing, knowledge, poetry, royalty, the runic alphabet, sorcery, and wisdom; he enhanced it with magical runes. Gungnir was thrown at the onset of every battle to signify the start of the conflict; it never missed its mark.

Sources: Grimes, *The Norse Myths*, 273; Hawthorne, *Vikings*, 19; Keightley, *World Guide to Gnomes, Fairies, Elves, and Other Little People*, 68; Norroena Society, *Asatru Edda*, 354

Gwenn

In Welsh Arthurian lore, Gwenn ("White") is the cloak of King Arthur; when Arthur tells Culhwch that he may ask and receive anything of him, the king makes a short list of his prize possessions that are the seven exceptions to his offer: CALADBOLG, his sword; CARNWENNAN, his dagger; Gwenhwyfar, his wife; Gwenn, his cloak; PRYDWEN, his ship; RHONGOMIANT, his spear; and WYNEBGWRTHUCHER, his shield. Gwenn was named second. The text "The Thirteen Treasures of the Island of Britain" claims that Gwenn has the magical ability to render its wearer invisible. Arthur inherited this cloak (figuratively, if not literally) from Caswallawn, the chieftain who battled against Julius Caesar.

Sources: Matthews and Matthews, *The Complete King Arthur*, n.p.; Padel, *Arthur in Medieval Welsh Literature*, n.p.

Hafr, al

According to Islamic mythology, the prophet Muhammad owned at least three half-pikes at the time of his death; their names were al ATRA, al Hafr, and al NAB'A. Beyond its name, nothing else is known of al Hafr.

Sources: Osborne et al., *A Complete History of the Arabs*, Volume 1, 254; Sale et al., *An Universal History, Part 2*, Volume 1, 185

halahala

In Hindu mythology, halahala—an exceedingly lethal poison—was created during the Samudra Manthan ("Churning of the Ocean"); black in color, it was so potent that it could destroy all of creation. It is the opposite of AMORTAM. The poison took fiery form as a wrathful manifestation of its potential. One version of the myth says that Brahma uttered the long syllable "Hum," which caused the terrible being to explode into thousands of pieces. Some of the larger bits were claimed by the *naga* (a race of demonic beings described as human with the lower body of a snake). The smallest particles transformed into all forms of poisonous creatures and plants. Another version claims that the god Shiva consumed the halahala; being whole, it lodged in his throat and caused him to turn blue. This act gave Shiva one of his epithets: Nilakantha (the Blue-Throated One).

Sources: Beer, *The Handbook of Tibetan Buddhist Symbols*, 232; Feller, *Sanskrit Epics*, 180, 189

Halteclere

Variations: Hauteclaire, Hauteclairn, Hauteclare, Hauteclere

One of the swords of Oliver, Halteclere ("High and Neat"/"Very Bright") is described as having burnished steel, a golden guard and a crystal hilt. In one story, while Roland and his faithful companion Oliver were battling Saracens (Muslims), Oliver, in a single motion, dropped his broken lance, drew Halteclere from its scabbard and cleaved Justin de Val Ferree from the crown of his head straight down through his body and into the saddle, ending the stroke only after severing the spine of the horse upon which his enemy was mounted.

In *The Legend of Croquemitaine*, the celebrated swordsmith Galas created three swords: FLAMBERGE, Halteclere, and JOYEUSE. Each sword took three years to make, and each was eventually used to test the edge of the sword GLORIOUS, which managed to hack into each of them.

Sources: "Ancient Literature of France," 296; Brewer, *Dictionary of Phrase and Fable* 1900, 1197; L'Epine, *The Days of Chivalry*, n.p.; Pendergrass, *Mythological Swords*, 43

halter of Clydno Eiddyn

Variations: Cebystr Clydno Eiddin (Welsh), Kebystr Clyddno Eiddyn, Kebystr Klydno Eiddin

In British and Welsh folklore, there is a series of items (always thirteen in number) called the THIRTEEN TREASURES OF THE ISLAND OF BRITAIN (in Welsh, they are called *Tri Thlws ar Ddeg Ynys Prydain*). Although in more modern times the items listed are different, the original thirteen items from the fifteenth century were the CAULDRON OF DYRNWCH THE GIANT, CHARIOT OF MORGAN MWYNFAWR, CHESSBOARD OF GWENDDOLEU AP CEIDIO, COAT OF PADARN BEISRUDD, CROCK AND DISH OF RHYGENYDD YSGOLHAIG (two items), halter of Clydno Eiddyn, HAMPER OF GWYDDNO GARANHIR, HORN OF BRAN GALED, KNIFE OF LLAWFRODEDD FARCHOF, MANTLE OF ARTHUR IN CORNWALL, sword of Rhydderch Hael (DYRNWYN), and WHETSTONE OF TUDWAL TUDGLYD.

The halter of Clydno Eiddyn (a onetime ruler of Edinburgh, Scotland) is typically the fifth item on the list of treasures. According to the legend, the halter was affixed to the owner's bed by a staple, and whatever horse he wished for would then be found in the halter. Sir Gawain (Gawaine), the knight who embodied courtly love, had a horse from this halter, Ceincaled (Gringolet in French); this animal is named in the Welsh Triads as one of the Three Spirited Horses of Britain.

Sources: Dom, *King Arthur and the Gods of the Round Table*, 110; Pendergrass, *Mythological Swords*, 25; Stirling, *King Arthur Conspiracy*, n.p.

hamper of Gwyddno Garanhir

Variations: hamper of Gwyddno Longshanks, Mwys Gwyddno Garanir

In British and Welsh folklore, there is a series of items (always thirteen in number) called the THIRTEEN TREASURES OF THE ISLAND OF BRITAIN (in Welsh, they are called *Tri Thlws ar Ddeg Ynys Prydain*). Although in more modern times the items listed are different, the original thirteen items from the fifteenth century were the CAULDRON OF DYRNWCH THE GIANT, CHARIOT OF MORGAN MWYNFAWR, CHESSBOARD OF GWENDDOLEU AP CEIDIO, COAT OF PADARN BEISRUDD, CROCK AND DISH OF RHYGENYDD YSGOLHAIG (two items), HALTER OF CLYDNO EIDDYN, hamper of Gwyddno Garanhir,

HORN OF BRAN GALED, KNIFE OF LLAWFRODEDD FARCHOF, MANTLE OF ARTHUR IN CORNWALL, sword of Rhydderch Hael (DYRNWYN), and WHETSTONE OF TUDWAL TUDGLYD.

Gwyddno Garanhir (also known as Long Shanks) was the legendary ruler of a sunken island said to be off the western coast of Wales, known as Cantre'r Gwaelod; he owned a hamper (a large basket with handles and a hinged lid) that had the magical ability to multiply one hundred times whatever food was placed inside of it. The hamper is similar to items such as the CAULDRON OF THE DAGDA, the CLOTH OF PLENTY, and the CORNUCOPIA.

Sources: Dom, *King Arthur and the Gods of the Round Table*, 110; Pendergrass, *Mythological Swords*, 24–25

Haoma

Variation: Horn

A magical drink from the folklore of ancient Persia and the mythology of Zoroastrianism, Haoma is said to grant immortality. Made by combining the haoma plant with milk and water, Haoma is also personified as a deity.

The haoma plant is described as fragrant with golden-green leaves; it matures tall and grows in the mountains. Medicinally, it is said to enhance strength, improve alertness, maintain sexual arousal, sharpen awareness, and speed healing. Notorious, this mild intoxicant can be consumed without any unwanted side effects.

Yazata Haoma (also known as Horn Yazad) is the deity of the haoma plant made manifest. Appearing as a handsome man with golden-green eyes, he "furthers righteousness," as he is himself righteous and wise and grants insight to others. He is the guardian of the plants on the highest mountain peaks.

Sources: Boyce, *Zoroastrians*, n.p.; Dhalla, *History of Zoroastrianism*, n.p.; Taillieu and Boyce, "Haoma," 502

hardmandle (plural: hardmandlene)

In Swiss fairy lore, dwarfs are said to use cow's milk to make an excellent and well-formed cheese known as hardmandle. When a wedge is cut from the whole, the remaining hardmandle will regrow and fill in the missing space. As long as there remains enough of the original form, the hardmandle will continue to replenish itself.

Sources: Keightley, *World Guide to Gnomes, Fairies, Elves, and Other Little People*, 264

harp of Binnorie, the

In the British folktale *Binnorie*, two unnamed princesses were being courted by Sir William; when it was apparent to the older sister that her younger sister was going to be the one proposed to, she convinced her sibling to go boating with her. While out on the millstream of Binnorie, the older princess drowned her younger sister and left her body upon the shore. A skilled harper happened by, came upon the drowned sister, and fell in love with her beautiful face. He never forgot her and, years later, returned to the place where he had found her remains. He made a harp from her breastbone and golden hair. Later that night, the harper played in the hall of Sir William. When the harper laid his new harp down, it began to play and sing and told the tale of how the older sister had murdered her younger sibling to win the hand of Sir William.

Sources: Creeden, *Fair Is Fair*, 155; Jacobs, *English Fairy Tales*, 46–47

harp of Bragi, the

The god of eloquence, poetry, and song, as well as patron of the *skalds* (poets), Bragi was, according to Norse mythology, the best of the poets. A son of Odin (the god of battle, death, frenzy, the gallows, healing, knowledge, poetry, royalty, the runic alphabet, sorcery, and wisdom) and Frigg ("Beloved"), Bragi was gifted with a golden, magical harp by the dwarfs on the day of his birth. When Bragi played his harp, he had the power to "bring the world back to life," causing trees and flowers to bloom—that is, the season of spring would begin.

Sources: Andrews, *Dictionary of Nature Myths*, 175; Lindow, *Handbook of Norse Mythology*, 87, 169

harp of Jack, the

In the British folktale "Jack and the Bean Stalk," there was a golden harp that would play the most beautiful and soothing music (accompanied by its own sweet voice) when its owner, the giant, said, "Play." When the harp was grabbed by Jack as he attempted to steal it, the harp cried out in a human voice for help.

Sources: Jacobs, *English Fairy Tales*, 65–66

harp of King David, the

Variation: lyre of David

One of the relics associated with the ARK OF THE COVENANT, the harp of King David was said to play music of its own accord. With this instrument, David would produce soothing music to ease King Saul's suffering when the evil spirit that resided in him would torment and cause him pain.

Harpe

Sources: Boren and Boren, *Following the Ark of the Covenant*, 14; Friedmann, *Music in Biblical Life*, 63

Harpe

Variations: Cronus's sickle, Gaea's sickle, Perseus's sickle, SCYTHE OF CRONUS, sickle of Cronus, sickle of Gaea, sickle of Perseus, SICKLE OF ZEUS, Zeus's sickle

In classical Greek mythology, Harpe was the ADAMANTINE sword used by Cronus ("Time"; Chronos/Cronos/Kronos/Saturn), a Titan and the god of time, to castrate his father, Uranus ("Heaven"; Ouranos). Harpe is more notably recognized, however, as the characteristic sword wielded by a famous grandson of Cronus, the demigod and hero Perseus—this was the sword he used to decapitate the Gorgon, Medusa. The demigod and legendary hero Heracles was also a great-grandson of Perseus; he used Harpe when he fought the multi-headed hydra.

Hermes (Roman god Mercury), the god of animal husbandry, commerce, eloquence, fertility, language, looters, luck, sleep, thieves, trade, travel, and wealth, used Harpe to kill the giant Argus. In addition, Zeus (Roman god Jupiter), the god of fate, kings, lightning, sky, and thunder, used Harpe in his battle against Typhon (Typhoes/Typhaon/Typhos).

In art, Harpe was originally depicted as a khopesh-like Egyptian sickle-sword.

Sources: Tatius, *Achilles Tatius*, 151; Viltanioti and Marmodoro, *Divine Powers in Late Antiquity*, 110, 118; Wilk, *Medusa*, 28, 241

harpoon of Isis, the

Variation: Isis's harpoon

In Egyptian mythology, Isis, the goddess of death, fertility, healing, magic, motherhood, and rebirth, created a magical harpoon to protect her son Horus from Set, the god of chaos, darkness, desert, disorder, earthquakes, eclipses, foreigners, thunderstorms, violence, and war. Isis created the harpoon first by braiding yarn into rope; next, she smelted copper and created a harpoon. The rope was then tied to the end of the harpoon. Her weapon had the ability to release anyone she had hit with it.

Sources: Mercatante, *Who's Who in Egyptian Mythology*, 63; Regula, *The Mysteries of Isis*, 55, 58

Harr

Variations: Haar, Har, Hor

In Norse mythology, Harr ("High One") was one of the halls of Odin (the god of battle, death, frenzy, the gallows, healing, knowledge, poetry, royalty, the runic alphabet, sorcery, and wisdom); it was the place where the witch Gullveig was judged, spat upon, and then burned. In this secondary hall, Odin had many rooms constructed, each serving a separate purpose, such as one for poetry reading, another for sporting contests, one for specifically wrestling, and so on. At the end of the hall stood three thrones. The name of Odin's main hall was VALASKJALF.

Sources: Grimes, *The Norse Myths*, 18, 36, 272

hat of the yech, the

In the folklore of India, the yech is a humorous, powerful fairy animal described as looking like a dark civet cat with a small white hat on its head. If someone manages to gain possession of the creature's hat, the yech will then become their devoted servant; wearing the hat will make a person invisible.

Sources: Crooke, *Popular Religion and Folk-Lore of Northern India*, Volume 2, 80; Shepard et al., *Encyclopedia of Occultism and Parapsychology*, 1005; Zell-Ravenheart and Dekirk, *Wizard's Bestiary*, 104

Hatel, al

Variations: Halef, Hatef, Hatf

Al Hatel ("the Deadly") was said to have been one of the three swords of the prophet Muhammad; the other two swords were al BATTER and al MEHDHAM. These three swords, along with other treasures, came into his possession as wealth confiscated from the Jewish tribe Banu Kainoka prior to their banishment to Syria.

In other sources, the prophet Muhammad owned a collection of nine different swords at the time of his death: al ADHAB, al Battar (see BATTER), Dhu'l Fakar (see DHUAL-FIRQAR), al Hatf, al KADIB, KOLAITE, MABUR, al MEHDHAM, and al ROFUB. Beyond its name, nothing else is known of the sword al Hatel.

Sources: Brewer and Harland, *Character Sketches of Romance, Fiction and the Drama*, Volume 4, 378; Irving, *Works of Washington Irving*, Volume 9, 132; Sale et al., *An Universal History, Part 2*, Volume 1, 184

hauberk of gold

Variation: hauberk of glittering gold

One of the items taken by the Norse hero Sigurd (Siegfried/Sigmund) from the treasure of the dragon god Fafnir (Fafner) and the dragon's brother, Regin, was the hauberk of gold. Other items in the hoard were the AEGIS OF FAFNIR,

ANDVARANAUT, coins from ancient cities, other suits of golden armor, and many magic bracelets and rings. Sigurd was easily distinguished on the field by his fair hair flowing from beneath the AEGIS OF FAFNIR and his wearing of the glittering hauberk of gold.

Sources: Bradish, *Old Norse Stories*, 180, 205, 230; Guerber, *Myths of the Norsemen*, 242, 243, 246

head of Medusa, the

In classical Greek mythology, the severed head of the Gorgon Medusa became a powerful weapon. King Polydectes challenged the young hero Perseus to retrieve for him the head of Medusa, whose appearance (or gaze—sources conflict) was so horrific that it would literally turn a person to stone. Favored by the gods and gifted with items to assist him in his quest, Perseus was successful; the blood shed during Medusa's decapitation gave birth to both Chrysaor and the winged horse Pegasus. The head was kept in a leather bag called a KIBISIS ("wallet"), and Perseus would use it as a weapon to turn his enemies into stone: King Polydectes and his army, the Titan Atlas, and the sea monster to whom Andromeda was offered as a sacrifice. When Perseus finished his days of adventuring, he made a gift of the head to Athena (Roman goddess Minerva), the goddess of crafts, military victories, war, and wisdom; she had it embedded on the face of her shield, the AEGIS OF ATHENA.

Sources: Daly and Rengel, *Greek and Roman Mythology, A to Z*, 22, 114; Roberts, *Encyclopedia of Comparative Iconography*, n.p.; Sears, *Mythology 101*, n.p.

healing stone of the uktena, the

According to the folklore of North Carolina and Tennessee, a species of winged horned serpents called uktena feed upon children and fishermen who venture too near their homes. Stories claim that within the skull of these creatures is a stone or crystal with the magical ability to cure any disease. The crystal is dangerous to acquire, as the uktena have toxic breath. Additionally, in order to maintain the magical property of the stone, it must be bathed in human blood daily.

Sources: Sierra, *Gruesome Guide to World Monsters*, 8; Zell-Ravenheart and Dekirk, *Wizard's Bestiary*, 98

Heaven Bridge

Variations: Bridge of Difficulties, Bridge of the Dead, Brig o' Dread, Rainbow Bridge, Soul Bridge

A heaven bridge, of some description, is mentioned in numerous belief systems: ancient Persian mythology (CHINWAT BRIDGE); Burmese folklore; Hawaiian, Indonesian, Melanesian, and Polynesian mythology (Bridge of the Gods); Hindu beliefs; the Idaan of Borneo; the Inuit of Greenland; Islamic mythology (al SIRAT); Japanese legend (Floating Bridge of Heaven); Javanese folklore; the Karens of Birmah; Norse mythology (BIFROST, GJALLARBRU); numerous native American tribes such as the Chactaw, the Ojibwa, and the Minnetarees; rabbinical literature; Sardinian mythology; Vedic beliefs; and Zend-Avesta, to name some examples.

This archetypical heaven bridge is simply a path, walkway, or space that must be traversed; the starting point is in this earthly world, with the goal being to reach the other side in order to enter into an afterlife in another realm. Sometimes this journey acts as a means of crossing over into some otherwise unattainable "other world," such as the world of the fay. If the crossing of the bridge is treacherous, it represents a test of one's worthiness; in such cases, this object is sometimes referred to as a "Bridge of Difficulties."

The bridge need not always be a literal bridge; it may be a path, a lake, or even a gaping abyss.

Sources: Stuart, *New Century Reference Library*, Volume 3, 151; Todd and Weeks, *The Romanic Review*, 177; Tylor, *Researches into the Early History of Mankind and the Development of Civilization*, 359–61

heifer of Ilmarinen, the

In a legend from Finland found in the epic poem *The Kalevala*, Ilmarinen, a god with remarkable smithing abilities, used the magical elements in his forge to create many items. One such item was a heifer; it had a perfectly formed head and horns of gold. Unfortunately, the animal was ill tempered and would run through the forests and swamps, spilling her milk as she went. Displeased with the result, Ilmarinen cut his creation into pieces and threw it back into his magical forge.

Sources: Friberg et al., *The Kalevala*, 99; Mouse, *Ilmarinen Forges the Sampo*, 55

Hel Cake

In Norse mythology, Hel Cake was the treat-bread the deceased would give to Garmr, the guardian of Niflheimr, in order to pass by while he was distracted. Only those who gave bread to the poor or aided those who were in need while they lived were able to obtain Hel Cake in death.

Sources: Abel, *Death Gods*, 68; Grimes, *The Norse Myths*, 275; Sherman, *Storytelling*, 185

hel keplein

hel keplein

Variation: CAP OF INVISIBILITY

In German folklore, the dwarf king Laurin owned many magical items, one of which was a magical cap known as a hel keplein; it had the ability to make him invisible at will.

Sources: Keightley, *World Guide to Gnomes, Fairies, Elves, and Other Little People*, 207; Pope, *German Composition*, 71–73; Wagner, *Great Norse, Celtic and Teutonic Legends*, 69–77

Hel shoons

Variations: Hel shoes, helsko, Helskot

In Scandinavian folklore, Hel shoons are the footwear that a deceased person must wear in order to traverse the moor that lays before Hel, the land of the dead. It was at one time a custom to burn a pair of shoes with a corpse so the deceased would arrive on the "other side" with them. In Icelandic lore, Hel shoons were absolutely necessary for the journey down the rough road into VALHALLA.

Sources: Brewer, *Dictionary of Phrase and Fable*, Volume 1, 597; Grimes, *The Norse Myths*, 275; Sidgwick, *Old Ballads*, 174

Helgrindr

Variations: Corpse Gate, Gates of Hel, Hel Gate, Heldgrindr, Helgate, Helgrind, NAGRINDR, VALGRIND

In Norse mythology, Helgrindr ("Death Gate"/ "Hel Gate") is the gated wall that stands on the far side of GJALLARBRU, the bridge that connects the world of the living and that of the deceased (see HEAVEN BRIDGE). This is the primary gate leading into Hel, the realm of those who die of disease or old age; it is located at the end of Hel-Way. Sitting atop the gate is a rooster named Sooty-Red whose call stirs the dead; on the other side of this gate is the Hrymthursar (frost giant) Hrimgrimnir.

Sources: Anderson, *Norse Mythology*, 449; Bennett, *Gods and Religions of Ancient and Modern Times*, Volume 1, 389; Grimes, *The Norse Myths*, 73; Lindow, *Norse Mythology*, 172; Norroena Society, *Asatru Edda*, 357

Helheim

In Norse mythology, Helheim ("Home of Hel" or "House of Hel") is the physical home of the goddess Hel. Those who were wicked in life or who died of old age or disease report to Hel in Helheim. One of the nine worlds of Norse cosmology, the realm of Helheim is located directly below Mannaheim and between Niflheimr and Svartalfaheim.

Sources: Anderson, *Norse Mythology*, 187, 391, 449; Bennett, *Gods and Religions of Ancient and Modern Times*, Volume 1, 389

hell broth

Variation: brorth

In American and European folklore, hell broth is a magical mixture concocted by evil witches for malevolent purposes. In the Shakespearian play *Macbeth*, the witches list the ingredients as adder's fork (tongue), blind-worm's sting(er), lizard leg, and owlet wing, among others.

Sources: Johnson, *A Dictionary of the English Language*, Volume 2, n.p.; *New and Enlarged Dictionary of the English Language*, 485

helmet of Rostam, the

In the Persian epic *Shahnameh* (*Shahnama*), the mythical hero Rostam (Rustam) undertakes seven labors in order to free his king. The final challenge he faces is against the chieftain of the Divs (demons) of Mazandaran, Div-e-Sepic ("White Demon"). After defeating the Div, the hero uses the creature's blood and heart to cure the blindness of his king, Kay Qubad; then Rostam uses Div-e-Sepic's severed head as his helmet.

Sources: Khan, *Who Killed Kasheer?*, n.p.; Warner and Fernández-Armesto, *World of Myths*, Volume 2, 125–26

Helvegir (HEL-vehg-ir) (plural: Helvegr)

In Norse mythology, Helvegir ("Hel Ways") refers to the many paths in the region of Hel, the land of the goddess of the underworld (also named Hel).

Sources: Norroena Society, *Asatru Edda*, 359; Rydberg, *Teutonic Mythology* Volume 1 , 299

Helyes book, the

A powerful book of magic from Arthurian lore, the Helyes book was owned by Helyes of Thoulouse. Although the book was reputed to hold powerful magic, it was scarcely used. On one occasion in the Vulgate cycle, Helyes used it to conjure up a demonic apparition in order to learn how long Duke Galeholt would live (at his own request).

Sources: Karr, *Arthurian Companion*, 245

Heorot (hay oh roht)

Variation: Herot

The palace and mead hall of the legendary Danish king Hrothgar in the Anglo-Saxon epic *Beowulf*, Heorot ("Hall of the Hart") is described as the "foremost of halls under Heaven." This is the hall in which Beowulf confronts (and ultimately defeats) the monster Grendel.

Sources: Bjork and Niles, *A Beowulf Handbook*, 225, 277; Orchard, *A Critical Companion to Beowulf*, 172, 206, 216

herb of Gaea, the

In classical Greek mythology, the primordial goddess Gaea, the personification of the Earth, was the mother of an indomitable race of beings known as the Gigante; they were created when the blood of Uranus ("Heaven"; Ouranos) fell upon her. These massive humanoids, often described as having serpents for feet, were made invincible by Gaea through her use of a special herb. This herbal application protected them in battle against the Olympian gods during the Gigantomachy.

Sources: Hansen, *Handbook of Classical Mythology*, 177; Lurker, *Dictionary of Gods and Goddesses, Devils and Demons*, 69; Smith and Brown, *The Complete Idiot's Guide to World Mythology*, 238

herb of Sir Gawain, the

In Arthurian lore, there is an unnamed, magical herb known to Sir Gawain (Gawaine) that has remarkable healing properties; it is described as potent enough to heal a sick tree. Sir Gawain uses this herb to help the wounded Greoreas. The herb is said to grow in shady areas near hedges.

Sources: Karr, *Arthurian Companion*, 193; Pickens, *Perceval and Gawain in Dark Mirrors*, 107

hide of Leviathan, the

Originating in ancient Hebrew folklore and popularized in medieval demonology, Leviathan ("the Crooked Serpent"/"the Piercing Dragon"), the demon of envy and faith, was an aquatic she-demon who was also said to be one of the fallen angels of the order of seraphim. In Judeo-Christian lore, the hide of Leviathan, after its inevitable defeat, will be divided up; God will make tents with it for the first rank of the faithful, girdles for the second rank, chains for the third rank, and necklaces for the fourth. The remaining hide will be hung on the temple walls, and the world will "shine with its brightness."

Sources: Singer and Adler, *The Jewish Encyclopedia*, Volume 8, 38

hide of the Nemean Lion, the

In classical Greek mythology, it is said there once lived a lion larger and fiercer than any other;
its golden hide was impervious to any weapon, and its claws could shred any shield. One of the labors of the demigod and hero Heracles was to go to Nemea, where this creature lived, and slay it. Knowing none of his weapons would harm the beast, Heracles grabbed the lion by the waist and, using his godlike strength, literally squeezed the life out of it. Using the lion's own claws, Heracles then fashioned for himself a garment from its pelt. (It should be noted that some authors claim the lion pelt Heracles wore came from the lion from Mount Kithaeron that he slew in his youth.)

Sources: Daly and Rengel, *Greek and Roman Mythology, A to Z*, 63; Fiore, *Symbolic Mythology*, 175

Hildigolt

Variations: Hildegolt, Hildisvin ("Battle Pig")

According to Norse legend, Swedish King Adils enlisted the assistance of his stepson, King Hrolf Kraki, to defeat King Ali of Norway; he promised to pay his stepson's entire army in addition to giving Hrolf any three Swedish treasures. Hrolf accepted and sent his twelve best berserkers. Adils defeated Ali and on the battlefield claimed his opponent's helmet, HILDIGOLT, and his warhorse, Raven. When the time for payment came, the berserkers asked for three pounds of gold each for themselves and the treasures FINNSLEIF, Hildigolt, and SVIAGRIS for their king.

Sources: Anderson, *The Younger Edda*, 215; Byock, *The Prose Edda*, 36

Hildigrim

In Continental Germanic mythology, Hildigrim is the helmet worn by Sir Thidrek, the son of Thettmar and Olilia. According to the *Thidrekssaga*, Thidrek captured the dwarf Alfrek, from whom he received the sword Naglhring (see NAGELRING) as well as the promise of treasure should he defeat the berserker Grimr and his wife, Hildr. Victorious, Thidrek discovered the helmet Hildigrim in their treasure hoard.

Sources: de Beaumont and Allinson, *The Sword and Womankind*, 8; McConnell et al., *The Nibelungen Tradition*, 127

Himinbjorg

Variations: Himinbjord, Himinbrjodr, Himmelbjerg

In Norse mythology, Himinbjorg ("Heaven's Cliffs"/"Mount of Heaven") was Heimdallr (Heimdal)'s fortress-like hall; it was the eighth hall of the Asgard ("Enclosure of the Aesir") and was located at the keystone of Bifrost.

Hindarfiall

Sources: Anderson, *Norse Mythology*, 186, 449; Grimes, *The Norse Myths*, 276; Lindow, *Norse Mythology*, 174

Hindarfiall (hin'dar-fyal)

Variation: Hindfell

In Norse mythology, Hindarfiall is the place where Odin, the god of battle, death, frenzy, the gallows, healing, knowledge, poetry, royalty, the runic alphabet, sorcery, and wisdom, took the Valkyrie Brynhildr (Brunnehilde) after piercing her with a SVEFNPORN; he then surrounded her with a wall of fire known as the VAFRLOGAR. As she lay awaiting the arrival of a husband brave enough to pass through the flames, Brynhildr retained her beauty and youth. Hindarfiall is described as a tall mountain whose cloud-top summit also had a halo of flames.

Sources: Guerber, *Myths of the Norsemen*, 280, 284; Sturluson, *Younger Edda*, 134

Hippocrene

Variation: the fountain of the Muses

A spring from classical Greek mythology, Hippocrene ("Horse Fountain") was sacred to the Muses because it possessed the power of poetic inspiration. Said to have been created when the winged horse Pegasus landed upon the earth for the first time, this sweet-tasting spring became a water source the legendary animal would return to whenever it needed to refresh itself. The water of the spring was so pure and delicious that when shepherds drank from it, they would abandon their flocks to the mercy of the wolves and wander off babbling rhyme and verse, hoping someone would listen to them.

Sources: Evslin, *Gods, Demigods, and Demons*, 92; Howey, *The Horse in Magic and Myth*, n.p.

Hlidskjalf (LITH-skyahlv)

Variations: Hlidskialf, Hlithskjalf, Hlithskjolf, Lidskialf, Lidskialfa, Lidskjalf, the Terror of Nations

In Norse mythology, Hlidskjalf ("Battle Shelf"/ "Gate-Tower"/"Heaven's Crag"/"Hill Opening") was the throne of Odin, the god of battle, death, frenzy, the gallows, healing, knowledge, poetry, royalty, the runic alphabet, sorcery, and wisdom; it was located in the watchtower of his hall VALA-SKJALF. Anyone who sat upon the throne would be able to see all the nine worlds of Norse mythology. Although only Odin's wife, Frigg ("Beloved"), had open permission to sit upon Hlidskjalf, Freyr (Frey/Yngvi), the god of fertility, peace, rain, and sunshine, did sit upon the throne once. Odin was accompanied in this hall when he sat upon Hlidskjalf by his two wolf companions, Freki ("Ravenous") and Geri ("Ravenous"), and his two ravens, Hugin ("Thought") and Munin ("Memory"). Each day the ravens would fly throughout the nine worlds and report back to Odin everything they saw.

Sources: Anderson, *Norse Mythology*, 231, 445; Daly, *Norse Mythology A to Z*, 25–26, 41; Grimes, *The Norse Myths*, 277; Guerber, *Myths of the Norsemen from the Eddas and Sagas*, 119; Lindow, *Norse Mythology*, 176

Hnitbjorg

Variation: Hnitbergen

In Norse mythology, Hnitbjorg ("Lock Box") was the treasure chamber belonging to Suttungr; it was here that his daughter Gunnlod guarded the PRECIOUS MEAD. Hnitbjorg was located within the mountain of the same name.

Sources: Daly, *Norse Mythology A to Z*, 43, 50; Grimes, *The Norse Myths*, 277; Sturluson, *The Prose Edda*, 94

hoarfrost

Variation: rimfrost

In Norse mythology, hoarfrost was a particular type of frost; it looked as if many needles made of ice were intersecting. When the searing heat of Muspellsheimr and the frigid cold of Ginnungagap met, the hoarfrost melted and, mixing with the rime of the area, created the evil Ymir ("Groaner"; Aurgelmir). Finding he had nothing to eat but rime, Ymir used the hoarfrost to create the first cow, Audhumla.

Sources: Grimes, *The Norse Myths*, 3–4, 278

hodd Goda (HAWD GAWTH-a)

Variation: hoddgoda

In Norse mythology, the hodd Goda ("Hoard of the Godin") is a treasure chamber located in Mimir's realm; it contains many divine artifacts. The exact location of the concealed hodd Goda is difficult to pin down, as details are scant. It is said to be in the southern region of Hel and surrounded by "Hel-rivers" originating from Hvergelmer, but their names are not given. The myth suggests the crossing of the rivers creates a barrier that keeps out anything from the region that does not belong there.

Sources: Norroena Society, *Asatru Edda*, 361; Rydburg, *Norroena*, Volume 3, 416; Rydberg, *Teutonic Mythology* volume 1 , 285

hodd Niflunga (HAWD NIV-lung-a)

Variations: Nibelunge hort, Niflung treasure, Niflungr hoard, Volund treasure

In Norse mythology, the hodd Niflunga ("Niflunga hoard") is a significant stockpile of gold and magical items typically owned collectively by three brothers. There are many stories that mention the hodd Niflunga, each featuring the treasure as a prize to be won by the hero (usually Siegfried). It is common for the AEGISH-JALMR to be found hidden in the gold or serving as the reason why the hero went seeking the hoard. In traditional German tales, the three brothers are named Egil, Slagfin-Gjuke, and Volund; in another version, only one of the brothers is named—King Euglin (Eugel)—and he is said to be "an interpreter of the stars."

Sources: Norroena Society, *Satr Edda*, 25, 333; Rydberg, *Teutonic Mythology* Volume 1 , 662

Hofud

Variations: Bifrost Sword, Hofund

In Norse mythology, Hofud ("Human Head," "Man Head") is the deadly and flashing sickle-shaped sword of Heimdallr (Heimdal), the guardian of Bifrost (the Rainbow Bridge).

Sources: Hawthorne, *Vikings*, 19; Simek, *Dictionary of Northern Mythology*, 155

Holy Grail, the

The Holy Grail is an important recurring theme in Arthurian lore and literature; it has been variously described as a cup, dish, plate, and stone. The Grail was first used in an unfinished romance penned by the French poet and troubadour Chretien de Troyes (1130–1191), who described it as a low and wide cup or dish. It was featured in his work *Perceval, le Conte du Graal* (*Story of the Grail*). While dining with the Fisher King (Crippled King/Maimed King/Wounded King/Anfortas/Bron/Evelake/Parlan/Peliam/Pellam/Pelles), Perceval saw the Grail being carried by a beautiful young girl; it was used much like a platter to carry a large Communion Wafer, the only food consumed by the Fisher King's aged father (alluding to the man's sainthood). In this story it was not the Grail that was holy or special, but rather the item it carried.

It was the German knight and poet Wolfram von Eschenbach (1170–1220) who made the Grail a stone that fell from the heavens. He claimed the stone (which he called the *lapis exillis*) was the sanctuary for those angels who did not side with either God or Lucifer during the rebellion.

It was not until the late twelfth century that the Grail became holy and associated with Jesus and the chalice of the Last Supper. According to this version, Joseph of Arimathea received the Grail from Jesus in a vision. Taking it, he and his family traveled to Great Britain. Later, other authors said it was the cup used to catch the blood of Christ during the Crucifixion, and a line of guardians was founded to keep the item safe; this line would eventually include Perceval.

In the Vulgate Cycle, the Holy Grail was symbolic of divine grace, and Sir Galahad, the greatest and most pure of the knights, was destined to receive it. It was this interpretation of the Grail that in the fifteenth century was picked up by Sir Thomas Mallory in his *Le Morte d'Arthur* and is still popular today.

Sources: Barber, *The Holy Grail*, 93; Loomis, *The Grail*, n.p.; Sayce, *Exemplary Comparison from Homer to Petrarch*, 143

Holy Lance, the

Variations: Holy Spear, Lance of Longinus, Spear of Destiny, Spear of Longinus

According to the Gospel of John, the Holy Lance is the weapon that pierced the side of Jesus as he hung dead on the cross. It was customary to break the legs of a person who was crucified in order to hasten their death; this practice was known as *crurifragium*. The Roman soldiers wanted to be sure Jesus was dead, so one of them (a centurion later named Longinus in biblical lore) pierced the body with his lance, and from the wound poured forth blood and water.

Legends associated with the Holy Lance claim that whoever possesses it and can solve its mysteries holds "the destiny of the world in their hands, for good or evil."

Sources: Ravenscroft, *Spear of Destiny*, n.p.; Smith and Piccard, *Secrets of the Holy Lance*, n.p.

homunculus (plural: homunculi)

An artificial human created through the use of alchemy, the homunculus ("little human being") was said to be the greatest possible achievement for an alchemist, as it represented the dream of achieving "nature through art."

To create a homunculus, the alchemist would place a certain amount of human semen into a flask, seal it, and gently heat it over a flame for forty days; at that point, it would begin to move and resemble a human being in form. The creature was then fed a specially prepared chemical diet consisting largely of human blood for forty weeks; after this stage, it would be a fully formed homunculus. Although it looked like a human child, the creature had innate knowledge and powers, such as knowing all of the arts required to create itself. The homunculus would also have other deep and great knowledge, as it was not created with the "taint" of the female element. It is said that if the same experiment was conducted using menstrual blood rather than semen, the result would produce a creature known as a basilisk.

Sources: Draaisma, *Metaphors of Memory*, 212; Principe, *Secrets of Alchemy*, 131–32

Horn Hilt

In Scandinavian folklore, Val, the brother of Raknar, owned a sword named Horn Hilt; the weapon was heavily inlaid with gold, and whenever he swung at an opponent, he always hit his mark. Using this sword, Val slew Svidi the Bold, a son of Thor, the god of thunder. In one popular folktale, Thorir Oddsson and his comrades went on a great adventure to find Val's treasure cave. After defeating the guardian dragon, Thorir searched the vast treasure for three days before discovering Horn Hilt; he claimed it and the largest share of the hoard.

Sources: Craigie, *Scandinavian Folk-lore*, 249; Palsson and Edwards, *Seven Viking Romances*, n.p.

horn of Bran Galed, the

Variation: horn of Gawlgawd

In British and Welsh folklore, there is a series of items (always thirteen in number) called the THIRTEEN TREASURES OF THE ISLAND OF BRITAIN (in Welsh, they are called *Tri Thlws ar Ddeg Ynys Prydain*). Although in more modern times the items listed are different, the original thirteen items from the fifteenth century were the CAULDRON OF DYRNWCH THE GIANT, CHARIOT OF MORGAN MWYNFAWR, CHESSBOARD OF GWENDDOLEU AP CEIDIO, COAT OF PADARN BEISRUDD, CROCK AND DISH OF RHYGENYDD YSGOLHAIG (two items), HALTER OF CLYDNO EIDDYN, HAMPER OF GWYDDNO GARANHIR, horn of Bran Galed, KNIFE OF LLAWFRODEDD FARCHOF, MANTLE OF ARTHUR IN CORNWALL, sword of Rhydderch Hael (DYRNWYN), and WHETSTONE OF TUDWAL TUDGLYD.

The horn of Bran Galed ("the Stingy" or "the Niggard") had the magical ability to produce whatever drink was desired. According to the legend, the horn originally belonged to the Greek demigod and hero Hercules, who ripped it off the head of the centaur who had killed his wife.

While gathering together all the great treasures, Merlin (Merddyn/Myrddin) managed to obtain the drinking horn from Bran Galed, although the stories do not say how, and then retreated with it and the other items to Ty Gwydr ("Glass House") on Bardsey Island, where they were to remain forever.

Sources: Dom, *King Arthur and the Gods of the Round Table*, 105, 109, 125; Patton, *The Poet's Ogam*, 510; Pendergrass, *Mythological Swords*, 25

horn of Elephant Bone, the

In a tale by Sir Thomas Mallory, Sir Beaumains of Arthurian lore quested to free Dame Lyones from the Red Knight—Sir Ironside—who lived in Castle Dangerous. In the middle of a plane stood a lone sycamore tree from which there hung an intricately carved horn of elephant bone inlaid with gold. To blow the horn was to summon the Red Knight and challenge him to battle; he had the strength of seven men, as well as great combat prowess, and hated all true knights.

Sources: Gilbert, *King Arthur's Knights*, 94–95; Karr, *Arthurian Companion*, 237

horn of Gabriel, the

In biblical traditions, the horn of the Archangel Gabriel will be the instrument used to announce the arrival of Judgment Day; however, the Bible does not specifically name the angel who will signal the time when the dead will rise from their graves. The first designation of Gabriel as the trumpeter came in an Armenian manuscript from 1455 in which this event was illustrated. However, it was not until John Milton's *Paradise Lost* (1667) that English literature cited Gabriel as the trumpeter.

Sources: Koehler, *A Dictionary for the Modern Trumpet Player*, 67; McCasland, "Gabriel's Trumpet," 159–61

horn of Hades, the

Variation: Hades's horn

In Norse mythology, the horn of Hades was the vessel that held the combined liquids of SONAR DREYRI, SVALKALDR SAER, and URDAR MAGN.

Sources: Rydberg, *Teutonic Mythology* volume 1, 92

horn of Hoddrofnir, the

Variation: Hoddrofnir's horn

Only mentioned in the Eddic poem *Sigrdrifuma*, the horn of Hoddrofnir ("Hoard Tearer"/"One Who Breaks Up Treasure") was an item in Norse mythology stolen by a Jotun (giant) named Midvitnir ("Mead Wolf"/"Mid Wolf"/

"Sea Wolf"); upon returning to his own hall, he stored the horn in the SKULL OF HEIDRAUPNIR; both items were then placed under the protection of his son, Sokkmimir.

The exact nature of the horn of Hoddrofnir, with its dripping liquid, has long been open to speculation. Most authors and translators suggest that it is a drinking horn containing PRECIOUS MEAD, while a few feel the translation is referencing a fertility rite, with the dripping liquid being semen.

Sources: Grimes, *The Norse Myths*, 58; Larson et al., *Myth in Indo-European Antiquity*, 165; Terry, *Poems of the Elder Edda*, 163–64

horn of ivory, the

In a tale by Sir Thomas Mallory, the horn of ivory was found in the Castle of Maidens; richly bound with gold, the magically enchanted horn, when blown, could be heard for two miles in every direction. It was used to summon knights to the castle.

Sources: Anderson, *Norrœna*, 172; Karr, *Arthurian Companion*, 238

Hraeda

In Norse mythology, Hraeda was the rope used to hold the chains GLEIPNIR and GELGJA to the boulder GJOLL in order to bind Fenriswulf (Fenerriswulf/Fenrissulfrin).

Sources: Grimes, *The Norse Myths*, 279

hraki

In Norse mythology, hraki was the name given to the spittle that sealed the peace between the Aesir and the Vanir; the spittle was then transformed into Kvasir and given life. It is the blood of Kvasir mixed with honey that the goddess of poetic art and wisdom, Saga, uses to make PRECIOUS MEAD.

Sources: Grimes, *The Norse Myths*, 279; Grimm, *Teutonic Mythology*, Volume 1, 319

Hringham (RING-hawrn-i)

Variations: Hringhaune, Hringhorn, Hringhorni, Hringhornr, Hringthorn, RINGHORN, Ringhorni

In Norse mythology, *Hringham* (*Curved Prow/Ship with a Circle on the Stem*) was Balder's ship; it was the largest in the world. *Hringham* was used as Balder's funeral pyre: its masts were hung with tapestries telling the story of his life; gold, precious objects, silver, and weapons covered the ship as decorations; and it was heavily laden with garlands of flowers, a vast supply of food, and an array of tools. His favorite horse and hunting hounds were slain and placed on board as well. Nanna Nepsdottr, Balder's wife, saw the sad sight of the funeral ship and died of grief; she, too, was then placed aboard.

The vessel was too large for the gods to launch it themselves, so the giantess Hyrrokkin ("Fire Smoke") of Jotunheimr was summoned. Using her great strength, she pushed the ship into the water with such force that the friction caused *Hringham* to catch fire. Also set ablaze in the funeral pyre was DRAUPNIR, the arm-ring of Odin, the god of battle, death, frenzy, the gallows, healing, knowledge, poetry, royalty, the runic alphabet, sorcery, and wisdom.

Sources: Bassett, *Wander-ships*, 118–19; Grimes, *The Norse Myths*, 208, 210, 280; Norroena Society, *Asatru Edda*, 362; Simek, *Dictionary of Northern Mythology*, 159

Hrotti (RAWT-i)

A sword from Norse mythology, Hrotti ("Springing Rod") belonged to Hodr; he retrieved it from the hoard of the dragon god Fafnir (Fafner) after Sigurd (Siegfried/Sigmund) slew the creature with GRAM. Hrotti was described as having a wrinkled or wavy pattern upon its blade.

Sources: Davidson, *The Sword in Anglo-Saxon England*, 167; Norroena Society, *Satr Edda*, 364; Pendergrass, *Mythological Swords*, 45

Hrunting

Variation: Baedoleoma ("Battle Light")

In the Old English epic *Beowulf*, the titular hero wields the sword Hrunting, given to him by Unferth, a thane of King Hrothgar. Hrunting is described as an ancient and rare iron blade, galvanized in venom and covered with "ill-brooding patterns"; its hilt has snake imagery. Although Hrunting had never failed its wielder in battle, it proved useless against Grendel's mother. Despite its ineffectiveness, Beowulf sang the praises of the sword when he returned it.

Sources: Davidson, *The Sword in Anglo-Saxon England*, 129, 131, 142, 144; Pendergrass, *Mythological Swords*, 3

Huldraslaat

Variation: Huldras Laat

Norwegian fairy lore says the name of the music of the fay is Huldraslaat; it is played in a minor key and produces a dull and mournful sound.

Sources: Keightley, *World Guide to Gnomes, Fairies, Elves, and Other Little People*, 79; von Wildenbruch, *Poet Lore*, Volume 3, 183

Hulidshjalmr (HUL-iths-hyahlm-r)

In Norse mythology, the helm Hulidshjalmr ("Helm of Invisibility"/"Secret Helm"), created by the dwarfs, allows its wearer to become invisible.

Sources: Eliasson and Jahr, *Language and Its Ecology*, 441; Norroena Society, *Asatru Edda*, 364

Hungr (HUNG-r)

In Norse mythology, Hel, the goddess of the underworld, has an enormous hall named ELJUD-NIR ("Preparer of Pain"/"Sprayed with Snow-storms"), which is fully decorated with many named items. The name of her dish is Hungr ("Hunger").

Sources: Byock, *The Prose Edda*, 34; Norroena Society, *Satr Edda*, 365; Thorpe, *Northern Mythology*, 50

Hvergelur Well (VER-gehlm-ir)

Variations: Hveigilmer, Hvengelmir, Hvergel-men, Hvergelmer Well, Hvergelmin, Hwergelmr, Kvergjelme, Vergelmir

In Norse mythology, Hvergelur Well ("Bubbling Kettle"/"Roaring Kettle") was the well located near the center of Niflheimr, beneath the Grotti (World Mill); it was from here that the river Elivagar flowed and nourished the northern roots of the tree YGGDRASIL. The well was said to give those who drank from it endurance.

Sources: Grimes, *The Norse Myths*, 282; Norroena Society, *Asatru Edda*, 365; Orchard, *Dictionary of Norse Myth and Legend*, 93

Hvitingr (VEET-ing-r)

Variation: Hwytingus

In *Kormaks saga*, Bersi, one of the two husbands of Steingerd, wields a sword by the name of Hvitingr ("the White" or "Whitting"); in its pommel is the life-stone, a magical stone that has the ability to heal any wound caused by the blade.

Sources: Davidson, *The Sword in Anglo-Saxon England*, 177; Eddison, *Egil's Saga*, 281; Norroena Society, *Asatru Edda*, 365

ichor

In ancient Greek mythology, the gods, their horses, and a few of their favorite mortals did not consume the food of the mortal world, but rather a substance known as AMBROSIA (as well as the food offered up to them in sacrifice). The properties of AMBROSIA caused the gods to stop aging once they reached physical maturity, granting them immortality as long as they continued to regularly consume AMBROSIA. This diet caused the bodies of the gods to be physically different from those of mortals; rather than blood flowing through their veins, they had a type of immortal fluid known as ichor—thinner than human blood and almost colorless. In addition to immortality, it grants a bounding heart and joy. The most popular story involving ichor was the tale of TALOS, the gigantic bronze automaton created to guard the coastline of Crete.

Sources: Hansen, *Classical Mythology*, 35, 101, 145; Nardo, *Greek and Roman Mythology*, 156; Shahan, *Myths and Legends*, 167

Indraastra

Variation: Indra Astra

In Hindu mythology, an ASTRA is a supernatural weapon created or gifted by the gods to someone who then presides over the weapon. The wielder of an ASTRA is known as an astradhari.

Indraastra was an ASTRA from Indra, the god of the heavens, lightning, rains, river flows, storms, and *vajra* ("thunder"). Indraastra was said to have the ability to bring about a "shower" of arrows from the sky. According to the Indian epic *Mahabharata*, during the battle between Ashvatthama and the heroic archer Arjuna ("Spotless and Shining like Silver"), Ashvatthama used Indraastra, which shot a web of arrows out over the Pandava army. In retaliation, Arjuna used his own ASTRA, MAHENDRA, which neutralized Indraastra's effect.

Sources: Edizioni, *Vimanas and the Wars of the Gods*, n.p.; Kotru and Zutshi, *Karna*, n.p.

invisibility stone of the tokoloshe, the

The Xhosa people of Lesotho, Africa, have in their folklore a vampiric creature known as a tokoloshe, which is said to make an excellent familiar for a witch. Always male, these baboon-like, hairy, and short creatures have the ability to use magic to create a magical stone that will allow them to become invisible at will. The tokoloshe will keep the stone hidden in its mouth at all times. If the creature can be destroyed, the stone makes for a valuable prize.

Sources: Broster, *Amagqirha*, 60; Knappert, *Bantu Myths and Other Tales*, 173-74; Mack, *Field Guide to Demons*, 35; Scobie, *Murder for Magic*, 80-82; St. John, *Through Malan's Africa*, 152-53

Ir

In the Irish epic *Tain Bo Cuailnge* (*The Cattle Raid of Cooley*/*The Tain*), Ir was presumably the sword of Cordere, as it is described only as "angry" (a characteristic attributed to a weapon). Ir is named as being among the many cups, drinking horns, goblets, javelins, shields, and swords kept in Tete Brec, one of the three households of the Ulster hero Cuhullin (Cu Chulaind/Cu Chulainn/Cuchulainn).

Sources: Kinsella and Le Brocquy, *The Tain*, 5

Isarnkol (EES-arn-kawl)

In Norse mythology, Isarnkol ("Ice-Cold Iron") was the bellows or the cooling substance (sources conflict) used to cool down Alsvin and Aarvak, the horses who pulled Sol's sun chariot across the sky.

Sources: Grimes, *The Norse Myths*, 282; Norroena Society, *Asatru Edda*, 366

Jacob's ladder

As described in the book of Genesis, this is a ladder that stands upon the earth but ascends to the Gate of Heaven, which is flanked by angels. The biblical patriarch Jacob claimed to have seen this ladder in a vision sent to him by God.

Sources: Ryken et al., *Dictionary of Biblical Imagery*, 433

Jana, al

According to Islamic mythology, the prophet Muhammad owned a quiver at the time of his death by the name of al Jana ("the Collection"); beyond its name, nothing else is known of it.

Sources: Sale et al., *An Universal History, Part 2*, Volume 1, 185

Jarngreipr

Variations: Iarn Greiper, Iarngreiper, Jarnglofar ("Iron Gauntlets"), Jarn-Greiper

In Norse mythology, Jarngreipr ("Iron Gripper") was the name of the iron gauntlets belonging to the god of thunder, Thor; they, along with the belt of strength, MEGINGJARDAR, were a gift from the *asynjr* (female Jotun, or giant) Gridr to assist him in thwarting the plot of (and then killing) Geirrod.

With these items, not only was Thor able to throw his hammer, MJOLNIR, at his enemies, but the hammer would also return to him. Jarngreipr was essential in wielding the hammer because MJOLNIR was created with its handle too short; Jarngreipr compensated for this shortcoming. The other prized possessions of Thor were GRIDARVOLR and MEGINGJARDAR.

When Geirrod threw a glowing hot iron at Thor, the god of thunder was able to catch it without hurting his hands because he was wearing Jarngreipr at the time. Although Geirrod was hiding behind an iron pillar, Thor threw the hot iron back at him, striking and killing him.

Sources: Grimes, *The Norse Myths*, 272, 284; Norroena Society, *Asatru Edda*, 353; Norroena Society, *Satr Edda*, 25; Orchard, *Dictionary of Norse Myth and Legend*, 10; Simek, *Dictionary of Northern Mythology*, 178

jars of fluid, the

In medieval French folklore, the jars of fluid were the last two of their kind; they had allegedly been used on Christ. The fluid was said to have magical properties that could cure any illness and close any wound. The Saracen (Muslim) giant Fierabras (Fierbras), son of the giant Balan, stole the jars when he sacked the city of Rome with his father. Ultimately, Fierabras was defeated by Oliveros, who gave the balm to Charlemagne so it could be returned to Rome.

Sources: Daniels and Stevens, *Encyclopedia of Superstitions, Folklore, and the Occult Sciences of the World*, Volume 2, 1376; Mancing, *Cervantes Encyclopedia: A–K*, 57, 294; Rose, *Giants, Monsters, and Dragons*, 37–38

javelin of Procris, the

Artemis (Roman goddess Diana), the goddess of children, hunting, virginity, unmarried girls, and wild animals from classical Greek mythology, gave two gifts to Procris, the daughter of King Thespius, on her wedding day to see whether it would cause a rift between Procris and her new husband, Cephalus. The first gift was Laelaps, a hunting dog so swift it could catch any game it was sent after; the other gift was a magical javelin that, when thrown, would never miss its mark. The Roman poet Ovid (Publius Ovidius Naso) describes the javelin as being made of a strange-looking wood and tipped in gold. He also states that the javelin will return to its thrower after a successful strike.

Sources: Ovid, *The Essential Metamorphoses*, 92–93; Westmoreland, *Ancient Greek Beliefs*, 761

jenglot

Depending on which source is consulted, a jenglot of Malaysian lore is either an actual vampiric creature or a magical item with vampiric needs.

In the case of the jenglot being an undead creature, this unique species begins its existence about the size of a doll; over time it will grow to human proportions as it consumes blood. This creature is described as having conjoined feet and a skeletal face. Some people claim to keep a jenglot as a "pet."

jewels of Ryujin

The other school of thought on the jenglot claims it is a magical creation, a fetish doll that is symbolic of the langsuir or the pontianak (two species of regional vampires).

In either case, the jenglot is fed a diet of blood; although animal blood is said to be acceptable, lore claims that the owners of one of these creatures (or items) can purchase human blood from the Red Cross. The jenglot does not consume the blood in a traditional manner; rather, it magically absorbs the necessary unlife-giving properties from the blood through an invisible and highly mystical means. After the blood has been "consumed," it is rendered useless for any other purpose.

Sources: Maberry and Kramer, *They Bite*, 76; Sherman, *Vampires*, 72

jewels of Ryujin, the

A dragon king from Japanese mythology, Ryujin was a gigantic creature said to be a beautiful shade of deep blue; he was so magnificent to behold that no human could look upon him in his full majesty and survive the experience. Among his possessions, Ryujin owned magical jewels that allowed him to control the weather.

Sources: Andrews, *Dictionary of Nature Myths*, 165; Barber and Riches, *Dictionary of Fabulous Beasts*, 125; Niles, *Dragons*, 77–78; Rose, *Giants, Monsters, and Dragons*, 312

Jiuchidingpa

In the classic Chinese tale *Journey to the West*, Zhu Bajie ("Eight Prohibitions") is one of the characters who assist the Buddhist monk Xuanzang on his journey to claim and return with the Buddhist sutras. Zhu Bajie (Zhu the Pig/Zhu Wuneng) carries as his weapon Jiuchidingpa ("Nine-Tooth Iron Rake"), a rake or spear (depending on the translation).

Sources: Huang, *Snakes' Legs*, 61; Wu, *Journey to the West*, 72, 176; Wu, *Monkey King's Amazing Adventures*, n.p.

Jokulsnaut

The sword of Grettir Asmundarson, the outlaw hero of the Icelandic tale *Grettis saga* (dating to the thirteenth and fourteenth centuries), Jokulsnaut was used to defeat a *draugr* ("after-goer"—a type of vampiric revenant). According to the story, when Grettir descends into the tomb of Karr the Old to plunder the burial treasure, he is attacked by the "howedweller" Karr. A long and dramatic battle ensues, but, in the end, Grettir is able to draw Jokulsnaut and behead the creature, the only means by which it can be destroyed.

Sources: Lecouteux, *The Return of the Dead*, n.p.; Redfern and Steiger, *The Zombie Book*, 126–27

Joyeuse

Variations: Fusberta Joiuse, Joyean, Joyense

Traditionally, Joyeuse ("Joyous") is the name given to the personal sword of Charlemagne. Legend claims that the pommel was forged to contain a bit of the BLEEDING LANCE; other lore asserts that the sword was made of the same materials as DURANDAL and COURTAIN. The *Song of Roland* (*La Chanson de Roland*, circa 1040–1115) describes Joyeuse as unmatched in beauty and "chang[ing] colors thirty times a day."

In *The Legend of Croquemitaine*, the celebrated swordsmith Galas created three swords: FLAMBERGE, HALTECLERE, and Joyeuse. Each sword took three years to make, and each was eventually used to test the edge of the sword GLORIOUS, which managed to hack into each of them.

Sources: Brewer, *Dictionary of Phrase and Fable* 1900, 1197; Evangelista, *The Encyclopedia of the Sword*, 577; L'Epine, *The Days of Chivalry*, n.p.; Pendergrass, *Mythological Swords*, 48–49

Kabeirian horses

Variations: Cabeirian horses, Hippoi Cabeirici, Hippoi Kabeiroi, the horses of the Cabeiri

In ancient Greek mythology, AUTOMATONS ("self-acting") were statues of animals, humans, and monsters that were then animated or otherwise brought to a kind of life by one of the gods; usually this was done by Hephaistos (Hephaestus; Roman god Vulcan), the god of bindings, the art of sculpture, fire, forges, metalworking, stonemasonry, and talismans. Other AUTOMATONS were the CAUCASIAN EAGLE, the GOLDEN MAIDENS, the GOLDEN TRIPODS, the KELEDONES, KHRYSEOS AND ARGYREOS, the KOLKHIS BULLS, and TALOS.

Hephaistos created four bronze horse AUTOMATONS to pull the ADAMANTINE chariot of his sons, collectively known as the Kabeiroi; the son named Eurymedon was the driver. The horses made a dry whinny and shot fire from their mouths.

Sources: Bonnefoy, *Greek and Egyptian Mythologies*, 88–89; Westmoreland, *Ancient Greek Beliefs*, 54

Kadib, al

Variation: al Mokhazzem ("the Piercing")

According to Islamic mythology, the prophet Muhammad owned a collection of nine different swords at the time of his death: al ADHAB, al Battar (see BATTER), Dhu'l Fakar (see DHUAL-FIRQAR), al Hatf (see Hatel), al Kadib, Kolaite, Mabur, al Mehdham, and al Rofub. Beyond its name, nothing else is known of the sword al Kadib ("the Thin").

Sources: Sale et al., *An Universal History, Part 2*, Volume 1, 184

Kagami

Variation: Yata no Kagami

In Japanese mythology, Kagami was a mirror used to entice the goddess of the sun, Amaterasu O Mi Kami, out of the cave Ame-no-Iwato ("Sky Rock Cave"). The goddess Ame-no-uzume-no-Mikoto (also known as Ama-no-Uzume, or "Heavenly Alarming Female") placed Kagami and a necklace named Yasakani no Magatama in the branches of a nearby tree and performed a frenzied dance so seductive, wild, and humorous that it caused the gods watching to laugh uproariously, creating curiosity in Amaterasu O Mi Kami. When she came out to see who the beautiful woman was, she caught sight of her own reflection in Kagami.

Sources: Coulter and Turner, *Encyclopedia of Ancient Deities*, 40, 241

kakh

In Iranian lore, there was a gigantic bird known as a simurgh that lived upon Mount Albur; it was said to be the guardian spirit of Rustam and Zal. The nest of this creature is known as a kakh; it is made of columns of aloe wood, ebony, and sandalwood.

Sources: Houtsma et al., *The Encyclopaedia of Islam*, 427; Rosen, *Mythical Creatures Bible*, 152

Kaladanda

Variations: Kala-Danda, the staff of Death

In Hindu mythology, Kaladanda—an especially lethal and ferocious club—was the weapon of Yama, the god of Naraka; it was given to him by Brahma, the god of creation. The power of Kaladanda was quite remarkable, as it could kill anyone it struck, no matter what boons had been granted to the target. This weapon was so powerful that even the sight of it was fatal, as anyone who saw it would die within the hour.

Sources: Smith, *Hinduism*, n.p.; Venkatesananda, *The Concise Ramayana of Valmiki*, 364

Kalichi

In Hindu and Vedic mythology, Kalichi is the huge palace where the god of death, Yama, lives; it is located in the city of Yamapuri in Pitriloka. It is here that Yama sits upon his throne of judgment, Vichara-bhu.

Sources: Dalal, *Religions of India*, 398; Dowson, *Classical Dictionary of Hindu Mythology and Religion*, 374

Kalpa Tarou

Variations: Kalpadruma, Kalpapadapa, Kalpataru, Kalpavriksha

There is a mythical tree in Indian lore from which a person may gather whatever they desire; this tree, created during the Samudra Manthan ("Churning of the Ocean"), is known as the Kalpa Tarou ("Tree of Imagination").

Sources: Brewer, *Dictionary of Phrase and Fable 1900*, 623; Scatcherd, *A Dictionary of Polite Literature*, Volume 2, 87

kantele of Vainamoinen, the

Variation: vinens

In Finnish mythology, the mage Vainamoinen created a zither-like musical instrument by using the jawbone from a giant pike and some hairs from the mane of his stallion, Hiisi; the instrument was called a kantele. When Vainamoinen played it, the music he created was so wonderful that it drew the attention of the animals of the forest, the birds of the sky, and the fish of the sea; every man, woman, and child gathered near to hear the beautiful music. Even Vainamoinen himself was brought to tears, and each teardrop that landed in the water was transformed into a pearl.

Sources: Pentikainen, *Kalevala Mythology*, 55; Seal, *Encyclopedia of Folk Heroes*, 259

Kasthuba

Variation: Kaustubha

The Kasthuba was one of the items created as a result of the Samudra Manthan ("Churning of the Ocean") of Hindu mythology. Described as a radiantly beautiful gem, the Kasthuba is located in the chest of the god Narayana.

Sources: Sutton, *Religious Doctrines in the Mahabharata*, 148, 152

Kaumodaki

In Hindu lore, the god of preservation, Vishnu, carries a *gada* (a blunt mace or club made of wood or metal) named Kaumodaki in one of his four hands; it was given to him by Varuna, the god of justice, sky, truth, and water. As it was swung through the air, the weapon roared like *vajra* ("thunder") and was capable of killing daityas. Kaumodaki is personified as a woman named Gadadevi (Gadanari).

Keledones

Sources: Gonda, *Aspects of Early Visnuism*, 99; Iyer, *Bhasa*, n.p.; Krishna, *The Book of Vishnu*, 17, 18, 19, 25, 26

Keledones, the

Variations: Iynges, Keledones Khryseai (Golden Celedones)

In ancient Greek mythology, AUTOMATONS ("self-acting") were statues of animals, humans, and monsters that were then animated or otherwise brought to a kind of life by one of the gods; usually this was done by Hephaistos (Hephaestus; Roman god Vulcan), the god of bindings, the art of sculpture, fire, forges, metalworking, stonemasonry, and talismans. Other AUTOMATONS were the CAUCASIAN EAGLE, the GOLDEN MAIDENS, the GOLDEN TRIPODS, the KABEIRIAN HORSES, KHRYSEOS AND ARGYREOS, the KOLKHIS BULLS, and TALOS.

Created by Hephaistos, the Keledones ("Charmers") were a choir of six female singers that stood in the bronze temple of Athena (Roman goddess Minerva), the goddess of crafts, military victories, war, and wisdom. The Keledones would entrance men when they sang and have a deleterious effect on them. Some older sources claim that the Keledones also played the lyre and liken them to the Sirens.

Sources: Bonnefoy, *Greek and Egyptian Mythologies*, 88–89; Gilhuly and Worman, *Space, Place, and Landscape in Ancient Greek Literature and Culture*, 46–47; Millingen, *Ancient Unedited Monuments Illustrated and Explained*, 30, 31; Westmoreland, *Ancient Greek Beliefs*, 54

Kema

In Arabic folklore, *Kema* is the name of the book that allegedly holds the secrets of the djinn (genie). Because these creatures were fascinated by the concept of love, they shared with mankind the marvels of nature; for this act, they were damned.

Sources: Brewer, *Dictionary of Phrase and Fable* 1900, 472

kenne

According to European folklore, a kenne is a stone said to form in the eye of a stag; once extracted, it is believed to be a powerful antidote to poisons.

Sources: Brewer, *Dictionary of Phrase and Fable* 1900, 472

keris of Mpu Gandring, the

Variations: Kris Mpu Gandring

In Indonesian folktales, a legendary keris (or kris—a type of dagger) was forged by the famous eleventh-century dagger maker Mpu Gandring. According to the tale, the weapon was commissioned by a man named Ken Arok so he could kill Tunggll Amrtung and marry his exceptionally beautiful wife, Ken Dedes, who, it had been foretold, would be the mother of a line of kings. Mpu Gandring took the commission and promised the blade would be ready within a year, but Ken Arok, an impatient man, returned in five months. The keris had been shaped and was powerful enough to be considered an exceptional weapon, but Mpu Gandring insisted he needed more time to layer in additional magic and spells to ensure that it did not become an evil weapon. Ken Arok took the keris and killed Mpu Gandring, but before he died, the artisan used his last breath to curse the weapon so that it would slay his murderer and seven generations of his lineage. In the end, however, the keris did not take the lives of any of Ken Arok's descendants, though it was involved in the murders of six people before it went missing.

Sources: Khan, *The Malay Ancient Kingdoms*, n.p.; Muljana, *A Story of Majapahit*, 15–17

kettle of Medea, the

Variations: caldron of Medea, potion of Medea

In classical Greek mythology, Medea (the daughter of King Aeetes of Colchis, niece of Circe, priestess of the goddess Hecate, and a sorceress) possessed a magical kettle. A skilled herbalist, she—at the request of her husband, Jason—drained the blood of his aged father Aeson and, after boiling it in her kettle with certain herbs, returned it to his body; this process restored Aeson to his youth. The daughters of the aged and failing Pelias, Aeson's murderous brother, wished to do the same for their father. Medea bade them to kill him and boil his body in her kettle. The daughters did as she said, but Medea did not utilize her magic kettle or special herbs, assisting her husband in gaining the revenge he sought against Pelias for murdering so many members of his family. Consequently, Pelias's body was consumed by flames and deprived of a proper burial.

Sources: Lempriere, *Bibliotheca Classica*, 737–38; Westmoreland, *Ancient Greek Beliefs*, 761–62; Williams, *Chambers's New Handy Volume American Encyclopædia*, Volume 7, 964–65

Kherna, al

According to Islamic mythology, the prophet Muhammad owned at least seven cuirasses (a piece of armor made of a breastplate and back-plate hinged or otherwise fastened together) at the time of his death; their names were al BETRA, DHAT AL FODHUL, DHAT AL HAWAFHI, DHAT AL WELHAL, al FADDO, al Kherna, and al SA'ADIA. Beyond its name and the fact that it was covered with hare fur, nothing else is known of al Kherna.

Sources: Osborne et al., *A Complete History of the Arabs*, Volume 1, 254; Sale et al., *An Universal History, Part 2*, Volume 1, 185

Khryseos and Argyreos

Variations: KUON KHRYSEOS and Kuon Argyreos, Kuones Khryseos and Kuones Argyreos ("Gold and Silver Dogs")

In ancient Greek mythology, AUTOMATONS ("self-acting") were statues of animals, humans, and monsters that were then animated or otherwise brought to a kind of life by one of the gods; usually this was done by Hephaistos (Hephaestus; Roman god Vulcan), the god of bindings, the art of sculpture, fire, forges, metalworking, stonemasonry, and talismans. Other AUTOMATONS were the CAUCASIAN EAGLE, the GOLDEN MAIDENS, the GOLDEN TRIPODS, the KABEIRIAN HORSES, the KELEDONES, the KOLKHIS BULLS, and TALOS.

Crafted to be guardians, Khryseos ("Golden") and Argyreos ("Silvery"), a pair of ageless gold and silver dogs, were given to King Alkinous to watch over his palace, which was the resting place of the golden jar that housed the bones of the demigod and hero Achilles.

Sources: Bonnefoy, *Greek and Egyptian Mythologies*, 88–89; Seymour, *Life in the Homeric Age*, 433; Westmoreland, *Ancient Greek Beliefs*, 54

kibisis

In ancient Greek mythology, the kibisis ("wallet") was the sack carried by Hermes (Roman god Mercury), the god of animal husbandry, commerce, eloquence, fertility, language, looters, luck, sleep, thieves, trade, travel, and wealth. The demigod and hero Perseus also used the kibisis to carry the severed head of the Gorgon Medusa; inside of this deep leather pouch, the severed head lost all of its power, as it could neither see nor be seen by a victim.

Sources: Garber and Vickers, *The Medusa Reader*, 24, 224; Smith and Brown, *The Complete Idiot's Guide to World Mythology*, 240

kirtle of the giant of Saint Michael's Mount, the

Described as a *kirtke* (coat) emblazoned with gems and beautifully embroidered with the beard-hair of the 15 kings whom the giant of Saint Michael's Mount had vanquished, this garment and the giant's iron club were taken as trophies by King Arthur after he slew the giant (see CLUB OF IRON OF THE GIANT OF SAINT MICHAEL'S MOUNT).

Sources: Karr, *Arthurian Companion*, 115

kladenets

Variations: samosek, samosyok

In Russian and Slavic fairy tales and folklore, there are often references to magical swords, but unlike in other cultures, these weapons are not given names; rather, they are simply called *kladenets* ("made of steel" or "self-swinging sword"). These special swords, wielded by heroes, are oftentimes said to be magical, but seldom are specific abilities or properties given.

Sources: Afanasyev, *Russian Folktales from the Collection of A. Afanasyev*, 157

knife of Llawfrodedd Farchof, the

In British and Welsh folklore, there is a series of items (always thirteen in number) called the THIRTEEN TREASURES OF THE ISLAND OF BRITAIN (in Welsh, they are called *Tri Thlws ar Ddeg Ynys Prydain*). Although in more modern times the items listed are different, the original thirteen items from the fifteenth century were the CAULDRON OF DYRNWCH THE GIANT, CHARIOT OF MORGAN MWYNFAWR, CHESSBOARD OF GWENDDOLEU AP CEIDIO, COAT OF PADARN BEISRUDD, CROCK AND DISH OF RHYGENYDD YSGOLHAIG (two items), HALTER OF CLYDNO EIDDYN, HAMPER OF GWYDDNO GARANHIR, HORN OF BRAN GALED, knife of Llawfrodedd Farchof, MANTLE OF ARTHUR IN CORNWALL, sword of Rhydderch Hael (DYRNWYN), and WHETSTONE OF TUDWAL TUDGLYD.

Llawfrodedd ("Melancholy" or "Sadness") Farchof is mentioned only in passing in the Arthurian tales *Culhwch and Olwen* and *The Dream of Rhonabwy*, in which he appears in Arthur's retinue as an advisor. The knife of Llawfrodedd Farchof (in Welsh, *Cyllell Llawfrodedd Farchog*) is not a weapon, but rather a serving utensil; it had the magical ability to serve twenty-four people at one time.

Kodandam

Sources: Dom, *King Arthur and the Gods of the Round Table*, 111, 255; Patton, *The Poet's Ogam*, 510; Pendergrass, *Mythological Swords*, 24, 26

Kodandam

Variation: bow of Rama

In Hindu mythology, Kodandam was Rama's bow; it was said to be as "sturdy as a diamond," a reference to the stiffness of the bow and the strength that would be required to draw back the bowstring.

Sources: Hande and Kampar, *Kamba Ramayanam*, 50

Kolaite

Variation: Kola'ite

According to Islamic mythology, the prophet Muhammad owned a collection of nine different swords at the time of his death: al ADHAB, al Battar (see BATTER), Dhu'l Fakar (see DHUAL-FIRQAR), al Hatf (see HATEL), al KADIB, Kolaite, MABUR, al MEHDHAM, and al ROFUB. Kolaite was named after the city of Kola, famed for its excellent swords.

Sources: Sale et al., *An Universal History, Part 2*, Volume 1, 184

Kolkhis Bulls, the

Variations: Colchis Bulls, Khalkotauroi, Tauroi Khalkeoi (Bronze Bulls)

In ancient Greek mythology, AUTOMATONS ("self-acting") were statues of animals, humans, and monsters that were then animated or otherwise brought to a kind of life by one of the gods; usually this was done by Hephaistos (Hephaestus; Roman god Vulcan), the god of bindings, the art of sculpture, fire, forges, metalworking, stonemasonry, and talismans. Other AUTOMATONS were the CAUCASIAN EAGLE, the GOLDEN MAIDENS, the GOLDEN TRIPODS, the KABEIRIAN HORSES, the KELEDONES, KHRYSEOS AND ARGYREOS, and TALOS.

The Kolkhis Bulls were sculpted out of bronze with flaming hooves and the ability to breath fire; they lived in an underground lair beneath the Field of Ares, a four-acre plot of land; located upon this field was a plow of silver with a bronze harness. In order to obtain the GOLDEN FLEECE, the Greek hero Jason needed to wrestle the two bulls into the harness and have them plow the Field of Ares so he could sow the field with DRAGON TEETH.

Sources: Apollonius, *Argonautica*, 116; Bonnefoy, *Greek and Egyptian Mythologies*, 88–89; Bruce, *Jason and the Argonauts*, 106–7; Hunter, *Argonautica of Apollonius*, 16; Westmoreland, *Ancient Greek Beliefs*, 54

Kongo

In Japanese mythology, Kongo ("Diamond") was the trident-like staff that belonged to the mountain god Koya-no-Myojin. This item had the magical ability to not only emit a bright light but also grant the gift of insight and wisdom.

Sources: Knappert, *Pacific Mythology*, 159

Kor (KUHR)

Variation: Sickness

In Norse mythology, Hel, the goddess of the underworld, has an enormous hall named ELJUDNIR ("Preparer of Pain"/"Sprayed with Snowstorms"), which is fully decorated with many named items. Kor ("Sick Bed") is the name of her bed; its curtains are named BLIKJANDABOL.

Sources: Daly, *Norse Mythology A to Z*, 21; Norroena Society, *Asatru Edda*, 369

Krisaswas

Variation: Krisasva

An ASTRA described in the ancient Sanskrit epics *Mahabharata* and the *Ramayana*, Krisaswas was the most powerful of the AGNEYASTRA. As described in the *Ramayana*, Krisaswas was alive and had been endowed with intelligence.

Sources: Blavatsky, *The Theosophical Glossary*, 180

Kuon Khryseos

Variations: Cyon Chryseus, Golden Dog, Golden Hound

A golden dog from ancient Greek mythology, Kuon Khryseos was created by the Kouretes Daktylo (daimones, spirits) for the Titan Rhea so it might be the guardian of the goat Amalthea as it nursed the infant Zeus (Roman god Jupiter), the god of fate, kings, lightning, sky, and thunder. After the Titanomachy (the war against the Titans), Zeus assigned the canine to watch over his sanctuary in Crete. Kuon Khryseos was then stolen by Pandareos and taken to Mount Sipylos to be held in safekeeping by Tantalos. When Zeus discovered the theft, he found the two collaborators together; Pandareos was transformed into a pillar of stone where he stood and Mount Sipylos was picked up and brought crashing down on Tantalos's head.

Sources: Graves, *The Greek Myths*, 26; Smith, *A Classical Dictionary of Greek and Roman Biography, Mythology and Geography*, 853; Trzaskoma et al., *Anthology of Classical Myth*, 14–15

Kusanagi-no-Tsurugi

Variations: Ama-no-Murakumo-no-Tsurugi ("Sword of the Gathering Clouds of Heaven"), Kusanagi, Tsumugari no Tachi

In Japanese mythology, the legendary Kusanagi-no-Tsurugi was originally the sword of the god of sea and storms, Susanoo (Susanowo/Susa-no-wo no Mikoto). He used his sword WOROCHI NO ARA-MASA to slay the gigantic eight-headed serpent of Koshi, Yamata-no-Orochi. While dismembering the serpent, Susanoo discovered another sword within the creature's fourth tail; he named the weapon Ama-no-Murakumo-no-Tsurugi and made a gift of it to his consort and sister, the goddess of the sun, Amaterasu O Mi Kami, to settle an old grievance between them. Eventually, Okuni-Nushi, their son, tricked his father and gained possession of the sword.

Many generations later, the sword was said to pass on to the great warrior Yamoto Takeru. When he had been trapped by a warlord in an open field that was set ablaze, Yamoto used the sword to desperately cut back the grass; in doing so, he discovered that he was able to control the direction and speed of the wind and used this knowledge to turn the fire back against his would-be assassin. To commemorate his victory, Yamoto renamed the weapon Kusanagi-no-Tsurugi ("Grass Cutting Sword").

Sources: Aston, *Nihongi*, 56; Pendergrass, *Mythological Swords*, 50; Smith and Brown, *The Complete Idiot's Guide to World Mythology*, 29

Kvad Galdra

In Norse mythology, Kvad Galdra was the song used to summon the dead in order to gain their knowledge.

Sources: Grimes, *The Norse Myths*, 284

kvikudropar (KVIK-u-drawp-ar)

In Norse mythology, kvikudropar ("Poison Drops") is the frozen water from the rivers of Elivagar; it is described as looking like a slag of cinders spilling from a furnace. Layer by layer, the kvikudropar grew and eventually formed Ginnungagap. According to the myth, when the kvikudropar of Elivagar and the warm winds of Muspellsheimr met, the kvikudropar melted in tiny droplets that slowly accumulated and, over time, because of the heat, *likandi* or "came alive," forming the first giant, Ymir ("Groaner"; Aurgelmir).

Sources: Norroena Society, *Asatru Edda*, 1, 3, 369; Ross, *Prolonged Echoes*, 155

La Ok Litr

In Norse mythology, La Ok Litr ("Blood and Healthy Hue") was the gift Ve gave to Askr and Emble.

Sources: Grimes, *The Norse Myths*, 284

Laedingr (LAITH-ing-r)

Variations: Ladine, Laeding, Leding, Leuthing, Loeding, Loedingr

In Norse mythology, Laedingr ("Cunningly Binding") was the first ADAMANTINE chain forged in Asgard ("Enclosure of the Aesir") by the god of thunder, Thor, in his attempt to bind and hold the son of the god Loki known as Fenriswulf (Fenerriswulf/Fenrissulfrin); it failed. The other chain created for the same purpose was DROMI; it, too, was forged by Thor, and it also failed. However, GLEIPNIR, a rope woven by the dwarfs, was successful.

Sources: Anderson, *Norse Mythology*, 452; Grimes, *The Norse Myths*, 284; Hawthorne, *Vikings*, 20; Lindow, *Handbook of Norse Mythology*, 145; Norroena Society, *Asatru Edda*, 369

Laeradr

Variation: Laerad

In Norse mythology, Laeradr ("Giving Protection") was the primary tree growing in VALHALLA, the hall of Odin, the god of battle, death, frenzy, the gallows, healing, knowledge, poetry, royalty, the runic alphabet, sorcery, and wisdom; it is often identified with YGGDRASIL. The she-goat Heidrun eats the needles of this tree, causing her to produce enough milk to fill a *tun* (130 gallons; 491 liters) every day. The hart Eikthyrnir also eats from the branches of Laeradr, and, in doing so, his horns drip so much water as to create a river.

Sources: Grimes, *The Norse Myths*, 284

Laevateinn

A sword from Norse mythology, Laevateinn ("Devious Twig"/"Guileful Twig") belonged to the god Loki; beneath NAGRINDR ("Corpse Gate"), he carved magical runes upon the weapon to increase its power. Laevateinn is the only weapon that can slay Gullinkambi ("Goldcomb"; Vidofnir), the rooster that will alert the *einherjar* ("lone fighters"—the spirits of brave warriors who died in battle), gods, and heroes as Ragnarok begins. The giantess Sinmora (Sinmara), wife of Surtr, is the guardian of the sword; she will only release it from her protection if she is presented with the tail feathers of Gullinkambi—a paradox.

Lafing

Sources: Crossley-Holland, *The Norse Myths*, 124; Frankel, *From Girl to Goddess*, 49; Gray et al., *The Mythology of All Races*, Volume 2, 136; Grimes, *The Norse Myths*, 284; Hawthorne, *Vikings*, 20; Loptson, *Playing with Fire*, n.p.; Welch, *Goddess of the North*, 60

Lafing

A sword named in the Old English epic *Beowulf*, Lafing ("Battle Flasher") was the weapon that the half-Dane rebel chief Hun (Hunlaf) presented to Hengest as a symbol of Hengest's newly sworn allegiance to Hun as well as his breaking of the oath given to Finn. However, in a different interpretation of this passage, Hengest was slain by Hun, a follower of Finn, with the sword Lafing.

Sources: Child, *Beowulf and the Finnesburh Fragment*, 31, 91; Olrik, *The Heroic Legends of Denmark*, Volume 4, 524; Sedgefield, *Beowulf*, 122

Lagulf

In the *Thidrekssaga* (*Saga of Thiethrek*, circa 1205), the tale of the German hero Thidrek, Lagulf was the sword of Hildebrand, Thidrek's old master-at-arms. This is the sword Hildebrand uses to kill Gernoz.

Sources: Anderson, *The Saga of the Völsungs*, 223; Hatto, *The Nibelungenlied*, 338

lamp of Aladdin, the

Variations: Aladdin's lamp, Aladdin's wonderful lamp, magic lamp

Originating in a Middle Eastern folktale and popularized in a story appearing in the book *Tales of Sheherazade, or A Thousand and One Nights*, the magical lamp of Aladdin was a wondrous item. Although there are many versions of the tale, basically Aladdin and his mother are poor people living in "one of the cities of China"; one day they are met by a man claiming to be the long-lost brother of Aladdin's late father. The stranger befriends them and requests Aladdin's assistance with an unusual task. He loans the boy a magic ring and convinces him to enter a strange cave to retrieve an oil lamp whose flame burns red, white, and yellow. In his greed and haste to double-cross the boy, the stranger accidently traps Aladdin inside the cave with the lamp. Wringing his hands in worry, Aladdin inadvertently rubs the magic ring on the lamp and frees the djinn (genie) trapped in the ring; this magical being frees him from the cave. Aladdin returns home with the lamp; his mother takes it to clean so they can sell it to buy food and releases the powerful djinn who is bound to the lamp. By use of the djinn of the lamp, Aladdin becomes powerful and rich; he also marries the sultan's beautiful daughter, Princess Badroulbadour. The djinn has the ability to make endless amounts of precious gems, create magnificent palaces, summon loyal servants, and give quality advice.

When the stranger hears of Aladdin's good fortune, he returns and tricks the princess (who is unaware of the power of the lamp) into giving it to him. The stranger then ruins Aladdin's life and undoes all the splendor he once held; fortunately, with the aid of the lesser djinn from the magic ring, the cunning princess uses her "womanly wiles" to recapture the lamp and kills the stranger.

In the climax, the stranger's older and more evil brother seeks out Aladdin to avenge his sibling's death; he begins by tricking the princess and capturing her. Fortunately, the djinn of the lamp warns Aladdin of the murderous plot and assists him in killing this would-be assassin. In the end, Aladdin and the princess are reunited and Aladdin inherits the throne of his father-in-law.

Sources: *Library of Famous Fiction*, 954–1019; Marzolph, *The Arabian Nights in Transnational Perspective*, 331–41

Lamthapad

In the Irish epic *Tain Bo Cuailnge* (*The Cattle Raid of Cooley/The Tain*), Lamthapad ("Swift to Hand") was the sword—or possibly the shield or spear—of Conall Cernach; it is named as being among the many cups, drinking horns, goblets, javelins, shields, and swords kept in Tete Brec, one of the three households of the Ulster hero Cuhullin (Cu Chulaind/Cu Chulainn/Cuchulainn).

Sources: Kinsella and Le Brocquy, *The Tain*, 5; Mountain, *The Celtic Encyclopedia*, Volume 2, 465

Landvidi

Variations: Landithi, Landvide

In Norse mythology, Landvidi ("Broadland"/"Whiteland") was the name of the hall of Vidarr, the god of silence, located in a secluded forest; he lived in it with his mother, Gridr. Landvidi was also how the area was referenced; it contained many fields with tall grasses and greenwoods.

Sources: Grimes, *The Norse Myths*, 284; Kaldera, *The Pathwalker's Guide to the Nine Worlds*, n.p.

lantern of Diogenes, the

Variation: candle of Diogenes

Diogenes of Sinope (circa 404–323 BCE) was a Greek Cynic philosopher who, according to popular legend, would carry a lantern in the middle of the day in his attempt to find an honest man as he walked the streets of Athens.

Sources: Diogenes the Cynic, *Sayings and Anecdotes*, ix

lasso of sixty loops, the

Variation: Rustam's lasso of sixty loops

The Persian epic poem *Shahnameh* (*Shahnama*), written by the poet Ferdowsi (circa 977 CE), tells of the events of the historical and mythical Persian past. In the poem, the celebrated hero Rostam (Rustam) has many adventures. In art, the hero is easily recognized for the iconic items that accompany him: his lasso of sixty loops, his leopard-skin hat, his MACE OF A SINGLE BLOW, and his wondrous rose-colored horse, Rakhsh. The lasso, difficult to render in art, is most often written of in his physical description. Rostam uses the lasso most prominently in performing his fifth labor—capturing the brave warrior Aulad, who rules the border lands.

Sources: Ferdowsi, *Shahnameh*, n.p.; Melville and van den Berg, *Shahnama Studies II*, 41; Renard, *Islam and the Heroic Image*, 61, 142, 208

lattice of Momus, the

Variation: Momus's window

The personification of mockery and satire from Greek mythology, Momus was known to have bemoaned to Hephaistos (Hephaestus; Roman god Vulcan), the god of bindings, the art of sculpture, fire, forges, metalworking, stonemasonry, and talismans, that he had not fashioned a lattice into the human chest enabling him to see people's secrets and know their thoughts.

Sources: Brewer, *Dictionary of Phrase and Fable* 1900, 851

Latyr stone, the

Variations: ALATYR, white stone Latyr

A mysterious and legendary stone mentioned in Russian folklore and songs, the Latyr stone is where all sorts of diseases and magical powers are concentrated. Illnesses and impurities are magically gathered and embedded into the stone. It is said that if a snake bite victim goes to the stone, the venom will be magically extracted and pulled into the stone.

Sources: Bailey, *An Anthology of Russian Folk Epics*, 37, 398; Frog and Stepanova, *Mythic Discourses*, 461, 462

Laufi

In Icelandic folklore, and as mentioned in the *Biarkarimur* (fifteenth century), there is the tale of a hero named Biarki who is in the service of King Hrolf Kraki; this warrior had the ability to change into a white bear and, while in this form, was nearly impervious to blades. When challenged by the fierce warrior Agnar, Biarki took several sword blows to the head but received no damage from the attacks. Biarki then quickly changed back into human form, drew his sword Laufi, and ran it through Agnar, who died laughing. As a reward, King Hrolf gave his vassal twelve estates and the hand of his daughter in marriage.

Sources: Byock, *Saga of King Hrolf Kraki*, n.p.; Olrik, *The Heroic Legends of Denmark*, Volume 4, 76

leash of Cors Cant Ewin, the

In the Welsh Arthurian legends, Cors Cant Ewin ("Hundred Claws") owned the singular leash worthy of being matched with the CHAIN OF CILYDD CANASTYR. These items, along with the COLLAR OF CANHASTYR CANLLAW, would be used by the houndsman Mabon in order to handle the hound of Greid, Drudwyn. All of these items and the hound needed to be gathered together in order for Culhwch to hunt the boar Twrch Trwyth.

Sources: Bruce, *The Arthurian Name Dictionary*, 131; Ellis, *The Chronicles of the Celts*, 327; Mountain, *The Celtic Encyclopedia*, Volume 3, 764

leffas

In occult lore, leffas is the vapor of the Earth, which allows plants to flourish and grow; it is also said to be the name of the astral body of a plant.

Sources: Drury, *The Dictionary of the Esoteric*, 180; Gaynor, *Dictionary of Mysticism*, n.p.; Paracelsus, *Hermetic Medicine and Hermetic Philosophy*, Volume 2, 372

Legbiter

When the Norwegian king Magnus III (Magnus Olafsson/Magnus Barefoot) was ambushed and slain in 1103 by the men of Ulster, his sword, Legbiter, was allegedly salvaged from the fray and returned home.

Sources: Pendergrass, *Mythological Swords*, 54; Sturluson, *Heimskringla*, 685

Leifnis Elda (LAYV-nis EHLD-a)

Variations: Leifnir's Flames

A magical potion from Germanic lore, Leifnis Elda ("Leifnir's Fire"/"The Smeared on Fire") will allegedly give a person the ability to escape from any sort of restraint with merely their breath.

Dietrich of Bern, a popular character in German literature and legend, was said to have consumed this potion; it enabled him to literally breathe fire from his mouth, which would burn

Leochain

off any chain that might hold him. The potion was so powerful that when Dietrich grew angry in combat, the heat and flames from his breath would make the blades of his enemy's swords glow red hot.

Sources: Norroena Society, *Asatru Edda*, 370; Rydberg, *Teutonic Mythology*, Volume 1 of 3, n.p.

Leochain

In the Irish epic *Tain Bo Cuailnge* (*The Cattle Raid of Cooley/The Tain*), Leochain was the sword of Fergus; it is named as being among the many cups, drinking horns, goblets, javelins, shields, and swords kept in Tete Brec, one of the three households of the Ulster hero Cuhullin (Cu Chulaind/Cu Chulainn/Cuchulainn). Leochain is described only as a "hacking" sword.

Sources: Kinsella and Le Brocquy, *The Tain*, 5; Pendergrass, *Mythological Swords*, 16

Lerbrimr

Variation: Lerbrimer

In Norse mythology, Lerbrimr were the limbs of Ymir ("Groaner"; Aurgelmir), the progenitor of the Hrymthursars (frost giants) and the Aesir (gods). His limbs served as the base for the walls of Asgard ("Enclosure of the Aesir") and were sufficient protection against both the frost giants and the mountain giants. It was in this wall that the gate GASTROFNIR was located.

Sources: Grimes, *The Norse Myths*, 285; Rydberg, *Teutonic Mythology* Volume 1, 162, 512

Lerna

In classical Greek mythology, Lerna is one of the many hidden springs of the beautiful nymph Amymone; it, along with the others, were gifted to her as a courtship offering by Poseidon (Roman god Neptune), the god of earthquakes, horses, and the seas. Lerna is not only the spring where Amymone resides but also one of the entrances into the realm of Hades.

Sources: Hard, *The Routledge Handbook of Greek Mythology*, 235; Illes, *Encyclopedia of Spirits*, 171

Lettach

In the Irish epic *Tain Bo Cuailnge* (*The Cattle Raid of Cooley/The Tain*), Lettach was the sword— or possibly the shield—of Errge; it is named as being among the many cups, drinking horns, goblets, javelins, shields, and swords kept in Tete Brec, one of the three households of the Ulster hero Cuhullin (Cu Chulaind/Cu Chulainn/Cuchulainn).

Sources: Eickhoff, *The Red Branch Tales*, 50; Kinsella and Le Brocquy, *The Tain*, 5

Lia Fail

Variations: Coronation Stone, Coronation Stone of Tara, Stone of Destiny, Stone of Fal

According to Irish lore, when the Tuatha de Danann came to Ireland, they carried with them four magical treasures: the CAULDRON OF THE DAGDA, CLAIDHEAMH SOLUIS, Lia Fail, and LUIN; each of these magical items came from one of their cities—Falias, Findias, Gorias, and Murias—and each item was carried by a druid.

Falias is the mythical city on the island of Fal ("Destiny") where Lia Fail originated; it was protected by the druid Morfessa (Fessus). The fabulous stone was said to be imbued with magical powers. According to legend, when the rightful high king of Ireland placed his feet upon Lia Fail, it would "roar out in joy." Additionally, the stone was able to grant the king a long reign and rejuvenate his body.

An actual stone monument called Lia Fail is located on the Hill of Tara in Meath County, Ireland; this site is said to have been the location where Irish kings were crowned.

Sources: Anonymous, *From the Book of Invasions*, n.p.; Ellis, *Brief History of the Druids*, 73, 124; Spence, *The Magic Arts in Celtic Britain*, 99

Liobhanach

In Celtic lore and Irish mythology, Liobhanach ("the Polisher") was the sword of Diarmuid Ua Duibhne (Diarmid O'Dyna), a Fianna in the Fenian Cycle. Liobhanach was one of the six swords made by Lon Lonnrach the *beangruagach* ("giant woman"); the other swords were CEARD-NAN GALLAN, CHRUAIDH COSGARREACH, DRUIDHE LANNACH, FASDAIL, and MAC AN LUINE.

Sources: Gregory and MacCumhaill, *Gods and Fighting Men*, 268; Leodhas, *By Loch and by Lin*, n.p.

lotus tree fruit, the

Mentioned in *The Odyssey*, the ancient Greek epic attributed to Homer, the lotus tree was said to bear fruit that, when consumed, would cause a pleasant lethargy; it was the only food that the island people known as the Lotophagi ("lotus eaters") would eat. Lotus fruit is described as about the size of a lentisk berry, with the sweet taste of a date. In the story, this fruit has the power to make a person forget their families and friends, their memories of home, and their past. The lotus fruit also had an addictive property, as shown when Odysseus wanted to leave the island; he had to bind the hands and feet of his crewmen who had consumed the fruit, as they cried and fought to remain.

Sources: Brewer, *Dictionary of Phrase and Fable* 1900, 526; Mandzuka, *Demystifying the Odyssey*, 252; Osborne, *Tales from the Odyssey*, Part 1, n.p.

love potion of Deianeira, the

Deianeira was the wife of the demigod and legendary hero Heracles in classical Greek mythology. One day she was informed by Heracles's herald, Lichas, that her husband was coming home from an adventure and was returning with the beautiful Princess Iole, with whom Lichas suspected Heracles was in love. Alarmed, Deianeira remembered the love potion she had created with blood of the dying centaur Nesso (Nessus). Nesso had assured her it would guarantee her husband's fidelity. Unfortunately, the potion Nesso had Deianeira create was an infectious poison, as his blood had been tainted by the BLOOD OF THE HYDRA. Deianeira used the supposed love potion to coat the robe her husband intended to wear while making a ritual sacrifice. As Heracles approached the ritual fire, the heat activated the potion, which began burning away his skin. Suffering from unendurable pain, he tried to remove the robe, but it had melted into his bones and muscles. Realizing what she had done, Deianeira, full of remorse, committed suicide by hanging (or stabbing—sources conflict).

Sources: Hard, *The Routledge Handbook of Greek Mythology*, 284; Westmoreland, *Ancient Greek Beliefs*, 327

Luin

Variations: Fiery Spear of Lugh, Gae Assail ("Spear of Assal"), Gae Bolga ("Spear of Lightning"), Lightning Spear, Luin Celtchair, Luin of Celtchar, Sleg of Lug, Spear of Assal, Spear of Destiny, Spear of Fire, Spear of Lugh, Sun's Rays at Midsummer

According to Irish lore, when the Tuatha de Danann came to Ireland, they carried with them four magical treasures: the CAULDRON OF THE DAGDA, CLAIDHEAMH SOLUIS, LIA FAIL, and Luin; each of these magical items came from one of their cities—Falias, Findias, Gorias, and Murias—and each item was carried by a druid.

Gorias was a city said to be located in the Otherworld; Luin was created here. The druid Urias (Esras) of the Noble Stature traveled with the spear.

In the stories of the Ulster Cycle, Luin was the flaming spear (or lance) belonging to the Celtic god of the sun, Lugh ("Bright" or "Light") of the Long Arms (Artful Hands or Long Hands). Forged by the weapon smith of Falias, the mythical city on the island of Fal ("Destiny"), for Lugh to use in his battle against Balor the Strong-Smiter, Luin needed to be kept submerged in water when not in use, as there was no other way to quench the flames it emitted. Other heroes also wielded the weapon, such as Celtchar mac Uthechar, Dubthach, Fedlimid, and Mac Cecht.

Detailed descriptions of the spear come from the texts *Mesca Ulad* (*The Intoxication of the Ulstermen*) and *Togail Bruidne Dd Derga* (*The Destruction of the Hostel of Da Derga*); it was said to be as tall as a great warrior and had fifty rivets through a shaft that would have been a heavy burden for "a team of oxen." Before and after each use, it was dipped in "an appalling dark liquid" suspected of being poison or the blood of cats, dogs, and druids prepared with sorcery by night. In battle, whoever wielded the spear would smack the shaft three times against his palm, after which sparks "as big as eggs" shot forth. Each time the lance was thrust, it would kill its target, even if the blow itself fell short; on occasion it could kill a group of up to nine men. Afterward, the spear needed to be submerged and remain in its cauldron, or else the flames would backtrack along the shaft with the heat and intensity of "a house fire." When the hero Celtchar hefted the weapon, the fluid from the cauldron dripped and fell on his body, killing him.

Luin, made of yew wood, was invincible and unstoppable; lore held that whoever wielded this weapon in battle would be guaranteed victory. The spear was constantly generating heat, so when not in use, Lugh kept the spear in a vat of water to cool it. The spear also had magical properties—for example, when thrown, if Lugh cried out the incantation *Ibar* ("Yew"), the weapon would fly true and hit its mark with deadly precision. To make the spear return, he would call to it with the incantation *Athibar* ("Re-Yew").

Luin was only one of the spears utilized by Lugh; the other spears he owned were AREADBHAIR and SLEA BUA.

Sources: Bruce, *The Arthurian Name Dictionary*, 337; Ellis, *Brief History of the Druids*, 73, 124; Gantz, *Early Irish Myths and Sagas*, 97; Knott, *Togail Bruidne Da Derga*, 37–38; Koch, *The Celtic Heroic Age*, 106–27; Leviton, *The Gods in Their Cities*, 236; Watson, *Mesca Ulad*, 120

lute of Vasunemi, the

In the Hindu fairy tale *Kathasaritsagara*, a naga (a race of demonic beings described as human with the lower body of a snake) by the name of Vasunemi ("Folly of the Gods") was the owner of a wonderful lute; this instrument was said to produce the sweetest sounds, as its strings were arranged according to the divisions of the quarter tones and betel leaf. Out of gratitude, Vasunemi gifted his prized possession to the human king Udayana as a reward for saving him from the clutches of a snake charmer.

Sources: Gandhi, *Penguin Book of Hindu Names for Boys*, 665; Vogel, *Indian Serpent-lore*, 191

luz

Variation: Luez

According to rabbinical lore, there is an indestructible bone in the human body called luz; it is the starting location from which God will reform and resurrect a person. Located in the backbone and said to be the shape of an almond or hazelnut, the luz cannot be consumed by fire, ground by a mill, smashed with a hammer and anvil, or softened by water.

Sources: Brewer, *Dictionary of Phrase and Fable* 1900, 784; Butler, *Hudibras*, Volume 3, 136–37

lyngurium

Variation: ligurium

A stone named in medieval lore, the lyngurium is a powerful object created when a lynx urinates on gravel from the sea; over time, it hardens into a gem. Lyngurium is used to make an angry person calm in addition to staunching a bleeding wound and lessening intense menstrual symptoms. It also has magical properties that are attributed to sharp vision, one of the supposed attributes of the lynx.

The Greek philosopher Theophrastus (372–287 BCE) claimed that lyngurium was clear, cold, and harder than most stones, and it allegedly had the magical ability to "attract other objects to it." It worked not only on a bed of leaves and straw but also on thin sheets of copper and iron. Additionally, it was believed that, due to reasons of diet and exercise, wild male lynxes produced better lyngurium than domesticated males or wild females.

Sources: Taylor, *Chaucer Translator*, 148; Young, *A Medieval Book of Magical Stones*, 60–61

lyre of Apollo, the

In classical Greek mythology, Hermes (Roman god Mercury), the god of animal husbandry, commerce, eloquence, fertility, language, looters, luck, sleep, thieves, trade, travel, and wealth, created a lyre from the shell of a tortoise and the intestines of some of the cows under the protection of Apollo ("to destroy" or "to drive away"), the god of archery, art, healing, hunting, knowledge, medicine, music, oracles, plague, prophecy, sun and light, truth, and young unmarried men. Apollo managed to discover who had stolen and slaughtered the cows, but Hermes denied it repeatedly. In order to prevent the two gods from coming to blows over the matter, Zeus (Roman god Jupiter), the god of fate, kings, lightning, sky, and thunder, made them go in search of the livestock together. Hermes pulled the lyre from his sack and played and sang as they traveled to where he had hidden the remaining cows. Apollo was so impressed with the quality of the instrument and the beauty of its music that he promised to forgive Hermes if the lyre was given to him along with the promise that it would never be stolen from him. Hermes agreed to the deal; in turn, he accepted a staff along with the right to herd cattle and sheep.

Sources: Allan and Maitland, *Ancient Greece and Rome*, 101; Orr, *Apollo*, 35

Lysingr (LEES-ing-r)

Variation: Lysingus

In Eddaic and Germanic traditions, Lysingr ("the Shining") was the sword that belonged to Jarl, the father of the hero Konr (Gramr/Halfdan/Helgi/Mannus/Rigr), who used it slay Hildibrandr-Hildigir (Hildingr Hildigir; "Descendants of Hildur"). Lysingr was the only weapon that had the ability to slay them.

Sources: Davidson, *The Sword in Anglo-Saxon England*, 177; Norroena Society, *Satr Edda*, 164, 74, 373

Mabur

According to Islamic mythology, the prophet Muhammad owned a collection of nine different swords at the time of his death: al ADHAB, al Battar (see BATTER), Dhu'l Fakar (see DHUAL-FIRQAR), al Hatf (see HATEL), al KADIB, KOLAITE, Mabur, al MEHDHAM, and al ROFUB. Beyond its name, nothing else is known of the sword Mabur ("Sharp").

Sources: Sale et al., *An Universal History, Part 2*, Volume 1, 184

Mac an Luine

Variation: Mac an Luin ("Son of the Waves")

In Celtic lore and Irish mythology, Mac an

Luine ("Son of the Surge") was the sword of Fionn mac Cumhaill (Finn MacCool/Finn Mac-Cumhail), a legendary warrior and the leader of the Fianna in the Fenian Cycle. This sword was wielded in tandem with the shield SGIATH GAIL-BHINN. Mac an Luine was one of the six swords made by Lon Lonnrach the *beangruagach* ("giant woman"); the other swords were CEARD-NAN GALLAN, CHRUAIDH COSGARREACH, DRUIDHE LANNACH, FASDAIL, and LIOBHANACH.

Sources: Gregory and MacCumhaill, *Gods and Fighting Men*, 268; Leodhas, *By Loch and by Lin*, n.p.

mace of a single blow, the

Variation: Rustam's mace

The Persian epic poem *Shahnameh* (*Shahnama*), written by the poet Ferdowsi (circa 977 CE), tells of the events of the historical and mythical Persian past. In the poem, the celebrated hero Rostam (Rustam) has many adventures. In art, the hero is easily recognized for the iconic items that accompany him: his LASSO OF SIXTY LOOPS, his leopard-skin hat, his mace of a single blow, and his wondrous rose-colored horse, Rakhsh. As the name of this weapon implies, more often than not, when a combatant was struck a single time with the mace, it caused enough damage to kill whoever it hit. When Rostam was seen wielding the mace, it was not uncommon for his enemies to turn and flee in terror; this mace was also the weapon he used to slay the demon Mazanderan. In literature it is described as heavy and massive.

Sources: Ferdowsi, *Shahnameh*, n.p.; Kinsella and Le Brocquy, *The Tain*, 5; Renard, *Islam and the Heroic Image*, 61, 142, 208

mace of Bhima, the

In Hindu mythology, the king of the asura, daitya, and raksasa, Mayasura, presented the hero Bhima with a mace of gold (or adorned with gold—sources conflict). When striking an opponent, sparks of fire were emitted by the weapon, and it made a loud sound comparable to a thunderbolt. When striking the ground, the mace would cause the earth to tremble. Bhima used his great strength to wield the mace to destroy city gates and kill literally countless elephants, men, and war steeds; in one battle alone, he slew 10,000 steel-clad war horses and an untold number of soldiers.

Sources: Roy, *The Mahabharata*, Volumes 8–11, 221–27; Valmiki, *Delphi Collected Sanskrit Epics*, n.p.

madhu vidya

Variation: MAHAUSHADI

In Hindu mythology, madhu vidya ("honey"/ "honey doctrine"/"knowledge of honey") was one of the AUSADHIRDIPYAMANAS that had the power to make a mortal into an immortal.

Sources: Garrett, *A Classical Dictionary of India*, 241

magic beans

In the English fairy tale "Jack and the Bean Stalk," a poor and simple boy named Jack trades his mother's only milking cow for magic beans. After being planted in the yard, the beans take root overnight and miraculously grow impossibly large and tall, reaching up into the clouds and unintentionally penetrating into another realm of existence. In ascending the stalk, Jack enters a different world populated by giants; it is filled with danger, but, through the use of his wits, he is able to obtain a great deal of wealth to provide for his mother. In order to retain his newly acquired treasure, Jack chooses to chop down the bean stalk and close the portal between his world and the other, presumably forever.

Sources: Lewis and Oliver, *The Dream Encyclopedia*, 252; Telesco, *The Kitchen Witch Companion*, 15

magic bullet

Variations: freischutz ("freeshooter" or "marksman"), zauberkugel

According to German folklore, the Devil has crafted seven magic bullets that he is prepared to barter for a human soul. Six of the bullets will perform with hyper accuracy, but the seventh will cause some sort of startling twist that will lead to unanticipated results.

Another type of magic bullet, said to made of silver (or at least silver coated), appears in other German folktales as a means of killing a werewolf.

Sources: Humez and Humez, *On the Dot*, 40; Kay et al., *New Perspectives on English Historical Linguistics*, 88

mahaushadi

In Hindu mythology, mahaushadi ("great medicine") was one of the much-celebrated AUSADHIRD-IPYAMANAS; it grew on the northern mountain Gandha-mandana. Mahaushadi was able to bring those who were dying or dead back to full health. When prepared for usage, the patient would inhale its vapors to recover.

Sources: Garrett, *A Classical Dictionary of India*, 241

Mahendra

Variation: Mahendra Astra

In Hindu mythology, an ASTRA is a supernatural weapon created or gifted by the gods to someone who then presides over the weapon. The wielder of an ASTRA is known as an astradhari.

Mahendra was an ASTRA belonging to the heroic archer Arjuna ("Spotless and Shining like Silver"); it had the ability to neutralize the effects of Ashvatthama's divine weapon, INDRAASTRA.

Sources: Edizioni, *Vimanas and the Wars of the Gods*, n.p.; Kotru and Zutshi, *Karna*, n.p.

Maheshwarastra

Variation: Maheshwar astra

In Hindu mythology, an ASTRA is a supernatural weapon created or gifted by the gods to someone who then presides over the weapon. The wielder of an ASTRA is known as an astradhari.

Maheshwarastra was an ASTRA from the god Shiva the Destroyer; it was said to contain the god's third eye. This weapon would generate an instantaneous beam of fire so intense that it could turn even one of the devas (demigods) to ash. Although infallible, Maheshwarastra's effects could be nullified by an ASTRA from Shiva or one from the god of preservation, Vishnu.

Sources: Edizioni, *Vimanas and the Wars of the Gods*, n.p.

mail coat of Manannan, the

Variations: leaf-armor shirt of Manannan, mail of Manannan

Manannan mac Lir (Mannanan,Mannanos), god of the sea and guardian of the Underworld in Celtic mythology, was a master of shape shifting and had many varied powers and magical items. One of his possessions was a coat of mail; it was said that whoever wore this coat could not be wounded through it, above it, or below it.

Sources: Kittredge and Bodleian Library, *Arthur and Gorlagon*, 42; Macbain, *Celtic Mythology and Religion*, 97

Maltet

In the Matter of France (also called the Carolingian cycle), Maltet ("Evil") was the lance of Baligant, a legendary Arabic king. It is described as having a shaft as thick as a club with an iron head weighing as much as a mule could carry.

Sources: Auty, *Traditions of Heroic and Epic Poetry*, Volume 1, 96; Sayers, *The Song of Roland*, 38

Manavastra

In Hindu mythology, an ASTRA is a supernatural weapon created or gifted by the gods to someone who then presides over the weapon. The wielder of an ASTRA is known as an astradhari.

Manavastra was an ASTRA from the god of the human race, Manu. Manavastra was said to have the ability to travel to its target from hundreds of miles away. It could also infuse wickedness into humans and cause evil beings to have human traits.

In the *Ramayana* (*Rama's Journey*), an ancient Indian epic poem dating between 500 and 100 BCE, Rama shot Manavastra like an arrow into the chest of a rakshasa; it lifted the creature into the air, set it ablaze, and propelled it against the wind for a distance of one hundred *yojanas* (approximately 746 miles), at which point it landed, barely alive, in the ocean.

Sources: Edizioni, *Vimanas and the Wars of the Gods*, n.p.; Menon, *The Ramayana*, 29

Mandjet

Variations: Boat of Millions of Years, mandjet-barque

In Egyptian mythology, *Mandjet* ("Growing Strong") was the morning solar boat that carried the god of the sun, Ra (Re), across the heavens; he was accompanied on this daily journey by the gods Horus, Maat, and Toth, who would set his course and steer the boat. *Mandjet* was the "boat of the east" and said to be the left eye of the sun. This was one of two solar boats Ra utilized; the other was MESEKTET.

Sources: Hart, *A Dictionary of Egyptian Gods and Goddesses*, 182; Remler, *Egyptian Mythology, A to Z*, 117, 180

Mani Bhitti

Variation: Mani Mandapa ("Jewel Palace")

In Hindu mythology, Mani Bhitti ("Jewel Walled") is the palace of Seesha, king of the infernal region known as Patala, and his wife Ananta-Sirsha. It is described as having clear but bejeweled walls whose worth is incalculable.

Sources: Balfour, *The Cyclopædia of India and of Eastern and Southern Asia*, Volume 3, 584; Dowson, *A Classical Dictionary of Hindu Mythology and Religion*, 291–92

manna

Variations: angel's food, bread of the mighty, food of angels, mana, maria

According to the Old Testament of the Bible, as the Israelites wandered in the desert wilderness, they had a constant supply of a food substance they called manna. This substance was sent by God each morning to his people, appearing with the dew. It was said to be as fine "as hoarfrost on the ground … like coriander seed" and white; its taste was described as similar to honey and wafers. Rabbinical lore claims the manna would change taste according to the person who consumed it, taking on the flavor of anything they wished.

Manna could be baked or stewed and served as a supplement to the Israelites' daily diet. The manna was supplied from Heaven each day for forty years and ceased the day after the Israelites arrived in the land of Canaan and ate the food produced there. A precise amount of manna fell each day and needed to be eaten; any manna that remained by the following day would have a horrible smell and be filled with worms.

Sources: Boren and Boren, *Following the Ark of the Covenant*, 11; Lockyer, *All the Miracles of the Bible*, 66

Mannigfual

In north Frisian traditions, *Mannigfual* was a gigantic ship, so large that it was practically its own world; it constantly cruised the Atlantic Ocean. The *Mannigfual* was described as having masts as tall as a mountain. When young sailors would climb up the masts to unfurl the sails, they would descend as old men with long white beards; fortunately, there were resting houses at each block and pulley. The captain of this massive vessel would ride over the deck on horseback to bark out orders. According to the tales, there was always plenty to eat and the crew was content.

Sources: Anderson, *Norse Mythology*, 87; Guerber, *Myths of the Norsemen from the Eddas and Sagas*, 235; Kingshill, *The Fabled Coast*, n.p.

mantle of Arthur in Cornwall, the

Variations: Gwenn, Lien Arthyr yng Nghernyw, Llen Arthyr yng Nghernyw, mask of Arthur, veil of Arthur

In British and Welsh folklore, there is a series of items (always thirteen in number) called the Thirteen Treasures of the Island of Britain (in Welsh they are called *Tri Thlws ar Ddeg Ynys Prydain*). Although in more modern times the items listed are different, the original thirteen items from the fifteenth century were the cauldron of Dyrnwch the Giant, chariot of Morgan Mwynfawr, chessboard of Gwenddoleu ap Ceidio, coat of Padarn Beisrudd,

crock and dish of Rhygenydd Ysgolhaig (two items), halter of Clydno Eiddyn, hamper of Gwyddno Garanhir, horn of Bran Galed, knife of Llawfrodedd Farchof, mantle of Arthur in Cornwall, sword of Rhydderch Hael (Dyrnwyn), and whetstone of Tudwal Tudglyd.

The mantle of Arthur in Cornwall ("Llen Arthyr yng Nghernyw") had the magical ability to render anyone who covered themselves with it invisible; yet they were able to clearly see through it. The mantle is mentioned in two tales: *Culhwch and Olwen* and *The Dream of Rhonabwy*. In the former, the mantle is the only item named that Arthur will not give to Culhwch, and it is not otherwise described. In the latter story, the mantle is named Gwen ("Blessed," "Sacred," or "White").

Sources: Dom, *King Arthur and the Gods of the Round Table*, 95, 106; Pendergrass, *Mythological Swords*, 26; Taylor, *The Fairy Ring*, 389

mantle of fidelity, the

Variation: mantle of matrimonial fidelity

An item from Arthurian lore, the mantle of fidelity was presented to King Arthur by a small boy; he told the king that it would "become no wife that was not *leal*" (i.e., loyal and honest). The women of the court attempted to wear the mantle, but it would not fit any of them, as it became too wrinkled to wear, changed to a hideous color, grew too small, rose up too short in the back, or shredded itself. Only the wife of Sir Caradoc Briefbras (Caradoc of the Shrunken Arm), Guimier (Guignier/Tegau Eurfon), was able to wear the garment because she confessed to the court that she had kissed her husband before they were wed. On her the mantle shone like gold and suited her perfectly.

Sources: Brewer, *Dictionary of Phrase and Fable* 1900, 549; Bruce, *The Arthurian Name Dictionary*, 465; Gerwig, *Crowell's Handbook for Readers and Writers*, 104, 129

mantle of Tegau Eurfon, the

Variation: Tegau Gold-Breast

In late Arthurian lore, the mantle of Tegau Eurfon is said to be one of the Thirteen Treasures of the Island of Britain (in Welsh, they are called *Tri Thlws ar Ddeg Ynys Prydain*); this object appears in post-fifteenth-century manuscripts, replacing one of the original items. Typically this change occurs when the crock and dish of Rhygenydd Ysgolhaig are combined and counted as a single item rather than the traditional two. This mantle, similar to the MANTLE OF FIDELITY, had the ability to prove whether a woman was chaste or unchaste. Tegau Eurfon was the standard of medieval chastity in King Arthur's court; she was better known as Guimier (Guignier), the wife of Sir Caradoc Briefbras (Caradoc of the Shrunken Arm).

Sources: Ashley, *The Mammoth Book of King Arthur*, n.p.; Bruce, *The Arthurian Name Dictionary*, 465; Ellis, *Celtic Women*, 62; Pendergrass, *Mythological Swords*, 25

Mantramukta

In ancient Hindu mythology, there were six weapons known collectively as the Mantramukta; they were said to be so powerful that nothing could frustrate or subdue them. The Mantramukta are projected by spells. Their individual names are BRAHMAASTRA (the missile of Brahma), Kalapasaka (the noose of death), NARAYANASTRA (the missile of Narayana), Pasupatastra (missile of Pasupati), Vajrastra (the thunderbolt), and Vishnucakra (the discus of Vishnu, which was created by Vishvakarman from superfluous rays of the sun).

Sources: Hall, *The Vishnu Purana*, Volume 3, 22; Oppert, *On the Weapons*, 30

Mardallr Gratr

Variations: Mardallar Gratr ("Mardoll's Weeping"), Mardaller Grate

In Norse mythology, Mardallr Gratr ("Tears of Gold"/"Tears of Mardal") was the name given to the bits of gold that fell from the eyes of Mardoll when she cried.

Sources: Billington and Green, *The Concept of the Goddess*, 70; Grimes, *The Norse Myths*, 286

Margleis

Variations: Murgleys ("Death Glave"), sword of Ganelon

Margleis ("Death Brand"/"Moorish Sword"/ "Valiant Piercer") was the sword of the traitorous Count Ganelon in the French epic poem *Song of Roland* (*La Chanson de Roland*, circa 1040–1115). The sword is described as having some sort of holy relic in its golden pommel, which also sported a carbuncle. Margleis was forged by Madelger in Regensburg.

Sources: Pendergrass, *Mythological Swords*, 56; Sayers, *The Song of Roland*, 38

Marmiadoise

Variations: Marmydoyse

In the French romances of King Arthur, Mar-

miadoise was the "good sword" of King Rion of Ireland, a man described as twenty-four feet tall. The sword, said to be one of the best in the world, was forged by Hephaistos (Hephaestus; Roman god Vulcan), the god of bindings, the art of sculpture, fire, forges, metalworking, stonemasonry, and talismans; it was the very sword that mythical Greek demigod and legendary hero Heracles had used to slay the giants in the land where Jason brought Medea.

Marmiadoise was made so that it would never bend or rust and any wound it caused would never heal. When Arthur beheld the weapon, he desired it "more than any city" and battled Rion for possession of it. When Marmiadoise was won, Arthur gave EXCALIBUR to Sir Gawain.

Sources: Warren, *History on the Edge*, 203, 205

Matahourua

According to Maori tradition, Matahourua was the canoe used by the legendary Polynesian hero and navigator Kupe when he left his cousin Hoturapa to drown while fishing deep out in the ocean. Kupe then returned to shore; kidnapped his cousin's wife, Kuramaro-tini; and crossed Kiwa (the Pacific Ocean), discovering Aotearoa (New Zealand) in the process.

Sources: Best, *Journal of the Polynesian Society*, Volume 10, 110; Craig, *Dictionary of Polynesian Mythology*, 127

Mawashah, al

According to Islamic mythology, the prophet Muhammad owned two helmets at the time of his death—an interior one and an exterior one. The interior helmet is not named; however, the exterior helmet was called al Mawashah ("the Fillet," "the Wreath," or "the wreathed Garland"). This helmet was the one Muhammad was said to have worn in the Battle of Ohod.

Sources: Osborne et al., *A Complete History of the Arabs*, Volume 1, 254; Sale et al., *An Universal History, Part 2*, Volume 1, 185

Med Sviga Laevi

In Norse mythology, Med Sviga Laevi ("Consumer of Branches"/"Danger to Branches") was name of the fiery sword belonging to Surtr, one of the Eldjotnar (fire giants); it was given to him by Angroboda in the Jarnvidr Forest.

Using the guise of Svidrir, Odin, the god of battle, death, frenzy, the gallows, healing, knowledge, poetry, royalty, the runic alphabet, sorcery, and wisdom, recovered the PRECIOUS MEAD after it was stolen by the Jotun (giant) Midvitnir, decapitating Midvitnir's son Sokkmimir in the process with Med Sviga Laevi.

It is said that in the final battle of Ragnarok, on the Vigridr Plain, Surtr will kill Freyr (Frey/Yngvi), the god of fertility, peace, rain, and sunshine, and then throw Med Sviga Laevi, letting it consume the nine worlds in fire.

Sources: Grimes, *The Norse Myths*, 58, 287, 300; Rydberg, *Teutonic Mythology* Volume 1, 443–44

Sources: Brewer and Harland, *Character Sketches of Romance, Fiction and the Drama*, Volume 4, 378; Irving, *Works of Washington Irving*, Volume 9, 132

Megingjardar (MEHG-ing-yarth-ar)

Variations: girdle of Might, Megingiord, Megingiord, Megingjarpar, Megingjord

One of the three prized possessions of Thor, the Norse god of thunder, Megingjardar ("Belt of Strength" or "Power Belt") doubled the god's mighty strength when worn around his waist. It was given to him, along with JARNGREIPR, by the *asynjr* (female Jotun, or giant) Gridr to assist him in thwarting the plot of (and then killing) Geirrod.

Sources: Hall et al., *Saga Six Pack*, 103, 141; Hawthorne, *Vikings*, 20; Norroena Society, *Satr Edda*, 374; Orchard, *Dictionary of Norse Myth and Legend*, 10

Mehdham, al

According to Islamic mythology, the prophet Muhammad owned a collection of nine different swords at the time of his death: al ADHAB, al Battar (see BATTER), Dhu'l Fakar (see DHUAL-FIRQAR), al Hatf (see HATEL), al KADIB, KOLAITE, MABUR, al Mehdham, and al ROFUB. Mehdham ("the Keen") was taken from the Jewish tribe Banu Kainoka prior to their banishment to Syria. This was the same tribe that once claimed the lance al MONTHARI, which was also taken from them by Muhammad.

Sources: Brewer and Harland, *Character Sketches of Romance, Fiction and the Drama*, Volume 4, 378; Irving, *Works of Washington Irving*, Volume 9, 132; Sale et al., *An Universal History, Part 2*, Volume 1, 184

Memory of Blood, the

In Arthurian lore, the SWORD WITH THE STRANGE HANGINGS was an item sought by Sir Galahad, Sir Percival, and Sir Bors; it was discovered on the SHIP OF KING SOLOMON. In some versions of the tale, it was Percival's sister who led the knights to the sword, explaining to them the history of the weapon and how she had removed its former shabby hangings and replaced them with weavings of gold thread and her own hair. In this version, the sheath of the sword was called the Memory of Blood.

Sources: Loomis, *Celtic Myth and Arthurian Romance*, 246, 275; Sommer, *The Vulgate Version of the Arthurian Romances*, 162

Merry Dun of Dover, the

In Scandinavian folklore, the *Merry Dun of Dover* was described as a gigantic sailing ship; it was so large that it was responsible for knocking down the Calais steeple while cruising through the Straits of Dover. Its pennant flag was said to have once swept a flock of sheep off the Dover cliffs, dropping them into the sea. Like the MANNIGFUAL, it was said that if a young sailor climbed up to the very top of the ship's main mast, when he finally descended, he would be an old man.

Sources: Brewer, *Dictionary of Phrase and Fable* 1900, 570; Farmer, *Slang and Its Analogues Past and Present*, Volume 4, 303

Merveilleuse

In the Charlemagne romances, the hero Doolin de Mayence wielded the sword Merveilleuse ("That Marvelous"), which was created in the forge of Galant by one of his apprentices but was nevertheless magical. The mother of Galant, a fairy, said her prayers over the weapon, enchanted it with her magic, and made the Sign of the Cross over it. Then she placed the sword on a tripod to rest for the night. When she returned in the morning, she found the sword had cut through the tripod. So impressed with the magically enhanced cutting edge she had given the sword, she named it Merveilleuse and declared that there was no substance in the world the weapon would not be able to cut unless God himself intervened.

Sources: Brewer, *Dictionary of Phrase and Fable* 1900, 1197; Depping, *Wayland Smith*, lxv; Urdang and Ruffner, *Allusions*, 344

Mesektet

In Egyptian mythology, *Mesektet* ("Growing Weaker") was the evening solar boat that carried the god of the sun, Ra (Re), across the heavens and into the Netherworld, the land of the dead; unlike the daytime journey, during which Ra was accompanied by friendly gods, he traveled alone during the evening, surrounded by his enemies. *Mesektet* was the "boat of the west" and was said to be the right eye of the sun. This was one of two boats Ra utilized; the other was MANDJET.

Sources: Remler, *Egyptian Mythology, A to Z*, 117, 180

Mi-Kuratana-no-Kami

In Japanese mythology, the young goddess of the sun, Amaterasu O Mi Kami, received from her father, Izanagi, a jeweled necklace of fertility known as Mi-Kuratana-no-Kami ("August-Store house-Shelf-A'aw").

Sources: Coulter and Turner, *Encyclopedia of Ancient Deities*, 52. ; Holtom, *The Political Philosophy of Modern Shinto*, 142

Mimirsbrunnr Well

Variations: Mimesbrunn Well, Mimir's Well, Mimisbrunnar Well, Mimis-Brunnar, Mimisbrunnr Well, Mimis-Brunnr Well, Well of Mimir, Well of Mimisbrunnr, Well of Wisdom

In Norse mythology, Mimirsbrunnr Well is the font of all wisdom and wit; it is located at Mimir's Grove, next to the Jotunheimr root in the land of Odainsaker. This is one of the three wells that nourish YGGDRASIL (HVERGELUR WELL and URDARBRUNNR WELL being the other two). The water of Mimisbrunnr Well is so clear that the future can be seen in it. The well's spring is considered the headwater of memory, and when Odin, the god of battle, death, frenzy, the gallows, healing, knowledge, poetry, royalty, the runic alphabet, sorcery, and wisdom, desired great wisdom, he exchanged one of his eyes for a drink from it. Mimirsbrunnr Well is guarded by the god Mimir himself.

Sources: Grimes, *The Norse Myths*, 287; Guerber, *Myths of the Norsemen*, 13, 30–31

Mimmung

Variations: Mimming, Mimung

According to German mythology, Mimmung was the good sword that belonged to and was forged by legendary master blacksmith Wayland (Gofannon/Volund/Weiland/Weyland) the Smith; it was left as an inheritance to his son, Wudga (Witga). In one tale, when the sword was placed against the invulnerable helmet of Amilias, the smith of King Nidung, Wayland cut through the helm and straight through to Amilias's waist. When asked how he felt, Amilias replied, "As if cold water has been poured over me"; when he stood and shook himself, Amilias fell apart in two cleanly cut pieces.

In the Nibelungen tradition, Mimmung was known as Mimung; this was the sword Velent forged while he was in Nithung, which he then passed on to his son, Vithga, when he set off to become a knight. In one story, Vithga challenges Thidrek to a duel and, using Mimung, cuts Thidrek's helmet HILDIGRIM in two. Over the course of his adventures, Vithga loses Mimung several times, only to reclaim it again. By the end of the story, however, Vithga has made a grave enemy of Thidrek, so he flees into the sea, carrying Mimung with him; neither is ever seen again.

Sources: Brewer, *Dictionary of Phrase and Fable* 1900, 1197; Anonymous, *Curious Stories about Fairies and Other Funny People*, 85, 92; Grimes, *The Norse Myths*, 287; McConnell et al., *The Nibelungen Tradition*, 164; Pendergrass, *Mythological Swords*, 3

Minnihorn (MIN-i-hawrn)

In Norse traditions, Minnihorn ("Memory Horn") was a mead of remembrance; in addition to honoring ancestors, it was used to recall and retain information.

Sources: Norroena Society, *Satr Edda*, 375

mirror of Alasnam, the

Variation: Touch-Stone of Virtue

In "The Tale of Zayn Al-Asnam" in the work *Tales of Sheherazade, or A Thousand and One Nights*, Prince Zeyn Alasnam (Zayn Al-Asnam) is given a mirror by a djinn (genie) that will dim when a woman who is not chaste and pure minded gazes into it. If the mirror remains brilliant, the prince will know the woman is not faithless or wanton.

Sources: Brewer, *Dictionary of Phrase and Fable*, Volume 1, 26; Brewer and Harland, *Character Sketches of Romance, Fiction and the Drama*, Volume 8, 215; Hyamson, *A Dictionary of English Phrases*, 9

Mistilteinn

Variations: Miseltein, Misteltan, Misteltein, Mistilein, Mistilleinn, Mystletainn

In Norse mythology, Mistilteinn ("Mistletoe") was the sprig of mistletoe from which Frigg ("Beloved") forgot to secure a promise not to harm Balder. Because of this oversight, the god Loki took the sprig and forged it into a weapon that Hodr then used against Balder, killing him.

In *Hromundar saga Gripssonar* (*Saga of Hromund Gripsson*), Mistileinn was the name of the sword that the legendary hero Hromund won from King Prainn, a barrow-wight or draugr ("after-goer"—a type of vampiric revenant); the sword had the magical ability to always retain a sharp edge.

Sources: Grimes, *The Norse Myths*, 288; Pendergrass, *Mythological Swords*, 3

Mjolnir (MYUHL-nir)

Variations: hammer of Donar (Thor), Miollnir, Miolnir, Mjohiir, Mjollnir, Mjolne, Mjolner, Mul-

licrusher, Thrudhammer, Thrudnamarn, Thruth-
amer, Vigdi ("Hallowed")

In Norse mythology, Mjolnir ("Crusher"/"Pul-
verizer"/"That Which Smashes") was a magical
hammer created by the dwarf brothers Brokkr
and Eitri in order to win a bet they made with
the god Loki. Because Loki cheated by distract-
ing Brokkr during a critical part of the forging
process, the hammer's shaft was made too short;
this meant the weapon could only ever be wielded
one handed at best. However, in spite of this flaw,
Mjolnir was imbued with magical abilities. It
could be folded up and squeezed into small locations (usually kept inside of Thor's shirt). More
interestingly, whenever the hammer was thrown,
not only would it always hit its mark, but it would
also return automatically to its owner. Given to
the god of thunder, Thor, Mjolnir was only ever
used to slay Jotuns (giants) and consecrate sacred
events, such as births, funerals, and weddings.
This was the second hammer Thor brandished;
the first, made of stone, was known as VINGNIR'S
MJOLNIR.

Typically, the weapon was red hot to the touch.
The thunder and lightning that shot from it when
used was known as FULMINEN. To compensate for
the weapon's short shaft, Thor would use a set of
iron gloves known as JARNGREIPR; they allowed
him to lift and properly utilize Mjolnir.

After the Battle of Ragnarok, the hammer
would become the property of Thor's sons, Magni
and Modi.

Sources: Grimes, *The Norse Myths*, 288, 308; Keightley,
*World Guide to Gnomes, Fairies, Elves, and Other Little
People*, 68; Norroena Society, *Satr Edda*, 25; Orchard, *Dic-
tionary of Norse Myth and Legend*, 255

Mjotudr (MYEUT-oodr)

In Norse mythology, Mjotudr ("Measure
Exhausting") is the name given to YGGDRASIL
during its dying stage.

Sources: de Santillana and von Dechend, *Hamlet's Mill*,
158

Mjotvidr (MYEUT-veedr)

In Norse mythology, Mjotvidr ("Measure Increasing" or "Measure Tree") is the name given to YGG-
DRASIL during its growing stage.

Sources: de Santillana and von Dechend, *Hamlet's Mill*,
158

Mo Ye

Variation: Moye

According to Chinese legend, GAN JIANG and
Mo Ye were a pair of twin swords named after
their creators, a husband-and-wife swordsmith
duo. Legend says that all blacksmiths can distinguish the sex of metal when objects are commissioned to be made in pairs; in these cases, the
Genie of the Bellows operates the bellows, the
jiao dragon heats up the furnace, the Master of
the Rain washes down and sweeps, and the Red
Sovereign loads the furnace with charcoal.

The story goes that the king of Chu commissioned twin swords from the husband, Gan Jiang,
who collected iron from five mountains and gold
from the ten directions. The wife, Mo Ye, sacrificed
her hair and nails to the fire, which had 300 boys
and girls working the bellows. As the three-year
process drew to an end, and after giving birth to
Chibi, their son, Mo Ye leaped into the furnace, as
a human sacrifice was required to make the different metals meld together. The female (yin) sword
is described as having an eel-skin texture.

Sources: Bonnefoy, *Asian Mythologies*, 258; Wagner,
Iron and Steel in Ancient China, 113–14

Mohini

In Hindu mythology, an ASTRA is a supernatural weapon created or gifted by the gods to someone who then presides over the weapon. The
wielder of an ASTRA is known as an astradhari.

Mohini was an ASTRA from Mohini, an avatar
of the god of preservation, Vishnu. This weapon
was said to have the ability to dispel any sort of
magic or sorcery in its vicinity.

Sources: Edizioni, *Vimanas and the Wars of the Gods*,
n.p.

Mokkerkalfe (MUHK-ur-kahlv-i)

Variations: Mokker Kalfe, Mokkurkalf, Mok-
kurkalfi

A Jotun (giant) made of clay in Norse mythology, Mokkerkalfe ("Cloud-Calf"/"Mist Wader")
was created by Hrungnir to assist him in his battle against the god of thunder, Thor; the clay giant
was nine *rasts* (63 miles) tall and three *rasts* (21
miles) wide. Although he was created with the
heart of a mare, when Mokkerkalfe accompanied
his creator, he sweated with nervousness before
the battle and, upon arriving and seeing Thor,
urinated on himself in fear. Mokkerkalfe was
destroyed by Thor's servant Thjalfe, shattered into
many pieces.

Sources: Anderson, *Norse Mythology*, 55, 309; Anderson, *The Younger Edda*, 171; Norroena Society, *Asatru
Edda*, 375; Oehlenschläger, *Gods of the North*, lv

moly

Variations: herb of virtue, molu

Mentioned in *The Odyssey*, the ancient Greek epic attributed to Homer, moly (the herb of virtue) was given to Odysseus by Hermes (Roman god Mercury), the god of animal husbandry, commerce, eloquence, fertility, language, looters, luck, sleep, thieves, trade, travel, and wealth. This divine herb, which needed to be consumed, protected Odysseus from the magic of the sorceress Circe. Moly is described as having black roots and a milk-white flower; mortals are unable to dig it up from the earth.

Sources: Anderson, *Finding Joy in Joyce*, 471; Naddaf, *The Greek Concept of Nature*, 13, 14

Monthari, al

Al Monthari ("the Disperser") was said to have been one of the lances of the prophet Muhammad. It, along with other treasures, came into his possession as wealth confiscated from the Jewish tribe Banu Kainoka prior to their banishment to Syria.

Sources: Irving, *Works of Washington Irving*, Volume 9, 132; Osborne et al., *A Complete History of the Arabs*, Volume 1, 254; Sale et al., *An Universal History, Part 2*, Volume 1, 185

Monthawi, al

Al Monthawi ("the Destroyer") was said to have been one of the lances belonging to the prophet Muhammad. It, along with other treasures, came into his possession as wealth confiscated from the Jewish tribe Banu Kainoka prior to their banishment to Syria. Al Monthawi was listed as one of the items Muhammad owned at the time of his death.

Sources: Irving, *Works of Washington Irving*, Volume 9, 132; Osborne et al., *A Complete History of the Arabs*, Volume 1, 254; Sale et al., *An Universal History, Part 2*, Volume 1, 185

moon drop

Variation: virus lunare

According to ancient Roman lore and medieval demonology, a moon drop was a bit of dew or foam that was believed to have fallen from the moon and would land on certain herbs and items when enticed by magical incantations.

Sources: Brewer, *The Reader's Handbook of Famous Names in Fiction, Allusions, References, Proverbs, Plots, Stories, and Poems*, 723; Liddell, *The Elizabethan Shakespeare*, 136; Rolfe, *Tragedy of Macbeth*, 223

Moralltach

Variation: Noralltach

Two swords were given to Diarmuid Ua Duibhne (Diarmid O'Dyna) by his father, Angus of the Brugs, in Celtic mythology: BEAGALLTACH ("Little Fury") and Moralltach ("Great Fury"). Diarmuid carried each weapon for a different purpose; BEAGALLTACH was taken on his small adventures when he did not foresee much danger, and Moralltach was taken on affairs he considered to be of life and death.

Sources: Joyce, *Old Celtic Romances*, 302; MacCulloch et al., *Celtic Mythology*, Volume 3, 66

Morglay

In the folklore of sixth-century England, Morglay ("Big Sword") was the sword wielded by the giant Ascpart.

Sources: Brewer, *Dictionary of Phrase and Fable* 1900, 1197; Evangelista, *The Encyclopedia of the Sword*, 577

mortar and pestle of Baba Yaga, the

In Slavic mythology, Baba Yaga ("old woman Yaga" or "old woman Jadwiga"), a character originating in Hungarian lore, was more often than not whatever the storyteller needed her to be, whether it was a cannibalistic old crone or witch, a kind and benevolent fairy, or a race of evil fay. No matter how she was described, Baba Yaga owned a gigantic mortar and pestle that had the magical ability to fly. It moved through the air amazingly fast, and she would steer it with her right hand by moving the pestle.

Sources: Dixon-Kennedy, *Encyclopedia of Russian & Slavic Myth and Legend*, 23–28; Evan-Wentz, *Fairy Faith in Celtic Countries*, 247; Rose, *Spirits, Fairies, Leprechauns, and Goblins*, 29; Rosen, *Mythical Creatures Bible*, 234

Myrkvan Vafrloga

In Norse mythology, Myrkvan Vafrloga ("Flickering Fire") was the high wall of magical fire that surrounded Gymirsgard, the land owned by the Jotun (giant) Gymir; his lovely daughter Gerdr lived there with two hounds made of fire that were kept tethered to the flaming entrance.

Sources: Grimes, *The Norse Myths*, 164, 289

Nab'a, al

According to Islamic mythology, the prophet Muhammad owned at least three half-pikes at the time of his death; their names were al ATRA, al HAFR, and al Nab'a. Beyond its name, nothing else is known of al Nab'a.

Sources: Osborne et al., *A Complete History of the Arabs*, Volume 1, 254; Sale et al., *An Universal History, Part 2*, Volume 1, 185

Naegling

Variations: Nsegling, the sword of Beowulf'

In the Old English epic *Beowulf*, the titular hero used many swords, one of which was the magical blade named Naegling ("Kinsman of the Nail"/"Nail"/"Nailer"). A fine weapon, this old heirloom with a venerable history is described as "bright," "excellent," "gleaming," "grey-colored," "mighty," "sharp," and "strong." In spite of its excellent qualities, Naegling ultimately fails its user in his final battle against the dragon: Beowulf's strength is so great that when he strikes the creature, the sword cannot withstand the impact and breaks (a sword failing its wielder was a common motif in works from this time period).

It has been suggested by some researchers that Naegling may be the sword NAGELRING, a weapon from the *Vilkina saga*.

Sources: Frankel, *From Girl to Goddess*, 49; Garbaty, "The Fallible Sword," 58–59; Mullally, *Hrethel's Heirloom*, 228–44; Portnoy, *The Remnant*, 25

Nagaastra

Variation: Naga astra

In Hindu mythology, an ASTRA is a supernatural weapon created or gifted by the gods to someone who then presides over the weapon. The wielder of an ASTRA is known as an astradhari.

Nagaastra was an ASTRA from the naga (a race of demonic beings described as human with the lower body of a snake); an arrow, it was said to never miss its target. This missile would assume the form of a snake the moment it struck its target, mortally wounding its victim. In the *Ramayana* (*Rama's Journey*), an ancient Indian epic poem dating between 500 and 100 BCE, Nagaastra was used by Ravana's son, Indrajit, against Rama. In the *Mahabharata*, Nagaastra was described as having the shape of a cobra's head, and it contained great destructive powers because it had been devotedly worshiped and tended to by Karna, who intended to use it to slay Arjuna ("Spotless and Shining like Silver"). Unknown to Karna, a snake of princely blood by the name of Ashwasena slithered into the quiver containing Nagaastra, intent on assisting Karna. Courageous and determined, Ashwasena sought justice for the death of his mother against Arjuna, who had killed her when he burned the Khandava Vana forest. The presence of the snake increased Nagaastra's potency but threw off the weapon's balance, causing it to strike its mark without inflicting any real harm on Arjuna.

Sources: Edizioni, *Vimanas and the Wars of the Gods*, n.p.; Narlikar and Narlikar, *Bargaining with a Rising India*, 40–41

Nagapasha

Variation: Naga pasha

In Hindu mythology, an ASTRA is a supernatural weapon created or gifted by the gods to someone who then presides over the weapon. The wielder of an ASTRA is known as an astradhari.

Nagapasha ("Cobra Noose") was an ASTRA from the naga (a race of demonic beings described as human with the lower body of a snake). Nagapasha was said to have the ability to bind its target in coils of living, venomous snakes.

Sources: Edizioni, *Vimanas and the Wars of the Gods*, n.p.; Kulkarni, *The Epics*, 149

Nagelring

Variation: Naglhring

According to Germanic mythology, the magical sword Nagelring once belonged to a giant by the name of Grim; it was stolen from him by a dwarf named Alberich (Alferich/Alpirs/Elbegast), who in turn gave it to a young and heroic Prince Dietrich von Bern so he would slay the giant known as Grim. Nagelring was described as having a hilt covered in hammered gems.

In Continental Germanic mythology, Naglhring is the sword used by Sir Thidrek, the son of Thettmar and Olilia. According to the *Thidrekssaga*, Thidrek captured the dwarf Alfrek, from whom he received the sword as well as the promise of more treasure should he defeat the berserker Grimr and his wife, Hildr. Victorious, Thidrek discovered the helmet HILDIGRIM in their treasure hoard.

Sources: Brewer, *Dictionary of Phrase and Fable* 1900, 1197; de Beaumont and Allinson, *The Sword and Womankind*, 8; Grimes, *The Norse Myths*, 277; Guerber, *Legends of the Middle Ages*, 111, 112

Naglfar (NAG-l-var)

Variations: *Nagelfar* ("Ship of Death"), *Nagilfar*, *Naglfare*, *Nalgfar*

In Norse mythology, *Naglfar* (*Nail Ship*) was a ship constructed entirely from the untrimmed finger- and toenails of the deceased; it was built at Nastrond near Hvergelur in Niflheimr. *Naglfar* carried the dead from Niflheimr to the Vigridr Plain, where the last battle will take place during Ragnarok, with the rising of the waters carrying the god Loki and a horde of others. The Jotun (giant) Hrymr ("Decrepit") steered the vessel.

Sources: Grimes, *The Norse Myths*, 289; Norroena Society, *Asatru Edda*, 375

113

Nagrindr

Variations: Nagates, Nagrinodr, Nigrind

In Norse mythology, Nagrindr ("Corpse Gate") was the gate that contained the dead in the various regions. The gate leading into Niflheimr was named Nagrindr; the sooty-red rooster that would crow the start of Ragnarok lived here, as did the Hrymthursar Hrimgrimnir. Other such gates were called Helgrindr and Valgrind.

Sources: Grimes, *The Norse Myths*, 289

Nandaka

Variation: Nandaki

In Hindu mythology, an ASTRA is a supernatural weapon created or gifted by the gods to someone who then presides over the weapon. The wielder of an ASTRA is known as an astradhari.

The ASTRA Nandaka ("Source of Joy") was the indestructible and sacred sword of Vishnu, the god of preservation. This weapon was utilized by Krishna to kill countless demons; its brilliance was said to put the sun to shame.

Sources: Dalal, *Hinduism*, 163; Iyer, *Bhasa*, n.p.; Jobes, *Dictionary of Mythology, Folklore, and Symbols*, Part 1, 425

naphtha

Variation: Medea's oil

According to Euripides, one of the three best-known ancient Greek tragedians, Medea was the niece of Circe, a priestess of the goddess Hecate, and a sorceress who was abandoned by her husband, the hero Jason, in favor of a new and more politically advantageous wife: Glauce, a Theban princess. Pretending not to be offended, Medea coated the GOLDEN CROWN AND WHITE GOWN OF GLAUCE with a special type of poison known as naphtha and presented the items to the couple as a wedding present. When Glauce donned Medea's gifts, they smoldered and burst into supernatural flames that could not be extinguished, nor could the items be removed from her burning but still living body. The princess suffered in terrible agony until her death, her face scorched beyond recognition and her flesh bubbled and burned away from her body.

Sources: Graves, *The Greek Myths*, 355; Smith, *A Classical Dictionary of Greek and Roman Biography, Mythology and Geography*, 1004; Stuttard, *Looking at Medea*, 196–97

Narayanastra

Variation: Narayan astra

In Hindu mythology, an ASTRA is a supernatural weapon created or gifted by the gods to someone who then presides over the weapon. The wielder of an ASTRA is known as an astradhari.

Narayanastra was an ASTRA from the god of preservation, Vishnu. This item was said to have the ability to create a downpour of arrows and discs. Its power is described as increasing with the amount of resistance that opposes it; thus, attacking Narayanastra will make it grow stronger and more deadly. When the weapon is loosed upon the enemy, the earth shakes and the sky seems to catch fire. A hundred thousand arrows rain down, as do tornadoes of flames, taking many lives.

Narayanastra can only be used once; if a second usage is attempted, the weapon will turn against its wielder and his army. The only way to weaken the terrible power of this weapon is to lie prostrate before it and worship it; doing so will cause its attack to become less dangerous.

Sources: Edizioni, *Vimanas and the Wars of the Gods*, n.p.; Menon, *The Mahabharata*, Volume 2, 352–53

nartsane

In the regional folklore of the Caucasus mountains, and according to Abkhazian legends, the Nart heroes who lived in the mountains drank a type of wine known as nartsane ("Nart's Drink"); it contained small bits of red snakes. This beverage was said to have the ability to give beauty to women, strength to the young, health to the sick, and perpetual youth to the aged and elderly. This remarkable wine was kept in earthenware pitchers, the largest of which was magical and named AWADZAMAKAT.

Sources: Belyarova, *Abkhazia in Legends*, n.p.

Nathach the Wonder

In the Irish epic *Tain Bo Cuailnge* (*The Cattle Raid of Cooley*/*The Tain*), Nathach the Wonder was the sword—or shield—of Laegaire; it is named as being among the many cups, drinking horns, goblets, javelins, shields, and swords kept in Tete Brec, one of the three households of the Ulster hero Cuhullin (Cu Chulaind/Cu Chulainn/Cuchulainn).

Sources: Kinsella and Le Brocquy, *The Tain*, 5

nebelkap

According to fairy lore, there is a magical stone known as a nebelkap ("mist cloak") that, when held, will made the person carrying it invisible.

Sources: Edwards, *Hobgoblin and Sweet Puck*, 65; Keightley, *World Guide to Gnomes, Fairies, Elves, and Other Little People*, 215

necklace of Harmonia, the

When Hephaistos (Hephaestus; Roman god Vulcan), the god of bindings, the art of sculpture, fire, forges, metalworking, stonemasonry, and talismans, discovered that his wife, Aphrodite (Roman goddess Venus), the goddess of love, was having an affair with the god of war, Ares (Roman god Mars), he sought revenge—especially since the affair resulted in Aphrodite bearing a daughter she named Harmonia. Hephaistos created a beautifully wrought gold necklace inlaid with jewels that was shaped like two serpents whose mouths formed the clasp. The necklace was magically crafted to give its wearer eternal beauty and youth; it would also bring great misfortune to anyone who wore or owned it.

When she came of age, Harmonia was betrothed to Cadmus of Thebes, and, as a gift, Hephaistos presented her with the necklace. Soon thereafter, the couple were transformed into dragons (or serpents—sources conflict). The necklace then went to Semele, the daughter of Harmonia; she was inadvertently slain by Zeus (Roman god Jupiter), the god of fate, kings, lightning, sky, and thunder. Some generations later, it was owned by Queen Jocasta, who unknowingly married her own son, Oedipus, and later committed suicide when she discovered what she had done. The necklace was always passed to a new owner, each of the House of Thebes, and all met a terrible fate. The last recorded owner of the necklace was Phayllus, a Phocian tyrant who stole it from the Temple of Athena at Delphi, where it was being held in safekeeping to prevent further deaths. Phayllus made a gift of the necklace to his unnamed mistress. Shortly thereafter, her son was afflicted with a kind of madness and set fire to their home, killing his mother and destroying all of her worldly possessions.

Sources: Daly and Rengel, *Greek and Roman Mythology, A to Z*, 8, 29–30, 52, 63, 132; Graves, *The Greek Myths*, 159.; Menoni, *Kings of Greek Mythology*, 13, 39

necklace of the Lady of the Lake, the

Variation: necklace of Lady Nymue

In Arthurian lore, Nymue, the foremost of the Ladies of the Lake, assumed the guise of an old woman to test the honor, knightliness, and nobility of Sir Pelleas (Pellias). Greatly pleased with him for passing her test, she gave to him her own necklace of emeralds, gold, and opals, which hung down to his chest. This powerful magical item had to ability to make anyone who looked upon the person wearing the necklace love him dearly. Sir Pelleas was unaware of the power of the jewelry but treasured it for its beauty.

Sources: Pyle, *The Story of King Arthur and His Knights*, 239; Smithmark Publishing, *Robin Hood/King Arthur's Knights*, 189

nepenthe

In *The Odyssey*, the ancient Greek epic attributed to Homer, nepenthe is a drug mentioned as a remedy for grief; it was said to be able to ease one's pain by inducing forgetfulness of past sorrows. Helen received this opiate from Polydamma, an Egyptian queen.

Sources: Maginn, *Miscellanies: Prose and Verse*, Volume 2, 37; Oswald, *The Legend of Fair Helen as Told by Homer, Goethe and Others: A Study*, Volume 10, xx

Nes

Variation: Nes Scoit ("Swelling Matter")

In Celtic mythology, Nes ("Swelling") was the spear that Goibniu (Gaibne/Gaibniu/Gobha/Goibhnionn/Goibnenn/Goibniu Sear), the god of blacksmithing, was holding when he heard his wife was not faithful to him. In his anger and jealousy, Goibniu sang magical songs over the spear, enchanting it so that anyone who was struck with it (and survived) would subsequently experience a "swelling" that would fill up with pus and burn the victim as if they were on fire.

Sources: Gregory and MacCumhaill, *Gods and Fighting Men*, 57, 81; Stokes, *Three Irish Glossaries*, xlv

Nesr

Variation: Nesrem

An idol from the lore of southern Arabia, Nesr was said to have been responsible for giving the gift of divination to the Arabs, allowing them to know what will happen in the future as well as what a person has dreamed. Nesr, made in the shape of an eagle (or vulture—sources conflict), is said to be perpetually weeping, as tears fall from its eyes in great sorrow.

Sources: Baring-Gould, *Curious Myths of the Middle Ages*, 156; Lane, *Selections from the Kur-án*, 32

net of Caligorant, the

An item of mixed lore, the net of Caligorant was said to have originated in Greek mythology. Hephaistos (Hephaestus; Roman god Vulcan), the god of bindings, the art of sculpture, fire, forges, metalworking, stonemasonry, and talismans, created a magical net so as to capture his wife, Aphrodite (Roman goddess Venus), the goddess of love, and her lover Ares (Roman god Mars), the god of war. Before the item could be used, however, it was stolen by Hermes (Roman god Mercury), the god of animal husbandry, commerce, eloquence, fertility, language, looters, luck, sleep, thieves, trade, travel, and wealth, so he could capture his beloved nymph, Chloris. Once successful, Hermes left the net in the Temple of Anubis, where it was then stolen by the Egyptian giant and cannibal Caligorant. He made ill use of it, ensnaring people to consume until, according to the lore of Charlemagne, he was defeated by the fictional paladin Astolpho and thereafter used as a beast of burden.

Sources: Daniels and Stevens, *Encyclopedia of Superstitions, Folklore, and the Occult Sciences of the World*, Volume 2, 1375–38; Reddall, *Fact, Fancy, and Fable*, 82

never-failing purse

The steward of King Arthur, Sir Launfal, was known to be a spendthrift; he was given a never-failing purse by the fairy Tryamoug as a sign of her affection for him. This magical pouch always contained untold riches. As long as Launfal kept their romance a secret, the bag would provide coins and Tryamoug would remain his lover, coming to him whenever he wished and remaining unseen so that no one would ever be able to catch them together.

Sources: Fulton, *A Companion to Arthurian Literature*, 246; Keightley, *World Guide to Gnomes, Fairies, Elves, and Other Little People*, 37

Nibelungen Hoard, the

Described in the Middle High German epic poem *Nibelungenlied* (*The Song of the Nibelungs*) as consisting of one hundred wagonloads of precious gems and many more wagons of red gold, the Nibelungen Hoard was given by Sigurd (Siegfried/Sigmund) to Kriemhild as his bridal gift. It is also associated with the sword BALMUNG. This treasure appears at key moments in the tale and eventually becomes the focal point as the lust for gold makes men betray their country, king, and principles. Whoever possessed the hoard was known as the Nibelunger.

After the death of Sigurd, his widow moved the hoard to Worms, where it was seized by Hagen, who buried it in a secret location for later use. However, before the treasure could be accessed, Kriemhild married Etzel, a king, and sought revenge. When Hagen came for a visit,

Kriemhild created a stir that grew into a terrible slaughter.

Sources: Brewer, *Dictionary of Phrase and Fable* 1900, 613; McConnell et al., *The Nibelungen Tradition*, 153

Nide's Plain

According to Norse mythology, Nide's Plain was a hall of glittering gold situated at the base of the Nida Mountains and within sight of those individuals who dwelt in Niflheimr; it was a source of hope for them.

Sources: Grimes, *The Norse Myths*, 290

Nihingo

Variation: Nippongo

In Japanese folklore, Nihingo was counted as one of the *tenka-sanso* ("Three Greatest Spears Under the Heaven") along with OTEGINE and TONBOGIRI.

Sources: Nagayama, *The Connoisseur's Book of Japanese Swords*, 31; Sesko, *Encyclopedia of Japanese Swords*, 460

Noatun

In Norse mythology, Noatun ("Boathouse"/"Place of Ships"/"Ship's Haven") was the home of Njordr, the god of fire, the fury of the sea, the ocean, seafarers, and the winds; it was located by the seaside and was a noisy place, the air full of the sounds of seabirds and the wind. Skade, the wife of Njordr, could only live in the joyous and bustling shipyard for nine days before having to leave; the noise and commotion was too much for her.

Sources: Clare, *Mediaeval History*, 180; Daly, *Norse Mythology A to Z*, 73, 74; Grimes, *The Norse Myths*, 291

Nothung

Variations: BALMUNG, GRAM

Nothung was the sword wielded by the hero of the Middle High German epic poem *Nibelungenlied* (*The Song of the Nibelungs*), Sigurd (Siegfried/Sigmund). The sword was imbued with magical powers by Wotan, which he could also draw on at will; this was explained to Siegmund by Brynhildr (Brunnehilde) in the Wagnerian opera *Die Walkure* (*The Valkyrie*). When that power was withdrawn and the sword shattered against Wotan's spear, known as SPEER, Brynhildr gathered up the broken pieces. Later, Sigurd, the son of Siegmund, under the guidance of Mime, took the pieces of Nothung and reforged the sword so he could slay Fafnir (Fafner), the dragon. With this weapon he also slew Mime and broke SPEER.

Sources: Grimes, *The Norse Myths*, 291; Lewsey, *Who's Who and What's What in Wagner*, n.p.

nucta

Variation: Miraculous Drop

According to Egyptian folklore, nucta is a drop of dew that falls from the moon on Saint John's Day; it is believed to have the ability to stop the plague.

Sources: Brewer, *Dictionary of Phrase and Fable* 1900, 901; Folkard, *Plant Lore, Legends, and Lyrics*, 51

Ocean Sweeper

In Celtic mythology, *Ocean Sweeper* (*Aigean Scuabadoir*) was the ship of Manannan mac Lir (Mannanan,Mannanos), the god of the sea and guardian of the Underworld; this vessel was able to follow his commands without oars or sails. In addition to using his ship to travel and trade between Ireland and Wales, the *Ocean Sweeper* was used to ferry deceased heroes to Tir Tairnigiri ("the Land of Promise"), their final resting place in the Otherworld.

Sources: Mountain, *The Celtic Encyclopedia*, Volume 4, 840; Rolleston, *Myths & Legends of the Celtic Race*, 125

Ochain

In Celtic mythology, Ochain ("Beautiful Ear" and "Moaning One") was the magical shield of Conchobar, which hung in his feasting hall. Whenever Conchobar was in danger, Ochain would moan, and all the shields in the army of Ulster would moan along with it.

Sources: Barber, *Myths & Legends of the British Isles*, 270, 288–89; Gregory, *Cuchulain of Muirthemne*, 43, 130

Ochnech

In the Irish epic *Tain Bo Cuailnge* (*The Cattle Raid of Cooley/The Tain*), Ochnech was the sword of the goddess of the forest beasts, Flidais; it is named as being among the many cups, drinking horns, goblets, javelins, shields, and swords kept in Tete Brec, one of the three households of the Ulster hero Cuhullin (Cu Chulaind/Cu Chulainn/Cuchulainn).

Sources: Kinsella and Le Brocquy, *The Tain*, 5; Mountain, *The Celtic Encyclopedia*, Volume 3, 685

Odrerir

Variations: Odhaerir, Od-hroerir, Odraer, Odraerir, Odrcerir, Odreyrer, Odroerer ("That Which Moves the Spirit"), Odroerir, Odrorir, Osrerir

In Norse mythology, Odrerir ("Heart Stirrer") was one of the three bronze kettles under the protection of the *asynjr* (female Jotun, or giant) Gun-nlod that held part of the PRECIOUS MEAD; the others were BODN and SON.

In the "Skaldskaparmal" portion of the *Prose Edda*, Icelandic historian Snorri Sturluson explicitly states that Odrerir was a bronze kettle in which the blood of Kvasir was fermented, while BODN and SON were barrels.

The name Odrerir is used interchangeably to indicate both the kettle and the mead within it.

Sources: Anderson, *Norse Mythology*, 252; Grimes, *The Norse Myths*, 292; Hawthorne, *Vikings*, 20; Lindow, *Norse Mythology*, 252; Murphy-Hiscock, *The Way of the Hedge Witch*, 60–61

Ofdokkum Ognar Ljoma (OHV-duhk-um OHG-nar LYOHM-a)

Variation: VAFR ("Quickness")

In Norse mythology, Ofdokkum Ognar Ljoma ("Black-Terror Gleam") is the material used to construct the VAFRLOGAR ("Bickering Flames")— the lightning bolts that surround fortresses and lash out at enemies. These bolts are "smart," and they never miss their mark.

Sources: Norroena Society, *Asatru Edda*, 396

Ogress of War

Variation: Rimmu Gugr ("War Ogress")

Named in the thirteenth-century Icelandic epic *Njals saga* (*The Story of Burnt Njals*), the Ogress of War is said to be the axe of Skarphedinn; with it, he slew Hallstein, cutting him in half and severing his spine; Sigurd (Siegfried/Sigmund), striking a blow from his shoulder to his waist; Thrain Sigfus's son, cleaving his head in two; and eight other unnamed men. Later in the story, Thorgeir Craggier used the Ogress of War to slay Thorwalld, cleaving into his chest with the upper horn of the axe, a blow that killed him before he fell to the ground. With the hammer side of the axe, he also caved in the skull of Thorkel Sigfus's son.

Sources: Dasent, *The Story of Burnt Njal*, 80, 173, 195, 220, 291, 300; Eddison, *Egil's Saga*, 281

Okolnir

In Norse mythology, Okolnir ("Uncold") was the region where the beer hall of the giant Brimir; it was said to always have plenty of good drink.

Sources: Larrington et al., *A Handbook to Eddic Poetry*, n.p.; Jones, *Medieval Literature in Translation*, n.p.

Olivant

Variation: Olifant

In the French epic poem *Song of Roland* (*La Chanson de Roland*, circa 1040–1115), which retells

Omphalos

the events of the Battle of Roncevaux Pass in 778 CE, Olivant was the ivory horn belonging to Roland, a paladin of Charlemagne, which he won from the giant Jutmundus. When Olivant was sounded, the noise was so loud that it could be heard thirty miles away; it would not only kill any birds that were flying overhead but also put armies to flight.

Sources: Brewer and Harland, *Character Sketches of Romance, Fiction and the Drama*, Volume 6, 310

Omphalos

Variation: Navel of the Earth

A BAETYLUS from ancient Greek mythology, Omphalos was the stone that Rhea presented to her husband, the Titan Cronus, in place of their newborn child Zeus (Roman god Jupiter), the god of fate, kings, lightning, sky, and thunder. Rhea was fearful that her husband would eat the child, as he had done to their other children, Demeter, Hades, Hera, Hestia, and Poseidon (Roman gods Ceres, Dis/Pluto, Juno, Vesta, and Neptune, respectively), because he had learned that one of his children would eventually kill him.

Sources: Daly and Rengel, *Greek and Roman Mythology, A to Z*, 152; Doniger, *Merriam-Webster's Encyclopedia of World Religions*, 106; Palmer, *Rome and Carthage at Peace*, 99

Omumborombonga

The primordial tree from Namibian mythology, Omumborombonga created the first man, Makuru ("Sorcery"), and the first woman, Kamangundu; it was from the latter that the Betshuana, Herero, Nama, Ovaherero, Ovambo, Ovatyaona, and Tswana tribes were created. Oxen likewise arose from this tree.

Sources: Beiderbecke, "Some Religious Ideas and Customs of the Ovaherero," 92–93; Frazer, *The Golden Bough*, Volume 2, 213, 218–19

Orderg

In the Irish epic *Tain Bo Cuailnge* (*The Cattle Raid of Cooley/The Tain*), Orderg was the shield made of red gold belonging to Furbaide; it is named as being among the many cups, drinking horns, goblets, javelins, shields, and swords kept in Tete Brec, one of the three households of the Ulster hero Cuhullin (Cu Chulaind/Cu Chulainn/Cuchulainn).

Sources: Kinsella and Le Brocquy, *The Tain*, 5; Orel, *Irish History and Culture*, 9

orichalcum

Variation: aurichalcum ("gold copper")

The classical Greek philosopher Plato (428–347 BCE) stated that the metal orichalcum ("mountain brass") was second only in value to gold; it was described as having the "color of fire"—a shining dark yellow or reddish yellow. Ancient writings are divided as to whether it was a natural ore versus a blend of metals. It was referenced by many ancient writers, including the Greek poets Hesiod and Homer. Marcus Tullius Cicero (106–43 BCE), the ancient Roman lawyer, orator, and philosopher, mentioned that a bit of gold and orichalcum were so close in appearance that a person could easily mistake one for the other, but in his time the orichalcum was worth very little. Pliny the Elder (23–79 CE), a Roman army commander, author, natural philosopher, naturalist, and naval commander, claimed the metal lost its value because the mines had all run out. If orichalcum ever existed, there was none to be found by the time that Plato embarked on an active search for it.

Sources: Polehampton, *The Gallery of Nature and Art*, Volume 6, 272, 280; Zhirov, *Atlantis*, 45, 46

Orna

In Celtic mythology, Orna was the sword of King Tethra of the Fomorians. After the battle of Mag Tured, the champion Oghma recovered the weapon. According to the story, he unsheathed the blade and cleaned it; Orna, a magical sword possessed of intelligence, then recounted to Oghma all of its adventures and deeds.

Sources: Akins, *The Lebor Feasa Runda*, 71; Gregory and MacCumhaill, *Gods and Fighting Men*, 60; Sjoestedt, *Celtic Gods and Heroes*, n.p.

Otegine

Variation: Otegine-no-yari

In Japanese folklore, the great swordsmith Masamune (circa late thirteenth century) was said to have created the greatest swords ever forged. Although Masamune was a real person, the legendary sword Otegine was not. Otegine was the sword of the swordsmith Shimada Yoshisuke, and it was counted as one of the *tenka-sanso* ("Three Greatest Spears Under the Heaven") along with NIHONGO and TONBOGIRI.

Sources: Nagayama, *The Connoisseur's Book of Japanese Swords*, 31; Pauley, *Pauley's Guide*, 130; Sesko, *Encyclopedia of Japanese Swords*, 460

paatuwvota

In the Hopi oral traditions, the paatuwvota ("magic flying shield") is a means of transportation utilized by shamans. This item is made of lightweight cotton and woven in the same manner as a traditional robe. The shaman sits upon it and tugs on some strings while speaking an incantation. The shield then rises up from the ground and takes the shaman wherever he wishes to travel.

Sources: Lomatuway'ma, *Earth Fire*, 152; Malotki and Gary, *Hopi Stories of Witchcraft, Shamanism, and Magic*, xl

Palladium, the (pal-LA-de-um)

In classical Greek mythology, the Palladium was a wooden pillar (or statue) given by Zeus (Roman god Jupiter), the god of fate, kings, lightning, sky, and thunder, to Dardanus, the founder of the Trojan line. It was believed to protect national welfare, and as long at it remained in the city, Troy would never fall. During the Trojan War, the Palladium was stolen by Diomedes and Odysseus.

Sources: Berens, *Myths and Legends of Ancient Greece and Rome*, 299, 301; Scull, *Greek Mythology Systematized*, 133, 354

panacea (pan-ah-SEE-ah)

Variation: panchrest

A magical drug named after the goddess of the universal remedy—specifically of the materials used to cure the sick—panacea ("all healing") was said to have the ability to cure any disease and to prolong life indefinitely.

Sources: Loar, *Goddesses for Every Day*, 25, 40

Pancakala

According to Hindu mythology, one day while Bhima, the second born of the Pandavas, was walking along a bank, he was attacked by a giant dragon (or serpent) that lived in the lake. Upon seizing the creature, Bhima used his thumbnail, named Pancakala, and stabbed the monster in the neck, slaying it.

Sources: Darmawan, *Six Ways toward God*, 21

Panchajanya

Variation: Paanchajanyam

In Hindu mythology, Panchajanya ("Possessing Control Over the Five Classes of Beings") is the conch belonging to the god of preservation, Vishnu. Said to be as pure as a moonbeam and a source of majestic sound, it also had the ability to emit fire.

Sources: Beer, *The Handbook of Tibetan Buddhist Symbols*, 10; Iyer, *Bhasa*, n.p.; Varadpande, *Mythology of Vishnu and His Incarnations*, 19

Pantao

Variations: Immortal Peache, Longevity Peach, Magical Peache, p'an-t'ao, Peach of Immortality

In Taoist mythology, Pantao was the peach of immortality; it was said that every 3,000 years (or 10,000 years—sources conflict), the fruit, which grew in the garden of Hsi wang mu (Xiwangmu), the Queen Mother of the West, would ripen. This event would be celebrated with a grand banquet held by the Pa Hsien ("Eight Immortals").

Sources: Campbell, *Gods and Goddesses of Ancient China*, n.p.; Duda, *Traditional Chinese Toggles*, 104; Yu, *Journey to the West*, 74

Pan-the-ra comb of Reynard the Fox, the

Variations: panther comb, panthera comb

Written of in the fifteenth century by Hermann Barkhusan of Rostock, Reynard the Fox possessed a Pan-the-ra comb that he wished to present as a gift to the king. The comb was said to be made from a single bone taken from the remains of a panther. According to Reynard, the animal had traits so admirable and desirous that all the creatures of the jungle walked in its wake. When the panther died, all its wonderful traits settled down into a single bone, from which the glossy blue-black comb was made. It was as light as a feather but so indestructible that none of the natural elements could destroy it. The comb, like the panther, gave off a scent so wonderful that it would cure all the ailments to which the human body was susceptible. Additionally, if its user's body was weak, it would suddenly grow strong, and their heart, if full of grief, would thereafter only be filled with gladness.

Sources: Brewer, *Dictionary of Phrase and Fable* 1900, 819; Day, *The Rare Romance of Reynard the Fox*, 122–23; de Sanctis, *Reynard the Fox*, 137; Hyamson, *A Dictionary of English Phrases*, 263

panther-skin sack

In Chinese Buddhist mythology, there are four brothers known collectively as the Diamond Kings of Heaven (*Ssu Ta Chin-kang* or *T'ien-wang*); statues of them stand guard in pairs on the left and right sides of the entrances to Buddhist temples. The god and guardian of the north, Mo-li Shou (Ch'ih Kuo; known in Sanskrit as Vaisravana), carries twin whips and a magical panther-skin sack containing a creature known as the Hua Hu tiao. While in the magical sack, the creature is a white rat, but once removed it assumes its true form: a large, carnivorous, winged elephant.

Sources: Buckhardt, *Chinese Creeds and Customs*, 163; Werner, *Myths and Legends of China*, 122

Paran-ja

In Hindu mythology, Paran-ja was the sword of Indra, god of the heavens, lightning, rains, river flows, storms, and *vajra* ("thunder"); he is also the king of the devas (demigods) and Svarga (Heaven).

Sources: Dowson, *Classical Dictionary of Hindu Mythology and Religion*, 127; Rengarajan, *Glossary of Hinduism*, 191

Parashu

Variation: Parasu

In Hindu mythology, an ASTRA is a supernatural weapon created or gifted by the gods to someone who then presides over the weapon. The wielder of an ASTRA is known as an astradhari.

Parashu was the divine battle-axe of Shiva the Destroyer; it was an indestructible and unbeatable weapon. Shiva made of gift of Parashu to Parashurama ("Rama with an axe"), who passed it on to Ganesha, the god of obstacles. Parashu is described as having four cutting edges; there was a blade on each end of the axe head and one on each end of the shaft.

Sources: Knappert, *Indian Mythology*, 191

Parvataastra

Variation: Parvata astra

In Hindu mythology, an ASTRA is a supernatural weapon created or gifted by the gods to someone who then presides over the weapon. The wielder of an ASTRA is known as an astradhari.

The ASTRA Parvataastra was said to have the ability to cause a mountain to fall out of the sky and land on the enemy; it was wielded by Pradyumna, the son of Krishna and the incarnation of the god of love, Kamadeva.

Sources: Edizioni, *Vimanas and the Wars of the Gods*, n.p.

pasha

In Hindu mythology, a pasha ("lasso" or "noose") is a divine weapon utilized by such gods as Ganesha, the god of obstacles; Varuna, the god of justice, sky, truth, and water; and Yama, the god of death.

Sources: Dallapiccola and Verghese, *Sculpture at Vijayanagara*, 38, 39; Moor, *The Hindu Pantheon*, 274

pasha of Yama, the

Variations: noose of Yama, Yama Paasha, Yama's noose

Yama, the god of death in Hindu mythology, carried a pasha (noose) that had the innate ability to drain the life out of any living being; no one could escape this powerful weapon except for the Trimurtis (the collective name for the three gods Brahma, Shiva, and Vishnu).

Sources: Moor, *The Hindu Pantheon*, 274; Nahm, *Dealing with Death*, 69, 199

Pashupatashastra

Variation: Pashupatas astra

In Hindu mythology, an ASTRA is a supernatural weapon created or gifted by the gods to someone who then presides over the weapon. The wielder of an ASTRA is known as an astradhari.

Pashupatashastra, an arrow or magical staff, was the primary weapon of Mahakali ("Goddess Who Is Beyond Time"), the consort of Shiva the Destroyer. On two occasions, Shiva allowed this ASTRA to be called as a boon—once to Arjuna ("Spotless and Shining like Silver") and another time to Indrajit. Pashupatashastra was a dreadful weapon, as it had the ability to shoot thousands of arrows, maces, and spears at the same time.

Sources: Mani, *Memorable Characters from the Ramayana and the Mahabharata*, 49; Vaidya, *The Mahabharata*, 45

Pashupatastra

In Hindu mythology, an ASTRA is a supernatural weapon created or gifted by the gods to someone who then presides over the weapon. The wielder of an ASTRA is known as an astradhari.

Pashupatastra was an ASTRA from the god Shiva the Destroyer. It was said to have the ability to completely destroy its target no matter its nature; in this it was infallible. This ASTRA would release several demons and a huge spirit that personified the weapon. The destruction caused by Pashupatastra has been compared to a hydrogen bomb explosion. Each time the ASTRA appeared, its head would look different. Pashupatastra could only be obtained directly from Shiva.

Sources: Edizioni, *Vimanas and the Wars of the Gods*, n.p.

Pattayudha

Variation: Patta-Yudha

In Hindu mythology, an ASTRA is a supernatural weapon created or gifted by the gods to someone who then presides over the weapon. The wielder of an ASTRA is known as an astradhari.

Pattayudha was a metallic weapon Shiva the Destroyer gave to the leader of his armies, Lord Virabhadra (Veerabhadra).

Sources: Kramrisch, *The Presence of Siva*, 323, 324, 364, 365

Pelian spear, the

Variations: Pelias, the spear of Achilles

In Greek mythology, the Pelian spear, a divine weapon, was so named because it was made by the centaur Chiron from the wood of a tree from Mount Pelion and given to Peleus on the day of his wedding to Thetis. When Chiron gave the ashen spear to Peleus, he intended it to be the "death of heroes"; Peleus later passed the weapon to his son, Achilles.

The Pelian spear is described in the *Iliad* (1260–1180 BCE), the ancient Greek epic attributed to Homer, as "huge, heavy, and massive … like Athena's"; in one instance, it is said to be "heavy with bronze." No Achaean aside from Achilles can use the spear due to its unwieldiness. This is why Patroclus did not take the spear with him when he used Achilles's armor to confront Hector.

Sources: Homer, *Homer: Iliad*, Book 22, 93, 141; Mueller, *Objects as Actors*, 134

peridexion tree, the

According to medieval folklore, there was a tree in India known as the peridexion whose fruit was pleasant and sweet; it had the unique ability to attract doves. These birds would eat the fruit and live within the tree's branches. This tree also had the ability to repel dragons (or snakes—translations vary), who were so fearful of the tree that they would not even stand in its shade.

Sources: Curley, *Physiologus*, 28; Hassig, *The Mark of the Beast*, 146; Porteous, *The Forest in Folklore and Mythology*, 196

Perilous Seat, the

Variation: Siege Perilous

A chair from Arthurian lore, the Perilous Seat was one of four different types of chairs placed around the ROUND TABLE. According to the Italian romances, the Perilous Seat was to be at the table but would remain empty, symbolic of Judas Iscariot's vacated seat at the Last Supper, and it was to be filled by the knight who would find the HOLY GRAIL.

Sources: Ashley, *The Mammoth Book of King Arthur*, n.p.; Bruce, *The Arthurian Name Dictionary*, 430; Dom, *King Arthur and the Gods of the Round Table*, 93

Philippan

The celebrated sword of Marcus Antonius Marci filius Marci nepos ("Marcus Antonius, son of Marcus, grandson of Marcus") was named Philippan in William Shakespeare's tragedy *Antony and Cleopatra*. The sword, it is said, was named after Anthony's defining battle, Philippi, at which he defeated Brutus and Cassius.

Sources: Brewer, *Dictionary of Phrase and Fable* 1900, 1197; Rosenberg, *The Masks of Anthony and Cleopatra*, 94, 262; Shakespeare, *The Tragedy of Anthony and Cleopatra*, 75, 199

Philosopher's Stone, the

Variations: afternoon light, ALKAHEST, Alome of Spaine, Antidotus, Antimonium, aqua benedicta, aqua volans per aeram, Arcanum, Argentvive fixt, Atramentum, attrement, Auripigment, Auripigmentum, Autumnus, Ayre, Azot, bark of the sea, Basilicus, Beyia, blacker than black, bloud, body cynaper, body of Magnesia, Borax, Brasse of Philosophers, Brutorum cor, Bufo, burnt brass, calculus albus, Camelion, Capillus, Capistrum auri, Carbones, Celestial Ruby, Certore of the earth, Cinis cineris, crowne overcoming a cloud, Cucurbite with his Alimbeck, Denne, dew of heavenly gate, divine quintessence, Dominus philosophorum, dregs of the belly, dry water, dun salt, earth found on the dunghill putrefied, Egge, Elephas, elixir of immortality, elixir of life, Ethell, everlasting water, eyes of fishes, Father of minerals, ferment of elixir, Filius ignis, filthiness of the dead bloud, Fimus, first matter, flying Volatile, Folium, Gold, Granum, Granum frumenti, green lion, greene vitriol, Haematites, Hepar, herbalis, Hermes bird, high man with a sallet, Hypostasis, joyning water, kybrik, Lac, lapis noster, lapis occultus, lapis philopharum, Lead of Philosophers, lesse world, light of lights, Lune, Magnesia, Maptha, Marvelous Father, masculine, materia prima, Melancholia, menstruousm Brazill, Mercury corporall, Metteline, most strong vinegar, most vivid black, old water, our gold, our stone Lunare, our Sulphur, ovum philosophorum, Panacea salutifera, philosophic mercury, poison, pure body, Purified Stone, quintessence, radicall humidity, Radices arboris solares, red earth, red lead, Red Lion, red water of sulpur, Rex regum, rubie stone, Sal armoniack, Sal metallorum, Sal niter, Salarmoniack, Salvator terrenus, Secundine, seminall, shadow of the sun, Sol, Sperme, spittle of Lune, stinking menstrues, stinking spirit, stinking water, Stone of the Wise, Sulpher red, Sulphur incombustible, taile of the dragon, thing of vile price, tincture of the philosophers, unctuous moisture, Ventus hermetis, Vermilion white, vessel of the philosophers, vine of the wise, vine sharp, vinegar of life, virgin's milk, vitriol, water metelline, water of Sulphur, water of the world, water of wise men, white fume, white gumme, white Jayre, white lead, white stone, wind of the belly (and scores of additional names)

A legendary alchemical substance said to have the ability to turn simple base metals into gold or silver, the Philosopher's Stone was also believed to be a key ingredient in an elixir of life that would have the ability to restore a person to their perfect youthful state and heal them of all illnesses; in addition, there was the belief that should a person consume a small portion of the stone, they would be granted immortality. More mundane uses of the Philosopher's Stone include being able to create a HOMUNCULUS, fuel perpetually burning lamps, revive dying plants, transform crystals into diamonds, and render glass flexible.

The stone appears in writing dating back to 300 CE, but the legend is believed to be older. Its physical appearance is hard to pin down, as it is never described directly; alchemists were intentionally mysterious and vague regarding this object. Their texts used allegory and obscure terms and words, as well as pages filled with symbols that were inconsistent from work to work.

The stone's origin is equally mysterious. Some alchemists believed it was hatched from a concoction of magical ingredients, some thought it oozed down from the moon, and others believed it was the remnant of a star that fell from the heavens. However, no matter its origins, alchemists would devote their lives to re-creating the stone to reap its alleged rewards.

Sources: Figulus, *Book of the Revelation of Hermes*, n.p.; Guiley, *Encyclopedia of Magic and Alchemy*, 10, 104, 252; Steiger and Steiger, *Gale Encyclopedia of the Unusual and Unexplained*, 206–8

pigskin of Tuis, the

A magical item belonging to the Celtic god of the sun, Lugh ("Bright" or "Light") of the Long Arms (Artful Hands or Long Hands), the pigskin of Tuis (a king in Greece) had the ability to heal the sick and wounded as well as to transform water into wine. Lugh acquired the item through an act of revenge against the sons of Tuireann, who had murdered his father. Lugh tasked the brothers with retrieving a list of rare items in exotic locations. To conclude the quest, the brothers were each to call out three times to him from atop the hill of Modhchaoin in Lochlann. Unbeknownst to the Tuireann brothers, Modhchaoin and his family were bound to prevent anyone

from shouting out upon that hill. Although the brothers succeeded in calling out to Lugh, they were all fatally wounded by the Modhchaoin family. The Tuireanns begged Lugh to use the pigskin of Tuis on them, but he coldly refused, confronting them with the murder of his father and watching as they died.

Sources: Asala, *Celtic Folklore Cooking*, 288; Ellis, *The Mammoth Book of Celtic Myths and Legends*, n.p.; Williams, *Ireland's Immortals*, 261

Pill of Immortality, the

Variation: Elixir of Jade

In Chinese, Japanese, and Korean folklore, Moon Rabbit is said to live on the moon beneath a cassia tree; there he sits eternally with a mortar and pestle, pounding gold, jade, and jewels to make the Pill of Immortality. This tablet is said to give everlasting life and has many of the same properties as the PHILOSOPHER'S STONE.

Sources: Bredon and Mitrophanow, *Moon Year*, 409; Newman, *Food Culture in China*, 165

Pillar of Cloud

A manifestation of the divine presence of God, the Pillar of Cloud guided the Israelites through the wilderness by day; at night, it would transform into the PILLAR OF FIRE. On one occasion, near the Red Sea, the Pillar of Cloud did not change, instead moving behind the Israelites into a defensive position to prevent a nighttime attack by the Egyptian army. After the construction of the tabernacle, the Pillar of Cloud would descend upon it, which was taken as a sign to stop and make camp. When the cloud ascended, it was time to break camp and move again.

Sources: Freedman, *Eerdmans Dictionary of the Bible*, 1059; Mahusay, *The History of Redemption*, 339

Pillar of Fire

A manifestation of the divine presence of God, the Pillar of Fire guided the Israelites through the wilderness by night; by day it led them as the PILLAR OF CLOUD.

Sources: Freedman, *Eerdmans Dictionary of the Bible*, 461, 1059; Mahusay, *The History of Redemption*, 339

Pinaka

Variations: Pinakin, Shiva Dhanush

In Hindu mythology, Pinaka was the sacred bow and personal weapon of the god Shiva; it was given to him by Parashurama. When wielding this particular bow, Shiva was known as Pinakavan. Pinaka was described in texts as large and black; in addition to being invincible, it was able to strike terror into the hearts of Shiva's enemies and could not be strung or carried by a mortal. Pinaka was created by Vishvakarman, the cosmic architect and the maker of weapons.

Sources: Garg, *Encyclopaedia of the Hindu World*, Volume 1, 264; Satish, *Tales of Gods in Hindu Mythology*, n.p.

plow of Balarama, the

Variation: hala

In Hindu mythology, the god of agriculture, propriety, and social decorum, Balarama (the older brother of Krishna), had two primary weapons: a plow (hala) and a pestal (musala). Balarama used the plow on his enemies, literally plowing a bloody path into their bodies. Most notably, he used his plow to divert the Yamuna River.

Sources: Beck, *Alternative Krishnas*, 93, 94; Sharma, *Essays on the Mahabharata*, 73, 74

plow of Ilmarinen, the

In a legend from Finland found in the epic poem *The Kalevala*, Ilmarinen, a god with remarkable smithing abilities, used the magical elements in his forge to create many items. One such item was a plow of gold with silver handles and a shaft of copper; unfortunately, this item plowed up the barley fields and the richest meadows. Displeased with his creation, Ilmarinen destroyed it and hurled the bits back into his magical forge.

Sources: Friberg et al., *The Kalevala*, 99; Mouse, *Ilmarinen Forges the Sampo*, 56

pole of heaven and earth, the

There is a prophecy in Brazilian folklore stating that the end of the world will come when Sinna, a hybrid monstrosity born of the union between a woman and a gigantic jaguar, removes the pole that separates the heavens from the earth.

Sources: Cotterell, *Dictionary of World Mythology*, 288; Rose, *Giants, Monsters, and Dragons*, 335

Precieuse

Variations: Preciuse, sword of Baligant

In the Matter of France (also known as the Carolingian cycle), Precieuse ("Precious") was the sword of Baligant, a legendary Arabic king. According to the story, after meeting Charlemagne and learning that his sword was called Joyeuse, Baligant felt inferior and, at that moment, gave his sword a similar sort of name: Precieuse. The sword's name was also Baligant's war cry, and in more intense battles, his knights would yell "Precieuse" as well.

Sources: Auty, *Traditions of Heroic and Epic Poetry*, 96; Pendergrass, *Mythological Swords*, 61; Sayers, *The Song of Roland*, 38

Precious Mead

Variations: Dwarfs' Drink, Dwarfs' Fill, Ferry Boat of Dwarfs, Foundation of Poetry, Hinn Dyri Mjodr, Kvasir's Blood, Liquid of Bond, Liquid of Odrerir, Liquid of Son, Liquor of Hintbjorg, Mead of Inspiration, Mead of Poetry, Odhroeris Drecker, Odhroeris Dreckr, Odthroeris Dreckr, Suttungr's Hoard, Suttungr's Mead

In Norse mythology, the Precious Mead was a beverage created by the two dwarfs Fjalar and Galarr; it was a combination of honey, rum, the saliva of all the gods, and the blood of Kvasir. Whoever drank this concoction was said to become a great poet.

The Precious Mead was given as weregild to the Jotun (giant) Suttungr as payment from the two dwarfs for having murdered his father and mother. Suttungr kept the drink safe in his treasure chamber, Hnitbjorg, which was guarded by his daughter Gunnlod until Odin, the god of battle, death, frenzy, the gallows, healing, knowledge, poetry, royalty, the runic alphabet, sorcery, and wisdom, managed to steal it and flee with it back to Asgard ("Enclosure of the Aesir"). From there, the Precious Mead was stolen by Midvitnir, who had his son Sokkmimir guard it, but, again, it was stolen by Odin.

Sources: Grimes, *The Norse Myths*, 284, 287, 292, 293; Murphy-Hiscock, *The Way of the Hedge Witch*, 60; Sturluson, *The Prose Edda*, 94

Preserver of Life, the

In the epic poem from ancient Mesopotamia known as the *Epic of Gilgamesh* (2100 BCE), the *Preserver of Life* was the ship that Enki, the god of art, crafts, creation, exorcism, fertility, fresh water, healing, intelligence, magic, trickery and mischief, virility, and wisdom, told Utnapishtim to build in order to save his animals, craftsmen, family, grain, and seeds from the impending flood. Constructed by Utnapishtim and his craftsman in seven days out of solid timbers, the *Preserver of Life* is described as 200 feet in height, length, and width, with seven interior stories, each floor of which was divided into nine sections.

Sources: Abulhab, *The Epic of Gilgamesh*, 161; Rosenberg, *World Mythology*, 196–200

Prima Materia

Variations: Abzernad, Adarner, Agnean Alartar, Albar Evis, Alcharit, Alembroth, Alinagra, Alkaest,

Promethean Fire

Almialudel, Almisada, Alun, Amalgra, Anatron, Androgyne, Anger, Animal Stone, Antimony, Aremaros, Arnec, Arsenic, Asmarceh, Asrob, AZOTH, Bath, Belly of the Ostrich, Bird of Hermes, Boiling Milk, Borax, Boritis, the Bride, the Bull, Butter, Caduceus, Cain Chyle, Chamber, Chaos, Clouds, the Cock, Creature of God, Crystal, Dew, Dissolved Refuse, the Doing, the Dragon, a Drop, Dung, Eagle, Eagle Stone, Ebisemeth, Embryo, Euphrates, Eve, Feces, Fiery and Burning Water, the Fig, First Matter, Flower of the Sun, Fog, the Garden, Glass, Golden Wood, Heart of the Sun, Heaven, Honey, Hyle, Indian Gold, Infinite, Isis, Kibrish, the Lamb, Laton, Lead, Lion, Lord of the Stones, Lucifer, Lye, Magnes, Magnesia, Magnet, Marble, Mars, Materia Prima, Matter of All Forms, May Blossom, Medicine, Menstruum, Mercury, Mermaphrodite, Metallic Entity, Microcosmos, Milk of Virgin, the Moon, Mother, Nebula, Ore, Orient, Permanent Water, Philosophical Stone, Poison, Pure and Uncontaminated Virgin, Rainbow, Salamander, Salt of Nitre and Saltpetre, Scottish Gem, the Sea, Serpent, Shade, Shadow of the Sun, Silver, Son of the Water of Life, Soul and Heaven of the Elements, Soul of Saturn, Spirit, Spiritual Blood, Spittle of the Moon, the Spouse, Spring, Stella Signata, Sulphur, Sulphur of Nature, Summer, Sun and the Moon, Syrup, Tartar of the Philosophers, Tin, Tincture of Metals, the Tree, Urine, Vapour, Vegetable Liquor, Venom, Venus, Vinegar, Water of Gold, Water of Life, the West, White Ethesia, White Moisture, White Smoke, Whiteness, the Woman

When constructing a PHILOSOPHER'S STONE, the first ingredient required is Prima Materia; it is said to be found in nature, and its few imperfections can be removed by use of alchemical arts. In its pure form, Prima Materia has the ability to remove imperfections from other forms of matter. Descriptions of what Prima Materia looks like in its original and altered forms have changed throughout history, but it is alleged to contain within it all colors and all metals.

Additionally, formulas often do not directly use Prima Materia's name, but rather an alias, as alchemists have gone to great lengths to obscure what this element may be. Martin Ruland the Younger (1532–1602), a German alchemist and physician, listed more than fifty names for Prima Materia in his dictionary of alchemy, along with a short explanation of why each name was chosen. Adding to the confusion, some alchemists believed Prima Materia and the PHILOSOPHER'S STONE to be the same, while others, believing the items to be different, overlapped the aliases they used for each.

Sources: Atwood, *A Suggestive Inquiry into Hermetic Mystery*, 72; Kugler, *The Alchemy of Discourse*, 112; Ruland, *Lexicon Alchemiae*, 93

Promethean Fire

In Greek mythology, Promethean fire was the flame used by the cultural hero, Titan, and trickster Prometheus ("Forethought") to bring his clay sculptures to life.

Sources: Brewer, *Dictionary of Phrase and Fable* 1900, 1010; Draco, *The Dictionary of Magic and Mystery*, n.p.

Promethean Unguent

According to classical Greek mythology, when the cultural hero, Titan, and trickster Prometheus ("Forethought") was chained to a boulder as part of his punishment for giving humanity the gift of fire, some of his blood fell upon an herb. This plant gained magical properties that Medea was able to discern and use. She made an unguent that would protect its user from fire and warlike instruments and gave it to the hero and Argonaut Jason.

Sources: Brewer, *Dictionary of Phrase and Fable* 1900, 1010; Draco, *The Dictionary of Magic and Mystery*, n.p.

prophetic stone of Unhcegila, the

Unhcegila was a dragon-like, female monster in the mythology of the Lakota; her body was covered with scales of flint, her heart was a crystal, and her eyes could produce flames. According to the lore, she lived in the ocean but several times a year would swim along the shore, causing tidal waves and turning the water brackish and unfit for human use. Only one place on her body was vulnerable to attack—the seventh point beneath her head. Two brothers learned of this weakness and, armed with arrows and magic to slow her reactions, set off to slay her. While one brother chanted the magical incantations, the other shot his arrow into the vulnerable place on Unhcegila's head, killing her. Taking her crystal heart, the brothers gained the gift of prophecy.

Sources: Rose, *Giants, Monsters, and Dragons*, 374; Walker, *Lakota Belief and Ritual*, 122

Prydwen

Variations: *Pridwen, Priwen, Pryd-wen*

In Welsh Arthurian lore, *Prydwen* (*Fair Face/ Fair Form/[of] White Aspect*) is the ship of King

Arthur; however, in later Arthurian lore, Sir Thomas Malory (1415–1471) gives "Prydwen" as the name of his shield. The later translation of the name suggests a form of invisibility and a means of traveling to the Underworld.

When Arthur tells Culhwch that he may ask and receive anything of him, the king makes a short list of his prize possessions that are the seven exceptions to his offer: CALADBOLG, his sword; CARNWENNAN, his dagger; Gwenhwyfar, his wife; GWENN, his cloak; *Prydwen*, his ship; RHONGO-MIANT, his spear; and WYNEBGWRTHUCHER, his shield. *Prydwen* was named first.

In the Welsh poem *Preiddeu Annwn* (*Spoils of Annwn*), Arthur and his men travel to the Underworld in *Prydwen* to retrieve the CAULDRON OF ANNWN.

Sources: Karr, *Arthurian Companion*, 408; Padel, *Arthur in Medieval Welsh Literature*, n.p.

pukku

The magical drum of Gilgamesh, the pukku, was a gift from the goddess Inanna (Ishtar). According to the myth "Gilgamesh and the Huluppu Tree," Inanna planted a huluppu tree in her personal garden with the intention of making a bed and chair from its wood. When hostile forces thwarted her plans, Gilgamesh intervened and assisted Inanna. As a reward for his services, the goddess made the shamanic pukku from the base of the tree and an accompanying mikku (drumstick) from the tree's crown. The ability or powers the drum may have possessed are highly debatable; one idea is that the drum could entice men to rally to war, while another is that it gave Gilgamesh some sort of tyrannical hold over the city.

When, according to the myth, the pukku and mikku disappeared into the underworld, Gilgamesh lamented their loss; his friend Enkidu then ventured into the underworld to retrieve them.

Sources: Gardner, *Gilgamesh*, n.p.; Hooke, *Middle Eastern Mythology*, 55

Pushpaka Vimana

Variations: DHADU MONARA, Pushpa Vimana ("Flight of Flowers")

In Hindu mythology, Pushpaka Vimana was the flying machine originally belonging to the demon Ravana; it was taken from him by Rama and commanded by Raghira. The vessel was described in *Ramayana* (*Rama's Journey*), an ancient Indian epic poem dating between 500 and 100 BCE, as

"taking off" with a loud noise and carrying twelve people. The poem says that it left Lanka in the morning and nine hours later arrived in Ayodhya, traveling 1,118 miles (1,800 kilometers) at 124 miles per hour (200 kilometers per hour).

The vehicle was said to look like a cloud, painted and shiny. It had two floors, each with many rooms and each room having many windows. Travel on board was comfortable and spacious. As Pushpaka Vimana flew through the upper atmosphere, it made a sound much like a whisper. Able to move of its own accord, it would take passengers wherever they wished to go.

In the fifth book of *Mahabharata*, entitled "Vimanapala" ("Guardian of the Aircraft"), a highly specialized individual is given the responsibility of caring for the vimana.

Sources: Baccarini and Vaddadi, *Reverse Engineering Vedic Vimanas*, n.p.; Childress, *Vimana*, n.p.

qengmerping

In the Inuit folklore of Greenland, an evil spirit by the name of Idlirvirissong lives in a house in the sky where she waits for the newly dead to arrive. She is described as having a turned-up nose and owning many dogs. When the recently deceased arrive, she steals their intestines, places them on her dish (known as *qengmerping*), and feeds them to her dogs.

Sources: Krober, "Tales of the Smith Sound Eskimo," 180–81

Quadriga

According to the Latin narrative poem *Metamorphoses* (2.153) written by the Roman poet Ovid (Publius Ovidius Naso; 43 BCE–17 CE), the sun god and second-generation Titan, Helios (Sol), had his golden chariot, Quadriga, pulled across the sky by several flying horses: Aethon, Astrope, Bronte, Chronos, Eous, Lampoon, Phaethon, Phlegon, and Pyrois. All of these horses are described as pure white with flaring nostrils that can bring forth flame.

Sources: Breese and D'Aoust, *God's Steed*, 86; Coulter and Turner, *Encyclopedia of Ancient Deities*, 76; Rose, *Giants, Monsters, and Dragons*, 178

Que Qiao

In Chinese folklore, the Que Qiao (Bridge of Magpies) in described in the story of Niulang (Cowherd; N'gow) and Zhinu (Weaver Girl; Yehr N'geu), the beautiful seventh-born daughter of a goddess. The two fell in love, married, and had two children; they enjoyed a wonderful, love-filled life until the goddess discovered her daughter had married a mere mortal and commanded her to return to the heavens. Niulang was distraught over the disappearance of his wife. At this time, his ox suddenly gained the ability to speak and told him to kill it and wear its hide; doing so would enable Niulang to enter the heavens. Doing as instructed, Niulang carried his two children with him in search of Zhinu. However, the goddess discovered what was happening and, using her hairpin, scratched the universe, creating the Milky Way and forever separating the two lovers. Zhinu sadly sits on one side, working her loom, while Niulang sits on the other with the children. However, once a year, the magpies take pity on the couple and gather together in the heavens, building a bridge across the Milky Way that will let Niulang and Zhinu reunite for one day.

Sources: Bernardin, "Portfolios," 431; Bhagavatananda, *A Brief History of the Immortals of Non-Hindu Civilizations*, 136

Quern Biter

Variation: Kvernbitr

A sword from Norse mythology, Quern Biter ("Foot Breadth") belonged to King Hakon Athelstane I of Norway and his follower, Thoralf Skolinson the Strong. Quern Biter was said to have an edge so keen it could cut through quernstones (stones used since the Iron Age to hand grind a wide variety of materials).

Sources: Brewer, *Dictionary of Phrase and Fable* 1900, 1197; Eddison, *Egil's Saga*, 281

Quickborn

Variation: FOUNTAIN OF YOUTH

An ancient Norse fairy tale tells that Hulla (Hulda) was queen of the Kolbolds, appointed to be their ruler by Odin, the god of battle, death, frenzy, the gallows, healing, knowledge, poetry, royalty, the runic alphabet, sorcery, and wisdom. A poem from the Middle Ages says she lives in the Mountain of Venus, and it is there that she has the fountain Quickborn. Should one bathe in this fountain, their full ability, power, and strength would be restored; it would also wash away old age and return a person to the height of their youth.

Sources: Macdowall, *Asgard and the Gods*, 113

Qumqam

According to the medieval Persian saga of Amir Hamza, Qumqam was one of the four swords once held by King Suleiman, the others being AQRAB-E SULEIMANI, SAMSAM, and ZUL-HAJAM. Qumqam was used in tandem with SAMSAM by the cultural hero Amir to slay an entire army of infidels in a two-hour-long battle.

Sources: Jah, *Hoshruba*, 58, 243, 380

Rainbow Sling, the

One of the weapons of the Celtic god of the sun, Lugh ("Bright" or "Light") of the Long Arms (Artful Hands or Long Hands), the Rainbow Sling was used to slay the Fomorian Balor the Strong-Smiter. Astride his white horse, Lugh charged Balor and let loose his slingstone, which penetrated into the Fomorian's eye with such force that it exploded out of the back of his skull (see TATHLUM).

Sources: Macdonald, *Heroes, Gods and Monsters of Celtic Mythology*, n.p.; O'Farrell, *Ancient Irish Legends*, n.p.

Randarr

Variations: Hrungnir's shield, Randarr Iss, shield of Hrungnir

In Norse mythology, Hrungnir ("Noisy") was not only the largest of all the rock Jotuns (giants) but also the chief of the Hrymthursars (frost giants); among his possessions was a shield called Randarr. Made of stone, it had sharp edges and three corners.

Sources: Daly, *Norse Mythology A to Z*, 52; Grimes, *The Norse Myths*, 280, 294; Selbie and Gray, *Encyclopædia of Religion and Ethics*, Volume 12, 253; Vigfússon and Powell, *Court Poetry*, Volume 2, 425

Rate

Variation: Rati

In Norse mythology, Rate ("the Traveler") was the enchanted auger of Odin, the god of battle, death, frenzy, the gallows, healing, knowledge, poetry, royalty, the runic alphabet, sorcery, and wisdom. This item was used to drill a hole in order to enter HNITBJORG, the treasure chamber of Suttungr, so Odin could steal the PRECIOUS MEAD.

Sources: Anderson, *Norse Mythology*, 249; Grimes, *The Norse Myths*, 294

Rathachal

Variation: chariot of Brahma

Tripurasura, a demon from Hindu mythology, gained a tremendous amount of power through gathering many *siddhis* (spiritual powers); he could not be defeated in battle. The demon built three cities—one of gold, one of iron, and one of silver—which collectively became known as the

Tripura. He and his two brothers each ruled a city, and they were jointly referred to as the Tripurasura. When Tripurasura went to war against the gods and defeated Indra, god of the heavens, lightning, rains, river flows, storms, and *vajra* ("thunder"), the rest of the pantheon sought the help of Brahma. Together, under the guidance of the god of preservation, Vishnu, they constructed a mystical chariot named Rathachal ("Chariot Mountain"); its frame was made of the earth and its wheels were made from the moon and the sun. Brahma was the charioteer, driving the four Vedas—Indra (Svargapata), Kubera, Varuna, and Yama—transformed into the horses who pulled it. To ensure their victory over Tripurasura, Vishnu transformed himself into an arrow to be shot from the bow of Shiva (likely not AJAGAV). With the remaining gods engaged in devotional prayer, the arrow was released and Tripurasura was defeated, his cities and brothers falling with him.

Sources: Haas, *Rudraksha*, 26–27; Javeed, *World Heritage Monuments and Related Edifices in India*, Volume 1, 151; Kosambi, *Intersections*, 27, 41

Ratna Maru

In Hindu mythology, Ratna Maru was a divine sword without equal; it was created by Mahadeva and given to Kalki, the tenth incarnation of the god of preservation, Vishnu.

Sources: Chaturvedi, *Kalki Purana*, 18

Raudskinna

Variations: *Book of Power*, the *Red Skin*

In Scandinavian folklore, *Raudskinna* (*Redskin*) was a book of black magic said to have been written by Bishop Gottskalk grimmi Nikulasson (Gottskalk the Cruel) of Holar in the sixteenth century; legend claims that he was buried with it. The book supposedly contains all of the spells of black magic handwritten in gold ink and bound in red leather. According to the story, if a person were to read and master the contents of *Raudskinna*, they would have mastered magic to such a degree that they would be able to summon and control Satan himself. There was also a section in the book about *stave magic* (the symbols peculiar to Icelandic magic in that time).

Sources: Curran, *A Haunted Mind*, n.p.; Hayes, *Folklore and Book Culture*, 51, 52; Ross, *You Can't Read This*, n.p.

Razin, al

According to Islamic mythology, the prophet Muhammad owned at least three shields at the time

of his death; their names were al FATUK, al Razin, and al ZALUK. Beyond its name, nothing else is known of al Razin ("the firm" or "the strong").

Sources: Osborne et al., *A Complete History of the Arabs*, Volume 1, 254; Sale et al., *An Universal History, Part 2*, Volume 1, 185

Refanu

In Swedish folklore, the *Refanu* was a gigantic sailing ship so large it would take three weeks to travel from one end of the vessel to the other; fortunately, there was a pub located at every pulley. In one tale, a schooner was said to have been lost in the *Refanu*'s cooking pot. However, there was always plenty to eat and the crew was content.

Sources: Bassett, *Wander-ships*, 26–27; Kingshill, *The Fabled Coast*, n.p.

Refil

Variation: Ridill

According to "Skaldskaparmal," the second part of Snorri Sturluson's *Prose Edda*, Refil was the sword of Regin, brother of Fafnir (Fafner).

Sources: Anderson, *The Younger Edda*, 196; Pendergrass, *Mythological Swords*, 62

Rhongomiant

Variations: Rhongomynad, Rhongomyniad ("Slayer Spear" or "Spear Striker"), Rhongowennan, Ron

In Welsh Arthurian lore, Rhongomiant was the heavy spear of King Arthur; it was thought to be among the triad of weapons given to him by God (CALADBOLG and CARNWENNAN being the other two).

When Arthur tells Culhwch that he may ask and receive anything of him, the king makes a short list of his prize possessions that are the seven exceptions to his offer: CALADBOLG, his sword; CARNWENNAN, his dagger; Gwenhwyfar, his wife; GWENN, his cloak; PRYDWEN, his ship; Rhongomiant, his spear; and WYNEBGWRTHUCHER, his shield. Rhongomiant was named fourth.

Sources: Bromwich and Evans, *Culhwch and Olwen*, 64; Padel, *Arthur in Medieval Welsh Literature*, n.p.

ring of Aine, the

The daughter of King Egobagal (one of the Tuatha de Danann), Aine ("Bright"), a beautiful fairy queen of Knockaine in Limerick County in West Munster, was already one of the Sidhe when she was taken and enchanted by the fay; when she was still part mortal, she possessed a magical ring that could reveal fairies.

ring of Aladdin

Sources: Evan-Wentz, *Fairy Faith in Celtic Countries*, 79; Mountain, *The Celtic Encyclopedia*, Volume 2, 301

ring of Aladdin, the

Originating in a Middle Eastern folktale and popularized in a story appearing in the book *Tales of Sheherazade, or Thousand and One Nights*, the ring of Aladdin contained a djinn (genie) with the ability to grant wishes. In the beginning of the tale, this ring is owned by a man pretending to be the uncle of Aladdin; it is given to the boy as a show of good faith, meant to indicate that he will not abandon Aladdin once he has the lamp. The stranger knows the ring contains a djinn but assumes that he will be able to reclaim it after he has possession of the lamp. The djinn of the ring, described as black and large, has the ability to swiftly carry anyone the wielder wishes to any destination he chooses.

Sources: Dawood, *Aladdin and Other Tales from the Arabian Nights*, n.p.; Kelly, *The Magical Lamp of Aladdin*, 18–19

ring of Cambalo, the

Variation: ring of Cambel

A character from Geoffrey Chaucer's (circa 1340s–1400) unfinished "Squire's Tale," Cambalo was the second-born son of Cambuscan (Cambyuskan). The ring was originally a gift from the king of Arabia and India to Canacee, the sister of Cambalo. The ring would allow its wearer to have knowledge of all the healing properties of plants in addition to allowing the wearer to communicate freely with birds.

When Edmund Spenser (1552/1553–1599) attempted to finish "The Squire's Tale," the ring was described as having the magical ability to heal wounds and restore stamina. In this version, Cambalo challenged every one of his sister's suitors, defeating them all, except for Triamod.

Sources: Brewer, *Dictionary of Phrase and Fable* 1900, 203; Rossignol, *Critical Companion to Chaucer*, 254, 255

ring of dispelling, the

Variations: ring of Lancelot, Lancelot's ring

In Arthurian lore, the Lady of the Lake gave Sir Lancelot a ring that had the magical ability to dispel any enchantment; in some versions of the tale, the gift came from an unnamed fairy. Lancelot used the ring to cross the bridge at Gorre.

Sources: Gerritsen and Van Melle, *A Dictionary of Medieval Heroes*, 163; Lacy et al., *The New Arthurian Encyclopedia*, 269

ring of Eluned, the

Variation: ring of Sunet

The Middle English Arthurian romance titled *Ywaine and Gawaine* features the ring of Eluned (Luned or Lunete); this item had a stone in it that, when covered or turned inward toward the palm, would make the wearer invisible. Gawain (Gawaine) gave the ring to Ywaine, the Knight of the Lion, to aid him in his adventures and noble deeds.

Sources: Jones, *Finger-ring Lore*, 96; Taylor, *The Fairy Ring*, 389

ring of Gyges, the

Variation: Gyges's ring

The classical Greek philosopher Plato (428–347 BCE) refers to the mythological ring of Gyges in Book 2 of *The Republic* (circa 380 BCE) to prove that justice has a "relative value due to our inability to do wrong." In this book, Plato's brother Glaucon wonders whether there can ever be a man so virtuous that he would not commit murder, rape, or theft if he could do so without detection (and therefore consequences); suspecting not, he claims that man practices justice unwittingly.

To explain his point, Glaucon tells the tale of an unnamed ancestor of the historical King Gyges of Lydia, who ruled between 687 BCE and 654 BCE. This ancestor (perhaps a great-grandfather also named Gyges) was a shepherd in service to the current ruler of Lydia, King Candaules. After an earthquake, the ancestor discovered a lost tomb. Within were the remains of a very large man wearing a golden ring. The ancestor took the ring and discovered that it had the magical ability to make him invisible. Using the ring, he was able to get into the palace, seduced the queen, conspired with her to murder Candaules, married her, and became king himself.

Sources: Irwin, *Plato's Ethics*, 184–85; Plato, *The Republic*, Volume 1, 70, 126

ring of Laurin, the

In German folklore, the dwarf king Laurin owned many magical items; one of these was a magical ring that gave him the ability to see through illusions and anyone or anything that was invisible.

Sources: Jiriczek, *Northern Hero Legends*, 83; Keightley, *World Guide to Gnomes, Fairies, Elves, and Other Little People*, 207

ring of Mudarra, the

The epic poem *Cantar de los Siete Infantes de Lara* (*Song of the Seven Lara Princes*) is based on the legend of a family feud driven by revenge and the murder of seven princes of Lara or Salas, Spain. In the poem, Gonzalo Gusto cuts a ring in two and gives one half to his infant son, Mudarra, so he will be able to recognize him in the future. Eventually, Mudarra comes to his father, and when the two halves of the ring meet, they magically repair themselves. In this same episode, Gonzalo's sight is restored and he is finally able to (literally and figuratively) recognize his son.

Sources: Ganelin and Mancing, *The Golden Age Comedia*, 185

ring of Reynard, the

Written of in the fifteenth century by Hermann Barkhusan of Rostock, Reynard the Fox possessed a magical ring. The band of this ring was solid gold and had three names written upon it. When the names were spoken aloud (and only a master of the black arts could correctly pronounce them), the spell embedded in the ring would activate and protect the person who wore it from bolts of lightning, claps of thunder, any harmful effects from cold or heat, and any "weird" charm that might be placed upon him. There was a singular stone set in the ring with three distinct bands of color. The first was a red so intense that it shined at night as if it were the noon sun. The next color was a glossy white that had the innate ability to cure any sort of bloat, discomfort, or pain that might be caused by overindulging in drink, drugs, or food. The last coloration was grass-green with red and blue spots; it was said to be able to safeguard the wearer from their enemies either in peacetime or when at war.

Sources: Day, *The Rare Romance of Reynard the Fox*, 121–22; Kozminsky, *Crystals, Jewels, Stones*, n.p.

ring of the Fairy Queen, the

In the story of Ogier the Dane, a Middle English Romance, Ogier is compelled to travel to Morgan La Fay, the queen of fairies. In her eternally perfect spring-day garden, she welcomes Ogier to live there with her forever. Upon his finger she places a magical ring; it melts away the years and restores Ogier to the prime of his youth. Upon his head she places the CROWN OF FORGETFULNESS, so he can live in the fairy dream of love and pleasure.

Sources: Cox, *Popular Romances of the Middle Ages*, 362

ring of the king of Lombardy, the

Variation: ring of Otnit

In Italian lore, King Otnit of Lombardy was said to wear a magical ring given to him by his mother; the ring allegedly had the ability to render its wearer invisible and to prevent them from ever losing their sense of direction or becoming lost.

Sources: Brewer, *Dictionary of Phrase and Fable*, Volume 1, 659; Kozminsky, *Crystals, Jewels, Stones*, n.p.

ring of Wayland, the

The Icelandic narrative poem *Volundarkuitha* tells the story of the hero and legendary master blacksmith Wayland (Gofannon/Volund/Weiland/Weyland) the Smith, who had taken and hidden the SWAN CLOAK of a Valkyrie who came to earth. After nine years of marriage, the Valkyrie discovered the hiding place of her magical cloak and, upon regaining it, returned to the heavens, but not before leaving Wayland a magical ring of the purest gold as a token of her eternal love for him. The ring enhanced Wayland's already impressive combat skills to be beyond the reach of mortal men. When the ring was placed atop his forge, he was able to produce weapons and armor with magical powers. The ring was also a source of infinite wealth for Wayland; when it was on his forge and struck with a hammer, it would create 700 gold rings of equal weight and value.

Sources: Day, *Tolkien's Ring*, n.p.; Edmison, *Stories from the Norseland*, 123–26

Ringhorn

In Norse mythology, the dragon-ship *Ringhorn* (*Ringed Horn*) was the personal ship of Odin, the god of battle, death, frenzy, the gallows, healing, knowledge, poetry, royalty, the runic alphabet, sorcery, and wisdom. According to one story, when Balder died, Odin placed the young god's body atop a funeral pyre on the deck of *Ringhorn*; Nanna Nepsdottr, Balder's wife, who had died of grief, was also placed on the ship. *Ringhorn* was set ablaze and pushed into the ocean by the giantess Thokk, who was actually the god Loki in disguise.

Sources: Guerber, *Myths of the Norsemen*, 206–07; Randolph, *Norse Myths and Legends*, 44

robe of Erec's coronation, the

Variation: Rhymer's Tower

This amazing robe, worn by the Arthurian knight Erec during his coronation as king of

Outre-Gales, was said to depict the four liberal arts in feminine personification—Arithmetic, Astronomy, Geometry, and Music. Allegedly made by four fairies out of watered fabric, the robe was lined with the multicolored skins of spice-eating barbioletes from India. The robe had four stones set in the tassels: two amethysts on one side, and two chrysolites on the other.

Sources: Karr, *Arthurian Companion*, 148

robe of Harmonia, the

In Greek mythology, Harmonia was the result of a love affair between Aphrodite (Roman goddess Venus), the goddess of love, and Ares (Roman god Mars), the god of war. Harmonia's marriage to Cadmus of Thebes was the first mortal wedding the twelve Olympian gods ever attended. As a wedding gift, Athena (Roman goddess Minerva), the goddess of crafts, military victories, war, and wisdom, gave Harmonia a beautiful gold robe woven by the Graces; it had the magical ability to bestow divine dignity upon its wearer. Eventually the robe fell into the possession of Thersander, son of Polyneices, who gifted it to Eriphyle on the condition that he go to war.

Sources: Brewer, *Dictionary of Phrase and Fable*, Volume 1, 582; Graves, *The Greek Myths*, 159

robe of immortality, the

In Greek mythology, the Graces (the personifications of beauty, charm, and grace) wove and created the robe of immortality for the goddess of love, Aphrodite (Roman goddess Venus).

Sources: Hard, *The Routledge Handbook of Greek Mythology*, 208; Littleton, *Gods, Goddesses, and Mythology* Volume 4, 582

robe of the fire-rat, the

In China there is a legend of a garment known as the robe of the fire-rat; it was made from the hide of the fire-rat (huo shu), an animal whose skin was said to be impervious to fire and heat.

A Japanese folktale from the Heinan period tells the story of a wealthy bamboo cutter's daughter by the name of Nayotake no Kaguya-hime ("Shining Princess of the Supple Bamboo") who wishes to marry only a man who truly loves her. She manages to whittle down her suitors to five and states that she will marry the one who is able to show her something special she wishes to see. The suitor named Udaijin Abe no Miushi, a man of wealth, is given the task of procuring the robe of the fire-rat. Even in this tale, it is said to be a beautiful, albeit legendary, item that will be difficult and expensive to obtain.

Sources: Rimer, *Modern Japanese Fiction and Its Traditions*, 285; Shirane, *Traditional Japanese Literature*, 117; Soothill and Hodous, *A Dictionary of Chinese Buddhist Terms*, 161

rod of Aaron, the

Variations: Aaron's rod, Aaron's staff, Khoter ("Branch" or "Twig")

In Hebrew mythology, the rod of Aaron was described as a shepherd's staff; traditionally, it would have been either between six and eight feet long or three feet long. Either version would have had a large knot on the end that would have been used for clubbing away wolves. The rod of Aaron was thrown down upon the floor before Pharaoh, where it transformed into a serpent to demonstrate the power of God. Jambres and Jannes, the magicians of Pharaoh, also transformed their rods into serpents, which were then consumed by the ROD OF MOSES.

According to the book of Exodus, the rod of Aaron was imbued with the power to bring about at least one of the plagues of Egypt: the creation of lice. The book of Numbers explains how the rod gained its powers; during the process, it grew flowering buds that yielded almonds. When not in use, God commanded that the rod be placed in the tabernacle; some scholars take this statement to mean that the rod was placed inside the ARK OF THE COVENANT, while others say the rod was placed beside it.

Sources: Boren and Boren, *Following the Ark of the Covenant*, 13; Calmet, *Calmet's Great Dictionary of the Holy Bible*, n.p.

rod of Hermes, the

Variation: staff of Mercury

In Greek mythology, Hermes (Roman god Mercury), the god of animal husbandry, commerce, eloquence, fertility, language, looters, luck, sleep, thieves, trade, travel, and wealth, served as the messenger of the gods; as such, he carried the symbol of his office—a rod—with him everywhere he went. According to the myth, one day while delivering a message, Hermes came upon two snakes copulating (or fighting—sources conflict) and, for reasons of his own, placed his rod between them. The snakes encircled his rod and have remained there ever since.

Sources: Cavanaugh, *Hippocrates' Oath and Asclepius' Snake*, n.p.; Westmoreland, *Ancient Greek Beliefs*, 204

rod of Moses, the

Variations: Shamir, Stone that Splits Rocks

In Hebrew mythology, the rod of Moses is said to be one of the items placed within the ARK OF THE COVENANT next to the EMERALD TABLET and the ROD OF AARON. It is described as one cubit (18 inches) long and made of metal. This rod was used by Moses while he led his people through the desert to engrave the stones inlaid in the high priest's breastplate; it was capable of cutting through the hardest substances without difficulty or heat and made no sound while it operated. The energy emitted by the rod was described in texts as a "worm of light." When not in use, the rod was wrapped in a woolen cloth and placed in a lead-lined wooden box.

In Islamic traditions, the rod of Moses was said to be able to levitate large stones into place during construction. The rod was also in Moses's hand when he sent the plagues upon Egypt, parted the Red Sea, and struck stones in the desert to have them produce fresh water, and it was held aloft over his head to ensure victory over the Amalakites. According to scripture (Numbers 17:6–10), the rod of Moses gave the ROD OF AARON its power.

Sources: Boren and Boren, *Following the Ark of the Covenant*, 11, 12, 13; McClintock and Strong, *Cyclopaedia of Biblical, Theological, and Ecclesiastical Literature*, Volume 9, 615

Rofub, al

According to Islamic mythology, the prophet Muhammad owned a collection of nine different swords at the time of his death: al ADHAB, al Battar (see BATTER), Dhu'l Fakar (see DHUAL-FIRQAR), al Hatf (see HATEL), al KADIB, KOLAITE, MABUR, al MEHDHAM, and al Rofub. Beyond its name, nothing else is known of the sword al Rofub ("the Penetrating").

Sources: Sale et al., *An Universal History, Part 2*, Volume 1, 184

Rosse

According to German folklore, Rosse was a sword that was part of the ransom that the captured and defeated King Elberich paid to Otnit. Rosse, forged on Mount Goickelsass, was said to have a bright hue and a blade as clear as glass, and it was adorned with gold. The sword was magically enchanted so that whoever struck out with it would not be ashamed of any blow that hit its target.

Sources: Keightley, *The Fairy Mythology by Thomas Keightley*, 208–9

Roth Fail

In Irish legend, Simon the Druid (Simon Magus/ Simon the Mage) assisted the druid Mog Ruith in the construction of Roth Fail ("Wheel of Light"); it was a wheel with magical enchantments enabling it to fly. According to legend, Mog Ruith used this wheel to fight against the Romans.

Sources: Forlong, *Faiths of Man*, Volume 2, 91; Spence, *The Magic Arts in Celtic Britain*, 36

Roth Ramach

Variations: Roth Ramhach

In medieval Irish mythology, *Roth Ramach* (*Rowing Wheel*) was a magical ship as capable on land as it was on the sea. It was said to be so large that it carried one thousand beds in its mid-cabin, with each gigantic bed sleeping one thousand sailors. According to the tales, there was always plenty to eat and the crew was content.

Sources: Kingshill, *The Fabled Coast*, n.p.

Round Table, the

In Arthurian mythology, the Round Table of King Arthur was the large circular table created with a singular purpose: when Arthur and his knights gathered, all would have a chair of the same creation and height, and, when seated at the table, their service would be equal—no knight would be closer to the head of the table to signify any greater or lesser degree of importance. The phrase "Round Table" was also used to refer to the collection of knights and noblemen in Arthur's service.

Robert Wace, the twelfth-century Norman cleric and teacher, presented to Eleanor of Aquitaine *Roman de Brut* (his translation of Geoffrey of Monmouth's *Historia Regum Britanniae*) in 1155; this work contained the first real mention of the Round Table as we know it today.

The Middle English poet and priest Layamon said the table was constructed by a carpenter who approached Arthur in court after the conquest of all the lands west of the Alps; the idea was presented after a fight broke out over who would sit at the end of the rectangular table then in use. However, according to the late twelfth-century French poet Robert de Boron and the Vulgate Cycle, it was Uther Pendragon who conceived the idea of the Round Table after hearing Merlin's tales of the Grail Table, a circular table that sat thirteen individuals. Uther gave the table to King Leodegan of Carmelide, who offered it as a wedding gift when his daughter Guenevere (Guinevere) married Arthur.

De Boron also says Merlin (Merddyn/Myrddin) enchanted the chairs of the Round Table with magical golden letters so that whoever sat in the chair would have his name magically appear upon it. In the Italian romances of Arthur, there are four types of chairs named: the Adventurous Seat for the active knight; the PERILOUS SEAT, which was to remain empty; the Royal Seat, which is reserved for Arthur; and the chairs for the infirm knights.

Likewise, the table was said to seat various numbers of people, depending on the Sources: 13 knights could be seated at the table according to Didot's *Perceval*; the Round Table of Castle Winchester lists the names of 25 knights; Robert de Boron claimed the number was 50; historian Jean d'Outremeuse (1338–1400) set the number at 60; in *The Legend of King Arthur* by Sir James Knowles (1831–1908), the number was 130; knight and poet Hartmann von Aue (1170–1210) claimed the number was 140; the Lancelot-Grail Cycle (circa 1210–1230) said the table could seat 150, while the Vulgate *Merlin* said it could seat 250; the Welsh tale of *Culhwch and Olwen* names some 200 knights; and the story of *The Knight with Two Swords* says there are 366 knights, one for each day of the solar year. Perhaps most remarkable of all, Layamon claimed the table could seat 1,600 and was portable. Members of the Round Table were bound to an oath outlined by Sir Thomas Malory (1415–1471). In it, the knights would swear toalways to speak the truth, avoid gossip and scandals, be loyal in friendship, cherish humility, defend those who cannot defend themselves, develop their life for the greater good. give to the poor honor and respect women, never to boast, once given to keep their word, place character above riches, remain faithful in love, and uphold justice by being fair to all. .

The ultimate fate of the Round Table is seldom discussed, but in the Post-Vulgate Cycle, when Mark destroys Camelot, he also destroys the Round Table.

Sources: Ashley, *The Mammoth Book of King Arthur*, n.p.; Bruce, *The Arthurian Name Dictionary*, 430; Dom, *King Arthur and the Gods of the Round Table*, 96–97

Rua-i-paku

In Polynesian lore, Rua-i-paku ("The Hole Where It Must Fall") was the magical ironwood spade owned by the hero Ono; with it he killed the demon of the ironwood forest, Vaotere ("Moving-Recess").

Sources: Beckwith, *Hawaiian Mythology*, n.p.; Porteous, *The Forest in Folklore and Mythology*, 142

ruby of Voivre, the

According to French lore, there was once a wyvern by the name of Voivre, described as having the upper body of a voluptuous woman; embedded in her forehead was a garnet or ruby that enabled her to navigate through the Underworld.

Sources: Dekirk, *Dragonlore*, 47

Rudastra

In Hindu mythology, an ASTRA is a supernatural weapon created or gifted by the gods to someone who then presides over the weapon. The wielder of an ASTRA is known as an astradhari.

Rama was an expert archer with extraordinary skill. In his battle against Ravana, he used the arrow Rudastra ("the Arm") against Ravana, hoping to pierce his opponent's golden armor; this ASTRA contained enough power to make the "earth and the nether-world tremble."

Sources: Aravamudan, *Pure Gems of Ramayanam*, 538

Rukma Vimana

There are five different types of vimana: PUSHPAKA VIMANA, Rukma Vimana, SHAKUNA VIMANA, SUNDARA VIMANA, and TRIPURA VIMANA.

In the fifth book of *Mahabharata*, titled "Vimanapala" ("Guardian of the Aircraft"), a highly specialized individual is given the responsibility of caring for the vimana. Just like SUNDARA VIMANA, Rukma ("Gold") Vimana is described as conical in shape and having three floors, each twenty feet tall, with the third floor being the cockpit. Ancient Sanskrit texts also say this vimana had four wings and eight propellers.

Sources: Baccarini and Vaddadi, *Reverse Engineering Vedic Vimanas*, n.p.; Becklake, *History of Rocketry and Astronautics*, 9; Childress, *Vimana*, n.p.

Ruyi Jingu Bang

Variations: Jingu Bang, Ruyi Bang

In the sixteenth-century Chinese novel *Journey into the West*, the rebellious hero Sun Wukong owns a magical iron rod known as Ruyi Jingu Bang ("As-You-Will Gold-Banded Cudgel" or "The Compliant Golden-Hooped Rod"). In addition to being able to fight of its own accord, create multiple copies of itself, and increase its size and mass to an eight-ton staff, it could shrink down to the size of a needle to conceal itself behind Sun Wukong's ear. The staff was taken from the Water Crystal Palace of the Dragon King of the Eastern Ocean so that Sun Wukong would be able to protect his feeble master, Xuanzang, as they traveled.

Sources: O'Bryan, *A History of Weapons*, 103; Wu and Yu, *Journey to the West*, Volume 1, 56, 104

Ryugu

The palace home of Japanese Dragon King Ryo-Wo, Ryugu ("Palace" or "Spool") is located beneath the sea; Ryo-Wo keeps the TIDAL JEWELS here.

Sources: de Visser, *The Dragon in China and Japan*, 142, 193; Dekirk, *Dragonlore*, 31

Sa'adia, al

According to Islamic mythology, the prophet Muhammad owned at least seven cuirasses (a piece of armor made of a breastplate and backplate hinged or otherwise fastened together) at the time of his death; their names were al BETRA, DHAT AL FODHUL, DHAT AL HAWAFHI, DHAT AL WELHAL, al FADDO, al KHERNA, and al Sa'adia. Al Sa'adia was taken from the Jewish tribe Banu Kainoka prior to their banishment to Syria; this item was said to have been the very one that David had worn when he confronted and slew the giant Goliath.

Sources: Sale et al., *An Universal History, Part 2*, Volume 1, 185

Sachs

According to German legend, Sachs was the sword of Dietrich of Bern; at one time, it (along with the swords BALMUNG and WELSUNG) was considered the best in the world in the hands of the proper wielder.

Sources: Mackenzie, *Teutonic Myth and Legend*, 424

saddle of Enide, the

Gulivret the Little, of Arthurian lore, gave to the heroine Enide a remarkable sorrel palfrey with an extraordinary saddle. The tack was described as decorated with gold, studded with emeralds, and bearing a bow of ivory; the complete story of Aeneas and Dido was carved onto it. The craftsman who made the saddle spent seven years creating it.

Sources: Karr, *Arthurian Companion*, 144; Kelly, *The Romances of Chretien de Troyes*, 74, 123–24

Saeg (SAIG)

Variations: Saeger, Saegr, Soeg, tub of Bil and Hiuki

In Norse mythology, Saeg ("the Noisy") is the bucket, cask, pail, or tub that Bil and Hjuki (Yuki) filled with water from the spring (or well) BYRGIR; together they carry Saeg using the carrying pole SIMUL.

Sources: Grimes, *The Norse Myths*, 295–96; Tangherlini, *Nordic Mythologies*, 194

Sagitta

Sagitta ("Arrow") was the weapon the demigod and legendary hero Heracles used to slay Aquila, the eagle (or vulture—sources conflict) that perpetually fed upon Prometheus's liver. This was the same arrow used in an act of revenge by Apollo, the god of archery, art, healing, hunting, knowledge, medicine, music, oracles, plague, prophecy, sun and light, and truth, to kill the Cyclopes that killed his son Asclepius.

Sources: Dixon-Kennedy, *Encyclopedia of Greco-Roman Mythology*, 40, 157, 273; Savill et al., *Pears Encyclopaedia of Myths and Legends*, 145

sakhrat

In Mohammedan lore, sakhrat is a holy emerald; it is the hue of green reflecting the deep blue tints of heavenly vapor. Lore claims that possessing even the smallest fragment of this stone will give its owner all the secret knowledge of the universe.

Sources: Kozminsky, *Crystals, Jewels, Stones*, n.p.

Sakradhanus

The bow of Indra, the god of the heavens, lightning, rains, river flows, storms, and *vajra* ("thunder"), is Sakradhanus, the rainbow, in Hindu mythology.

Sources: Dowson, *Classical Dictionary of Hindu Mythology and Religion*, 127

Sakti

In Hindu mythology, an ASTRA is a supernatural weapon created or gifted by the gods to someone who then presides over the weapon. The wielder of an ASTRA is known as an astradhari.

Sakti was a weapon of mass destruction created by Indra, the god of the heavens, lightning, rains, river flows, storms, and *vajra* ("thunder"), and given to Karna; it was an infallible dart, capable of destroying all hostile forces in a battle. Karna received this ASTRA in exchange for the golden breastplate and earrings he was born wearing (see ARMOR OF KARNA and EARRINGS OF KARNA). Sakti was thrown by hand and flew through the air roaring with fire; it would kill one powerful enemy and then return to its wielder. Unlike most ASTRAS, Sakti was given with a condition: if ever Karna were to throw Sakti in a state of anger, or when his life was not in mortal peril, the weapon would launch but turn against him.

Sources: Narasimhan, *The Mahabharata*, 70–71

saliva of the wolpertinger

Variations: elwedritsche, jackalope, rasselbock, skvader (Swedish), wolperdinger

A chimerical creature from Bavarian folklore, the wolpertinger is described as having bird feet, boar tusks, a coxcombed forehead, deer antlers, hawk wings, rabbit ears and hindquarters, and a rabbit-, squirrel-, or weasel-like body. It is believed that the saliva of this creature stimulates hair growth; to cure impotence, nectar is sipped through one of its shank bones, and then the person must urinate across the current of a stream.

Sources: Brunvand, *American Folklore*, 831; Zell-Ravenheart and Dekirk, *Wizard's Bestiary*, 102

Salmacis (SAL-muh-sihs)

A fountain or pool said to be located somewhere in Caria, Greece, Salmacis had the power to make anyone who dove into it effeminate.

According to classical Greek mythology, Salmacis was a sexually aggressive nymph. From the moment she saw Hermaphroditus, the son of Hermes (Roman god Mercury), the god of animal husbandry, commerce, eloquence, fertility, language, looters, luck, sleep, thieves, trade, travel, and wealth, and Aphrodite (Roman goddess Venus), the goddess of love, she fell instantly in love with him. Salmacis offered herself to Hermaphroditus, but he refused. Afterward, he wandered until he came upon a pool of refreshing water. Unaware that this was the home of Salmacis, he dove in; the nymph dove in immediately behind him and entwined her body about his. Passionately she prayed to the gods that they would never be separated. The gods answered her prayers and melded their bodies into one, creating the first hermaphrodite. What remained of Hermaphroditus then prayed that any man who bathed in this fountain would become *semivir* (an individual who has lost his masculinity and become infertile); his impassioned prayer was likewise answered.

Sources: Anderson, *Ovid's Metamorphoses, Books 1–5*, 442; Littleton, *Gods, Goddesses, and Mythology*, Volume 11, 1000; Parker, *Mythology: Myths, Legends and Fantasies*, 61

Sammohana

Variation: Pramohana

In Hindu mythology, an ASTRA is a supernatural weapon created or gifted by the gods to someone who then presides over the weapon. The wielder of an ASTRA is known as an astradhari.

Sammohana was an ASTRA said to have the ability to cause an entire army to collapse or fall into a trancelike state. Arjuna ("Spotless and Shining like Silver"), the heroic archer and main character in the Indian epic *Mahabharata*, first defeated the Kuru leader in hand-to-hand combat; then he let fly Sammohana from his bow, GANDIVA. Thanks to Sammohana, the opposing army fell unconscious. The soldiers were then field stripped; when they eventually came to their senses, they returned to Hastinapura.

Sources: Edizioni, *Vimanas and the Wars of the Gods*, n.p.; Narasimhan, *The Mahabharata*, 60

Sampo

Variation: Sampo Mill of Fortune

In a legend from Finland found in the epic poem *The Kalevala*, Ilmarinen, a god with remarkable smithing abilities, used the magical elements in his forge to create many items. One such item was Sampo, a mill. The bellows of the forge were fed continuously by the east, north, south, and west winds for three days. In addition to being a lucky item, the mill had three sides, one of which produced flour, while another created gold, and the last churned out salt. Each time it operated, it produced three measures of its product: one for daily use, one for market, and one for the storehouse. The lid of Sampo was like a rainbow, containing all the colors of nature. Sampo was created for Louhi the witch as a bridal gift for the hand of her daughter. Louhi took the mill to the hills of Lapland and hid it, binding it in place with three tree roots—two entwined to the mountain and one tied to the seashore.

Sources: Jennings, *Pagan Portals*, n.p.; Mouse, *Ilmarinen Forges the Sampo*, 56–77

Samsam

According to the medieval Persian saga of Amir Hamza, Samsam ("Sharp and Cutting Sword, Which Bends Not") was one of the four swords once held by King Suleiman, the others being AQRAB-E SULEIMANI, QUMQAM, and ZUL-HAJAM. Samsam was used in tandem with QUMQAM by the cultural hero Amir to slay an entire army of infidels in a two-hour-long battle.

Sources: Jah, *Hoshruba*, 58, 149, 243, 380

Samsamha

A legendary sword said to have been wielded by the caliph of Baghdad, Harour al Raschid (Aron the Just). In 802 CE, when Emperor Nicephorus advanced his army toward Baghdad, he sent a gift of five swords, showing his intent to attack. In response, the caliph drew Samsamha and attacked the offering, cutting the swords "like so many radishes"; this achievement speaks as much as to the arm strength of the caliph as it does to the ability of Samsamha.

Sources: Alexander, *Parallel Universal History*, 169; Brewer, *Dictionary of Phrase and Fable* 1900, 1197

sandals of Athena, the

The Greek mythological hero Perseus was tasked by Athena (Roman goddess Minerva), the goddess of crafts, military victories, war, and wisdom, with embarking on a seven-year quest to confront the Gorgon Medusa and behead her. To assist the young hero in his task, she loaned him some divine items, including her sandals, shield, and sword (see SHIELD OF PERSEUS and SWORD OF ATHENA). In some versions of this myth, the sandals are described as having wings or are the possessions of Hermes (Roman god Mercury), the god of animal husbandry, commerce, eloquence, fertility, language, looters, luck, sleep, thieves, trade, travel, and wealth (see SANDALS OF HERMES). Once the quest was completed, Perseus returned the borrowed items to their proper owners.

Sources: Mabie, *Young Folks' Treasury*, 194; Roman and Roman, *Encyclopedia of Greek and Roman Mythology*, 393; Westmoreland, *Ancient Greek Beliefs*, 170, 336

sandals of Hermes, the

Variations: Hermes's winged sandals, Talaria, winged sandals

In classical Greek mythology, Hermes (Roman god Mercury), the god of animal husbandry, commerce, eloquence, fertility, language, looters, luck, sleep, thieves, trade, travel, and wealth, owned a pair of golden winged sandals; they, along with a golden winged helmet, were a gift from Zeus (Roman god Jupiter), the god of fate, kings, lightning, sky, and thunder, making the already swift god the fastest of them all. These sandals allowed him to not only move more quickly over the land than any other god, but also fly over the sea as well.

When the Greek mythological hero Perseus was tasked by Athena (Roman goddess Minerva), the goddess of crafts, military victories, war, and wisdom, with confronting Medusa and beheading her, Hermes, in some versions of the myth, loaned Perseus his winged sandals. Some versions say he also gave the hero his short sword (see SWORD OF HERMES). Once the quest was completed, Perseus returned all the items loaned to him.

Sources: Roman and Roman, *Encyclopedia of Greek and Roman Mythology*, 393; Westmoreland, *Ancient Greek Beliefs*, 57, 336, 826

Sanglamore

In the English epic poem *The Faerie Queene* (1590), written by Edmund Spenser, "the great and bloody" Sanglamore is the glaive belonging to Braggadocchio, a braggart and the personification of boasting.

Sources: Benét, *The Reader's Encyclopedia*, 1091; Brewer, *Dictionary of Phrase and Fable* 1900, 1197; Urdang and Ruffner, *Allusions*, 345

sanjeevani

A miracle herb from Hindu mythology, sanjeevani was said to grow on the Gandhamapdan hills of the Himalayas. Easily recognized, as it emits a natural light, sanjeevani has the ability to bring a person who is all but dead back to life.

In one story, the god of strength, Hanuman, was tasked by the medical expert Sushen with retrieving some of the herb so that he could use it to treat Sushen, who was wounded and rendered unconscious in battle. Unable to quickly find the herb, Hanuman lifted up the entire hill and flew it back to Sushen.

Sources: Agarwal, *Tales from the Ramayan*, n.p.; Venu, *The Language of Kathakali*, 295

Sarnga

In Hindu mythology, Sarnga was the celestial and divine bow of Vishnu; this powerful bow had the innate ability to strike fear into the hearts of an enemy army. Sarnga, described only as made of horn, was also wielded by Rama's younger brother Sauri and Hrsikesa.

Sources: Buitenen and Fitzgerald, *The Mahabharata*, Volume 3, 473; Dutt, *A Prose English Translation of Srimadbhagavatam*, Volumes 8–12, 365

Sauvagine

In the French epic poem *Song of Roland* (*La Chanson de Roland*, circa 1040–1115), which retells the events of the Battle of Roncevaux Pass in 778 CE, Sauvagine ("Relentless") was one of the two magical swords of Ogier the Dane.

In *The Legend of Croquemitaine*, the celebrated swordsmith Munifican created three swords: COURTAIN, DURANDAL, and Sauvagine.

scabbard of Excalibur

Each sword took three years to make, and each was eventually used to test the edge of the sword GLORIOUS, which managed to hack into each of them.

Sources: Benét, *The Reader's Encyclopedia*, 1091; Brewer, *Dictionary of Phrase and Fable* 1900, 1197; L'Epine, *The Days of Chivalry*, n.p.

scabbard of Excalibur, the

In Arthurian lore, the sword EXCALIBUR was the symbol of power held by King Arthur; however, the sword's unnamed scabbard was of far greater value. According to Merlin (Merddyn/Myrddin), the scabbard was in fact "ten times" more powerful than the sword. Whoever wore the scabbard would suffer no wound, as they would not lose so much as a single drop of blood.

During a troubled time in the reign of Arthur, his half-sister Morgan La Fay stole EXCALIBUR from him as an act of revenge for the death of her beloved Accolon. Although the sword was eventually recovered, the scabbard was lost to the king forever; many versions of the tale say Morgan threw it in a lake.

Sources: Evangelista, *The Encyclopedia of the Sword*, 577; Peterson and Dunworth, *Mythology in Our Midst*, 52–54

scepter of Erec, the

Variation: green scepter

Made from a single perfectly green and clear emerald, this scepter's head was said to be as large as a man's fist, and the likeness of every known mammal, bird, and fish was carved upon it. King Arthur put this scepter into Erec's hand at his coronation; it is unclear whether this was meant to be a gift to the new king or simply a loan.

Sources: Karr, *Arthurian Companion*, 148; Nolan, *Now Through a Glass Darkly*, 140

Schritt

Variation: Schrit

In the Middle High German heroic poem *Biterolf and Dietlieb*, Schritt ("the Lopper" or "Quick") is the named sword of Biterolf of Toledo.

Sources: Benét, *The Reader's Encyclopedia*, 1091; Brewer, *Dictionary of Phrase and Fable* 1900, 1197; de Beaumont and Allinson, *The Sword and Womankind*, 8

Sciatharglan

In the Irish epic *Tain Bo Cuailnge* (*The Cattle Raid of Cooley/The Tain*), Sciatharglan was the shield of Sencha; it is named as being among the many cups, drinking horns, goblets, javelins, shields, and swords kept in Tete Brec, one of the three households of the Ulster hero Cuhullin (Cu Chulaind/Cu Chulainn/Cuchulainn). Sciatharglan is described only as "resonant."

Sources: Gregory, *Cuchulain of Muirthemne*, 86; Kinsella and Le Brocquy, *The Tain*, 5

scythe of Cronus, the

Variations: harpe of Cronus, sickle of Cronus

In classical Greek mythology, Cronus ("Time"; Chronos/Cronos/Kronos/Saturn), a Titan and the god of time, received from his mother, Gaea, an ADAMANTINE (diamond) edged scythe, which he used to castrate his father, Uranus ("Heaven"; Ouranos), the personification of the universe.

According to the myth, Uranus refused to allow Gaea to give birth, but he continued to have relations and impregnate her. Gaea begged her unborn children for aid; of the eleven, only Cronus agreed to help her. Gaea gave her unborn son the scythe, and when next his father came to his mother, Cronus castrated him.

Sources: Berens, *Myths and Legends of Ancient Greece and Rome*, 17; Westmoreland, *Ancient Greek Beliefs*, 86

seal of Solomon, the

Variations: ring of Solomon, the shield of Solomon

According to Judeo-Christian mythology, King Solomon had among his possessions a magical ring; descriptions of the ring abound, but it is well documented to have been a seal ring, as Solomon used it to bind 72 demons into brass or copper vessels that were covered with lead and sealed with the ring's imprint. Early accounts say a pentagram was carved upon its bezel (the flat "top" of the ring), but later accounts say it was a hexagram. Some sources, such as Zohar (3:233 a–b), say the ring was carved with the four letters of Tetragrammaton: JHVH or YHWH (the Hebrew transliteration of the name of God). A description of the ring by Egyptologist and Orientalist Sir Ernest Alfred Thompson Wallis Budge (1857–1934) claims it was made of solid gold and bore a single *shamir* ("diamond"), which had the Tetragrammaton engraved upon it. Additionally, the ring had the ability to cut through any substance, including stone.

Sources: Budge, *Amulets and Talismans*, 281, 424; Kuntz, *Rings for the Finger*, 288–89

Secace

Variation: Seure

In the Arthurian story titled *Lancelot*, the sword

Arthur utilized in the battle at Saxon Rock was named Secace ("Sequence"); it was said that this "good and sharp sword" was only used in mortal combat. During this particular battle, EXCALIBUR (Arthur's usual sword) was being wielded by Sir Gawain. Typically in Arthurian lore, Secace is the sword of Sir Lancelot.

Sources: Bruce, *The Arthurian Name Dictionary*, 443; Corley, *Lancelot of the Lake*, 399; Sherman, *Storytelling*, 441; Warren, *History on the Edge*, 212

Sessrymnir (SEHS-room-nir)

Variations: Sesrumner, Sessrumnir

In Norse mythology, Sessrymnir ("Roomy-Seated"/"Seat Room"/"Seat Roomer"/"With Many Seats") was the hall of the beautiful and martial-minded goddess of beauty, death, fertility, gold, love, seidr (a type of sorcery), sex, and war, Freyja ("Lady"); able to easily accommodate all of her guests, this hall was located in the realm of FOLKVANGAR. Every day Freyja chose half of those slain to reside here with her. Sessrymnir was described only as "large and beautiful."

Sources: Anderson, *Norse Mythology*, 457; Bennett, *Gods and Religions of Ancient and Modern Times*, Volume 1, 396; Grimes, *The Norse Myths*, 266; Guerber, *Myths of the Norsemen*, 131

Setan Kober

In Javanese folklore, Setan Kober ("Devil of the Grave") was a keris (or kris—a type of dagger) forged by Empu Bayu Aji and owned by the adipati (duke) of Jipang, Arya Penangsang. Setan Kober is described as having 13 *luk* (or *lok*—waves on the blade). According to the tale, as the keris was being forged, the smith was distracted by the cries of a demon from a nearby graveyard. Although still a powerful weapon, the keris was tainted with an evil that caused its wielder to be ambitious and impatient.

Sources: Gardner, *Keris and Other Malay Weapons*, n.p.

seven kinds of silk

In Russian folklore, the phrase "of seven kinds of silk" is applied to any fabric with magical properties. In the workings of ancient Byzantium, using seven kinds of silk was not uncommon in spell crafting.

Sources: Bailey, *An Anthology of Russian Folk Epics*, 399; Petropoulos, *Greek Magic*, 76

seven lamps of sleep, the

Christian folklore tells of the Knight of the Black Castle, who keeps the castle's occupants in an enchanted sleep by ensuring that the seven lamps of sleep are maintained. According to the tale, as long as the lamps burn, the people within will not wake. The lamps can only be extinguished by water from an enchanted fountain. This story is told in *Seven Champions of Christendom* (1596) by Richard Johnson.

Sources: Brewer, *Dictionary of Phrase and Fable*, Volume 2, 725; Champlin, *Young Folks' Cyclopædia of Literature and Art*, 442

seven-league boots

Variations: canozu-cKopoxodhi ("fast-walker boots"—Russian), magic boots, shoes of swiftness (Scottish), sju mils stovler ("seven-league boots")

A fairly common bit of footwear in fairy tales and folklore of France, Germany, Great Britain, Holland, Italy, Portugal, and Scandinavia, seven-league boots are traditionally a pair of boots—or shoes—that will enable the hero of the story to travel a distance of seven leagues (24.1664 miles) in a single stride. This item is similar to the Russian fast-walker boots, which allow travelers to run at an incredible pace.

Sources: Haase, *The Greenwood Encyclopedia of Folktales and Fairy Tales*, 217; Toune and Adam, "Inquires Answered," 554; Urdang, *Three Toed Sloths and Seven League Boots*, 127

Sgiath Gailbhinn

Variation: Storm Shield

A shield from Celtic mythology, Sgiath Gailbhinn was wielded with the sword MAC AN LUINE by Fionn mac Cumhaill (Finn MacCool/Finn MacCumhail), the legendary warrior and leader of the Fianna in the Irish Fenian Cycle stories. When Sgiath Gailbhinn called out, it could be heard all over Ireland.

Sources: Gregory and MacCumhaill, *Gods and Fighting Men*, 269

Shakuna Vimana

There are five different types of vimana: PUSHPAKA VIMANA, RUKMA VIMANA, Shakuna Vimana, SUNDARA VIMANA, and TRIPURA VIMANA.

In the fifth book of *Mahabharata*, entitled "Vimanapala" ("Guardian of the Aircraft"), a highly specialized individual is given the responsibility of caring for the vimana. It also says that the 100-foot-tall Shakuna ("Bird") Vimana should be made only from the king of special metals, Raajaloha. The work gives a very detailed description on how to construct this vehicle (suitable for space travel) and its various components, including air heater, air suction pipes (vaatapaa yantra), direction-indicating banner (dikpradarsha dhwaja), domed window, electric generators (vidyud yantra), engine (owshmyaka yantra), floorboards (peetha), heater (chhullee), hollow mast, oil tank, pair of flapping wings, steam boiler, sun-ray-attracting bed (kiranaakarshana mani), three wheels, and a water jacket.

Sources: Childress, *Vimana*, n.p.; Childress, *Vimana: Aircraft of Ancient India & Atlantis*, 89

Shamshir-e Zomorrodnegar

A magical sword from Persian mythology, Shamshir-e Zomorrodnegar ("Emerald-Studded Sword") was said to have originally belonged to King Solomon. In addition to the sword being a charm against magic, any wound caused by this weapon could only be healed by use of a magical potion; one of the ingredients required to make the potion was the brains of the horned demon that guarded the sword, Fulad-zereh ("Possessing Steel Armor"). The demon's witch mother had made her son invulnerable to all weapons except for Shamshir-e Zomorrodnegar. In the tale, the hero Amir Arsalan manages to gain possession of the sword and slay the demon with it.

Sources: Chappell, *The Art of Waging Peace*, n.p.; Lindsay, *Giants, Fallen Angels, and the Return of the Nephilim*, n.p.

shank bone of the wolpertinger

Variations: elwedritsche, jackalope, rasselbock, skvader (Swedish), wolperdinger

A chimerical creature from Bavarian folklore, the wolpertinger is described as having bird feet, boar tusks, a coxcombed forehead, deer antlers, hawk wings, rabbit ears and hindquarters, and a rabbit-, squirrel-, or weasel-like body. It is believed that the saliva of this creature stimulates hair growth; to cure impotence, nectar is sipped through one of its shank bones, and then the person must urinate across the current of a stream.

Sources: Brunvand, *American Folklore*, 831; Zell-Ravenheart and Dekirk, *Wizard's Bestiary*, 102

Sharnga

Variations: Sharanga, Sharkha, Vaishnav Dhanush

In Hindu mythology, an ASTRA is a supernatural weapon created or gifted by the gods to someone who then presides over the weapon. The wielder of an ASTRA is known as an astradhari.

Sharnga was the bow of the god of preserva-tion, Vishnu; it was created by Vishvakarman, the cosmic architect and the maker of weapons. When Vishnu wielded Sharnga, he was known as Sharangapani.

Sharnga was beautifully made of bone and said to "thunder like the clouds"; when carried by Rama and Krishna, it was known as Vaishnav Dhanush. Prior to his death, Krishna threw the bow into the ocean, the domain of Vishnu, thus returning it to him.

Sources: Dalal, *Hinduism*, 163, 377, 416; Iyer, *Bhasa*, n.p.

Sharur

In ancient Sumerian mythology, Sharur ("Smasher of Thousands") was the mace of the sun god Ninurta; not only was it said to have the ability to communicate with Ninurta and fly unaided over great distances, but it was also sentient. Sharur was essential in gathering intelligence and reporting back to Ninurta before the commencement of battle. The sun god also used his mace to receive advice from his father, the god Enlil.

Sources: Dekirk, *Dragonlore*, 58; Kramer, *Sumerian Mythology*, 76, 79–80; Sherman, *Storytelling*, 331

sheep-wool shirt of Thorston, the

In fairy lore, a local hero by the name of Thorston rescued the child of a dwarf who was taken by a dragon; the unnamed dwarf insisted on rewarding his savior and made him accept several gifts. One of these gifts was a sheep-wool shirt. According to the story, as long as the shirt was worn next to the skin, the wearer would never receive a wound or tire while swimming.

Sources: Dunham, *The Cabinet Cyclopaedia*, Volume 26, 73; Keightley, *World Guide to Gnomes, Fairies, Elves, and Other Little People*, 72

shield of Achilles, the

Hephaistos (Hephaestus; Roman god Vulcan), the god of bindings, the art of sculpture, fire, forges, metalworking, stonemasonry, and talismans, created the shield used by the demigod Achilles; the famous warrior considered the shield one of his most prized possessions, even over Xanthos, his immortal war horse gifted with human speech.

According to the *Iliad* (1260–1180 BCE), the ancient Greek epic attributed to Homer, Hephaistos made the shield out of gratitude for Thetis, the woman who had raised him in his infancy. Achilles's previous armor had been borrowed by his comrade in arms, Patroclus, who had subsequently died in battle, and the armor was taken as spoils of war. Thetis asked Hephaistos to replace the armor so she could give it to her son.

The shield, heavy, huge, and round, was said to consist of five layers of bronze, and Homer gives a highly detailed description of each of the nine concentric circles of imagery. In the very center are the constellations, the earth, the moon, the sea, the sky, and the constellations of the Bear, Hyades, Orion, and the Pleiades. The next circle shows "two beautiful cities full of people. In one of the cities there are lawyers practicing their trade as well as a wedding taking place. The other city is being besieged. The next ring shows a field being plowed followed by the harvest growing on a king's estate with crops being reaped. The next layer shows a vineyard being harvested; the following circle shows a herd of straight-horned cattle; the lead bull is being attacked by lions who are in turn being attacked by a herdsman and his pack of dogs. Next is a pastoral scene of a sheep farm which is followed by the depiction of young men and women dancing. The outermost row shows the great stream of the ocean."

Publius Vergilius Maro (more commonly known as Virgil), a Roman poet from the Augustan period, wrote that Hephaistos made an entire set of armor for Achilles, including a breastplate, a crested helmet, a spear, a sword, and the shield. According to Virgil, carved upon the front surface of the shield was the entire history of Rome (see ARMOR OF ACHILLES).

Sources: Homer, *The Iliad*, 349–53; Roman and Roman, *Encyclopedia of Greek and Roman Mythology*, 43, 200

shield of Ajax, the

In classical Greek mythology, Ajax was the son of the king of Salamis, Telamon. The *Iliad* (1260–1180 BCE), the ancient Greek epic attributed to Homer, says Ajax was second in bravery and strength only to the demigod Achilles. The large, round shield Ajax carried had seven layers of ox hide trimmed in eight layers of brass; it was made in his home of Hyla. In the battle against Hector, a thrown spear penetrated six of the layers. The shield was also used to deflect a boulder that struck its center in the same battle.

Sources: Brennan, *The Delphian Course*, Volume 2, 253; Westmoreland, *Ancient Greek Beliefs*, 370

shield of darkness, the

In Norse mythology, the shield of darkness, along with the SHIRT OF INVISIBILITY and the SWORD OF HODR, was forged by the troll Mimring while he was in hiding on Balder's estate; they were later given to Hodr.

Sources: Green, *Myths of the Norsemen*, n.p.; Grimes, *The Norse Myths*, 287

shield of Evalach, the

Variation: shield of Galahad

In Arthurian lore, the marvelous shield of Evalach belonged to Sir Galahad; it is described as having a red cross upon a white field and could grant its wielder heavenly protection.

According to the tale, forty-two years after the death of Jesus, Joseph of Arimathea traveled to the city of Sarras, ruled by the Saracen (Muslim) king Evalach. Joseph told the story of Jesus to Evalach, who was then at war against King Tholomer. Joseph instructed that on the third day of battle, when all seemed lost, Evalach should say aloud, "Dear God, as I carry the sign of your death, protect me from this danger and lead me to safely receive your faith," as he uncovered his shield. Evalach did as he was instructed, and upon the face of the shield was the image of the crucified Christ. Evalach went on to honorably win the battle, and there were many converts because of this event. A man whose hand was severed placed his stump against the shield, and the lost appendage was instantly restored. When King Evalach converted to Christianity, the image on the shield disappeared, only to reappear on his arm. The years passed, and as Joseph lay on his deathbed, he bade Evalach bring him the shield. When it arrived, Joseph had a sudden, uncontrolled nosebleed; he used the blood to paint an image of the cross upon the shield and said that only those whom God appointed might use the shield from that on, as it would produce great wonders for a man of amazing prowess and virtue. He ordered the shield to be buried where Nascien was buried, and in five days' time, God's chosen knight would find it. And just as he described, Sir Galahad found the shield.

Sources: Jeffrey, *A Dictionary of Biblical Tradition in English Literature*, 412; Waite, *The Holy Grail, Its Legends and Symbolism*, 33, 502; Wood, *The Holy Grail*, 27

shield of Gawain, the

Variation: Gawain's shield

According to *Gawaine and the Green Knight*, an Arthurian tale written in the late fourteenth century, Sir Gawain (Gawaine) had a shield with the image of the Virgin Mother painted on the back so that he might look upon it and be inspired during battle. Typically, the shield of Gawain is described as having a pentagram upon its front.

Sources: Karr, *Arthurian Companion*, 193

shield of Gian Ben Gian, the

In ancient Persian mythology, Gian Ben Gian ("Occult Wisdom" or "True Wisdom") was said to have been the chieftain of the female *peris* as well as the governor of the world for the first two thousand years after the creation of Adam. Gian Ben Gian carried a shield that made her impervious to all forms of evil magic; however, it was useless against her personal adversary, Eblis.

Sources: Blavatsky, *Secret Doctrine*, Volume 2, 394; Brewer, *Dictionary of Phrase and Fable* 1900, 339

shield of Guenevere, the

Variation: Guenevere's shield

In Arthurian lore, the Lady of the Lake gave Queen Guenevere (Guinevere) a shield. The image upon it was that of a courtly lady and a knight who would be locked in a lover's embrace were it not for a cleft in the shield large enough for a man to pass his hand through without touching either side. Only when the knight became a member of Arthur's court and was able to earn the complete love of his lady would the fissure heal and close.

Sources: Brault, *Early Blazon*, 29; Karr, *Arthurian Companion*, 220

shield of Joseph of Arimathea, the

According to Arthurian legend, the shield of Joseph of Arimathea was carried by three maidens to King Arthur's castle, where it was then discovered by Sir Percival. It was said that the white shield had a red cross painted upon it. According to the thirteenth-century work *Perlesvaus* (also known as *Li Hauz Livres du Graal* and *The High History of the Holy Grail*), Joseph of Arimathea placed a cross upon the shield after the death of Jesus. It was also said to have belonged to Judas Maccabee. However, in the slightly older work *Queste del Saint Graal* (*Quest for the Holy Grail*), a shield of similar description and history is destined to belong to Sir Galahad.

Sources: Brault, *Early Blazon*, 50; Jeffrey, *A Dictionary of Biblical Tradition in English Literature*, 412

shield of Perseus, the

The Greek mythological hero Perseus was tasked by Athena (Roman goddess Minerva), the goddess of crafts, military victories, war, and wisdom, with embarking on a seven-year quest to confront the Gorgon Medusa and behead her. To assist the young hero in his task, she loaned him some divine items, including her sandals, shield, and sword (see SANDALS OF ATHENA and SWORD OF ATHENA). Medusa could turn into stone any creature who looked her in the eye (or even caught sight of her—sources conflict); however, it was safe to look upon her reflection. Therefore, the young hero used Athena's brazen shield (see AEGIS), as it was so highly polished and reflective that it was like looking into a mirror. Once Medusa was dead, the goddess intended to embed the head of the Gorgon onto the front of her shield.

Sources: Kirk, *Greek Myths*, 129; Mabie, *Young Folks' Treasury*, 193

ship of King Solomon, the

In the Grail Quest from Arthurian lore, the ship of King Solomon was discovered by Sir Galahad, Sir Percival, and Sir Bors; it was the vessel that took them to Sarras. The ship was described as built from the richest wood and adorned with curious inlaid gems. A red sail with a great white cross hung from the mast; it was bordered with scroll-work designs. The stern of this vessel had three spindles: one of green, one of red, and one of white. According to the lore, the spindles were made from wood harvested from the tree that grew in the Garden of Eden and bore the Forbidden Fruit, which Adam and Eve had consumed. This ship was where the knights found the SWORD AND SCABBARD OF KING DAVID.

Sources: Greenslet, *The Quest of the Holy Grail*, 71–73; Karr, *Arthurian Companion*, 124

Shiri-Kume-na-Nawa

In Japanese mythology, Shiri-Kume-na-Nawa ("Don't Retreat Rope") was the straw rope used to secure the entrance of the cave known as Ame-no-Iwato ("Sky Rock Cave"), where the goddess of the sun and personification of the light of the world, Amaterasu O Mi Kami, secluded herself after her brother, the god of sea and storms, Susanoo (Susanowo/Susa-no-wo no Mikoto), committed "atrocities" against her. Once Amaterasu O Mi Kami was lured out of the cave, the god Taiikaroo ("Prince Mighty Power") used Shiri-Kume-na-Nawa to block the entrance, preventing her from reentering the cave.

Sources: Coulter and Turner, *Encyclopedia of Ancient Deities*, 212

shirt of invisibility, the

In Norse mythology, the shirt of invisibility, along with the SHIELD OF DARKNESS and the SWORD OF HODR, was forged by the troll Mimring while he was in hiding on Balder's estate; they were later given to Hodr.

Sources: Grimes, *The Norse Myths*, 287

shoe of Vidarr, the

In Norse mythology, Vidarr, the god of silence, was a son of Odin, the god of battle, death, frenzy, the gallows, healing, knowledge, poetry, royalty, the runic alphabet, sorcery, and wisdom. Vidarr owned a remarkable left shoe that was "worked on for centuries by unseen hands." This remarkable shoe would be worn when the god shoved his foot into the jaws of Fenriswulf (Fenerriswulf/Fenrissulfrin) at Ragnarok, as it was absolute protection against both poison and teeth. The strength of the shoe came from an ancient custom: when shoes were created, a bit of leather was cut off from a place near the toe and the heal; this leather was then "given up" and applied toward the reinforcement of Vidarr's left shoe. The amount of power and strength the shoe would have on the day he needed to thrust it into Fenriswulf's mouth was solely dependent on the amount of leather given to this cause.

In another story of this powerful shoe, Vidarr received it as a gift from his mother, the *asynjr* (female Jotun, or giant) Gridr. Knowing her son would one day face the fires of Ragnarok, she designed this iron shoe to be impervious to fire, just like her own iron gauntlets (see JARNGREIPR).

Sources: Crossley-Holland, *The Norse Myths*, 216; Guerber, *Myths of the Norsemen*, 158-61; Wilkinson, *The Book of Edda Called Voluspa*, 83

shoes of Loki, the

Variation: sky shoes of Loki

In Norse mythology, Loki wore a pair of shoes that enabled him to travel through air and water, though they are seldom mentioned in the myths. In the story of how Honir, Loki, and Odin slew Ottar (Otter/Otr), Fafnir (Fafner) stole the shoes off Loki's feet, but the trickster god later recovered them.

Sources: Crossley-Holland, *The Norse Myths*, 186–189; Keightley, *World Guide to Gnomes, Fairies, Elves, and Other Little People*, 69; Rooth, *Loki in Scandinavian Mythology*, 45

Sibika

Variation: Sivika

In Vedic mythology, Sibika ("Litter") is the weapon of the god of wealth, Kuvera (Dhanada); it is described as a type of mace. This ASTRA was created by Vishvakarman from superfluous rays of the sun.

Sources: Blavatsky, *The Theosophical Glossary*, 298; Hall, *The Vishnu Purana*, Volume 3, 22

sickle of Zeus, the

Variation: ADAMANTINE sickle of Zeus

In classical Greek mythology, Zeus (Roman god Jupiter), the god of fate, kings, lightning, sky, and thunder, wielded an ADAMANTINE sickle (or the sword HARPE—sources conflict) in addition to his thunderbolts. While battling the Titan Typhon (Typhoes/Typhaon/Typhos), Zeus was able to land a fateful blow with his sickle. However, before Typhon succumbed to his wound, he wrestled the weapon out of Zeus's hands and used it to cut the sinews and remove them from the god's hands and feet.

Sources: Murgatroyd, *Mythical Monsters in Classical Literature*, 146; Viltanioti and Marmodoro, *Divine Powers in Late Antiquity*, 109

Sidrat al-Muntaha

Variation: Tree of Ultimate Boundary

According to Islamic mythology, Sidrat al-Muntaha is a very large lote tree that marks the boundary of the seventh heaven, "beyond [which] neither angel nor the Prophet may pass," as it marks the "farthest part of Paradise, to which, its farthest limit, extends the limit of knowledge, ancient and modern." Beyond this point, even divine inspiration (or *wahy*) disappears.

Sources: Adamec, *Historical Dictionary of Islam*, 406; Singh, *Sainthood and Revelatory Discourse*, 89

Sie-king T'ai

In Chinese mythology, the god Ts'en-kuag (Ts'in-kuang-wang/Ts'kuang-wang) uses his magical mirror named Sie-king T'ai when judging the dead. He is the first god to encounter the newly deceased; he places them before Sie-king T'ai, which reveals to him each person they ever caused to suffer. Based on what he sees, they are assigned to one of 10 hells.

Sources: Coulter and Turner, *Encyclopedia of Ancient Deities*, 430, 475

silk roll of Hidesato, the

In Japanese lore, there is a tale of man-eating centipede living in the mountains near Lake Biwa;

the cultural hero and famed monster-slayer Hidesato was asked by the Dragon King to destroy the creature. Hidesato coated one of his arrowheads in his own saliva, as it was widely believed that human saliva was poisonous to such creatures. He then shot the arrow into the head of the centipede, piercing its brain and killing it instantly. The hero was rewarded with three magical items, one of which was an endless roll of silk (see also CRIMSON COPPER PAN and ENDLESS BAG OF RICE). Upon receiving this reward, Hidesato began creating a new robe for himself; as he worked, he discovered that no matter how much of the fine fabric he used, it never ran out.

Sources: Kimbrough and Shirane, *Monsters, Animals, and Other Worlds*, n.p.; Roberts, *Japanese Mythology A to Z*, 22

silver branch

According to Celtic fairy lore, in order to enter the Otherworld before one's natural time, a passport was necessary; this usually took the form of a silver branch from a sacred apple tree bearing blossoms or fruit. A silver branch was typically given by the queen of the Land of the Ever Living and Ever Young to a mortal when she wished for a companion or lover. The silver branch also served as food and drink for the mortal who carried it. Additionally, the branch produced music so soothing that any mortal who heard its melody forgot all of their worries and ceased to grieve for family members who had been taken by the fairies.

Sources: Evan-Wentz, *Fairy Faith in Celtic Countries*, 336

Simul

Variation: Simmul

In Norse mythology, Simul was the carrying pole utilized by Bil and Hjuki (Yuki) when they retrieved water from the spring or well BYRGIR. The bucket that hung from Simul was named SAEG.

Sources: Grimes, *The Norse Myths*, 296; Tangherlini, *Nordic Mythologies*, 194

Singasteinn

According to Norse mythology, Singasteinn ("Chanting Stone" or "Singing Stone") is an item mentioned only in the skaldic poem *Husdrapa*, which records the account of Loki and Heimdallr (Heimdal) fighting while in the form of seals. While some scholars believe Singasteinn is the item the two gods were fighting over, others have

interpreted it as the name of the location where the fight took place, likely a skerry or rock jutting out of the water a short distance from land.

Sources: Norroena Society, *Asatru Edda*, 230, 231; Rydberg, *Teutonic Mythology* Volume 1, 558

singing sword of Conaire Mor, the

In Celtic mythology, the Irish hero Conaire Mor (Conaire/Conaire Mess Buachalla/Conare) owned a singing sword; it was said that in battle, the sword would sing, or whistle, in anticipation of bloodshed.

Sources: Classen, *Magic and Magicians in the Middle Ages and the Early Modern Time*, 124; Monaghan, *Encyclopedia of Celtic Mythology and Folklore*, 94

Sirat, al

Variations: Bridge of Jehennam, al Sirat Al-Mustaqim ("the Straight Path")

In Muslim mythology, al Sirat ("the Way") is the bridge that crosses over Hell and leads to Paradise; it is said to be no wider than a spider web but sharper than the edge of a sword. Those who are evil will fall from the bridge into the pits of Hell while those who are good will be able to walk across it quickly.

Sources: Netton, *Encyclopedia of Islamic Civilization and Religion*, n.p.

Sivamala

In Hindu mythology, Sivamala ("Siva's Garland") is the string of pearls that the goddess of science and wisdom, Sarasvati, holds in one of her two left hands; it serves as prayer beads.

Sources: Nath, *Encyclopaedic Dictionary of Buddhism*, Volume 3, 643; Wilkins, *Hindu Mythology*, 107

skald-fiflahlutr

In Norse mythology, skald-fiflahlutr ("poet-fool's portion") was the Fool's Portion of the PRECIOUS MEAD; it fell outside of the walls of Asgard ("Enclosure of the Aesir").

Sources: Grimes, *The Norse Myths*, 297

skatert-samobranka

According to Russian folklore, a skatert-samobranka was a magical tablecloth. When spread open, it would produce food and drink; when refolded; it would clean itself. If not treated with proper respect, this sentient item might spoil or taint the food. Over time, if allowed to become worn or full of holes, the skatert-samobranka would lose its magical abilities. In some tales, a magical incantation was required for its use.

Sources: Ryan, *Bathhouse at Midnight*, 199

skein of magical thread, the

In Arthurian lore, according to the German poem *Diu Crone* (*The Crown*), attributed to Heinrich von dem Turlin and dating from around the 1220s, Sir Gawain (Gawaine) defeated the wizard Laamorz of Janfruege and obtained a skein of magical thread in exchange for sparing the wizard's life.

Sources: Bruce, *The Arthurian Name Dictionary*, 273

Skidbladnir (SKEETH-blath-nir)

Variations: *Skidbladne, Skidbladner, Skidbladni, Skidhbladhnir, Skithbathnir, Skithblathnir*

In Norse mythology, *Skidbladnir* (*Assembled from Thin Pieces of Wood*/*Thin Planked*/*Wooden Blade*) was the magical sailing vessel commissioned by the god Loki and made by the dwarf Dvalin and his brothers (the Sons of Ivaldi) as reparation for having cut the long, golden hair of Thor's wife, Sif. *Skidbladnir* was ultimately given to Freyr (Frey/Yngvi), the god of fertility, peace, rain, and sunshine. *Skidbladnir* was considered the best ship ever constructed, as attested in both the *Prose Edda* and the *Heimskringla*, each written in the thirteenth century by Snorri Sturluson.

Although owned by Freyr, *Skidbladnir* was made magical by Odin, the god of battle, death, frenzy, the gallows, healing, knowledge, poetry, royalty, the runic alphabet, sorcery, and wisdom. The ship had the ability to contract and expand as desired, carry all of the Aesir, and move with equal ease in the air, on land, or at sea. When not in use, it could be folded up and placed inside a pocket or purse.

Sources: Faulkes, *Edda*, 36–37, 96–97; Hawthorne, *Vikings*, 21; Hollander, *Heimskringla*, 10–11; Keightley, *World Guide to Gnomes, Fairies, Elves, and Other Little People*, 68; Norroena Society, *Satr Edda*, 25, 386

skirar veigar (SKEER-ar VAYG-ar)

In Norse mythology, skirar veigar ("clear liquids") is the mead consumed in the underworld; it is a combination of the meads from the three underworld fountains. This brew was awaiting Balder upon his arrival in the underworld; it renewed his strength.

Sources: Norroena Society, *Asatru Edda*, 386; Rydberg et al., *Teutonic Mythology*, Volume 2, 358

Skofnung

Variations: Gunnlogi, Warflame

A mound weapon associated with the legendary Danish king Hrolf Kraki, the sword Skof-nung was said to have mystical properties; aside from being supernaturally hard and sharp, it was imbued with the souls of the king's 12 faithful berserker bodyguards. In accordance with ancient superstition, the sword could never be drawn in the presence of a woman, nor could sunlight be allowed to fall upon its hilt. Any wound made by Skofnung would never heal unless it was rubbed with the Skofnung Stone.

According to the *Kormaks saga*, the sword was retrieved from a burial mound by the Icelander Skeggi of Midfirth. In the *Laxdcela saga*, Eid of As removed Skofnung from the burial mound of Hrolf Kraki and loaned it to his kinsman, Thorkel Eyjolfsson, so he would slay the man who had murdered Eid's son, an outlaw by the name of Grom. Rather than killing him, the two men became friends and Skofnung was never returned to Eid. The sword was lost briefly when Thorkel's ship sank, but his son, Gellir, found it washed up on the shore stuck in a section of the mast. Skofnung was then buried with Gellir in Denmark and, according to the saga, is with him to this day.

Sources: Byock, *Saga of King Hrolf Kraki*, n.p.; Eddison, *Egil's Saga*, 281; Miller, *The Epic Hero*, 160, 211; Pendergrass, *Mythological Swords*, 64

Skrymir

In the Norse sagas, Steinar ("Stone") wielded a sword called Skrymir, named after a giant of Norse mythology; it was said to have been an excellent sword that had never been fouled or had any mishap come upon it.

Sources: Eddison, *Egil's Saga*, 281; Mouse, *The Saga of Cormac the Skald*, n.p.

skull of Heidraupnir

In Norse mythology, a Jotun (giant) by the name of Midvitnir ("Mead Wolf"/"Mid Wolf"/"-Sea Wolf") lived in a mead hall named Brimir in Okolnir, a region of Muspellsheimr. He stole the Precious Mead out of Asgard ("Enclosure of the Aesir") and returned to his hall with it, storing it in the skull of Heidraupnir and the Horn of Hoddrofnir, guarded by his son Sokkmimir.

Sources: Grimes, *The Norse Myths*, 58

Slatt yn Ree

Variations: Cliweny Sollys, Cliwe-ny-Sollys, Sword of Light

Slatt yn Ree, the symbol of all knowledge in Manx lore, was described as a great sword, blazing with gold and silver and emitting an otherworldly light. Whoever held the sword was invincible in battle, and anyone else who was touched by the blade would be instantly dispatched to the Otherworld, whether they were a mortal or immortal being. Slatt yn Ree was guarded by a warrior named Shelgeyr Mooar but was stolen by the hero Eshyn, who followed the careful instructions of Benrein na Sheem, the queen of the fairies.

Sources: Ellis, *The Mammoth Book of Celtic Myths and Legends*, n.p.

Slea Bua

Variation: Spear Invincible

One of the spears belonging to the Celtic god of the sun, Lugh ("Bright" or "Light") of the Long Arms (Artful Hands or Long Hands), Slea Bua ("Spear of Victory"), forged by the god of blacksmithing, Goibniu (Gaibne/Gaibniu/Gobha/Goibhnionn/Goibnenn/Goibniu Sear), was one of Lugh's most prized possessions; the other spears he owned were AREADBHAIR and Gae Assail ("Spear of Assal"; see LUIN). This magical spear was considered "alive," as it acted as if it had a mind of its own. Capable of self-propelled flight, it would seek out enemies and was so bloodthirsty that the only way to keep it still was to submerge the spearhead in a sleeping potion made from the pounded leaves of the poppy plant. As the time of battle approached, Slea Bua trembled to be used, and when pulled for that purpose, it would roar in delight.

Sources: Adams Media, *The Book of Celtic Myths*, 75; Mountfort, *Ogam*, 158

sleeve of Elaine, the

In the Arthurian tale *Sir Lancelot and Elaine the Fair*, Lancelot anonymously enters a tournament held in Winchester. Using borrowed armor, the knight wore the token of Elaine of Astolat (Elaine d'Escalot), who was profoundly in love with him. This was the first time he ever wore a lady's token, as he had dedicated his love and service to the queen. The sleeve was described as a flame-colored piece of satin embroidered with pearls of great value.

Sources: Karr, *Arthurian Companion*, 139; Pyle, *The Story of Sir Launcelot and His Companions*, 128, 129

sleeve of Guenevere, the

According to Sir Thomas Malory (1415–1471), Queen Guenevere (Guinevere) of Arthurian lore gave Sir Lancelot her token, or sleeve, to wear in tournaments, wrapped around the top of his crested helm, so he would always be recognized.

Sources: Karr, *Arthurian Companion*, 220

smith hook of Goibniu, the

Variation: knife hook of Goibniu

The smith hook of the Celtic god of blacksmithing, Goibniu (Gaibne/Gaibniu/Gobha/Goibhnionn/Goibnenn/Goibniu Sear), was kept in the CRANE BAG of Manannan mac Lir (Mannanan,Mannanos), god of the sea and guardian of the Underworld.

Sources: Gregory and MacCumhaill, *Gods and Fighting Men*, 202

Smoking Mirror

Tezcatlipoca ("Lord of the Smoking Mirror"), the supreme god of the Mesoamerican pantheon and the god of conflict and war, carries on his person a smoking mirror; sometimes it is depicted as attached to his forehead or replacing one of his feet. With the mirror, this invisible, ever-present lord of the shadows has the ability to divine the future, look into the hearts of men, and see the entirety of the cosmos.

Sources: Bezanilla, *A Pocket Dictionary of Aztec and Mayan Gods and Goddesses*, 8; Willis, *World Mythology*, 239

Sokkvabekkr

Variations: Soequabkeck, Sokvabekr, Soquabeck

In Norse mythology, Sokkvabekkr ("Singing Hall"/"Singing Stream"/"Sunken Hall") was the crystal hall of Saga, the goddess of poetic art and wisdom and drinking companion of Odin; it was located near the sea, with the waves constantly breaking against it.

Sources: Grimes, *The Norse Myths*, 299

solar barge of Ra, the

Variations: Atet, Barque of Ages, Boat of a Million Years, Bull of Millions, Madjet ("Becoming Strong"), MANDJET, Matet, MESEKTET, Sektet boat, Semektet ("Becoming Weak"), solar barque, sun barge, sun boat

In Egyptian mythology, the sun god Ra (Re) would use his solar barge to travel across the sky's twelve provinces each day; die; descend into Duat, the perilous underworld; and then, after traveling through the twelve regions each night, reappear in the eastern sky reborn, creating the morning. During the daylight hours, the barge was called Atet or Matet, while in the evening it was Seket.

Sources: Britannica Educational Publishing, *Egyptian Gods & Goddesses*, n.p.; Hart, *The Routledge Dictionary of Egyptian Gods and Goddesses*, n.p.

Soma

Variations: AMBROSIA, amrta, elixir of immortality, Haoma

In Hindu mythology, there is a certain "plant of immortality" that is the main ingredient of Soma, the elixir the gods quaff to become immortal. In early myths Soma was extracted in part from cows, plants, and water, and then combined and consumed. Later, it was created by removing the juices from the stalks of certain plants.

Properties attributed to the drink in addition to bestowing immortality were granting enhanced alertness and awareness, conferring great strength, healing the sick, bestowing paranormal abilities, and rejuvenating the aged.

Soma was also the name of the god described as a deity "of the highest strains of adulation and veneration. All powers belong to him; all blessings are his to bestow." Soma, a lunar god, was even worshiped by Indra, who was addicted to the drink and, along with Agni, consumed it in vast quantities.

Sources: O'Flaherty, *Hindu Myths*, 35, 273; Wilkins, *Hindu Mythology*, 59–63

Son

Variations: Sohn, Sonr

In Norse mythology, Son ("Blood") was one of the vats holding a portion of the PRECIOUS MEAD; the others were called BODN and ODRERIR. Son was said to be kept in the treasure chamber of Suttungr, HNITBJORG.

In the "Skaldskaparmal" portion of the *Prose Edda*, Icelandic historian Snorri Sturluson explicitly states that ODRERIR was a bronze kettle in which the blood of Kvasir was fermented, while BODN and Son were barrels.

Sources: Grimes, *The Norse Myths*, 299; Lindow, *Norse Mythology*, 252

Sonar Dreyri (SOHN-ar DRAYR-i)

In Norse mythology, Sonar Dreyri ("Son's Blood") was the mead of MIMIRSBRUNNR WELL, the fountain of Mimir. Anyone who consumed this mead would be granted wisdom. Sonar Dreyri was combined with SVALKALDR SAER and URDAR MAGN in the HORN OF HADES.

Sources: Norroena Society, *Asatru Edda*, 387; Rasums, *Norroena*, Volume 12, 138; Rydberg, *Teutonic Mythology* Volume 2, 92, 353

Sopasamhara

In ancient Hindu mythology, the Sopasamhara was a class of weapons connected with withdrawing or restraining; they are considered weapons that are thrown.

There are 44 different weapons in this classification, and each of them was given by Visvamitra to Rama: Anidracakra (the discus of Indra), Ardra (the Wet), Avidyastra (the missile of ignorance), Brahmasirsa (the head of Brahma), Dandcakra (the discus of punishment), Dharmacakra (the discus of light), Dharmapasa (noose of right), Gandharvastra (the Gandharva missile), GARUDASTRA (the missile of Garuda), Hayasirsa (the horse-headed missile), Isikastra (the reed missile), Kalacakra (the discus of Yama), Krauncastra (the Krauncastra missile), Manasa (the spiritual missile), MANAVASTRA (the missile of Manu), Mausala (the club-shaped missile), Mayastra (the missile of illusion), Modaki (the Charmer), NAGAASTRA (the missile of the serpent), Nandanastra (the joy-producing missile), Painakastra (the missile of Siva), Prasamana (the soothing missile), Prasvapana (the sleep-causing missile), Sailastra (the rocky missile), Samana (the conciliatory missile), Samhara (the missile of restraining), Samvarta (the rolling missile), Santapana (the tormenting missile), Satya (the missile of truth), Saura (the missile of the sun), Sikharastra (the flaming missile), Sjkhari (the Pointed), Somastra (the missile of the moon), Sosana (the drying missile), Sulavara (the spear of Siva), Suska (the Dry), Tamasa (the missile of darkness), The mathana (the churning missile), Tvastra (the missile of Vishvakarman), VARUNAPASHA (the noose of Varuna), Vassana (the rainy missile), Vayavya (the missile of Vayu), Vidyastra (the missile of knowledge), and vilapana (the wailing missile).

Sources: Oppert, *On the Weapons*, 25–28

spear of Ithuriel, the

Variations: detecting spear of Ithuriel, spear of the angel Ithuriel

According to John Milton (1608–1674), the angel Ithuriel had in his possession a spear with the ability to expose deceit in any form. In the epic poem *Paradise Lost*, when Ithuriel saw Satan sitting "like a toad" close to Eve, he placed the tip of the spear on him, causing Satan to reveal his true form.

Sources: Brewer, *Dictionary of Phrase and Fable*, Volume 2, 1165; Macaulay, *Miscellaneous Essays and Lays of Ancient Rome*, 323

Speer

In *Die Walkure* (*The Valkyrie*)—the second of the four musical dramas Richard Wagner wrote to create *Der Ring des Nibelungen*—the name of the spear of Wotan was Speer. In the drama, when the sword Nothung was wielded by Siegmund, it shattered upon striking the shaft of Speer. However, the son of Siegmund, Sigurd (Siegfried/Sigmund), took up the pieces of the broken weapon and reforged them. Then, when Sigurd confronted Wotan, the murderer of his father, the sword he created shattered the shaft of Speer.

Sources: Lewsey, *Who's Who and What's What in Wagner*, n.p.

staff of Moses, the

Variations: matei ha-Elohim ("rod of God"), staff of God

The staff of Moses from biblical lore was first mentioned in the book of Exodus, when God transformed it momentarily into a snake to persuade Moses to lead His people out of Egypt. It was also present when Moses brought forth the seventh and eighth plagues upon Egypt (hail and locusts, respectively). Moses held this staff when parting the Red Sea and when striking the rocks of the desert for water and battling the Amalekites. The staff became the symbol of the power and presence of God as well as the authority and leadership of Moses.

The exact nature of Moses's staff is a matter of scholarly debate; some argue that it was a miraculous item (perhaps created on the eve of the Sabbath by God), others that it was an item with inherent supernatural properties, and still others that it was simply an item present while miracles were being performed. There is also speculation regarding whether the ROD OF MOSES and the staff of Moses are the same item.

If the staff of Moses was the staff that God created on the eve of the Sabbath, it has been described as made of almond wood or sapphire and, in either case, bore the inscription of the Tetragrammaton and radiated light; once planted into the ground, only the rightful owner could pick it up. According to this lore, after its creation God gave it to Adam, who gave it to Enoch; he gave it to Methuselah, who passed it down to Noah, who gave it to his son Shem; it was then passed to Abraham, who gave it to Isaac, who passed it to Jacob, who gave it to Joseph. When Joseph died, the staff and all of his other possessions went into a vault of Pharaoh's. Jethro, a servant of Pharaoh, desired the staff and stole it from the vault; one day he planted it in the garden and

was unable to pull it up. There the staff remained until Moses came and removed it.

Sources: Dennis, *The Encyclopedia of Jewish Myth, Magic and Mysticism*, n.p.; Lim, *The Sin of Moses and the Staff of God*, 139, 152, 162

stone and ring of Eluned the Fortunate, the

Variations: Eluned's stone and ring, Modrwy a Charreg Eluned, ring of Sunset, stone ring of Eluned the Fortunate

In British and Welsh folklore, there is a series of items (always thirteen in number) called the THIRTEEN TREASURES OF THE ISLAND OF BRITAIN (in Welsh, they are called *Tri Thlws ar Ddeg Ynys Prydain*). The traditional list of thirteen items differs from the modern one with the inclusion of two additional items, one of which is Eluned's stone and ring and the other being the MANTLE OF TEGAU EURFON. When one of these items appears on the list, another is dropped from it. On some occasions, the CROCK AND DISH OF RHYGENYDD YSGOLHAIG are listed as a single item.

Eluned's stone and ring come from *Owain, or the Lady of the Fountain*. In this tale, the hero, Sir Owain, kills Esclados, the husband of Laudine, the Lady of the Fountain. While trying to make his escape, Owain is given the magical ring by Laudine's handmaiden, Eluned (Luned or Lunete). The ring is set with a stone that allows the wearer to become invisible when the ring is turned so that the stone is pointed inward and concealed from sight.

Sources: Dom, *King Arthur and the Gods of the Round Table*, 107, 150; Kozminsky, *Crystals, Jewels, Stones*, n.p.; Pendergrass, *Mythological Swords*, 25

stone begging bowl of the Buddha, the

A Japanese folktale from the Heinan period tells the story of a wealthy bamboo cutter's daughter by the name of Nayotake no Kaguya-hime ("Shining Princess of the Supple Bamboo") who wishes to marry only a man who truly loves her. She manages to whittle down her suitors to five and states that she will marry the one who is able to show her something special she wishes to see. The suitor named Ishitsukuri no Miko, a prince, is given the task of retrieving the stone begging bowl of the Buddha.

Sources: Rimer, *Modern Japanese Fiction and Its Traditions*, 285; Shirane, *Traditional Japanese Literature*, 117; Soothill and Hodous, *A Dictionary of Chinese Buddhist Terms*, 64

stone of Anansi, the

The mortal Anansi, an Ashanti folk hero who was the son of the god of the sky, Nyame, often acted as an intermediary between his father and the earth. Anansi taught mankind how to sow grain, married a princess, possessed endless resources, and owned a magical stone whose name, if ever said aloud, would kill the person who spoke it. He also had the ability to decrease or increase his size whenever he chose.

Sources: Haase, *The Greenwood Encyclopedia of Folktales and Fairy Tales*, 31; Penard, *Journal of American Folk-lore*, Volume 7, 241–42

stone of Giramphiel, the

In the Middle High German Arthurian tale *Diu Krone* (*The Crown*), attributed to the poet Heinrich von dem Türlin, Sir Gawain (Gawaine), during his Grail Quest, defeats Sir Fimbeus (Fimbeus) and wins from him a belt featuring a magical stone that will not only protect anyone who wears it from dragon's fire but also make them brave, charming, handsome, and strong. According to the poem, the belt and stone were created by Lady Saelde and gifted to her sister Giramphiel, who later gave it to her beloved, Sir Fimbeus. In an attempt to bed Queen Guenevere (Guinevere), the knight offers her the belt in exchange for becoming his lover. Desiring the belt, but not liking the terms, the queen asks Sir Gawain to win it for her in trial by combat. Reluctantly, he agrees and only by a lucky strike wins the match. The queen receives the belt from Gawain and gives it to her lover, Gasozein, but (in an undisclosed way) the belt is returned to Gawain; however, the stone that gave the belt its power was removed by Fimbeus and returned to Giramphiel. Gawain then sets off on a quest to recover the stone, which takes him to Sadinia, where he recovers the stone, defeats Fimbeus, and gains his fealty.

Sources: Bruce, *The Arthurian Name Dictionary*, 184; Thomas, *Diu Crône and the Medieval Arthurian Cycle*, 79

stone of Japheth, the

Variations: giudetasch, Jada Tas ("Rain Stone"), Japheth's stone, senkjede, Yadatash ("Rain-Stone")

In biblical traditions, Noah once possessed a stone given to him by the angel Gabriel, which had the ability to cause it to rain at will; in other tellings, the angel told Noah a divine word that would cause it to rain and Noah carved it onto a stone that he wore about his neck as a talisman. In both traditions, Noah made a gift of the stone to Japheth (Ipheth/Jepheth), one of his three sons.

According to more modern translations of the tale, when the proper incantation was said and the stone held to the sky, storm clouds would gather, and soon after it would rain.

Sources: Brewer, *Dictionary of Phrase and Fable* 1900, 455; *Journal of Indian History*, Volumes 13–14, 246; Molnar, *Weather-Magic in Inner Asia*, 12, 13, 55

stone of tongues, the

In Italian lore, King Otnit of Lombardy was said to possess a magical stone known as the stone of tongues, which was given to him by the dwarf Elberich. When placed in his mouth, this item would enable him to speak any foreign language perfectly.

Sources: Daniels and Stevens, *Encyclopedia of Superstitions, Folklore, and the Occult Sciences*, Volume 2, 753

stray sod

In Scottish fairy lore, stray sod is a fairy-enchanted lump of grass; stepping on it will trigger the magic, causing the person to suddenly become lost. Landmarks will no longer be familiar, and the trail or road you were just on will seemingly disappear. As a regional superstition, it is believed that wherever an unbaptized child is buried, the patch of earth above its grave will become an area of stray sod. In either case, the only way to break the enchantment is to wear your clothes inside out.

Sources: Bord, *Fairies*, 11–12; Jacobs et al., *Folk Lore*, Volume 4, 182

Suckling Tree

In the Aztec paradise known as Tomoanchan, which is ruled by the skeletal Itzpapalotl, there is a tree known as the Suckling Tree; it is covered with over 400,000 nipples and gently cradles deceased babies. Here, in its boughs, the infants rest and feed, regaining strength until they are ready for reincarnation.

Sources: Cotterell, *The Lost Tomb of Viracocha*, 102

Sudarsana

Variations: Chakkrath Azhwar ("Ring of God")

In Hindu mythology, Sudarsana ("Divine Vision") was the *chakra* (discus) of Vishnu, the god of preservation; it was described as a spinning disc with 108 serrated edges and was used to enforce law and order. With this ASTRA, Vishnu served as the keeper and protector of the celestial bodies and the heavens. Sudarsana was likely the most powerful of the ASTRAS, as neither Brahma nor Shiva could stop it once it was thrown.

The architect of gods, Vishvakarman, had to reduce the intensity of the god of the sun, Surya; with the dust created by the process, he made three ASTRAS: PUSHPAKA VIMANA, Sudarshana, and the TRISHUL.

Sudarsana was given by Shiva to Vishnu as a boon for his devotion to chanting the thousand sacred names of Shiva. With Sudarsana, Vishnu protected the god of fire, Agni, as he consumed the Khandava Vana forest and beheaded Shishupala. Sudarsana was also employed to cut Mandrachal Parvat, the celestial mountain, for the Samudra Manthan ("Churning of the Ocean").

Sources: Daniel, *The Akshaya Patra Series Manasa Bhajare*, n.p.; Kaur, *The Regime of Maharaja Ranjit Singh*, 15; Rajagopalachari, *Mahabharata*, 41, 43, 44

sugarcane bow of Shakti, the

According to the *Brahmanda Purana*, the goddess of power, Shakti, carries an unnamed sugarcane bow in her left hand; the arrows for the bow are tipped with flower petals.

Sources: Babu, *Sugar Cane*, 31

Sullt

In Norse mythology, Hel, the goddess of the underworld, has an enormous hall named ELJUDNIR ("Preparer of Pain"/"Sprayed with Snowstorms"), which is fully decorated with many named items. The name of her knife is Sullt ("Starvation").

Sources: Byock, *The Prose Edda*, 34; Norroena Society, *Satr Edda*, 365; Thorpe, *Northern Mythology*, 50

Sundara Vimana

There are five different types of vimana ("aerial car"): PUSHPAKA VIMANA, RUKMA VIMANA, SHAKUNA VIMANA, Sundara Vimana, and TRIPURA VIMANA.

In the fifth book of *Mahabharata*, titled "Vimanapala" ("Guardian of the Aircraft"), a highly specialized individual is given the responsibility of caring for the vimana. Sundara Vimana, just like RUKMA VIMANA, is described as conical in shape.

Sources: Becklake, *History of Rocketry and Astronautics*, 9; Childress, *Vimana*, n.p.

Suryastra

In Hindu mythology, an ASTRA is a supernatural weapon created or gifted by the gods to some-

one who then presides over the weapon. The wielder of an ASTRA is known as an astradhari.

Suryastra was an ASTRA from the god of the sun, Surya. It was said to have the ability to create a light so dazzling it would dispel the darkness and dry up all sources of water. Suryastra is described as having many sharpened edges and spinning wheels, and it discharges fire.

Sources: Aravamudan, *Pure Gems of Ramayanam*, 538; Edizioni, *Vimanas and the Wars of the Gods*, n.p.

Svalin (SVAL-in)

Variations: Svalinn

In Norse mythology, Svalin ("Chill"/"Cold"/ "Cooler") was the shield held between Earth and the sun. As the shield of the goddess Sol, Svalin was attached to her chariot to protect her horses, Aarvak and Alsvin, from the rays and heat of the sun as they ran across the sky. It was described in *Grimnismal* as being made of shining gold.

Sources: Coulter and Turner, *Encyclopedia of Ancient Deities*, 446; Grimes, *The Norse Myths*, 300; Hawthorne, *Vikings*, 21; Norroena Society, *Asatru Edda*, 388

Svalkaldr Saer (SVAL-kald-ur SAIR)

Variations: Svalkaldur Saer

In Norse mythology, Svalkaldr Saer ("Cool-Cold Sea") was the water from HVERGELUR WELL, the source fountain for all water, including the oceans. The well is located in the northernmost root of YGGDRASIL near the subterranean border. Svalkaldr Saer was combined with SONAR DREYRI and URDAR MAGN in the HORN OF HADES.

Sources: Norroena Society, *Asatru Edda*, 4, 35; Rydberg, *Teutonic Mythology* Volume 1, 92, 353

Svanhringar (SVAN-ring-ar)

In Norse mythology, Svanhringar ("Swan Rings") was the collective name of the rings given to Ivaldi's sons—Egill (Egil), Slagfinnr (Slagfin), and Volundr (Voldun)—by Svanmeyjar ("Swan Maiden") Auda, Idunn, and Siff. Each of the brothers was married to one of the Svanmeyjar and wore the Svanhringar as proof of such, symbolizing fertility. Egill was wed to Siff, Slagfinnr to Auda, and Volundr to Idunn, goddess of rebirth and spring.

Sources: Norroena Society, *Asatru Edda*, 113, 390; Rydberg, *Teutonic Mythology* Volume 1, 585, 661

svefnporn (SVEHV-n-thawrn)

Variations: thorn of sleep

In Norse mythology, svefnporn ("sleep thorn") was a thorn used to induce a magical sleep; the thorn was placed in a person's ear or on their clothing, and as long as it stayed in place, they would remain asleep.

In one story, Odin, the god of battle, death, frenzy, the gallows, healing, knowledge, poetry, royalty, the runic alphabet, sorcery, and wisdom, took the Valkyrie Brynhildr (Brunnehilde) to HINDARFIALL, a tall mountain whose cloud-top summit had a halo of flames. There, he pierced her with a thorn of sleep and surrounded her with a wall of fire known as the VAFRLOGAR. As she lay awaiting the arrival of a husband brave enough to pass through the flames, she retained her beauty and youth.

Sources: Guerber, *Myths of the Norsemen*, 280, 284; Keyser, *The Religion of the Northmen*, 270–71; Norroena Society, *Asatru Edda*, 389; Rydberg, *Teutonic Mythology* Volume 1, 489; Sturluson, *Younger Edda*, 134

Sviagris

One of the great treasures of the Uppsala Dynasty, the gold ring Sviagris ("Swede's Pig") was among the three prized possessions of King Adils of Sweden in the Hrolf Kraki saga of Norse mythology; FINNSLEIF and HILDIGOLT were the other two. Sviagris had been in the king's family since ancient times.

According to the legend, Adils enlisted the assistance of his stepson, King Hrolf Kraki, to defeat King Ali of Norway; he promised to pay his stepson's entire army in addition to giving Hrolf any three Swedish treasures. Hrolf accepted and sent his twelve best berserkers. Adils defeated Ali and on the battlefield claimed his opponent's helmet, HILDIGOLT, and his warhorse, Raven. When the time for payment came, the berserkers asked for three pounds of gold each for themselves and the treasures FINNSLEIF, HILDIGOLT, and Sviagris for their king.

Sources: Anderson, *The Younger Edda*, 215, 217; Byock, *The Prose Edda*, 232

swan cloak

Variation: swan dress

A popular convention in fairy tales and mythology alike is the magical vestment known as the swan cloak. Always worn by a woman of ravishing beauty, the cloak gives its user some magical abilities (usually being able to transform into a swan or travel between our world and some other, such as VALHALLA). It is common for the woman who owns the swan cloak to go to some secret glen, disrobe, and bathe in what she believes to be privacy; however, she is observed by the hero of tale, who immediately falls in love with her. After he steals the cloak, she is trapped and inevitably becomes the bride of her lovelorn captor. The only way for the woman to escape her marriage is to discover the hidden location of her cloak, steal it back, and flee.

Sources: Keightley, *World Guide to Gnomes, Fairies, Elves, and Other Little People*, 214–15; Kerven, *Viking Myths and Sagas*, n.p.; O hOgain, *Myth, Legend and Romance*, 424

sword and scabbard of King David, the

In the Grail Quest from Arthurian lore, the SHIP OF KING SOLOMON was discovered by Sir Galahad, Sir Percival, and Sir Bors; it was at the base of the altar on board the ship that the sword and scabbard of King David were discovered. According to the story, Solomon's wife bade her husband take the sword of King David and remove the precious stones from its scabbard and handle. Then she left a belt with the sword that was so thin it looked as if it would support nothing, but she assured Solomon that one day a damsel would add to the belt, building it up with the cords of her love. It would then be known as the SWORD WITH THE STRANGE HANGINGS.

Balin's sword was Galahad's first blade; his second sword was the sword of King David.

Sources: Hennig, *King Arthur*, 40; Karr, *Arthurian Companion*, 124

Sword in the Stone, the

Variations: Sword with the Red Hilt

According to Arthurian legend, there was once a sword that had been plunged into a stone, and only the true and rightful king of Britain would be able to pull it free. Although this sword is popularly misidentified as EXCALIBUR, they are in fact different objects.

The concept of the Sword in the Stone was introduced into Arthurian lore for the first time around the year 1200 by Robert de Boron in *Le Roman du Graal*. In this version, Uther Pendragon has died and left the land without a king. On Christmas Day, the bishops, knights, and noblemen gather to select a new king; before them appears a stone upon which rests an anvil pierced by a sword. It is determined that only the rightful king of Logres will be able to pull the sword free. Arthur, acting as squire to his older brother, Sir Kay, pulls the sword when sent to fetch his brother's weapon at a tournament. No one believes that Kay pulled the weapon, and eventually the council discovers that the deed was accomplished by Arthur. They decide to make him put the sword back and pull it out again at Candlemas, which he does. Again they make him return the sword and tell him he may try to retrieve it once more on Easter. When he is successful again, it is decided that Arthur will be recognized and crowned king at Pentecost.

According to Sir Thomas Malory (1415–1471), the Sword in the Stone is broken early in Arthur's reign while he is battling King Pellinor. Merlin (Merddyn/Myrddin) and Arthur then row to the island of Avalon, where a lady gives him a sword (likely Excalibur). In order to receive the sword, Arthur has to promise the lady that he will grant her a favor in the future. She also gives him the weapon's scabbard at this time.

Near the end of Arthur's reign, a second sword appears in a stone in a river outside of Camelot; it appears on the same day that Sir Galahad comes to court and sits in the Perilous Seat. As the knight has no sword, Arthur suggests Galahad attempt to retrieve the blade. He is successful, and the quest for the Grail begins.

Sources: Bruce, *The Arthurian Name Dictionary*, 43, 117, 213; Knowles, *The Legends of King Arthur and His Knights*, n.p.; Pendergrass, *Mythological Swords*, 29–30; Sherman, *Storytelling*, 440

sword of Athena, the

The Greek mythological hero Perseus was tasked by Athena (Roman goddess Minerva), the goddess of crafts, military victories, war, and wisdom, with embarking on a seven-year quest to confront the Gorgon Medusa and behead her. To assist the young hero in his task, she loaned him some divine items, including her sandals, shield, and sword (see SANDALS OF ATHENA and SHIELD OF PERSEUS). In some versions of the myth, it was Hermes (Roman god Mercury), the god of animal husbandry, commerce, eloquence, fertility, language, looters, luck, sleep, thieves, trade, travel, and wealth, who gave Perseus the sword.

Sources: Mabie, *Young Folks' Treasury*, 194; Simpson, *Guidebook to the Constellations*, 39

sword of Attila, the

Variations: sword of God, sword of Mars

The Roman bureaucrat-turned-historian Jordanes (Jordanis/Jornandes) claimed that a shepherd unearthed a sword and presented it to Attila; the Hun leader, in turn, believed it to be a symbol of the divine favor of the god of war and a sign that he would be the ruler of the world. The sword was both Attila's weapon and his scepter. In his writings, Jordanes said this legendary weapon was from the god Mars, but the Huns would not have worshiped a Roman god.

It was said that annually the sword was consecrated or rededicated to Mars by building a wood pile 300 yards long and wide. Upon it were sacrificed horse, sheep, and 100 captives. The human sacrifices had their arms severed at the shoulder and thrown onto the fire; where and how the limbs landed were read to divine the future, much like tea leaves.

Sources: Gibbon, *The History of the Decline and Fall of the Roman Empire*, Volume 4, 195; Jordanes, *The Origin and Deeds of the Goths*, 57

sword of Cheru, the

Variations: sword of Er, sword of Heru, sword of Tyr

Created by the same dwarfs who made the spear of Odin, the god of battle, death, frenzy, the gallows, healing, knowledge, poetry, royalty, the runic alphabet, sorcery, and wisdom, the sword of Cheru was said to ensure victory for those who wielded it. According to legend, the sword was hung in a temple where its blade caught and reflected the first rays of the sun—that is, until it was stolen. A priestess foretold that whoever possessed the sword would conquer the world but die by its blade. Among those who allegedly came to possess the sword of Cheru and fell victim to its legacy were the Roman emperor Vitellius, Attila the Hun, and the Duke of Alva, Charles the Great; the current owner of the sword is said to be the archangel Michael.

Sources: Guerber, *Myths of the Norsemen from the Eddas and Sagas*, 87–88

sword of Damocles, the

Variation: Damocles's sword

Marcus Tullius Cicero (106–43 BCE), the Roman consul, lawyer, orator, philosopher, prose stylist, and statesman, recorded the anecdote of the sword of Damocles. In the tale, Damocles was a flattering toady in the court of Dionysius II of Syracuse, Sicily, a tyrant who ruled in the fourth century BCE. To make a point to his pandering courtier, the king offered to switch places with him. Damocles was treated to a great feast with music and offered every amenity, but hanging directly over his throne was a sharpened sword suspended by a single horse hair. Damocles was afraid for his life and completely unable to enjoy any of the lush extravagances presented to him. He soon begged the king to switch back to their former positions. The lesson taught was that with great fortune and power also came great anxiety and peril, and great men with much to lose always live in constant fear.

Sources: Cicero, *Cicero's Tusculan Disputations*, n.p.; Cicero, *M. Tully Cicero's Five Books of Tuscan Disputations*, 216

sword of Hermes, the

The Greek mythological hero Perseus was tasked by Athena (Roman goddess Minerva), the goddess of crafts, military victories, war, and wisdom, with embarking on a seven-year quest to confront the Gorgon Medusa and behead her. To assist him in this undertaking, according to some versions of the myth, Hermes (Roman god Mercury), the god of animal husbandry, commerce, eloquence, fertility, language, looters, luck, sleep, thieves, trade, travel, and wealth, loaned Perseus his own short sword. This weapon was promised to be sharp enough to behead the Gorgon with a single swipe across the neck. It is described as a black-bound blade on a bronze belt.

Sources: Simpson, *Guidebook to the Constellations*, 39; Westmoreland, *Ancient Greek Beliefs*, 169

sword of Hodr, the

In Norse mythology, the sword of Hodr, along with the SHIELD OF DARKNESS and the SHIRT OF INVISIBILITY, was forged by the troll Mimring while he was in hiding on Balder's estate; they were later given to Hodr.

Sources: Grimes, *The Norse Myths*, 287; Norroena Society, *Asatru Edda*, 121–26

sword of Methuselah, the

Variations: the mighty sword of God, the sword of the Lord

In biblical lore, the sword of Methuselah was a mystical blade wielded by many people; it was handed down to Enoch, who used it to slay giants, and then passed on to Methuselah, from whom the sword took its name. Jacob, as well as other patriarchs, was likewise said to have possessed it.

According to legend, the sword could only be wielded by a rightful heir, as their handprint would fit perfectly upon the sword's hilt; the weapon would then make that person an invincible champion of just causes.

In the Misrash Abkir, Adam, having left Eve, took a *lilit* (a type of demon) by the name of Piznai as his lover; their firstborn of 92,000 djinn (genie) and lilit offspring was named Agrimas; he in turn took up with a lilit named Amarit, and she bore him 92,000 djinn and lilit. Their firstborn, Avalmas, likewise took up with a lilit named Gofrit, who bore him 88,000 djinn and lilit. Their firstborn, Akrimas, took up with Afizana, a daughter of Piznai. However, before more generations could continue, as they were tempting the humanity of mankind, Methuselah wrote the name of God upon his sword and slew 900,000 of the djinn and lilit. Agrimas then sought an audience with Methuselah, and it was agreed that, in exchange for the true names of the surviving djinn and lilit and the secret of iron so that the spirits might be bound rather than slain, Methuselah would let Agrimas and the rest of his kind go into hiding in the deepest parts of the ocean and the most remote part of the wilderness.

Christian and Hebrew tradition tells us that the ARK OF THE COVENANT contained items other than the two stone tablets listing the Ten Commandments. Although there is debate over whether the items were *in*, *beside*, or *near* the Ark, these items include a *bolide* (meteor) that fell from the heavens; the genealogy of the Jewish people; the ROD OF AARON, which magically flowered; the ROD OF MOSES; the URIM AND THUMMIM; the VESTMENT OF ADAM; and other relics. Less frequently mentioned items in the Ark are the EMERALD TABLET; the HARP OF KING DAVID, which played music of its own accord; and the flute of King David.

Sources: Boren and Boren, *Following the Ark of the Covenant*, 13–14; Dennis, *The Encyclopedia of Jewish Myth, Magic and Mysticism*, n.p.

sword of Paravataksha, the

A *nagaraja* (naga king) from Hindu mythology, Paravataksha lived in the northern quadrant of the Vindhya forest in a lake shaded by a holy acoka tree; he was described as clothed in dense clouds, with fiery eyes and a roar like *vajra* ("thunder"). Paravataksha carried a sword that had the ability to cause earthquakes; it was given to him by the asuras and the gods.

Sources: Coulter and Turner, *Encyclopedia of Ancient Deities*, 333; de Visser, *Dragon in China and Japan*, 17–18

sword of Peleus, the

In classical Greek mythology, the Argonaut Peleus was the son of King Aeacus and Emdeis. He

sword of Theseus

was given a magical sword created by Hephaistos (Hephaestus; Roman god Vulcan), the god of bindings, the art of sculpture, fire, forges, metalworking, stonemasonry, and talismans, as a reward for resisting the advances of Astydameia, the wife of Akastos. The sword had the magical ability to make its wielder victorious whether they were fighting or hunting. Peleus was the father of the hero Achilles.

Sources: Grant and Hazel, *Who's Who in Classical Mythology*, 403; Hansen, *Ariadne's Thread*, 126, 342

sword of Theseus, the

In classical Greek mythology, the Athenian hero Theseus was the son of King Aegeus of Athens and the princess of Troezene, Aethra. Before his birth, Theseus's father buried a sword and a pair of shoes beneath a great stone and told the princess that if a son was born and was eventually able to move the stone to retrieve the treasures, he would be recognized as Aegeus's heir. Their son Theseus grew up more beautiful, stronger, and wiser than most men; he was able to move the stone easily and claim his inheritance. En route to claim his birthright, using his sword, Theseus slew the giant Periphetes, a son of Hephaistos (Hephaestus; Roman god Vulcan), the god of bindings, the art of sculpture, fire, forges, metalworking, stonemasonry, and talismans. Once accepted as his father's heir, Theseus sought to free the city of Athens from its tribute of youths to be sacrificed to the Minotaur. Naturally, he succeeded; some tellings of the myth claim that he beat the monster to death with his bare hands, while others say he used the sword of his birthright.

Sources: Guerber, *The Myths of Greece and Rome*, n.p.; Hamilton, *Mythology*, n.p.

sword of Volund, the

In Norse mythology, the sword of Volund was one of his most powerful creations; it was said to have a constant stream of fire playing along its razor-keen edge. The blade was constructed so that it could never be blunted or broken, and anyone who used the weapon would be unbeatable in battle. Volund is also known as the legendary master blacksmith Wayland (Gofannon/ Weiland/Weyland) the Smith.

Sources: Day, *Tolkien's Ring*, n.p.; Edmison, *Stories from the Norseland*, 123–26

sword of Wrnach Cawr, the

In Welsh Arthurian folklore, the sword of the giant Wrnach Cawr was the only weapon that could bring about the death of Twrch Trwyth ("the boar Trwyth"), an enchanted boar. In the tale "How Culhwch Won Olwen" from *The Mabinogion*, the giant Ysbaddaden would only allow his daughter Olwen to marry the warrior Culhwch if he performed thirty-nine *anoethur* ("things hard to come by"); one of these tasks required gaining possession of the sword of Wrnach Cawr so Twrch Trwyth could be slain and his bristles and bones used to make combs and brushes for Ysbaddaden's personal grooming.

Sources: Bruce, *The Arthurian Name Dictionary*, 156, 477; Rhys, *Celtic Folklore: Welsh and Manx*, Volume 1, n.p.

sword with the strange hangings, the

In Arthurian lore, the sword with the strange hangings was an item sought by Sir Galahad, Sir Percival, and Sir Bors; it was discovered on the SHIP OF KING SOLOMON. In some versions of the tale, it was Percival's sister who led the knights to the sword, explaining to them the history of the weapon and how she had removed its former shabby hangings and replaced them with weavings of gold thread and her own hair. There were also two golden buckles. In this version, the sheath of the sword was called the MEMORY OF BLOOD.

According to one story, each of the two sides of the sword's hilt was decorated with a different creature. One side showed the image of a serpent that was only found in Calidoine (Scotland), while the other side had the image of an ortenax, a fish said to live only in the Euphrates River.

In a Dutch version of the tale, *Walewein*, the sword is described as having red strappings on the hilt, letters on the blade as red as blood, a sheath as red as rose petals, and the pommel containing a stone of all colors.

Sources: Bruce, *The Arthurian Name Dictionary*, 150, 286.; Loomis, *Celtic Myth and Arthurian Romance*, 246, 275; Sommer, *The Vulgate Version of the Arthurian Romances*, 162

Syamantaka

Variations: Syamantaka Mani

A magical jewel from Hindu mythology, Syamantaka was said to be able to protect its owner from harm if they were a good and virtuous person; however, if the owner was evil, it would bring evil to them. Syamantaka also had the ability to produce gold in its own weight eight times a day. The jewel was given to Prince Satrajit by the sun god for the prince's devotion. When worn, it created a bright radiance around the prince and, by association, his country of Dwarika; this effect eliminated all disease, distress, and poverty in his realm.

Sources: Meyer, *Sexual Life in Ancient India*, 400; Shama et al., *Tales from the Upanishads*, 35–36

table of the Fisher King, the

In Arthurian lore, the Fisher King (Crippled King/Maimed King/Wounded King/Anfortas/Bron/Evelake/Parlan/Peliam/Pellam/Pelles) is the last in a line of keepers of the HOLY GRAIL. His table, an example of the Fisher King's wealth, is described as a single board of ivory with trestles of ebony. When set, the cloth that covered the table was said to be whiter than any vestment of the pope.

Sources: Dom, *King Arthur and the Gods of the Round Table*, 127; Karr, *Arthurian Companion*, 160

Tablet of Destiny, the

Variations: Dup Shimati, Tablet of Destinies

In Mesopotamian mythology, the Tablet of Destiny was a clay tablet with inscriptions and seals that granted the god Enlil his supreme authority as the ruler of the universe; however, in the Sumerian poem *Ninurta and the Turtle*, it was the god of art, crafts, creation, exorcism, fertility, fresh water, healing, intelligence, magic, trickery and mischief, virility, and wisdom, Enki, who possessed the tablet. Ownership of the table was what conferred authority.

Sources: Black and Green, *Gods, Demons, and Symbols of Ancient Mesopotamia*, n.p.

tail feather of the zhar-ptitsa

A magical bird from Russian folklore, the zhar-ptitsa ("glow bird") is described as having feathers so beautiful as to make a person weep; they glow with a rich golden or silvery light, and the bird's eyes are like two brightly lit crystals. In nearly every story, it lives in a gold cage under the protection of a king or powerful ruler. The zhar-ptitsa has numerous magical abilities, which vary from story to story, but it is consistently said to bestow youth and beauty, carry the weight of a human safely upon its back as it flies, induce a deep sleep, and resuscitate the dead by use of the "dead" and "living" water it keeps stored in its beak. Additionally, its song can heal the gravely ill and restore sight to the blind as pearls fall from its beak.

Sources: Ralston, *Russian Folk-Tales*, 242, 289–92; Rosen, *Mythical Creatures Bible*, 152

Takarabune

Variation: *Takara-Bune*

A ship from Japanese lore, the *Takarabune* ("Ship of Good Fortune") is said to set sail on the second day of the New Year; it is hoped that it will carry a good and prosperous year into port. Early depictions of this vessel show it carrying bags of rice or rice plants—symbols of plenty. Over time, other images of plenty were added, such as the centipede, the lobster, and eventually the Seven Gods of Good Fortune. The sail of the ship features the character for the tapir, a creature said to consume bad dreams. It is common to put a small drawing of the *Takarabune* under one's pillow in the hope of having prophetic dreams of the coming year's fortune.

Sources: Allen, *Japanese Art Motives*, 152–53

Talos

Variations: Man of Brass, Talon, Talus

In ancient Greek mythology, AUTOMATONS ("self-acting") were statues of animals, humans, and monsters that were then animated or otherwise brought to a kind of life by one of the gods; usually this was done by Hephaistos (Hephaestus; Roman god Vulcan), the god of bindings, the art of sculpture, fire, forges, metalworking, stonemasonry, and talismans. Other AUTOMATONS were the CAUCASIAN EAGLE, the GOLDEN MAIDENS, the GOLDEN TRIPODS, the KABEIRIAN HORSES, the KELEDONES, KHRYSEOS AND ARGYREOS, and the KOLKHIS BULLS.

Talos was an AUTOMATON sculpted from bronze by Hephaistos and given as a wedding gift by Zeus (Roman god Jupiter), the god of fate, kings, lightning, sky, and thunder, to Europa, the queen of Crete; other versions of the myth said he was given to King Minos of Crete and was in the shape of a bull. In either case, Talos was designed to patrol the island and protect it from pirates. Usually this task was accomplished by hurling large boulders at their vessels. Should any unwanted person make their way to shore, Talos would super heat his body; then he would grab the person and hold them against his body, burning them alive.

Talos was designed with a large, singular vein beginning at his neck and extending down to his ankle. There are different versions of how his death was brought about. In some tales, Medea drove Talos insane with her magical drugs, while other versions claim she promised to make him immortal and then pulled out the plug that kept the vein in place, causing his ichor to drain out until he died. A few versions claim that Poeas shot him in the ankle, which caused him to bleed out.

Sources: Bonnefoy, *Greek and Egyptian Mythologies*, 88–89; Westmoreland, *Ancient Greek Beliefs*, 54

Taming Sari (TAH-ming SAH-ree)

In Malay literature, Taming Sari ("Beautiful Shield" or "Flower Shield") was allegedly the very first keris (or kris—a type of dagger) ever created; it was said to have been the weapon of the legendary hero Hang Tuah and was forged out of twenty-one different metals by a Javanese smith. The weapon was so expertly crafted that anyone wielding it was unbeatable.

Sources: Azman, *The Legend of Hang Tuah*, 122–24; Yousof, *One Hundred and One Things Malay*, n.p.

Tamsvondr

Variations: Gambanteinn, Laevateinn

In Norse mythology, Tamsvondr ("Taming Wand") was the magical sword of Freyr (Frey/Yngvi), the god of fertility, peace, rain, and sunshine; it had the ability to fight on its wielder's behalf. Originally the weapon's name was GAMBANTEINN, but it was changed to Tamsvondr after Skirnir carved runes onto the weapon and threatened Gerdr with it until she agreed to marry Freyr. In one version of the myth, her acceptance made Freyr so happy that he gave the sword to Skirnir; unfortunately, this action caused Freyr to be weaponless at the Battle of Ragnarok, leading to his defeat.

Sources: Grimes, *The Norse Myths*, 268, 300; Norroena Society, *Asatru Edda*, 348

Tarnhelm, the

In Richard Wagner's *Der Ring des Nibelungen*, the Tarnhelm is a magical helmet forged by Mime at the behest of his brother, Alberich, from the gold of the Rhinemaidens. In addition to allowing its wearer to become invisible, it grants the ability to change one's form and instantaneously travel great distances.

In the original Norse mythology, Tarnhelm does not exist.

Sources: Doniger, *The Ring of Truth*, 120–23; Fisher, *Wagner's The Ring of the Nibelung*, 44, 45

Tarnkappe

Variations: Hel-kaplein, TARNHELM, Tarn-kappe, Tarnkapppe

Tarnkappe is a type of magical red cap or helm from Norse mythology worn by some of the dwarfs because it would grant them invisibility; this quality was important because the magic of the tarnkappe ("mantle of invisibility") prevented the rays of the sun from finding the dwarfs and turning them into stone.

In Wagnerian lore, Tarnkappe (also called the CLOAK OF DARKNESS and the CLOAK OF INVISIBILITY) was the magical cloak originally belonging to the dwarf Alberich (Alferich/Alpirs/Elbegast) but was won by the human hero Sigurd (Siegfried/Sigmund); the cloak granted its wearer the power of invisibility.

Sources: Grimes, *The Norse Myths*, 301; Keightley, *World Guide to Gnomes, Fairies, Elves, and Other Little People*, 96, 207

Tathlum

In Celtic mythology, Tathlum was the slingstone utilized by the god of the sun, Lugh ("Bright" or "Light") of the Long Arms (Artful Hands or Long Hands). Tathlum was created by fusing and then polishing together purified sands from the Amorian Sea and the Red Sea into a concrete ball. A different version of the myth said the stone was created from the blood of bears, lions, "Osmurnn's trunk," toads, and vipers and was fiery, firm, and heavy. Lugh used this weapon to win his battle against Balor the Strong-Smiter. Tathlum was thrown into Balor's eye, blinding him.

Sources: Beaumont, *The Riddle of Prehistoric Britain*, 194; Squire, *Celtic Myth and Legend*, n.p.

tawiya

In Hopi oral traditions, the tawiya ("gourd") is a flying machine akin to the PAATUWVOTA; it is a means of transportation used by shamans. The passenger climbs into the lower portion of the vessel and closes the upper portion over his head. When the tawiya is closed, the sinew stretched between the roof and the seat is twisted between the shaman's hands, which causes the vessel to lift off and fly; as it travels, it makes a humming noise.

Sources: Malotki and Gary, *Hopi Stories of Witchcraft, Shamanism, and Magic*, xl

teen baan of Shiva

Variation: Shiva's teen baan (three infallible arrows)

In Hindu mythology, Barbarika (Babhruvahana/Baladhara Kunvara/Belarsen) was a skilled warrior and expert archer as well as a devoted follower of Shiva; as such, he was given the ASTRA teen baan—three infallible arrows. Each arrow had a different ability: The first arrow had a red mark upon its tail and would tag the enemy with a red dot before returning to Barbarika's quiver. The second arrow would kill all those marked by the first arrow and then return to the quiver. Conversely, the third arrow would mark all those Barbarika wished to protect.

Sources: Murty, *The Serpent's Revenge*, n.p.; Parmeshwaranand, *Encyclopaedic Dictionary of Puranas*, 155

Thirteen Treasures of the Island of Britain

In British and Welsh folklore, there is a series of items (always thirteen in number) called the Thirteen Treasures of the Island of Britain (in Welsh, they are called *Tri Thlws ar Ddeg Ynys Prydain*). Although in more modern times the items listed are different, the original thirteen items from the fifteenth century were the CAULDRON OF DYRNWCH THE GIANT, CHARIOT OF MORGAN MWYNFAWR, CHESSBOARD OF GWENDDOLEU AP CEIDIO, COAT OF PADARN BEISRUDD, CROCK AND DISH OF RHYGENYDD YSGOLHAIG (two items), HALTER OF CLYDNO EIDDYN, HAMPER OF GWYDDNO GARANHIR, HORN OF BRAN GALED, KNIFE OF LLAWFRODEDD FARCHOF, MANTLE OF ARTHUR IN CORNWALL, sword of Rhydderch Hael (DYRNWYN), and WHETSTONE OF TUDWAL TUDGLYD.

Sources: Dom, *King Arthur and the Gods of the Round Table*, 95, 106, 111, 255; Patton, *The Poet's Ogam*, 510; Pendergrass, *Mythological Swords*, 24, 26; Stirling, *King Arthur Conspiracy*, n.p; Taylor, *The Fairy Ring*, 389

throne of Aphrodite, the

Variation: Aphrodite's throne

In Greek mythology, Aphrodite (Roman goddess Venus), the goddess of love, had a throne in the council hall on Mount Olympus; it sat opposite the THRONE OF ARES and next to Athena (Roman goddess Minerva) on the left side of the hall (all the thrones of the goddesses were on the left). Created by Hephaistos (Hephaestus; Roman god Vulcan), the god of bindings, the art of sculpture, fire, forges, metalworking, stonemasonry, and talismans, the throne of Aphrodite was made of silver; to set it apart from the THRONE OF ATHENA, it had aquamarines and beryls set into it. The back of the throne was shaped like a scallop shell, and the cushion was made from swan's down. There was also a mat before the throne; it was woven with the images of apples, bees, and sparrows.

Sources: Graves, *Greek Gods and Heroes*, n.p.

throne of Apollo, the

Variation: Apollo's throne

In Greek mythology, Apollo ("to destroy" or "to drive away"), the god of archery, art, healing, hunting, knowledge, medicine, music, oracles, plague, prophecy, sun and light, truth, and young unmarried men, had a throne in the council hall on Mount Olympus; it sat next to that of Ares (Roman god Mars) on the right side of the hall (all the thrones of the male gods were on the right). Created by Hephaistos (Hephaestus; Roman god Vulcan), the god of bindings, the art of sculpture, fire, forges, metalworking, stonemasonry, and talismans, the throne of Apollo was made of well-polished gold. Upon its surface were magical inscriptions; its cushion was made of python skin. Suspended over the throne was a twenty-one-rayed sun disc, with each of the rays fashioned to resemble an arrow.

Sources: Graves, *Greek Gods and Heroes*, n.p.

throne of Ares, the

Variation: Ares's throne

In Greek mythology, Ares (Roman god Mars), the god of war, had a throne in the council hall on Mount Olympus; it sat opposite the THRONE OF APHRODITE (Roman goddess Venus) and next to Apollo on the right side of the hall (all the thrones of the male gods were on the right). Created by Hephaistos (Hephaestus; Roman god Vulcan), the god of bindings, the art of sculpture, fire, forges, metalworking, stonemasonry, and talismans, the throne of Ares was made of brass—strong but unattractive. The knobs upon it were made to look like human skulls; the cushion was made of human skin.

Sources: Graves, *Greek Gods and Heroes*, n.p.

throne of Artemis, the

Variation: Artemis's throne

In Greek mythology, Artemis (Roman goddess Diana), the goddess of children, hunting, virginity, unmarried girls, and wild animals, had a throne in the council hall on Mount Olympus; it sat opposite the THRONE OF APOLLO ("to destroy" or "to drive away") on the left side of the hall (all the thrones of the goddesses were on the left). Created by Hephaistos (Hephaestus; Roman god Vulcan), the god of bindings, the art of sculpture, fire, forges, metalworking, stonemasonry, and talismans, the throne of Artemis was made of silver; the back was shaped like the moon, and it

throne of Athena

was adorned with a date palm fronds on either side. The cushion she sat upon was made from a wolf pelt.

Sources: Graves, *Greek Gods and Heroes*, n.p.

throne of Athena, the

Variation: Athena's throne

In Greek mythology, Athena (Roman goddess Minerva), the goddess of crafts, military victories, war, and wisdom, had a throne in the council hall on Mount Olympus; it sat opposite the THRONE OF HEPHAISTOS (Hephaestus; Roman god Vulcan), the god of bindings, the art of sculpture, fire, forges, metalworking, stonemasonry, and talismans, on the left side of the hall (all the thrones of the goddesses were on the left). Created by Hephaistos, the throne of Athena was made of silver; the back and sides were decorated with golden baskets. The arms of the throne ended in the image of a smiling severed head of a Gorgon. Upon the top of the throne was a crown made of blue lapis lazuli. There was also an owl on the throne.

Sources: Graves, *Greek Gods and Heroes*, n.p.

throne of Demeter, the

Variation: Demeter's throne

In Greek mythology, Demeter (Roman goddess Ceres), the goddess of all useful fruits, grasses, and grains, had a throne in the council hall on Mount Olympus; it sat opposite the THRONE OF POSEIDON (Roman god Neptune) on the right side of the hall (all the thrones of the goddesses were on the left). Created by Hephaistos (Hephaestus; Roman god Vulcan), the god of bindings, the art of sculpture, fire, forges, metalworking, stonemasonry, and talismans, the throne of Demeter was made of bright green malachite and decorated with golden sculptures of barley and pigs (considered lucky) and blood-red gems, symbolic of poppy seeds.

Sources: Graves, *Greek Gods and Heroes*, n.p.

throne of Dionysus, the

Variation: Dionysus's throne

In Greek mythology, Dionysus (Roman god Bacchus), the god of fertility, the grape harvest, religious ecstasy, ritual madness, theater, winemaking, and wine, as well as a son of Zeus (Roman god Jupiter), the god of fate, kings, lightning, sky, and thunder, born of the mortal woman Semele, was given a throne in the council hall on Mount Olympus as a reward for having invented wine.

His throne was on the right side of the hall, with those of the other male gods. Created by Hephaistos (Hephaestus; Roman god Vulcan), the god of bindings, the art of sculpture, fire, forges, metalworking, stonemasonry, and talismans, the throne of Dionysus was made of gold-plated fir wood and decorated with amethysts carved to look like grapes along with snakes carved in serpentine and many horned animals carved from carnelian, jade, onyx, and sard.

Sources: Graves, *Greek Gods and Heroes*, n.p.

throne of Hephaistos, the

Variation: Hephaistos's throne

In Greek mythology, Hephaistos (Hephaestus; Roman god Vulcan), the god of bindings, the art of sculpture, fire, forges, metalworking, stonemasonry, and talismans, had a throne in the council hall on Mount Olympus; it sat next to the THRONE OF POSEIDON (Roman god Neptune) on the right side of the hall (all the thrones of the males gods were on the right). Created by his own hand, the throne of Hephaistos was made of every known kind of precious stone and rare metal; the seat of the throne could swivel, and it had the ability to move on its own by Hephaistos's will.

Sources: Graves, *Greek Gods and Heroes*, n.p.

throne of Hera, the

Variation: Hera's throne

In Greek mythology, Hera (Roman goddess Juno), the goddess of childbirth, family, marriage, and women, as well as the wife of Zeus (Roman god Jupiter), the god of fate, kings, lightning, sky, and thunder, had a throne at the far end of the council hall on Mount Olympus, opposite the doors, next to her husband's throne. Immediately upon walking into the chamber, the THRONE OF ZEUS was visible on the right and Hera's to the left. All the thrones of the female Olympians were on the left, facing right; these were the thrones of Demeter, Athena, Aphrodite, Artemis, and Hestia (Roman goddesses Ceres, Minerva, Venus, Diana, and Vesta, respectively).

The throne of Hera was made of ivory and had three steps made of crystal leading up to it. The back of the throne was decorated with carvings of cuckoos and willow leaves. Suspended overhead was a moon. The cushion upon which the goddess sat was made of cow hide; it could be shaken to cause rain to fall.

Sources: Graves, *Greek Gods and Heroes*, n.p.

throne of Hermes, the

Variation: Hermes's throne

In Greek mythology, Hermes (Roman god Mercury), the god of animal husbandry, commerce, eloquence, fertility, language, looters, luck, sleep, thieves, trade, travel, and wealth, had a throne in the council hall on Mount Olympus; it sat opposite the THRONE OF HESTIA (Roman goddess Vesta) on the right side of the hall (all the thrones of the male gods were on the right). Created by Hephaistos (Hephaestus; Roman god Vulcan), the god of bindings, the art of sculpture, fire, forges, metalworking, stonemasonry, and talismans, the throne of Hermes was made of stone; the arms were crafted to resemble rams' heads. On the back of the throne was a carving for the symbol of the fire dill—an invention of his. The cushion of the throne was made of goat skin.

Sources: Graves, *Greek Gods and Heroes*, n.p.

throne of Hestia, the

Variation: Hestia's throne

In Greek mythology, Hestia (Roman goddess Vesta), the goddess of architecture, family, hearth, home, the ordering of domesticity, and the state, had a throne in the council hall on Mount Olympus; it sat opposite the THRONE OF HERMES (Roman god Mercury) on the left side of the hall (all the thrones of the female gods were on the left). Created by Hephaistos (Hephaestus; Roman god Vulcan), the god of bindings, the art of sculpture, fire, forges, metalworking, stonemasonry, and talismans, the throne of Hestia was plain and made of wood; its cushion was crafted from undyed wool. Eventually, Hestia relinquished her throne for a simple tripod stool so she could sit next to the fire. This action allowed Zeus's son by a mortal woman, Dionysus (Roman god Bacchus), the god of fertility, the grape harvest, religious ecstasy, ritual madness, theater, winemaking, and wine, to take a throne as a reward for inventing wine.

Sources: Graves, *Greek Gods and Heroes*, n.p.

throne of Poseidon, the

Variation: Poseidon's throne

In Greek mythology, Poseidon (Roman god Neptune), the god of earthquakes, horses, and the seas, had the second largest of all the thrones in the council hall on Mount Olympus; it sat closest to the THRONE OF ZEUS (Roman god Jupiter), the god of fate, kings, lightning, sky, and thunder, on the right side of the hall (all the thrones of the males gods were on the right). Created by Hephaistos (Hephaestus; Roman god Vulcan), the god of bindings, the art of sculpture, fire, forges, metalworking, stonemasonry, and talismans, the throne of Poseidon was made of gray-green and white streaked marble adorned with coral, gold, and pearls. The arms of the throne were crafted to look like sea creatures, and the cushion was made of seal skin.

Sources: Graves, *Greek Gods and Heroes*, n.p.

throne of Zeus, the

Variation: Zeus's throne

In Greek mythology, Zeus (Roman god Jupiter), the god of fate, kings, lightning, sky, and thunder, as well as the king of the gods, and his wife Hera (Roman goddess Juno), the goddess of childbirth, family, marriage, and women, each had a throne at the far end of the council hall on Mount Olympus, opposite the doors. Immediately upon walking into the chamber, the throne of Zeus was visible on the right and Hera's on the left. To the right of the throne of Zeus were the thrones of Poseidon, Hephaistos, Ares, Apollo, Hermes, and (eventually) Dionysus. The hall was intended as place for the gods to meet to discuss mortal affairs, such as which army should win a war or whether a particularly petty king or vain queen should be punished. Typically, however, the gods were too involved with their own quarreling to intervene in mortal affairs as often as they would have liked.

Created by Hephaistos (Hephaestus; Roman god Vulcan), the god of bindings, the art of sculpture, fire, forges, metalworking, stonemasonry, and talismans, the throne of Zeus was made of the blackest marble inlaid with small bits of gold for decoration. The throne was enormous, and one had to ascend seven steps to reach it; each step was one of the colors of the rainbow. Over the throne was a large blue covering, symbolic of the sky. The right arm of the throne was carved to resemble an eagle; its eyes were inset with red rubies and its talons clutched jagged strips of tin, symbolizing Zeus's powerful lightning bolts. A purple ram's fleece was the throne's cushion; when the fleece was shaken, rain would fall upon the world.

Sources: Graves, *Greek Gods and Heroes*, n.p.

Thrudheimr

Variations: Thrandheim, Thrudheim, Thrudheimer, Thrudnamar, Thrudvang, Thrudvanga, Thrudvangar, Thrudvanger, Trudvang

Thrymgjoll

In Norse mythology, Thrudheimr ("Land of Might"/"Paddocks of Power") was the estate in Asgard ("Enclosure of the Aesir") that belonged to the god of thunder, Thor; the hall within the estate was known as BILSKIRNIR.

Sources: Grimes, *The Norse Myths*, 302–3.

Thrymgjoll (THREM-gyuhl)

Variations: Thrymgioll, VALGRIND

In Norse mythology, Thrymgjoll ("The Loud-Grating"/"Mighty Crash") was the gate to Asgard ("Enclosure of the Aesir") created by the three sons of the dwarf Solblindi. The gate is constructed in such a way that any unwanted guests will become entangled in its fetters and chains.

Sources: Edmison, *Stories from the Norseland*, 229–30; Norroena Society, *Asatru Edda*, 391

Thuan Thien

In Vietnamese lore, Thuan Thien ("Heaven's Will") was the legendary sword wielded by King Le Loi as he led a revolt against the Ming Dynasty. According to the lore, the sword belonged to a local god by the name of Long Vurong ("Dragon King"), who loaned it Le Loi but declared that it would not go directly to him; rather, Le Loi would need to locate the blade and the hilt separately. The blade was found by a fisherman, who gave it to Le Loi. Years later, while fleeing the enemy, Le Loi saw a glittering light up in a tree. Climbing it, he discovered a gem-encrusted sword hilt that fit the blade the fisherman had given him perfectly.

Thuan Thien not only had the ability to make Le Loi grow very tall but also gave him the strength of one thousand men. With it, he won battle after battle and was eventually able to free his land. Years later, a giant golden-shelled turtle approached Le Loi as he was sailing on Green Water Lake. The turtle told the king that it was time to return the sword to Long Vurong or become corrupted by the weapon. Le Loi gave the turtle the blade, and it swam away carrying Thuan Thien back to its owner. The lake was thereafter called Lake of the Returned Sword.

Sources: Pendergrass, *Mythological Swords*, 69–70; Vo, *Legends of Vietnam*, 120–21

Thviti (THVIT-i)

Variation: Thvite

In Norse mythology, Thviti ("Cut to the Ground"/"Thwacker") was the black boulder used to anchor the fetters holding Fenriswulf (Fenerriswulf/Fenrissulfrin).

Sources: Coulter and Turner, *Encyclopedia of Ancient Deities*, 465; Grimes, *The Norse Myths*, 303; Norroena Society, *Asatru Edda*, 393

Tidal Jewels

A set of jewels from Japanese mythology, the Tidal Jewels regulate the tides of the world; they are in the possession of the Dragon King, Ryo-Wo, who lives in his palace beneath the sea, RYUGU. With these jewels, he is able to control the tides. There are two jewels; one is called kanju ("tide-ebbing jewel"), and the other is manju ("tide-flowing jewel"). Each is said to be about the size of an apple and shines with a fiery light.

Sources: Aldersey-Williams, *The Tide*, n.p.; Dekirk, *Dragonlore*, 31

Tikarau

In Polynesian lore, Tikarau was the magical sword of Tiniraru.

Sources: Craig, *Dictionary of Polynesian Mythology*, 280

Tirfing (TEER-ving-r)

Variations: Tervingi, Tyrfing

The sword of Suaforlami—a hero who claimed to be a direct descendent of Odin, the god of battle, death, frenzy, the gallows, healing, knowledge, poetry, royalty, the runic alphabet, sorcery, and wisdom—Tirfing ("Tyr's Finger") was described as having a belt and a hilt of gold; it was said the sword would never miss anything it was swung at, ensuring victory in single combat. Tirfing would also never rust and could cut through iron and stone with ease. Most notably, it was cursed.

When Suaforlami slew Dwalin the dwarf, Dwalin cursed Tirfing, declaring that "this sword shall be the bane of man every time it is drawn, and with it shall be done three of the greatest atrocities. It shall also be thy bane." When Andgrim slew Suaforlami, he claimed Tirfing as his own; when he died, Andgrim had the sword entombed with him. When the twelve sons of Andgrim went to fight for Ingaborg, the daughter of King Inges, all were slain. However, Angantyr, one of the twelve slain brothers, had a daughter named Hervor who dressed like a man and took the name Hervardar. Knowing where Tirfing was buried, she recovered it. While visiting King Gudmund, a servant picked up Tirfing to admire it. A berserker rage then came over Hervor, and, taking up Tirfing, she beheaded the servant. Hervor eventually resumed her female role and married King Gudmund's son, Haufud. Two sons were born of their union: mild-mannered Angantyr and the violent Heidreker. When Heidreker was banished from his father's court, his mother gave him Tirfing. As he was leaving, the wicked brother slew his gentle-natured sibling in a sudden surge of rage. After distinguishing himself, Heidreker married Helga, the daughter of King Harold, but, again, the curse of Tirfing surfaced, and he killed his father-in-law, taking his throne. While boar hunting with his foster son, the prince of Russia, Heidreker thought he was slaying an animal, but his victim was in fact the unfortunate prince. Eventually, Scottish slaves killed Heidreker and ran off with the cursed weapon, but his son, Angantyr, found them as well as the sword and used Tirfing to kill them all. Angantyr also used Tirfing when he fought against the Huns; in the aftermath, it was revealed that among all the men he had slain was his own brother, Lundar.

Sources: Keightley, *World Guide to Gnomes, Fairies, Elves, and Other Little People*, 72–74; Norroena Society, *Asatru Edda*, 393; Tibbits, *Folk-lore and Legends: Scandinavian*, 189–92

Tizona

Variation: Tizon

In Spanish legend, Tizona was one of the magical swords own by Rodrigo Diaz de Vivar (circa 1043–1099), better known as El Cid Campeador ("the Champion"). According to the medieval poem *Cantar del mio Cid*, Tizona had a personality of its own; the strength and perception of the person wielding it varied as well. The sword was won in battle against the emir of Morocco and was said to be worth a thousand gold talents. El Cid made a gift of Tizona to his nephew, Pedro. The other sword of El Cid was COLADA.

Sources: Brewer, *Dictionary of Phrase and Fable* 1900, 1197; Frankel, *From Girl to Goddess*, 49; Harney, *The Epic of the Cid*, 89, 202; Pendergrass, *Mythological Swords*, 4

toadstone

Variations: bufonite, crepaidina, stelon

Medieval lore claimed that the toadstone—a gem or stone found in the head of a large toad—was an antidote to poison such as the kind from rats, spiders, and wasps; it was also used in the treatment of epilepsy. When poison was near, the toadstone was said to change color and sweat. According to the lore, the stone needed to be removed while the toad was alive. Toadstone was also allegedly a charm to ward off the ill attention and effects of fairies.

Sources: Daniels and Stevens, *Encyclopedia of Superstitions, Folklore, and the Occult Sciences*, Volume 2, 761; Simpson and Roud, *A Dictionary of English Folklore*, n.p.

toe of Aurvandil

Variations: Aurvandil's toe, toe of Orfandel, toe of Orvandill

In Norse mythology, Thor, the god of thunder, rescued the giant Aurvandil from Jotunheimr by carrying him in a basket across the river Elivagar. During the journey, one of Aurvandil's toes poked out of the basket and entered the freezing waters of the river. Thor snapped off the frostbitten toe and threw it into the heavens, creating the star known as Aurvandil's Toe.

Sources: Grimes, *The Norse Myths*, 256; Lindow, *Norse Mythology*, 65

Toflur

In Norse mythology, Toflur was a game that resembled draughts ("checkers"); the loss of the game marked the end of the Golden Age, but its rediscovery by Modi, son of Thor, was the first incident of the Rebirth of Discovery.

Sources: Grimes, *The Norse Myths*, 303

Tonbogiri

In Japanese folklore, the great swordsmith Masamune (circa late thirteenth century) was said to have created the greatest swords ever forged. Although Masamune was a real person, the legendary sword Tonbogiri ("Dragonfly Cutter") was likely not, as it was allegedly wielded by the legendary daimyo Honda Tadakatsu. According to the lore, when a dragonfly landed upon the blade, it was instantly sliced in two, attesting to the keen edge of the weapon and giving the sword its name. Tonbogiri is counted as one of the *tenka-sanso* ("Three Greatest Spears Under the Heaven") along with NIHONGO and OTEGINE.

Sources: Nagayama, *The Connoisseur's Book of Japanese Swords*, 31; Sesko, *Encyclopedia of Japanese Swords*, 460

tongs of Saint Dunstan, the

According to Christian lore, Saint Dunstan lived in a small earthen cell that contained a forge; there he was frequently harassed by the Devil in the guise of a bear, dog, fox, or serpent. One day, the Devil came to him as a woman and began a "wanton conversation to carnality." Saint Dunstan let the torment continue until the tongs he had placed in his forge were glowing hot; then he grabbed the Devil by the nose and held him fast until his cries of pain resounded throughout the region.

Sources: Robinson, *The Life of Saint Dunstan*, 10

Totsuka-no-Tsurugi

Belonging to the Shinto god of sea and storms, Susanoo (Susanowo/Susa-no-wo no Mikoto), Totsuka-no-Tsurugi ("Sword of Length Ten Times Its Handle") was the weapon used by Izanagi no Mikoto, father of the gods, to kill his own offspring, Kagu-tsuchi no Kami. Although there is no mention of who forged the sword, Susanoo found it when he was chopping a serpent to pieces near the River Hi. As he sliced through the tail section, the sword he was using broke. Examining the area, Susanoo discovered the great and sharp blade Totsuka-no-Tsurugi.

Sources: Aston, *Nihongi*, 57; Kammer, *Zen and Confucius in the Art of Swordsmanship*, n.p.

Touiafutuna

Variations: Touia-futuna, Touia-o-Futuna

According to the creation myth of the Polynesian people of Tonga, Touiafutuna was the primordial iron rock that separated the earth and seaweed floating on the surface of Vohanoa, the endless open sea. At some point, Touiafutuna began to tremble and shake violently, ultimately splitting open and revealing four sets of twins: Arungaki and his sister Maimoa'o Longona; Biki and his sister Kele; Fonua'uta and his sister Fonuaua; and Hemoana and his sister Lupe.

Sources: Reuter, *Sharing the Earth, Dividing the Land*, 348

treasure fan of pure yin

Variations: fan of yin, palm leaf fan, plantain-leaf fan, treasure fan

In the tale of Xuanzang, the monk who traveled from China to India to obtain Buddhist scriptures, the magical treasure fan of pure yin had a number of abilities; it was described as a spiritual treasure, twelve feet long, and made from the finest leaf of pure yin. When waved at the Mountain of Flames, it quenched the raging fires; the second wave of the fan produced a cool breeze; the third wave made it rain. When the flames were extinguished, the people of the region were able to harvest the five grains, but to ensure that the fires never started again, the treasure fan of pure yin had to be waved at the now extinguished Mountain of Flames forty-nine times. Should a man be fanned by the treasure fan of pure yin, he would

be blown for eighty-four thousand miles before the wind ceased. Normally the fan was of average size and easily carried; to make it expand to its full twelve feet in height, the seventh red string on the handle needed to be held while reciting the prayer "*hui-hsu-ho-his-his-ch'ui-hu*"; the fan would then become engulfed in a radiant light and charge the air. The handle was decorated with thirty-six plaited red strings.

Sources: Wu, *Journey to the West*, 136, 137, 145, 165, 185

Tree of Knowledge, the

Variations: Tree of Knowledge of Good and Evil, Tree of Wisdom

In Genesis, the first book of the Bible, there is mention of two trees that are often confused with one another: the Tree of Knowledge and the Tree of Life. The Tree of Knowledge was said to grow in the Garden of Eden, and its fruit was the only thing that the first humans, Adam and Eve, were forbidden to consume. This command was given to them directly by God himself. Consuming the fruit of this tree would open a person's eyes to the concept of good and evil, and they would "surely die" as a result. Although there was another tree "in the midst of the garden" (the Tree of Life), only the Tree of Knowledge was forbidden.

Sources: Mattfeld, *The Garden of Eden Myth*, 31, 32; Mettinger, *The Eden Narrative*, 3, 6, 7, 10

Tree of Life, the

Variation: Tree of Immortality

In Genesis, the first book of the Bible, there is mention of two trees that are often confused with one another: the Tree of Knowledge and the Tree of Life. The story of Adam and Eve consuming the forbidden fruit of the Tree of Knowledge is well known; the Tree of Life is mentioned only twice in this tale, once in the beginning of the story and again at the end. The location of the Tree of Life is given as "in the midst of the garden" (the same location as the other tree). After Adam and Eve ate from the Tree of Knowledge, the way to the Tree of Life was barred to them, as they were cast out of the garden.

Sources: Mattfeld, *The Garden of Eden Myth*, 31, 32; Mettinger, *The Eden Narrative*, 3, 6, 7, 10

Tree of Thorns, the

Variations: Calmali, Hantakadruma, Kantakadruma, Salmali, Tree of Hell, Tree of Punishment, Tree of Yama

In Hindu mythology, the Tree of Thorns is

described as very large and wide and covered in thorns; it is designed to snag and entrap the souls that pass near it. Yama, the god of death, is said to reside near this tree in the infernal regions.

Sources: Folkard, *Plant Lore, Legends, and Lyrics*, 189; Porteous, *The Forest in Folklore and Mythology*, 201

trident of Madhu, the

In Hindu mythology, an ASTRA is a supernatural weapon created or gifted by the gods to someone who then presides over the weapon. The wielder of an ASTRA is known as an astradhari.

Madhu Rakshasa, an extremely righteous daitya, was given a boon by the god Shiva—a trident that would reduce to ash anyone who opposed him as long as he did not oppose the gods or the sages.

Sources: Dalal, *Hinduism*, 227; Venkatesananda, *The Concise Ramayana of Valmiki*, 384

trident of Poseidon, the

In classical Greek mythology, Poseidon (Roman god Neptune), the god of earthquakes, horses, and the seas, is said to carry a trident; with it, he is able to literally stir up the ocean and create violent storms. There is some (albeit scant) literary evidence that this weapon was three pronged. However, there is no evidence to suggest that the trident was anything other than a visual representation of who Poseidon was—a means of differentiating him from the sea god Triton and Zeus (Roman god Jupiter), the god of fate, kings, lightning, sky, and thunder.

Sources: Roman and Roman, *Encyclopedia of Greek and Roman Mythology*, 418; Walters, "The Trident of Poseidon," 14

Tripura Vimana

There are five different types of vimana: PUSH-PAKA VIMANA, RUKMA VIMANA, SHAKUNA VIMANA, SUNDARA VIMANA, and Tripura Vimana.

In the fifth book of *Mahabharata*, entitled "Vimanapala" ("Guardian of the Aircraft"), a highly specialized individual is given the responsibility of caring for the vimana. Tripura Vimana, made of a flexible blend of three metals, was a hybrid vehicle usable in air, on land, in outer space, and under water.

Sources: Baccarini and Vaddadi, *Reverse Engineering Vedic Vimanas*, n.p.; Childress, *Vimana*, n.p.

trishul

Variations: Shiva's trident, trident of Shiva, trishula

In Hindu mythology, the three-pronged trident of Shiva is not only a weapon he wields to destroy ignorance but also a symbol of his three powers of action (*kriva*), knowledge (*jnana*), and will (*icca*), as well as transcendence over the three qualities of nature (*gunas*), which are dynamic (*rajas*), inert (*tamas*), and pure (*sattva*). Each prong is also symbolic of the three rivers Shiva is lord over: the Ganges, the Sarasvati, and the Yamuna. Unlike PINAKA (the named personal bow of Shiva), the trident is not named.

In early Hinduism, the serpent trident was the symbol of Shiva; it was depicted as having a green shaft with a single white serpent coiled around it, blood dripping out of its mouth.

Sources: Bansal, *Hindu Gods and Goddesses*, 62, 78; Beer, *The Handbook of Tibetan Buddhist Symbols*, 130, 134; Kaur, *The Regime of Maharaja Ranjit Singh*, 15

Trojan Horse, the

Athena (Roman goddess Minerva), the goddess of crafts, military victories, war, and wisdom, suggested to Prylis that entry into the walled city of Troy would be gained by means of a wooden horse. Epeius, under the direction of Athena, built the large wooden structure. Although Odysseus falsely took credit for the idea of its construction, he did manage to convince a small band of warriors to join him inside the horse, which was to be wheeled into the city. Numbers vary as to the size of the group (23, 39, 50, and even 3,000), but among them are named Acamas, Diomedes, Epeius, Menelaus, Neoptolemus, Polydamas, Sthenelus, and Thoas. Once the men were within, the horse was left on the beach to be found; the message inscribed on it read, "In thankful anticipation of a safe return to their homes, the Greeks dedicate this offering to the goddess." With the trap in place, the Greek army withdrew, burning their camps and setting sail. The citizens of Troy then opened the gates and accepted the colossal wooden horse made of fir planks, as the horse was sacred to their city and their patron god, Poseidon (Roman god Neptune), the god of earthquakes, horses, and the seas. That evening, the war band left the horse and opened the city gates, and the army, which had only pretended to leave, came into the city, massacring nearly everyone.

Sources: Dixon-Kennedy, *Encyclopedia of Greco-Roman Mythology*, 122; Graves, *The Greek Myths*, 259-260; Westmoreland, *Ancient Greek Beliefs*, 573

tsukumogami

From the Kamakura period (1185–1333) of Japanese folklore come tales of tsukumogami; these items are described as common household goods that have arms and legs and are alive. According to the lore, when an object reaches 100 years old, it develops a spirit (*seirei*) and has a life and mind of its own; it will be either benevolent or malicious depending on how it is treated. If the tsukumogami is not destroyed, the transformation will continue, and it will eventually become an otherworldly being known as an oni.

Sources: Foster, *The Book of Yokai*, 239–42; Foster, *Pandemonium and Parade*, 7–8

tusk razor of Ysgithyrwyn, the

In Welsh Arthurian lore, the giant Ysbaddaden would only allow his daughter Olwen to marry the warrior Culhwch if he performed thirty-nine *anoethur* ("things hard to come by"); the adventures of this quest are told in the story "How Culhwch Won Olwen" from *The Mabinogion*. One of these tasks required the construction of a razor made from the tusk of Ysgithyrwyn ("White Tusk"), the great boar, with the condition that the tusk would be pulled by Odgar, son of Aedd, while the creature was alive. Then the tusk was to be delivered to King Caw, who would shave the head of the giant with it. After the tusk was successfully pulled, the boar was killed by Cabal, the dog of King Arthur.

Sources: Bruce, *The Arthurian Name Dictionary*, 321, 501; Reno, *Arthurian Figures of History and Legend*, 63, 172

Twashtar

In Hindu mythology, an ASTRA is a supernatural weapon created or gifted by the gods to someone who then presides over the weapon. The wielder of an ASTRA is known as an astradhari.

Twashtar was an ASTRA from the god Twashtri, the Celestial Builder. When used against an enemy army, Twashtar allegedly had the ability to take on the form and appearance of their own loved ones; in doing so, it would cause infighting among the enemy soldiers.

Sources: Edizioni, *Vimanas and the Wars of the Gods*, n.p.

Uaithne (WEN-ya)

Variations: Asaithne, Coir Cetarchair ("Just Square"/"Fitting Rectangle"), Cor-cethair-chuir, Dagda's Harp, Daur Da Blao ("Oak of the Two Meadows"), Daurdabla, Four-Angled Music, Uaine

The magical harp of the Dagda, the Celtic god of abundance, artistry, banquets, death, excess, inspiration, life, music, the sky, and war, Uaithne ("Childbirth") was typically associated with the three songs it played. Only the Dagda himself was skillful enough to play the harp and bring forth its magical tunes. Each song is named after a stage of childbirth, as is each of the god's sons: Gentraiges ("Joy"), Goltraiges ("Sorrow"), and Suantraiges ("Sleep"). The harp, which the god carried with him everywhere he went—even into battle—was described as made of oak and covered in precious gems. It was also said to have the ability to cause the seasons to change.

In one story, Uaithne was stolen by the Fomorians (a fairy race then ruling over the country of Ireland) and hung as a trophy in their banqueting hall. The Dagda, Lugh, and Ogma came to retrieve it. When the Dagda reached the hall, he called out to his harp; it flew off the wall and came to him, killing nine of the Fomorians in the process.

Sources: Blamires, *The Irish Celtic Magical Tradition*, 223, 225; *Proceedings: Irish MSS. Series*, Volume 1, 141, 162

Uathach

In the Irish epic *Tain Bo Cuailnge* (*The Cattle Raid of Cooley*/*The Tain*), Uathach was the sword of Dubthach; it is named as being among the many cups, drinking horns, goblets, javelins, shields, and swords kept in Tete Brec, one of the three households of the Ulster hero Cuhullin (Cu Chulaind/Cu Chulainn/Cuchulainn). Uathach is described only as "fearful."

Sources: Kinsella and Le Brocquy, *The Tain*, 5

Uchide no kozuchi

Variation: Mallet of Luck

One of the Seven Gods of Good Fortune in Japanese folklore, Daikoku, the god of daily wealth, is depicted as obese and richly dressed, with a treasure sack slung over his shoulder. In art, he is often seen standing on two bags of rice (a symbol of wealth) and carrying the mallet Uchide no kozuchi ("Striking-Out Hammer") in his right hand. It is said that anything he struck with the mallet would turn to gold. When shaken, the mallet would drop riches. Some stories claim that Uchide no kozuchi has the ability to provide whatever item the wielder's heart desires.

In another tale, Momotaro, the peach boy, won Uchide no kozuchi on his personal quest to rid

Onigashima (Island of Ogres) of monsters; it was taken from their treasure hoard.

Sources: Mayer, *The Yanagita Kunio Guide to the Japanese Folk Tale*, 54; Pate, *Ningyo*, n.p.

Ukonvasara

Variation: Ukonkirves

In Finnish mythology, Ukonvasara ("Ukko's Hammer") was the symbol and weapon of the god of crops, harvest, sky, and weather, Ukko (Aijo/Isaimem/Isoiner/Pitkanen/Uko); with this weapon, Ukko could create and throw lightning bolts. Although the weapon is typically thought to have been a hammer, it is also possible that Ukonvasara was an axe or sword.

Sources: Salo, *Ukko*, n.p.

umbilical cord of Zeus, the

Variation: Zeus's umbilical cord

In classical Greek mythology, the infant Zeus (Roman god Jupiter), the god of fate, kings, lightning, sky, and thunder, was taken by the Curetes to Mount Ida, where he was raised by nymphs in secret. While traveling, the umbilical cord of the infant god fell into the river Triton and became a sacred place.

Sources: Parada, *Genealogic Guide to Greek Mythology*, 194; Siculus, *Delphi Complete Works of Diodorus Siculus*, 30–31

umbrella of chaos, the

In Chinese Buddhist mythology, there are four brothers known collectively as the Diamond Kings of Heaven (*Ssu Ta Chin-kang* or *T'ien-wang*); statues of them stand guard in pairs on the left and right sides of the entrances to Buddhist temples. The god and guardian of the south is Mo Li Hai (known in Sanskrit as Virudhaka, or "the Lord of Growth"); he carries the umbrella of chaos. When the umbrella is opened, universal darkness falls over the land. When the umbrella is turned inside out (or upside down—translations vary), violent windstorms accompanied by earthquakes and thunder occur.

Sources: Buckhardt, *Chinese Creeds and Customs*, 163; Werner, *Myths and Legends of China*, 122

Upasamhara

In ancient Hindu mythology, the Upasamhara was a class of weapon that restrained the SOPAS-AMHARA; there are 54 different weapons in this category, and each of them was given by Visvamitra to Rama: Alaksya (the Imperceptible), Avanmukha (the Down-Faced), Avarana (the Protecting), Avil (the Turbid), Daitya (the Fiendish), Dasaksa (the Ten-Eyed), Dasasirsa (the Ten-Headed), Dhanarati (the Desire of Wealth), Dhanya (the Grain), Dharmanabha (the Weapon with the Navel of Right), Dhrsta (the Bold), Dhrti (the Supporting), Drdhanabha (the Weapon with Firm Navel), Dundunabha (the Drum-Naveled); Jrmbaka (the Gaper), Jyotisa (the Luminous), Kamaruci (Following One's Own Wishes), Kamarupaka (the Shape Assumer), Kankalastra (the Skeleton Missile), Kankana (the Bracelet Weapon), Kapalastra (the Skull Weapon), Karavira (the Scimitar), Karsana (the Emaciating), Laksya (the Perceptible), Mahanabha (the Big-Naveled), Makara (the Monster), Mali (the Necklaced), Mausalastra (the Pestle Missile), Moha (the Fascinating), Nabhaka (the Naveled), Nirasys (the Discourager), Paisacastra (the Infernal Missile), Paranmukha (the Averted Face), Pitrya (the Paternal), Pramathana (the Churner), Pratihara (the Warding Off), Rabhasa (the Impetuous), Rucira (the Glittering), Sandhana (the Aimer), Sanidra (the Sleeping), Sarcirmala (the Garland of Energy), Sarpanathaka (the Missile Belonging to Serpents), Sarvadamana (the All-Subduer), Satavaktra (the Hundred-Mouthed), Satodara (the Hundred-Bellied), Satyakirti (the Truly-Famed), Satyavan (the True), Saumanasa (the Good-Minded), Sunabhaka (the Weapon with the Good Navel), Varuna (missile of Varuna), Vidhuta (the Vibrating), Vimala (the Stainless), Vrttima (the Abiding), and Yogandhara (the United).

Of these weapons, five are particular to demons (Kankalastra, Kankana, Kapalastra, Mausalastra, and Paisacastra), while another five are most effective in destroying demons (Alaksya, Kamarupaka, Sarvadamana, Satyavan, and Yogandhara).

The wielders of these weapons received supernatural powers of which the weapons themselves were only a solid manifestation.

Sources: Oppert, *On the Weapons*, 28–31

Urda

Variation: Urdan Fount

In Norse mythology, Urda was the sacred fount of heat and light; it was located over BIFROST, where it is guarded by three Norns: Skuld, Urda, and Verdandi. It is described only as too blindingly bright to look upon.

Sources: Brewer, *Dictionary of Phrase and Fable* 1900, 1108; Keary and Keary, *Tales of the Norse Warrior Gods*, 36

Urdar Magn (URTH-ar MAG-n)

Variations: Jardar Magn ("Earth's Strength")

In Norse mythology, Urdar Magn ("Ur's Strength") was the liquid from Urd's Fountain; it gives the warmth of life to YGGDRASIL, keeping it green, along with bestowing the strength to resist the cold. Urdar Magn was combined with SONAR DREYRI and SVALKALDR SAER in the HORN OF HADES.

Sources: Norroena Society, *Asatru Edda*, 394; Rydberg et al., *Teutonic Mythology*, Volume 2, 518

Urdarbrunnr Well

Variations: Udar-Brunnr Well, Urdar Fountain, Urdar-Brudar Well, Urdarbrunn Well, Urdarbrunnar Well, Urdarbrunnr, Urd-Fount, Urdr's Well, Weird's Well, Well of Fate, Well of Hydr, Well of Urd, Well of Urda, Well of Urdr

In Norse mythology, the Urdarbrunnr Well is located next to Mimir's hall and the root of Asgard ("Enclosure of the Aesir"); it was one of the three wells that nourished the tree YGGDRASIL; HVERGELUR WELL and MIMIRSBRUNNR WELL were the other two. Most of the meetings held by the Aesir were held at this location. Anything dipped into the sacred waters of Urdarbrunnr would turn white. Four harts lived in the area, browsing on the leaves and eating from YGGDRASIL.

Sources: Anderson, *Norse Mythology*, 460; Grimes, *The Norse Myths*, 304; Guerber, *Myths of the Norsemen*, 15

Urim and Thummim

In biblical lore, the Urim and Thummim ("Cursed or Faultless"/"Doctrine and Truth"/"Lights and Perfections"/"Revelation and Truth") were two items that worked in conjunction with one another to allow the high priest to directly communicate with God. They are first mentioned in Exodus 28:30. No description of the items is given in any text; the Urim is occasionally mentioned being used alone, but never the Thummim. On only a few occasions is the order of names reversed.

For the items to work, the high priest would wear an ephod (a garment similar to an apron in appearance); over it he would don a breastplate of fine gold, purple, and scarlet linen "folded square and doubled, a span in length and width." The breastplate was then set with 12 precious gems in four rows; by use of the ROD OF MOSES, the gems were engraved with the names of the twelve tribes of Israel. The Urim and Thummim were placed in a pocket deep within the ephod directly over the high priest's heart. When everything was secure, he would become an oracle, as he could literally hear the words of God. Some translations say the Urim and Thummim had the ability to also project images into the air (like a projection television) when near the Mercy Seat of the ARK OF THE COVENANT.

According to texts, the people would gather together and decide upon a question to be asked; typically, the questions were strategical in nature. These questions were then put to the high priest, whose answer was taken to be the Word of God; the answers were always brief, little more than a "no" or "yes." Only one question was asked at a time.

Sources: Boren and Boren, *Following the Ark of the Covenant*, 14–15; Peake, *A Commentary on the Bible*, 191; Smith, *Dr. William Smith's Dictionary of the Bible*, Volume 4, 3356–63

Vafr (VAV-r)

Variations: Ofdokkum Ognar Ljoma ("Black Terror Gleam")

In Norse mythology, Vafr ("Quickness") is the material from which the VAFRLOGAR and VAFRNIFL are made.

Sources: Norroena Society, *Asatru Edda*, 396

Vafrlogar (VAV-r-lawg-ar) (sing.: Vafrlogi [VAV-r-lawg-i])

Variations: Vafurloge

In Norse mythology, Vafrlogar ("Bickering Flames"/"Quick-Fires") is the flame that surrounds a fortress as a means of protection. In addition to being fire, it can shoot out blasts of white-hot lightning at a target; the bolts never miss what they aim at. Vafrlogar is often used in conjunction with VAFRNIFL and is said to be made of VAFR.

Sources: Norroena Society, *Asatru Edda*, 396; Sturluson, *Younger Edda*, 134

Vafrnifl (VAV-r-niv-l) (plural: Vafrniflar [VAV-r-niv-lar])

In Norse mythology, Vafrnifl ("Bickering Mist"/"VAFR-Mist") is the mist conjured to surround a fortress as a means of defense; it is often used in conjunction with VAFRLOGAR and is said to be made of VAFR.

Sources: Norroena Society, *Asatru Edda*, 396; Sturluson, *Younger Edda*, 134

Vaidurya

In Hindu mythology, Vaidurya ("Cat's Eyes") is a flawless green-gold gem belonging to Lakshmi, the goddess of abundance, beauty, contentment, fertility, luxury, material fortune, material fulfillment, power, and wealth. Vaidurya is worn in a girdle, hanging upon Lakshmi's hips and suspended just above her pubic hair.

Sources: Meulenbeld and Leslie, *Medical Literature from India, Sri Lanka, and Tibet*, 19–20

Vaijayanti

In Hindu mythology, Vaijayanti is the magical necklace worn by the god of preservation, Vishnu; it is composed of a series of five gems, each representing one of the elements, displayed in a specific order: pearl (water), ruby (fire), emerald (earth), sapphire (air), and diamond (ether). The wearer of this necklace is not dependent on or restricted by air, earth, ether, fire, or water.

Sources: Dalal, *Hinduism*, 436; Tagore, *Mani-mala*, 659

Vailixi

In Hindu mythology, Vailixi was a flying war machine used by the violent and warlike people known as the Asvins. Described as cigar shaped, it had the ability to fly in the air, in space, and under water.

Sources: Childress, *Vimana*, n.p; Ramsey, *Tools of War*, n.p.

Vajra

Variation: Vajrayudha

In Hindu mythology, an ASTRA is a supernatural weapon created or gifted by the gods to someone who then presides over the weapon. The wielder of an ASTRA is known as an astradhari.

Vajra, a hurling weapon, was an ASTRA from Indra, the god of the heavens, lightning, rains, river flows, storms, and thunder. According to the lore, Vajra could hit targets with Indra's lightning bolts; it was described as shining as brightly as the sun. After striking its target, Vajra would return to its wielder. This was the weapon that Indra used to slay the dragon and release the dawn, the sky, the sun, and water to the world.

Sources: Edizioni, *Vimanas and the Wars of the Gods*, n.p.; Olsen and Houwen, *Monsters and the Monstrous in Medieval Northwest Europe*, 98–100; Williams, *Handbook of Hindu Mythology*, 114

Valaskjalf

Variations: Valaskialf, Valaskjalv, Valaskjolf

In Norse mythology, Valaskjalf ("Shelf of the Slain") was the main hall belonging to Odin, the god of battle, death, frenzy, the gallows, healing, knowledge, poetry, royalty, the runic alphabet, sorcery, and wisdom; it was described as white with a silver roof. In the watchtower of this building was the throne HLIDSKJALF, where Odin would sit and be able to see all the worlds that branched out from YGGDRASIL. The goddess Frigg ("Beloved") had a throne in the watchtower as well, enabling her to also look over and see the events of all the worlds.

Sources: Grimes, *The Norse Myths*, 305

Valgrind

Variations: Vagrind, Valgrin, Valgrindr

In Norse mythology, Valgrind ("Gate of the Slain") was a barred gate that opened up into Niflheimr; the *einherjar* ("lone fighters"—the spirits of brave warriors who died in battle) passed through this gate on their way to VALHALLA. The Hrymthursar (frost giant) Hrimgrimnir lived near this location.

Sources: Grimes, *The Norse Myths*, 304

Valhalla

Variations: Valhall, Valhol, Walhalla

In Norse mythology, Valhalla ("Hall of the Slain") was the very last hall to be built; it was located near GLADSHEIM and was comparable in size to BILSKIRNIR, the hall of Thor, god of thunder. The walls of Valhalla were made from the shafts of spears, and its roof was shingled with shields. Each of the 540 gateways was wide enough for 800 armed warriors to pass through marching shoulder to shoulder. Over the main gate, a bear's head was mounted, and an eagle flew over the western door. In the center of the main hall grew the pine tree LAERADR. Standing upon the roof was a hart named Eikthyrnir, which constantly fed upon LAERADR. Valhalla was the hall where the *einherjar* ("lone fighters"—the spirits of brave warriors who died in battle, and who were selected by the Valkyries for this honor) awaited the coming of Ragnarok by battling one another, drinking, and feasting.

Sources: Daly, *Norse Mythology A to Z*, 111; Grimes, *The Norse Myths*, 305

Vartari (VAR-tar-i)

In Norse mythology, Vartari ("Lip-Tearer") was a leather thong used by the dwarf Brokkr to lace or sew together the lips of the trickster god Loki. A bet was made between the two, and if Loki lost,

Varunapasha

Brokkr would be able to cut off his head. Immediately upon losing the bet, Loki, adhering to the letter of the law, said the wager was for his head, but there was mention of harm coming to his neck. To compensate for his inability to collect what was rightly owed to him, Brokkr used Vartari to seal Loki's mouth shut.

Sources: Grimes, *The Norse Myths*, 307; Norroena Society, *Asatru Edda*, 396

Varunapasha

Variations: Astra Varunaastra, Pasa, PASHA, Varuna pasha

In Hindu mythology, an ASTRA is a supernatural weapon created or gifted by the gods to someone who then presides over the weapon. The wielder of an ASTRA is known as an astradhari.

Varunapasha was an ASTRA from Varuna, the god of justice, sky, truth, and water. It was said to have the ability to generate voluminous torrents of water. Usually this ASTRA is mentioned to contrast the AGNEYASTRA (weapons associated with fire).

Sources: Edizioni, *Vimanas and the Wars of the Gods*, n.p.; Moor, *The Hindu Pantheon*, 273

Varunastra

Variation: Varun astra

In Hindu mythology, an ASTRA is a supernatural weapon created or gifted by the gods to someone who then presides over the weapon. The wielder of an ASTRA is known as an astradhari.

Varunastra was an ASTRA from Varuna, the god of justice, sky, truth, and water. Like water, Varunastra could manifest in any form, but when used it would create a great wave of water, "bigger than a hill" at its target, dousing its victims in crushing water. Typically this ASTRA was used to counter AGNEYASTRA. Only experienced and highly skilled warriors would seek the use of Varunastra, as even a slight miscalculation would kill the wielder.

Sources: Menon, *The Mahabharata* Volume 2, 237, 274, 276

Vasavi Shakti

In Hindu mythology, an ASTRA is a supernatural weapon created or gifted by the gods to someone who then presides over the weapon. The wielder of an ASTRA is known as an astradhari.

Vasavi Shakti was an ASTRA from Indra, the god of the heavens, lightning, rains, river flows, storms, and *vajra* ("thunder"). This magical throwing dart, like many ASTRAS, would never fail to hit its target; however, it could be used only once. Vasavi Shakti was given to Karna by Indra. The weapon was used against the unstoppable warrior of the Kaurava army, Ghatotkacha.

Sources: Mani, *Memorable Characters from the Ramayana and the Mahabharata*, 56

Vayvayastra

Variations: Vayav astra, Vayavastra, Vayvay astra

In Hindu mythology, an ASTRA is a supernatural weapon created or gifted by the gods to someone who then presides over the weapon. The wielder of an ASTRA is known as an astradhari.

Vayvayastra was an ASTRA from Vayu, the god of the wind. It was said to have the ability to "raise an army by the land" by creating terrible gale-force winds. Vayvayastra was used primarily to counter VARUNASTRA.

Sources: Edizioni, *Vimanas and the Wars of the Gods*, n.p.

Vel ("vale")

In Hindu mythology, Vel (a javelin) was the invincible weapon of the god of war, Karthikeya (Murugan/Skanda/Subramanyam); it was given to him by his mother, Parvati. It was with Vel that Karthikeya was able to defeat the asura (demon) Taraka.

Sources: Kozlowski and Jackson, *Driven by the Divine*, 140, 309; Willford, *Cage of Freedom*, 59

vestment of Adam, the

Variations: Luminous Suit of Invulnerability, Luminous Suit of Adam

According to esoteric traditions, the vestment of Adam was a garment given to Adam by God; it had the ability to protect him from an attack by Satan. The vestment was said to have been handed down through the generations. Ham allegedly stole the vestment while his father, Noah, was in a drunken sleep. From Ham's line, the suit came into the possession of Nimrod. By use of the vestment and the ROD OF MOSES, Nimrod became a powerful king and constructed the Tower of Babel. According to the tale, God caused a beetle to crawl into the ear of Nimrod, which led him to go insane and enabled Abraham to take possession of the vestment and the rod. The vestment of Adam is said to be one of the items placed inside the ARK OF THE COVENANT.

Sources: Boren and Boren, *Following the Ark of the Covenant*, 11, 14

Vibhuti

In Hindu mythology, an ASTRA is a supernatural weapon created or gifted by the gods to someone who then presides over the weapon. The wielder of an ASTRA is known as an astradhari.

Vibhuti was the divine weapon given by Brahmin to Barbarika (Babhruvahana/Baladhara Kunvara/Belarsen), a skilled warrior and expert archer as well as a devoted follower of Shiva, so that he could use it against the Kauravas, who opposed the Pandavas. Vibhuti had the ability to "split the vital center of the body of an enemy."

Sources: Parmeshwaranand, *Encyclopaedic Dictionary of Puranas*, 155

Vichara-bhu

In Hindu mythology, Vichara-bhu is the throne of judgment in which Yama, the god of death, sits; it is located in his huge palace KALICHI.

Sources: Dalal, *Religions of India*, 398; Dowson, *Classical Dictionary of Hindu Mythology and Religion*, 374

Vijaya

Variation: Vijaya Dhanusha

In Hindu mythology, the powerful bow Vijaya ("Conquest"/"Victory") originally belonged to the god Shiva; it was made by Vishvakarman. It was so powerful and devastating that it commanded the respect of all beings in the universe.

The string of Vijaya could not be broken by any ASTRA; in fact, a mortal could not even lift it. The release of the bowstring created a sound similar to *vajra* ("thunder"), a noise so frightening that it could terrify the world. It would also create a flash of light bright enough to stun and blind the enemy.

Sources: Buitenen and Fitzgerald, *The Mahabharata*, Volume 3, 473; Dowson, *Classical Dictionary of Hindu Mythology and Religion*, 87, 356

Vingnir's Mjolnir

In Norse mythology, when Thor, the god of thunder, became too large and strong for his mother Frigg ("Beloved") to handle, he was sent to live with the Jotun (giant) Vingnir ("the Strong") and his wife, Hlor. Thor's first hammer, Vingnir's Mjolnir, came from his foster father; it was made of stone.

Sources: Grimes, *The Norse Myths*, 20, 194, 302; Norroena Society, *Asatru Edda*, 399

Vingolf

Variations: Vingolv, Vinjolf

In Norse mythology, Vingolf ("Friendly Floor"/ "Friendly Hall"/"Hall of Friends") was a hall built by Odin, the god of battle, death, frenzy, the gallows, healing, knowledge, poetry, royalty, the runic alphabet, sorcery, and wisdom; it stood next to GLADSHEIM. Vingolf was likely the hall and home of the goddess Frigg ("Beloved") and her *asynjes* (attendants): Eir, Fulla, Gefjun, Gna, Horn, Lin (Hlin), Lofn, Manglod, Menglod, Sage (Saga/Laga), Sjofn, Syn, and Vor.

Sources: Daly, *Norse Mythology A to Z*, 108; Grimes, *The Norse Myths*, 18, 309

Vitthakalai

Variation: golden flying coach of Kali

In the mythology of Ayyavazhi (a branch of Hinduism), Vitthakalai was the golden chariot of Kali, goddess of death, doomsday, sex, time, and violence.

Sources: Baccarini and Vaddadi, *Reverse Engineering Vedic Vimanas*, n.p.

wallet of Perseus, the

In classical Greek mythology, Hermes (Roman god Mercury), the god of animal husbandry, commerce, eloquence, fertility, language, looters, luck, sleep, thieves, trade, travel, and wealth, loaned the hero Perseus (in addition to his golden winged sandals) a leather wallet known as a KIBISIS (bag or satchel) to safely carry the severed head of the Gorgon Medusa (see SANDALS OF HERMES).

Sources: Dixon-Kennedy, *Encyclopedia of Greco-Roman Mythology*, 245–46; Sherman, *Storytelling*, 625

Waske

Variation: Waska

The sword of the Danish lord Iring, Waske is named in the Middle High German epic poem *Nibelungenlied* (*The Song of the Nibelungs*); it is described only as "a good as ever was made."

Sources: Brewer, *Dictionary of Phrase and Fable* 1900, 1197; Cobb, *The Nibelungenlied*, 554

Water of Heroes, the

In Russian fairy tales, the Water of Heroes is a beverage (typically old mead) that has the magical ability to inspire acts of bravery and heroism and bestow knightly qualities.

Sources: Falkayn, *Russian Fairy Tales*, 15

Water of Life and Death, the

According to Russian legend, Baba Yaga (a witch of vague and fluctuating morality) controls the fire-breathing dragon Chudo-Yudo, which she has set to guard the Water of Life and Death. This water not only has the magical property of granting beauty, strength, and even immortality but also can cure blindness, restore lost limbs, and even resurrect the dead.

There are many Russian fairy tales in which two heroes are horribly maimed, one having his eyes plucked out and the other having his hands or feet cruelly amputated. The pair then live together, helping one another. They encounter a snake or a forest crone who inevitably turns out to be Baba Yaga; she gives them a series of challenges that ends with the retrieval of the Water of Life and Death. Ultimately, the heroes are made whole again, and each manages to marry a beautiful princess before the tale is over.

In the story of the heroic Ivan the Pea, the hero slew the dragon to rescue his sister Vasilissa and fill a flask with the Water of Life and Death. When he came upon the remains of his two older brothers who had died attempting to carry out the same quest, he sprinkled the contents of the flask over the corpses and restored them to full and perfect life.

Sources: Dixon-Kennedy, *Encyclopedia of Russian & Slavic Myth and Legend*, 27, 132, 297; MacCulloch, *The Childhood of Fiction*, 52, 77

water of the zhar-ptitsa

A beautiful and magical bird from Russian folklore, the zhar-ptitsa ("glow bird") has a number of mystical innate abilities that vary from story to story. One such ability is the power to resuscitate the dead by means of the "dead" and "living" water the bird keeps stored in its beak.

Sources: Ralston, *Russian Folk-Tales*, 242, 289–92; Rosen, *Mythical Creatures Bible*, 152

Wave Sweeper

Variation: *Ocean Sweeper*

The Celtic god of the sun, Lugh ("Bright" or "Light") of the Long Arms (Artful Hands or Long Hands), had among his possessions a wonderful sailing vessel named *Wave Sweeper*. This ship had no mast or sails and required no crew to row it; yet it still propelled itself across the surface of the water as well as beneath the waves. When looking upon the ship, it seemed as small as a canoe, able to seat only two people at most; however, no matter how many people boarded it, there was always ample room. *Wave Sweeper* could also bring its occupants to any place they wished to visit, quickly and flawlessly navigating across the ocean and delivering them safely.

Sources: Spence, *A Dictionary of Medieval Romance and Romance Writers*, 274; Young, *Celtic Wonder Tales*, 50, 65, 87–89

well of Cassotis, the

In Greek mythology, the well of Cassotis, located in Delphi, gave off an intoxicating odor that was said to grant the priestess of Delphi her gift of prophecy. The well was named after the nymph Cassotis, who lived in and protected it.

Sources: Brewer, *Dictionary of Phrase and Fable* 1900, 220; Smith, *Dictionary of Greek and Roman Biography and Mythology: Abaeus–Dysponteus*, 627

Welsung

According to German legend, Welsung was the magical sword of Dietleib the Dane (Ditlieb of Steiner/Ditlieb von Steiner); at one time it (along with the swords BALMUNG and SACHS) was considered the best in the world in the hands of the proper wielder.

Sources: Brewer, *Dictionary of Phrase and Fable* 1900, 1197; Mackenzie, *Teutonic Myth and Legend*, 424

whetstone of Tudwal Tudglyd, the

Variations: Hogalen Tudwal Tudklyd, Hogalen Tudwal Tutklyd, Whetstone of Tudwal

In British and Welsh folklore, there is a series of items (always thirteen in number) called the THIRTEEN TREASURES OF THE ISLAND OF BRITAIN (in Welsh, they are called *Tri Thlws ar Ddeg Ynys Prydain*). Although in more modern times the items listed are different, the original thirteen items from the fifteenth century were the CAULDRON OF DYRNWCH THE GIANT, CHARIOT OF MORGAN MWYNFAWR, CHESSBOARD OF GWENDDOLEU AP CEIDIO, COAT OF PADARN BEISRUDD, CROCK AND DISH OF RHYGENYDD YSGOLHAIG (two items), HALTER OF CLYDNO EIDDYN, HAMPER OF GWYDDNO GARANHIR, HORN OF BRAN GALED, KNIFE OF LLAWFRODEDD FARCHOF, MANTLE OF ARTHUR IN CORNWALL, sword of Rhydderch Hael (DYRNWYN), and whetstone of Tudwal Tudglyd.

According to the lore, the whetstone of Tudwal Tudglyd had a different effect depending on the person using it. If the man who used the whetstone to sharpen his sword was brave, when the blade struck an opponent, it would pull from the victim their very life's blood. However, if the person was not brave, the sharpened sword would have no effect when it struck, no matter how masterful the blow.

Sources: Patton, *The Poet's Ogam*, 510; Pendergrass, *Mythological Swords*, 26; Stirling, *King Arthur Conspiracy*, n.p.

Wigar

In Arthurian lore, Wigar was Arthur's armor; it was named and described in the Middle English poem *The Chronicles of England*. According to this source, the bulk of the armor was a cuirass (a piece of armor made of a breastplate and backplate hinged or otherwise fastened together) of steel forged by an elf. It also had a pair of steel hose to cover Arthur's legs. The steel helmet, named GOSWHIT, was covered in gold and gemstones.

Sources: Harlow, *An Introduction to Early English Literature*, 34–35

wings of Daedalus, the

Apollodorus of Athens (circa 180 BCE–120 BCE), a Greek grammarian, historian, and scholar, and Ovid (Publius Ovidius Naso; 43 BCE–17 CE), the Roman poet, both wrote of Daedalus ("Ingenious"), the ancient Greek architect who designed the labyrinth that contained the monstrous Minotaur of Crete. Daedalus and his son Icarus were imprisoned in the labyrinth after a prisoner had escaped it. Although it was all but impossible to get away, Daedalus told his son that while "escape was checked by water and land, the air and sky are free." He therefore constructed for each of them a pair of wings made of beeswax and feathers. Daedalus warned Icarus that if they flew too high, the heat of the sun would melt the wax and the wings would fall apart; if they flew too close to the ocean, the moist sea air would dampen the feathers and make the wings too heavy to work. In spite of his father's warnings, Icarus soared up into the sky, and, as predicted, the wings failed him. The young man fell from a dizzying height into the ocean, and his anguished father flew on alone to freedom in Sicily.

Sources: Hamilton, *Mythology*, n.p.; Westmoreland, *Ancient Greek Beliefs*, 181

winnowing oar, the

Mentioned in *The Odyssey*, the ancient Greek epic attributed to Homer, the winnowing oar was in truth nothing but an ordinary oar. Odysseus was advised that after he returned home to Ithaca, he should take an oar from his vessel and journey until he was asked by a person who had never seen the ocean what sort of winnowing fan (a tool for separating wheat from chaff) he was carrying. On that spot, Odysseus was to plant the oar and sacrifice a boar, bull, and ram to Poseidon (Roman god Neptune), the god of earthquakes, horses, and the seas. Then Odysseus was to offer a hecatomb to every Olympian god. By doing so, he would be assured a gentle death at a great old age, surrounded by beloved and happy people.

Sources: Schein, *Reading the Odyssey*, 113; Westmoreland, *Ancient Greek Beliefs*, 492

wishing rod

In German folklore, a wishing rod is a magical rod made of hazel wood. Traditionally, a wishing rod was cut from a blackthorn tree and whoever wielded it would have their wishes granted. To use it, one needed to hold the rod and, while looking at a pile of hay, chant the magical rhyme while thinking about the desired wish. When the incantation was finished, the wielder had to leave the area without looking upon the hay again; if all these directions were followed, their wish would come true. However, in one source from Conrad of Megenberg titled *Buch der Natur*, when used as a spit to roast meat, the wishing rod would magically turn and rotate the food of its own accord. It was also said that the Nibelungs possessed a wishing rod of pure gold.

Sources: Daniels and Stevens, *Encyclopaedia of Superstitions, Folklore, and the Occult Sciences of the World*, Volume 2, 1445; Nielsen and Polansky, *Pendulum Power*, 21

Wondrous Bed, the

The Wondrous Bed ("Lit Marveile") of Arthurian lore resided in a chamber just beyond the DOORS OF EBONY AND IVORY in the castle of Queen Igraine. Sitting in the middle of a marble room with walls covered in silk, the bed itself was made entirely of gold except for the cords, which were silver; at the points where the cords crossed, there hung a small bell. On all four bedposts a carbuncle was fixed into place, each giving off as much light as four brightly burning candles. Each of the bed's legs was carved to resemble a grimacing dog with a fearsome maw, and each of the dogs was attached to four wheels. The bed, having so many wheels, was so easy to move that it could easily be pushed across the room with one finger.

To pass the test of the Wondrous Bed, a knight had to fight a lion and brave an onslaught of arrows; any taint of avarice, cowardice, flattery, or other type of sin would not survive this trial.

Sources: Karr, *Arthurian Companion*, 250; Kibler and Palmer, *Medieval Arthurian Epic and Romance*, 178

wooden cow of Daedalus, the

Daedalus ("Ingenious"), the architect and inventor of classical Greek mythology, once constructed a wooden cow to assist Queen Pasiphae of Crete. Because her husband, King Minos, refused to sacrifice a particular bull to Poseidon (Roman god Neptune), the god of earthquakes, horses, and the seas, the god cursed the queen to lust after the bull. At the behest of Pasiphae, Daedalus built the wooden cow and so artfully covered it with hide that it was easily mistaken for a living creature. This device was taken to the field where the bull of Poseidon grazed, and the queen crouched down within the wooden structure in the hope that the bull would be fooled, mount the false cow, and copulate with her. The plan worked, and Pasiphae became pregnant, giving birth to a son she named Asterion, better known as the Minotaur ("bull of Minos").

Sources: Bulfinch, *Bulfinch's Greek and Roman Mythology*, 122–23; Hard, *The Routledge Handbook of Greek Mythology*, 337–41, 347; March, *Dictionary of Classical Mythology*, 146

Worochi no Ara-Masa

Variations: Worochi no Kara-sabi ("Foreign Spade of the Serpent")

According to Japanese legend, Worochi no Ara-Masa ("Rough Perfect One of the Serpent") was the sword of the god of sea and storms, Susanoo (Susanowo/Susa-no-wo no Mikoto); it was the weapon he used to slay Yamata-no-Orochi, the gigantic eight-headed serpent of Koshi.

Sources: Aston, "Hideyoshi's Invasion of Kores," 213-22;Pendergrass, *Mythological Swords*, 50

Wynebgwrthucher

Variations: Wyneb Gwrthucher

In Welsh Arthurian lore, Wynebgwrthucher ("Face to Evening") is the shield of King Arthur; when Arthur tells Culhwch that he may ask and receive anything of him, the king makes a short list of his prize possessions that are the seven exceptions to his offer: CALADBOLG, his sword; CARNWENNAN, his dagger; Gwenhwyfar, his wife; GWENN, his cloak; PRYDWEN, his ship; RHONGOMIANT, his spear; and Wynebgwrthucher, his shield. Wynebgwrthucher was named fifth.

Sources: Dom, *King Arthur and the Gods of the Round Table*, 89, 92; Padel, *Arthur in Medieval Welsh Literature*, n.p.

Xiuhcoatl

In Aztec mythology, Xiuhcoatl ("Fire Snake") was the weapon wielded by the god Huitzilopochtli; he was born a full-grown adult armed with Xiuhcoatl and a war shield. Xiuhcoatl, a projectile weapon, was thrown and looked like a bolt of fire as it flew through the air.

Sources: Aguilar-Moreno, *Handbook to Life in the Aztec World*, 195; Koontz et al., *Landscape and Power in Ancient Mesoamerica*, 33–34

Yagrush

In Phoenician mythology, AYAMUR ("Driver") and Yagrush ("Chaser") were the two clubs created and named by Kothar; the weapons were then given to Baal ("Rider of the Clouds"), a god of storms, in order to defeat Yam, god of the sea.

Sources: Gowan, *Theology in Exodus*, 135; Pritchard and Fleming, *The Ancient Near East*, 109, 112

Yasakani no Magatama

In Japanese mythology, Yasakani no Magatama was the bejeweled and lovely necklace placed on the branch of a tree next to the mirror KAGAMI in order to entice the goddess of the sun, Amaterasu O Mi Kami, out of the cave Ame-no-Iwato ("Sky Rock Cave").

Sources: Bocking, *A Popular Dictionary of Shinto*, 115; Coulter and Turner, *Encyclopedia of Ancient Deities*, 445

Ydalir

Variations: Ydale, Ydaler, Yday

In Norse mythology, Ydalir ("Yew Clales" or "Yew Dales") was the hall belonging to the god of winter, Ullr ("Splendid"). The hall sat in a forest of yew trees, and, although small, it was said to be very comfortable to all who ever visited.

Sources: Daly, *Norse Mythology A to Z*, 109; Grimes, *The Norse Myths*, 18–19, 309

ye-she ral-gri

In Tibetan Buddhism, a ye-she ral-gri ("wisdom sword") is the weapon utilized by many *yidam* and wrathful deities; the purpose of this type of weapon is to destroy and sever enemies and hindering demons. A ye-she ral-gri is held in the right hand and symbolizes the eight great powers of psychic attainment: ability to traverse all realms of existence, alchemic immortality and transmutation of matter, clairvoyant vision, fleetness of foot, flight through the sky, invisibility, power to vanquish enemies, and translocation and multiple manifestations.

Sources: Beer, *The Handbook of Tibetan Buddhist Symbols*, 124

Yggdrasil (EG-dras-il)

Variations: Ash Tree of Existence, Ash Yggdrasil, Back Bone of the Cosmos, Mimamd, Mimameid, Mimameider ("Mimi's Tree"), Mimameidr, Mimameior, Mjifvitr ("Mead Tree"), Tree of Existence, Tree of Time, Ygdrasil, Yggdrasill, Yggdrasyll

Standing in the center of the nine worlds of Norse mythology, the ash tree known as Yggdrasil ("bearer of Ygg") binds the different planes together as its roots spread out in the past, present, and future. The tree was created when Bestla and Bor planted its seed under a rock moments before the tidal wave of Ymir's ("Groaner"; Aurgelmir) blood washed over them, drowning the couple. The blood nourished the seed, and the ash tree matured quickly. When this mighty tree finally falls, the universe will be destroyed.

There are three wells from which Yggdrasil draws its water: HVERGELUR WELL, MIMIRSBRUNNR WELL, and URDARBRUNNR WELL. When Odin needed to gain the knowledge and wisdom of the dead, he pierced his body with a spear dedicated to himself and hung from the branches of Yggdrasil for nine days.

In the topmost branches of Yggdrasil lives the rusty-yellow eagle Edgar; the hawk Vedrfolnir built its nest blocking Edgar's view. The serpent (or dragon) Nidhoggr has entwined itself around the roots of the tree in the realm of Niflheimr. Here, he and his sons (Goinn, Grabakr, Grafvolludr, Moinn, Ofnir, and Svafnir) chew on the roots of the mighty ash and eat the deceased who are deposited there. The red squirrel Ratatoskr runs up and down the trunk of tree, carrying gossip and rumors to Edgar and Nidhoggr in hopes of stirring up trouble so they will attack the tree. There are four harts that graze beneath Yggdrasil (Dainn, Duneyrr, Durathorr, and Dvallinn); the honeydew that drips from the branches of Yggdrasil to their horns nourishes the bees that live in the tree.

Each day the Aesir cross BIFROST and gather beneath Yggdrasil to hold council with one another.

Sources: Anderson, *Norse Mythology*, 74, 120, 190, 206, 370, 453; Evans, *Dictionary of Mythology*, 275; Grimes, *The Norse Myths*, 7, 15, 242, 261, 263, 281, 287, 291–92, 298

Yliaster (plural: Yliastri)

Variations: das grosse Yliaster, Iliaster, Magnus Limbus, Yliastrum

In alchemical workings, Yliaster ("prime matter of stars") was the *materia prima* from which the base elements were created; after the division

of Yliaster into the four parts, it was destroyed and the four elements went their separate ways. According to Paracelsus (1493–1541), a Swiss alchemist, astrologer, and physician who practiced Hermetic-Kabbalistic philosophy, Yliaster was created *ex nihilo* ("from nothing"). He was certain that searching for a fifth element was a fool's quest, as Yliaster was divided equally into four different elements. Paracelsus went on to explain how raw Yliaster remained in the elements in a vegetative state but was latently active; this is how, for example, rain makes seeds grow.

Sources: Granada et al., *Unifying Heaven and Earth*, 76–77, 99; Hartmann, *The Life and the Doctrines of Philippus Theophrastus*, 57–58

Ysetr (EE-seht-r)

Variations: Geirvadills setr, Geirvandills setr

In Norse mythology, Ysetr ("the chalet of the bow" or "of the bow") was the fortress of the hall YDALIR where the gods of Asgard ("Enclosure of the Aesir"), the Aesir, had an outpost against the Jotuns (giants). It was originally entrusted to Ivaldi and his sons, but later Ullr ("Splendid"), the god of winter and a superb archer, assumed the responsibility of protecting the borderland.

Sources: Anderson, *Norroena*, Volume 5, 867; Norroena Society, *Asatru Edda*, 401

Zakkum, al

Variation: Tree of Zaqqam

In Islamic mythology, this cursed tree, rooted in Hell, is covered with thorns and grows an extremely bitter fruit that is exceedingly ugly, as it resembles the heads of devils. This fruit is consumed by the souls of the damned, however their hunger remains unsatisfied and no nutritional value comes from having eaten it. It is said the buds of this tree taste like the paste of devils. Al Zakkum is the literal opposite of the TREE OF KNOWLEDGE that grows in the Garden of Eden. The tree grows by fire rather than water

Sources: Brewer, *The Reader's Handbook of Famous Names in Fiction, Allusions, References, Proverbs, Plots, Stories, and Poems*, 1127; Hughes, *A Dictionary of Islam*, 702; Porteous, *The Forest in Folklore and Mythology*, 209; Tyeer, 81–84, *The Qur'an and the Aesthetics of Premodern Arabic Prose*, 82

Zaluk, al

According to Islamic mythology, the prophet Muhammad owned at least three shields at the time of his death; their names were al FATUK, al RAZIN, and al Zaluk. Beyond its name, nothing else is known of al Zaluk ("the Repellant").

Zampun

Sources: Osborne et al., *A Complete History of the Arabs*, Volume 1, 254; Sale et al., *An Universal History, Part 2*, Volume 1, 185

Zampun

In Tibetan mythology, Zampun is the sacred tree of life. It has three roots: one reaches up into Heaven, the second reaches downward into Hell, and the third stays in the middle range between the other two.

Sources: Blavatsky, *Isis Unveiled*, 152; Wedeck, *Dictionary of Magic*, n.p.

Zul Fakar

Variations: Dhu-l-fiqar, Dhulfiqqr, Rhulfear, Zoulfikar, Zulfeqhar, Zulfikar, Zulfiquar

In Muslim lore, Zul Fakar was the legendary cloven-bladed sword given to the Prophet Muhammad by the angel Gabriel; it was then said to have been passed down to Ali ibn Abi Talbi. Historically, this weapon is depicted as crossed swords in an open scissor-like position.

Sources: Frankel, *From Girl to Goddess*, 49; Pendergrass, *Mythological Swords*, 79

Zul-Hajam

According to the medieval Persian saga of Amir Hamza, Zul-Hajam was one of the four swords once held by King Suleiman, the others being Aqrab-E Suleimani, Qumqam, and Samsam.

Sources: Jah, *Hoshruba*, 243

Bibliography

Abel, Ernest L. *Death Gods: An Encyclopedia of the Rulers, Evil Spirits, and Geographies of the Dead.* Westport, CT: Greenwood Press, 2009.

Abulhab, Saad D. *The Epic of Gilgamesh: Selected Readings from Its Original Early Arabic Language: Including a New Translation of the Flood Story.* New York: Blautopf, 2016.

Adamec, Ludwig W. *Historical Dictionary of Islam.* Lanham, MD: Rowman & Littlefield, 2016.

Adams Media. *The Book of Celtic Myths: From the Mystic Might of the Celtic Warriors to the Magic of the Fey Folk, the Storied History and Folklore of Ireland, Scotland, Brittany, and Wales.* Avon, MA: Adams Media, 2016.

Afanasyev, Alexander. *Russian Folktales from the Collection of A. Afanasyev: A Dual-Language Book.* Mineola, NY: Dover, 2014.

Agarwal, Himanshu. *Mahabharata Retold: Part 1.* Chennai: Notion Press, 2016.

Agarwal, Meena. *Tales from the Ramayan.* New Delhi: Diamond Pocket Books, 2016.

Aguilar-Moreno, Manuel. *Handbook to Life in the Aztec World.* Oxford: Oxford University Press, 2007.

Akins, Steven L. *The Lebor Feasa Runda: A Druidic Grammar of Celtic Lore and Magic.* Bloomington, IN: iUniverse, 2008.

Aldersey-Williams, Hugh. *The Tide: The Science and Stories Behind the Greatest Force on Earth.* New York: W. W. Norton, 2016.

Alexander, Prince Philip. *Parallel Universal History: Being an Outline of the History and Biography of the World, Divided into Periods.* London: Whittaker, 1838.

Allan, Tony, and Sara Maitland. *Ancient Greece and Rome: Myths and Beliefs.* New York: Rosen Publishing Group, 2011.

Allard, Joe, and Richard North. *Beowulf and Other Stories: A New Introduction to Old English, Old Icelandic and Anglo-Norman Literatures.* London: Routledge, 2014.

Allen, Maude Rex. *Japanese Art Motives.* Chicago: A. C. McClurg, 1917.

Altman, Nathaniel. *Sacred Trees.* San Francisco: Sierra Club Books, 1994.

"Ancient Literature of France." *Quarterly Review* 120 (1866): 283–324.

Andersen, Hans Christian. *The Fairy Tales and Stories of Hans Christian Andersen.* New York: Race Point Publishing, 2016.

Anderson, George Kumler. *The Saga of the Völsungs, Together with Excerpts from the Nornageststháttr and Three Chapters from the Prose Edda.* Newark: University of Delaware Press, 1982.

Anderson, John P. *Finding Joy in Joyce: A Reader's Guide to Ulysses.* Irvine, CA: Universal-Publishers, 2000.

Anderson, John P. *Joyce's Finnegans Wake: The Curse of Kabbalah,* Volume 9. Irvine, CA: Universal-Publishers, 2014.

Anderson, William S. *Ovid's Metamorphoses: Books 1–5.* Norman: University of Oklahoma Press, 1997.

Anderson, Rasmus B. *The Younger Edda: Also Called Snorre's Edda, Or the Prose Edda.* Chicago: Scott Foresman, 1897.

Anderson, Rasmus Bjorn. *Norroena: Embracing the History and Romance of Northern Europe,* Volume 5. London: Norroena Society, 1905.

Anderson, Rasmus Bjorn. *Norrœna: The Arthurian Tales. By Thomas Mallory.* London: Norroena Society, 1906.

Anderson, Rasmus Bjorn. *Norroena, the History and Romance of Northern Europe: A Library of Supreme Classics Printed in Complete Form,* Volume 2. London: Norroena Society, 1906.

Anderson, Rasmus Bjorn. *Norse Mythology: Or, The Religion of Our Forefathers, Containing All the Myths of the Eddas, Systematized and Interpreted. With an Introduction, Vocabulary and Index.* Chicago: C. S. Criggs and Company, 1884.

Andrews, J. B. "Neapolitan Witchcraft." In *Folklore: A Quarterly Review of Myth, Tradition, Institution, and Custom Being the Transaction of the Folk-Lore Society and Incorporating the Archaeological Review and the Folk-Lore Journal.* Volume 8, edited by David Nutt, 1–9. London: David Nutt, 1897.

Andrews, Tamra. *Dictionary of Nature Myths: Legends of the Earth, Sea, and Sky.* Oxford: Oxford University Press, 2000.

Anniversary Papers by Colleagues and Pupils of George Lyman Kittredge: Presented on the Completion of His Twenty-fifth Year of Teaching in Harvard University, June, MCMXIII. Boston: Ginn, 1913.

Anonymous. *The Black Pullet: Science of Magical Talisman.* Boston: Weiser Books, 2000.

Anonymous. *Curious Stories about Fairies and Other Funny People.* Boston: Ticknor, 1856.

Anonymous. *From the Book of Invasions: The Conquest of Nemed, The Conquest of the Fir Bolg, The Conquest*

Bibliography

of the Sons of Mil and The Conquest of the Tuatha De Danann. N.pag.: Library of Alexandria, n.d.

Anthon, Charles. *A Classical Dictionary.* New York: Harper & Brothers, 1872.

Apollodorus and Hyginus. *Apollodorus' Library and Hyginus' Fabulae.* Translated with introductions by R. Scott Smith and Stephen M. Trzaskoma. Indianapolis: Hackett, 2007.

Apollonius (Rhodius). *"The Argonautica" of Apollonius Rhodius.* Translated by Edward Philip Coleridge. London: George Bell, 1889.

Aravamudan, Krishnan. *Pure Gems of Ramayanam.* Gurgaon: Partridge India, 2014.

Ariosto, Lodovico. *The Orlando Furioso,* Volume 1. Translated by William Stewart Rose. London: John Murray, 1823.

Arrowsmith, Nancy. *Essential Herbal Wisdom: A Complete Exploration of 50 Remarkable Herbs.* Woodbury, MN: Llewellyn Worldwide, 2009.

Asala, Joanne. *Celtic Folklore Cooking.* St. Paul, MN: Llewellyn Worldwide, 1998.

Ashe, Geoffrey. *The Discovery of King Arthur.* New York: Henry Holt, 1987.

Ashley, Mike. *The Mammoth Book of King Arthur.* London: Little, Brown Book Group, 2011.

Ashton, John. *Curious Creatures in Zoology: With 130 Illustrations throughout the Text.* Strand: John C. Nimmo, 1890.

Aston, W. G. "Hideyoshi's Invasion of Kores: Chapter III: Negotiation." *Transactions of the Asiatic Society of Japan* 9–10 (1881): 213–22.

Aston, William George. *Nihongi: Chronicles of Japan from the Earliest Times to A.D. 697,* Book 1, Part 1. North Clarendon, VT: Tuttle, 1976.

Atwood, Mary Anne. *A Suggestive Inquiry into Hermetic Mystery: With a Dissertation on the More Celebrated of the Alchemical Philosophers, Being an Attempt towards the Recovery of the Ancient Experiment of Nature, also an Appendix Containing the [Table Talk and] Memorabilia of Mary Anne Atwood.* Belfast: W. Tait, 1918.

Auden, William C. *Reading Albrecht Durer's the Knight, Death, and the Devil Ab Ovum: Life Understood as Struggle.* Bloomington, IN: Archway Publishing, 2016.

Auty, Robert. *Traditions of Heroic and Epic Poetry,* Volume 1: *The Traditions.* London: Modern Humanities Research Association, 1980.

Azman, Ruzaini Fikri Mohd. *The Legend of Hang Tuah.* Kuala Lumpur: DBP, 2008.

Babu, C. N. *Sugar Cane.* New Delhi: Allied Publishers, 1990.

Baccarini, Enrico, and Kavya Vaddadi. *Reverse Engineering Vedic Vimanas: New Light on Ancient Indian Heritage.* Firenze, Italy: Enigma Edizioni, 2014.

Bailey, James. *An Anthology of Russian Folk Epics.* London: Routledge, 1998.

Bailey, James, and Tatyana Ivanova. *Anthology Russian Folk Epics.* Armonk, NY: M. E. Sharpe, 2006.

Baker, Alan. *The Enigmas of History: Myths, Mysteries and Madness from Around the World.* New York: Random House, 2012.

Balfour, Edward. *The Cyclopædia of India and of Eastern and Southern Asia: Commercial, Industrial and Scientific, Products of the Mineral, Vegetable, and Animal Kingdoms, Useful Arts and Manufactures,* Volume 3. New South Wales: Allen & Unwin, 1968.

Bandera, Cesareo. *Sacred Game: The Role of the Sacred in the Genesis of Modern Literary Fiction.* University Park: Penn State University Press, 2010.

Bansal, Sunita Pant. *Hindu Gods and Goddesses.* New Delhi: Smriti Books, 2005.

Barasch, Moshe. *The Language of Art: Studies in Interpretation.* New York: New York University Press, 1997.

Barber, Richard W. *The Holy Grail: Imagination and Belief.* Cambridge, MA: Harvard University Press, 2004.

Barber, Richard W. *Myths & Legends of the British Isles.* Sussex: Boydell and Brewer, 1999.

Barber, Richard W., and Anne Riches. *A Dictionary of Fabulous Beasts.* Sussex: Boydell and Brewer, 1996.

Baring-Gould, Sabine. *Curious Myths of the Middle Ages: The Sangreal, Pope Joan, the Wandering Jew, and Others.* Mineola, NY: Dover, 2005.

Barlow, Frank. *William Rufus.* New Haven, CT: Yale University Press, 2008.

Barnes, Charles Randall. *Dictionary of the Bible: Biographical, Geographical, Historical, and Doctrinal.* New York: Eaton & Mains, 1900.

Barrington, George. *Voyage to Botany Bay.* New South Wales: Sydney University Press, 2004.

Bartlett, Sarah. *The Mythology Bible: The Definitive Guide to Legendary Tales.* Sterling: New York, 2009.

Bassett, Wilbur. *Wander-ships: Folk-stories of the Sea, with Notes upon Their Origin.* Chicago: Open Court Publishing Company, 1917.

Bates, Roy. *All about Chinese Dragons.* Raleigh: Lulu.com, 2007.

Beaumont, Comyns. *The Riddle of Prehistoric Britain, Hardback.* Raleigh: Lulu.com, 1946.

Bechtel, John Hendricks. *A Dictionary of Mythology.* Philadelphia: Penn Publishing Company, 1917.

Beck, Guy L., editor. *Alternative Krishnas: Regional and Vernacular Variations on a Hindu Deity.* Albany: State University of New York Press, 2012.

Becklake, John. *History of Rocketry and Astronautics: Proceedings of the Twenty-Second and Twenty-Third History Symposia of the International Academy of Astronautics, Bangalore, India, 1988, Málaga, Spain, 1989.*

Beckwith, Martha Warren. *Hawaiian Mythology.* Honolulu: University of Hawaii Press, 1970.

Beer, Robert. *The Handbook of Tibetan Buddhist Symbols.* Chicago: Serindia Publications, 2003.

Beiderbecke, H. "Some Religious Ideas and Customs of the Ovaherero." *Folk-lore Journal* 1, Part 2 (1879): 88–97.

Bell, J. *Bell's New Pantheon; or Historical Dictionary of the Gods, Demi-gods, Heroes and Fabulous Personages of Antiquity: Also of the Images and Idols Adored in the Pagan World; Together with Their Temple, Priests, Alters, Oracles, Feasts, Festivals, Games, Etc, as well as Descriptions of their Figures, Representations, and Symbols, Collected from Statues, Pictures, Coins, and Other Remains of the Ancients. the Whole*

Designed to Facilitate the Study of Mythology, History, Poetry, Painting, Statuary, Medals, And Etc. and Compiled from the Best Authorities, in Two Volumes, Volume 2. London: J. Bell, 1790.

Bellows, Henry Adams. *The Poetic Edda: The Heroic Poems.* Mineola, NY: Dover, 2013.

Belyarova, Lina. *Abkhazia in Legends.* Moscow: LitRes, 2018.

Benét, William Rose. *The Reader's Encyclopedia.* New York: Crowell, 1955.

Bennett, Chris. *Liber 420: Cannabis, Magickal Herbs and the Occult.* Walterville, OR: TrineDay, 2018.

Bennett, De Robigne Mortimer. *The Gods and Religions of Ancient and Modern Times,* Volume 1. New York: D.M. Bennett, 1880.

Berens, E.M. *Myths and Legends of Ancient Greece and Rome.* Irvine, CA: Xist Publishing, 2015.

Berg, William J. *Literature and Painting in Quebec: From Imagery to Identity.* Toronto: University of Toronto Press, 2013.

Bernardin, Buchahan. "Portfolios." *Yale Literary Magazine* 83, Issue 9 (1918): 426–31.

Best, Elsdon. "Notes on the Art of War as Conducted by the Maori of New Zealand, with Accounts of Various Customs, Rites, Superstitions, and Pertaining to War as Practiced by the Ancient Maori, Part 2." *Journal of the Polynesian Society* 11 (1902).

Best, Elsdon. "Te Whanga-Nui-A-Tara: Wellington in pre-Pakeha Days" p 107-165. *Journal of the Polynesian Society* 10 (1901).

Bezanilla, Clara. *A Pocket Dictionary of Aztec and Mayan Gods and Goddesses.* Los Angeles: Getty Publications, 2010.

Bhagavatananda, Shri Guru. *A Brief History of the Immortals of Non-Hindu Civilizations.* Raleigh: Lulu. com, 2015.

Bigsby, Robert. *Old Places Revisited; Or the Antiquarians Enthusiast,* Volume 3. London: Wright, 1851.

Billington, Sandra, and Miranda Green, editors. *The Concept of the Goddess.* London: Routledge, 2002.

Bingham, Ann, and Jeremy Roberts. *South and Meso-American Mythology A to Z.* New York: Infobase Publishing, 2010.

Bjork, Robert E., and John D. Niles, editors. *A Beowulf Handbook.* Lincoln: University of Nebraska Press, 1998.

Black, J., and A. Green. *Gods, Demons and Symbols of Ancient Mesopotamia: An Illustrated Dictionary.* London: British Museum Press, 1992.

Blamires, Steve. *The Irish Celtic Magical Tradition.* Cheltenham: Skylight Press, 1992.

Blavatsky, Helena Petrovna. *Anthropogenesis.* London: Theosophical Publishing Company, 1888.

Blavatsky, Helena Petrovna. *Isis Unveiled: A Master Key to the Mysteries of Ancient and Modern Science and Theology.* New York: J.W. Bouton, 1877.

Blavatsky, Helena Petrovna. *The Secret Doctrine: The Synthesis of Science, Religion, and Philosophy,* Volume 2. Charleston, SC: Forgotten Books, 1893.

Blavatsky, Helena Petrovna. *The Theosophical Glossary.* Adelphi: Theosophical Publishing Society, 1892.

Blomberg, Catharina. *The Heart of the Warrior: Origins and Religious Background of the Samurai System in Feudal Japan.* Sandgate, UK: Psychology Press, 1994.

Boas, Franz, and Henry W. Tate. *Tsimshian Mythology.* Washington, DC: Government Printing Office, 1916.

Bocking, Brian. *A Popular Dictionary of Shinto.* Surrey: Curzon Press, 2005.

Bonnefoy, Yves, editor. *Asian Mythologies.* Chicago: University of Chicago Press, 1993.

Bonnefoy, Yves. *Greek and Egyptian Mythologies.* Chicago: University of Chicago Press, 1992.

Book of the Covenant, Volume 5. New York: KTAV Publishing House, 1928.

Booth, Daniel. *An Analytical Dictionary of the English Language: In Which the Words Are Explained in the Order of Their Natural Affinity.* London: Simpkin, Marshall, and Company, 1836.

Bord, Janet. *Fairies: Real Encounters with Little People.* New York: Carroll and Graf, 1997.

Boren, Kerry Ross, and Lisa Lee Boren. *Following the Ark of the Covenant: The Treasure of God.* Springville, UT: Bonneville Books, 2000.

Boult, Katherine F. *Asgard and the Norse Heroes.* New York: Biblo & Tannen, 1940.

Boyce, Mary. *A History of Zoroastrianism: The Early Period.* Leiden, Netherlands: Brill, 1989.

Boyce, Mary. *Zoroastrians: Their Religious Beliefs and Practices.* London: Routledge, 1979.

Bradish, Sarah Powers. *Old Norse Stories.* New York: American Book Company, 1900.

Brault, Gerard J. *Early Blazon: Heraldic Terminology in the Twelfth and Thirteenth Centuries with Special Reference to Arthurian Heraldry.* Woodbridge: Boydell & Brewer, 1997.

Brault, Gerard J. *The Song of Roland: An Analytical Introduction and Commentary.* University Park: Pennsylvania State University Press, 1996.

Bredon, Juliet, and Igor Mitrophanow. *The Moon Year: A Record of Chinese Customs and Festivals.* New York: Routledge, 2005.

Breese, Daryl, and Gerald D'Aoust. *God's Steed: Key to World Peace.* Raleigh: Lulu.com, 2011.

Brennan, J. K. *The Delphian Course: A Systematic Plan of Education, Embracing the World's Progress and Development of the Liberal Arts,* Volume 2: *Hebrew Literature. Greek Mythology.* Chicago: Delphian Society, 1913.

Brewer, Ebenezer Cobham. *Dictionary of Phrase and Fable: Giving the Derivation, Source, or Origin of Common Phases, Allusions, and Words That Have a Tale to Tell,* Volume 1. London: Cassell, 1898.

Brewer, Ebenezer Cobham. *Dictionary of Phrase and Fable: Giving the Derivation, Source, or Origin of Common Phases, Allusions, and Words That Have a Tale to Tell,* Volume 2. London: Cassell, 1898.

Brewer, Ebenezer Cobham. *Dictionary of Phrase and Fable: Giving the Derivation, Source, or Origin of Common Phrases, Allusions, and Words That Have a Tale to Tell.* London: Cassell, 1900.

Brewer, Ebenezer Cobham. *The Reader's Handbook of Famous Names in Fiction, Allusions, References, Proverbs, Plots, Stories, and Poems.* Philadelphia: J. B. Lippincott Company, 1910.

Brewer, Ebenezer Cobham. *The Wordsworth Dictio-*

nary of Phrase and Fable. Hertfordshire: Wordsworth Editions, 2001.

Brewer, Ebenezer Cobham, and Marion Harland. *Character Sketches of Romance, Fiction and the Drama*, Volume 2. New York: Selmar Hess, 1902.

Brewer, Ebenezer Cobham, and Marion Harland. *Character Sketches of Romance, Fiction and the Drama*, Volume 4. New York: Selmar Hess, 1902.

Brewer, Ebenezer Cobham, and Marion Harland. *Character Sketches of Romance, Fiction and the Drama*, Volume 6. New York: Selmar Hess, 1902.

Brewer, Ebenezer Cobham, and Marion Harland. *Character Sketches of Romance, Fiction and the Drama*, Volume 8. New York: Selmar Hess, 1902.

Britannica Educational Publishing. *Egyptian Gods & Goddesses*. New York: Rosen Publishing Group, 2014.

Brodeur, Arthur Gilchrist. *Snorri Sturluson: The Prose Edda*. New York: American-Scandinavian Foundation, 1916.

Bromwich, R., and D. Simon Evans. *Culhwch and Olwen: An Edition and Study of the Oldest Arthurian Tale*. Cardiff: University of Wales Press, 1992.

Bromwich, Rachel, editor. *Trioedd Ynys Prydein: The Triads of the Island of Britain*. Cardiff: University of Wales Press, 1961.

Broster, Joan A., and Herbert Bourn. *Amagqirha: Religion, Magic and Medicine in Transkei*. Cape Town: Afrika Limited, 1982.

Browning, Frank. *Apples*. New York: North Point Press, 1998.

Bruce, Christopher W., editor. *The Arthurian Name Dictionary*. New York: Garland, 1999.

Bruce, David. *Jason and the Argonauts: A Retelling in Prose of Apollonius of Rhodes' Argonautica*. Raleigh: Lulu.com, 2013.

Brunvand, Jan Harold, editor. *American Folklore: An Encyclopedia*. New York: Garland, 1996.

Bryant, Edwin F. *Krishna: A Sourcebook*. Oxford: Oxford University Press, 2007.

Buckhardt, Valentine Rodolphe. *Chinese Creeds and Customs*. London: Kegan Paul, 2006.

Budge, Ernest Alfred Thompson Wallis. *Amulets and Talismans*. Mineola, NY: Dover, 1978.

Buitenen, Johannes Adrianus Bernardus, and James L. Fitzgerald, editors. *The Mahabharata*, Volume 3: *Book 4: The Book of the Virata; Book 5: The Book of the Effort*. Chicago: University of Chicago Press, 1973.

Bulfinch, Thomas. *Bulfinch's Greek and Roman Mythology: The Age of Fable*. North Chelmsford: Courier Corporation, 2012.

Bullen, Margaret. *Basque Gender Studies*. Reno: Center for Basque Studies, University of Nevada, Reno, 2009.

Burton, Richard F. *The Book of the Sword*. Mineola, NY: Dover, 1987.

Butler, Samuel. *Hudibras by Samuel Butler; with Dr. Grey's Annotations. In Three Volumes*, Volume 3. Charles & Henry Baldwyn: London, 1819.

Byock, Jesse. *The Saga of the Volsungs*. London: Penguin, 1999.

Byock, Jesse L. *The Prose Edda*. London: Penguin UK, 2005.

Byock, Jesse L. *Saga of King Hrolf Kraki*. London: Penguin UK, 2005.

Cakrabarti, Bish⬛upada. *The Penguin Companion to the Ramayana*. New York: Penguin Books, 2006.

Calloway, Colin Gordon, and Frank W. Porter. *The Abenaki*. New York: Chelsea House Publishers, 1989.

Calmet, Augustin. *Calmet's Great Dictionary of the Holy Bible*. Charlestown, MA: Samuel Etheridge, 1813.

Campbell, John Gregorson. *Witchcraft & Second Sight in the Highlands & Islands of Scotland*. Glaswog: James MacLenose and Sons, 1902.

Campbell, Trenton, editor. *Gods and Goddesses of Ancient China*. New York: Encyclopaedia Britannica Educational, 2014.

Carlyon-Brotton, P. W. P., L. A. Lawrence, and W. J. Andrew, editors. *The British Numismatic Journal: Including the Proceedings of the British Numismatic Society*, Volume 1. London: British Numismatic Society, 1905.

Caro, Ina. *The Road from the Past: Traveling through History in France*. San Diego: Harcourt Brace, 1996.

Cavanaugh, T.A. *Hippocrates' Oath and Asclepius' Snake: The Birth of the Medical Profession*. New York: Oxford University Press, 2017.

Chambers's Encyclopaedia: A Dictionary of Universal Knowledge, Volume 10. London: Lippincott, 1912.

Chambers, Raymond Wilson. *Beowulf: An Introduction to the Study of the Poem with a Discussion of the Stories of Offa and Finn*. Cambridge: Cambridge University Press, 1921.

Champlin, John Denison. *The Young Folks' Cyclopædia of Literature and Art*. New York: Henry Holt and Company, 1901.

Chappell, Paul K. *The Art of Waging Peace: A Strategic Approach to Improving Our Lives and the World*. Westport, CT: Prospecta Press, 2013.

Charak, K. S. *Surya, the Sun God*. Delhi: Institute of Vedic Astrology, 1999.

Chaturvedi, B.K. *Kalki Purana*. New Delhi: Diamond Pocket Books, 2003.

Child, Clarence Griffin, editor. *Beowulf and the Finnesburh Fragment*. Boston: Houghton, Mifflin, 1904.

Childress, David Hatcher. *The Anti-Gravity Handbook*. Kempton, IL: Adventures Unlimited Press, 2003.

Childress, David Hatcher. *Vimana: Aircraft of Ancient India & Atlantis*. Kempton, IL: Adventures Unlimited Press, 1994.

Childress, David Hatcher. *Vimana: Flying Machines of the Ancients*. Kempton, IL: SCB Distributors, 2013.

Chisholm, Hugh, editor. "Baetylus." In *Encyclopedia Britannica 3*, 11th edition. Cambridge: Cambridge University Press, 1911.

Chopra, Ramesh. *Academic Dictionary of Mythology*. New Delhi: Gyan Books, 2005.

Churton, Tobias. *Gnostic Philosophy: From Ancient Persia to Modern Times*. New York: Simon & Schuster, 2005.

Cicero, Marcus. *Cicero's Tusculan Disputations*. Moscow: LitRes, 2018.

Cicero, Marcus. *M. Tully Cicero's Five Books of Tusculan Disputations, Done into English by a Gentleman of Christ Church College, Oxford.* London: Jonas Brown, 1715.

Clare, Israel Smith. *Mediaeval History.* New York: Union Book Company, 1906.

Clark, Nora. *Aphrodite and Venus in Myth and Mimesis.* Cambridge: Cambridge Scholars Publishing, 2015.

Classen, Albrecht. *Magic and Magicians in the Middle Ages and the Early Modern Time: The Occult in Pre-Modern Sciences, Medicine, Literature, Religion, and Astrology.* Boston: Walter de Gruyter, 2017.

Clauss, James J., and Sarah Iles Johnston. *Medea: Essays on Medea in Myth, Literature, Philosophy, and Art.* Princeton, NJ: Princeton University Press, 1997.

Cobb, Mary S., editor. *The Nibelungenlied.* Boston: Small, Maynard, and Company, 1906.

Codrington, Robert Henry. *The Melanesians: Studies in Their Anthropology and Folk-lore.* London: Clarendon Press, 1891.

Colum, Padraic. *The Children of Odin.* New York: Macmillan, 1920.

Colum, Padraic. *Nordic Gods and Heroes.* Mineola, NY: Dover, 2012.

Condos, Theony. *Star Myths of the Greeks and Romans: A Sourcebook.* Grand Rapids, MI: Red Wheel/Weiser, 1997.

Conley, Craig. *Magic Words: A Dictionary.* San Francisco: Weiser Books, 2008.

Conway, D. J. *Dancing with Dragons: Invoke Their Ageless Wisdom and Power.* St. Paul, MN: Llewellyn Worldwide, 1994.

Conway, D. J. *Maiden, Mother, Crone: The Myth and Reality of the Triple Goddess.* St. Paul, MN: Llewellyn Worldwide, 1994.

Coolidge, Olivia E. *Greek Myths.* Boston: Houghton Mifflin Harcourt, 2001.

Corley, Corin. *Lancelot of the Lake.* Oxford: Oxford University Press, 2000.

Cornell, Vincent J. *Voices of Islam: Voices of Life: Family, Home, and Society.* Westport, CT: Greenwood Publishing Group, 2007.

Cotterell, Arthur. *A Dictionary of World Mythology.* New York:G. P. Putman's Sons, 1980.

Cotterell, Maurice. *The Lost Tomb of Viracocha: Unlocking the Secrets of the Peruvian Pyramids.* New York: Simon & Schuster, 2003.

Coulter, Charles Russell, and Patricia Turner. *Encyclopedia of Ancient Deities.* Oxon: Routledge, 2013.

Coulter-Harris, Deborah M. *Chasing Immortality in World Religions.* Jefferson, NC: McFarland, 2016.

Courthope, William John. *The Marvellous History of King Arthur in Avalon: And of the Lifting of Lyonnesse. A Chronicle of the Round Table.* London: J. Murray, 1904.

Cox, George William. *Popular Romances of the Middle Ages, by G. W. Cox and E.H. Jones.* London: Kegan Paul, 1880.

Cox, George William, and Eustace Hinton Jones. *Popular Romances of the Middle Ages.* London: Longmans, Green, 1871.

Cox, George William, and Eustace Hinton Jones. *Tales of the Teutonic Lands.* London: Longmans, Green, 1872.

Craig, Robert D. *Dictionary of Polynesian Mythology.* New York: Greenwood Press, 1989.

Craigie, William Alexander. *Scandinavian Folk-lore: Illustrations of the Traditional Beliefs of the Northern Peoples.* Detroit, MI: Singing Tree Press, 1970.

Creeden, Sharon. *Fair Is Fair: World Folktales of Justice.* Little Rock, AR: August House, 1994.

Crisologo, Jonalyn, and John Davidson. *Egyptian Mythology—Ancient Gods and Goddesses of the World.* Mendon: Mendon Cottage Books, 2015.

Crooke, William. *The Popular Religion and Folk-Lore of Northern India,* Volume 2. Westminster: Archibald Constable and Company, 1896.

Crossley-Holland, Kevin. *The Norse Myths.* New York: Knopf Doubleday Publishing Group, 2012.

Crowther, Nigel B. *Sport in Ancient Times.* Westport, CT: Greenwood Publishing Group, 2007.

Crump, Marty, and Danté Bruce Fenolio. *Eye of Newt and Toe of Frog, Adder's Fork and Lizard's Leg: The Lore and Mythology of Amphibians and Reptiles.* Chicago: University of Chicago Press, 2015.

Curley, Michael J. *Physiologus: A Medieval Book of Nature Lore.* Chicago: University of Chicago Press, 1979.

Curran, Bob. *A Haunted Mind: Inside the Dark, Twisted World of H. P. Lovecraft.* Grand Rapids, MI: Red Wheel/Weiser, 2012.

Curtin, Jeremiah. *Myths and Folk-lore of Ireland.* Boston: Little, Brown, 1889.

Dalal, Roshen. *Hinduism: An Alphabetical Guide.* London: Penguin, 2014.

Dalal, Roshen. *Religions of India: A Concise Guide to the Nine Major Faiths.* London: Penguin, 2014.

Dallapiccola, Anna L. *Dictionary of Hindu Lore and Legend.* London: Thames & Hudson, 2002.

Dallapiccola, Anna Libera, and Anila Verghese. *Sculpture at Vijayanagara: Iconography and Style.* New Delhi: Manohar Publishers and Distributors for American Institute of Indian Studies, 1998.

Daly, Kathleen N. *Norse Mythology A to Z.* New York: Facts on File, 2009.

Daly, Kathleen N., and Marian Rengel. *Greek and Roman Mythology, A to Z.* New York: Infobase Publishing, 2009.

Daniel, Signet Il Y' Viavia. *The Akshaya Patra Series Manasa Bhajare: Worship in the Mind Part One.* Philadelphia: Xlibris, 2015.

Daniels, Cora Linn, and C. M. Stevens. *Encyclopedia of Superstitions, Folklore, and the Occult Sciences,* Volume 2. Honolulu, HI: University Press of the Pacific, 1903.

Daniels, Cora Linn, and C. M. Stevens. *Encyclopaedia of Superstitions, Folklore, and the Occult Sciences of the World: A Comprehensive Library of Human Belief and Practice in the Mysteries of Life,* Volume 2. Wisconson: J. H. Yewdale and Sons, Company, 1914.

Daniels, Cora Linn, and C. M. Stevens. *Encyclopedia of Superstitions, Folklore, and the Occult Sciences of the World,* Volume 2. Doral: Minerva Group, 2003.

Daniels, Cora Linn (Morrison), and Charles McClellan Stevens. *Encyclopedia of Superstitions, Folklore, and the Occult Sciences of the World: A Comprehensive Library of Human Belief and Practice in the Mysteries of Life.* Milwaukee: J.H. Yewdale and Sons Company, 1903.

Bibliography

Darmawan, Apollinaris. *Six Ways toward God*. Houston: Strategic Book Publishing, 2011.

Dasent, George Webbe. *Jest and Earnest: A Collection of Essays and Reviews*, Volume 2. London: Chapman and Hall, 1873.

Dasent, George Webbe. *The Story of Burnt Njal: From the Icelandic of the Njals Saga*. London: Grant Richards, 1900.

Dasent, George Webbe, editor. *The Story of Gisli the Outlaw*. Edinburgh: Edmonston and Douglas, 1866.

Davidson, Hilda Roderick Ellis. *Myths and Symbols in Pagan Europe: Early Scandinavian and Celtic Religions*. Syracuse, NY: Syracuse University Press, 1988.

Davidson, Hilda Roderick Ellis. *The Sword in Anglo-Saxon England: Its Archaeology and Literature*. Woodbridge: Boydel Press, 1962.

Davis, Graeme. *Knights Templar: A Secret History*. New York: Bloomsbury, 2013.

Dawood, N. J. *Aladdin and Other Tales from the Arabian Nights*. London: Puffin Books, 1982.

Day, David. *Tolkien's Ring*. London: Pavilion Books, 2012.

Day, Samuel Phillips. *The Rare Romance of Reynard the Fox, the Crafty Courtier: Together with the Shifts of His Son, Reynardine, in Words of One Syllable*. London: Cassell, Petter, and Galpin, 1870.

de Beaumont, Édouard, and Alfred Richard Allinson. *The Sword and Womankind: Being a Study of the Influence of "The Queen of Weapons" upon the Moral and Social Status of Women*. London: Society of British Bibliophiles, 1900.

de Genlis, Stéphanie Félicité comtesse. *Tales of the Castle: Or, Stories of Instruction and Delight. Being Les Veillées de Chateau*, Volume 3. Translated by Thomas Holcroft. London: G. G. J. and J. Robinson, 1798.

de Sanctis, translator. *Reynard the Fox*. London: W. S. Sonnenschein and Company, 1885.

de Santillana, Giorgio, and Hertha von Dechend. *Hamlet's Mill: An Essay on Myth and the Frame of Time*. Boston: David R. Godine Publisher, 1977.

de Visser, Marinus Willem. *The Dragon in China and Japan*. New York: Comico Classics, 2006.

Debroy, Bibek, translator. *The Mahabharata*, Volume 5. London: Penguin UK, 2015.

Dekirk, Ash. *Dragonlore: From the Archives of the Grey School of Wizardry*. Grand Rapids, MI: Red Wheel/Weiser, 2006.

Dennis, Geoffrey W. *The Encyclopedia of Jewish Myth, Magic and Mysticism*, 2nd edition. St. Paul, MN: Llewellyn Worldwide, 2016.

Depping, Georges-Bernard. *Wayland Smith: From the German of Oehleschaläger*. London: William Pickering, 1847.

Dhalla, Maneckji Nusserwanji. *History of Zoroastrianism*. New York: Oxford University Press, 1938.

Dieffenbach, Ernst. *Travels in New Zealand: With Contributions to the Geography, Geology, Botany, and Natural History of That Country*, Volume 2. London: Murray, 1843.

Diogenes the Cynic. *Sayings and Anecdotes: With Other Popular Moralists*. New York: Oxford University Press, 2012.

Dixon, Jeffrey John. *The Glory of Arthur: The Legendary King in Epic Poems of Layamon, Spenser and Blake*. Jefferson, NC: McFarland, 2014.

Dixon-Kennedy, Mike. *Encyclopedia of Greco-Roman Mythology*. Santa Barbara, CA: ABC-CLIO, 1998.

Dixon-Kennedy, Mike. *Encyclopedia of Russian & Slavic Myth and Legend*. Santa Barbara, CA: ABC-CLIO, 1998.

Dodds, Jeramy, translator. *The Poetic Edda*. Toronto: Coach House Books, 2014.

Dole, Nathan Haskell. *Young Folks' History of Russia*. Boston: Estes and Lauriat, 1881.

Dom, David. *King Arthur and the Gods of the Round Table*. Morrisville: Lulu.com, 2013.

Dong, Lan. *Asian American Culture: From Anime to Tiger Moms*, 2 volumes. Santa Barbara, CA: ABC-CLIO, 2016.

Doniger, Wendy. *Merriam-Webster's Encyclopedia of World Religions*. Springfield, MA: Merriam-Webster, 2000.

Doniger, Wendy. *The Ring of Truth: And Other Myths of Sex and Jewelry*. Oxford: Oxford University Press, 2017.

Dooley, Ann, and Harry Roe, editors. *Acallam Na Senorach*. Oxford: Oxford University Press, 1999.

Dowson, John. *A Classical Dictionary of Hindu Mythology and Religion, Geography, History, and Literature*. London: Trubner and Company, 1870.

Draaisma, D. *Metaphors of Memory: A History of Ideas about the Mind*. Cambridge: Cambridge University Press, 2000.

Draco, Melusine. *The Dictionary of Magic and Mystery*. Lanham, MD: John Hunt Publishing, 2012.

Drury, Nevill. *The Dictionary of the Esoteric: 3000 Entries on the Mystical and Occult Traditions*. Delhi: Motilal Banarsidass, 2004.

Dubois, Jean Antoine, Carrie Chapman Catt, and Henry K. Beauchamp. *Hindu Manners, Customs and Ceremonies: The Classic First Hand Account of India in the Early Nineteenth Century*. Mineola, NY: Dover, 2002.

Duda, Margaret B. *Traditional Chinese Toggles*. Singapore: Editions Didier Millet, 2011.

Dudley, Louise. *The Egyptian Elements in the Legend of the Body and Soul*. Baltimore: J. H. Furst Company, 1911.

Dudley, Marion Vienna Churchill. *Poetry and Philosophy of Goethe*. Chicago: S.C. Griggs & Company, 1887.

Dudley, William. *Unicorns*. San Diego: Reference Point Press, 2008.

Dunham, S. A. *The Cabinet Cyclopaedia*, Volume 26. London: Longman, Rees, Orme, Brown and Green, 1839.

Dunham, Samuel Astley. *History of Denmark, Sweden, and Norway*, Volume 2. London: Longman, Orme, Brown, Green and Longmans and John Taylor, 1839.

Dutt, Manmatha Nath, editor. *A Prose English Translation of Srimadbhagavatam*, Volumes 8–12. Calcutta: Elysium Press, 1896.

Eason, Cassandra. *Fabulous Creatures, Mythical Monsters, and Animal Power Symbols: A Handbook*. Westport, CT: Greenwood Publishing Group, 2008.

Eccles, John. *Rinaldo and Armida*. Middleton: A-R Editions, 2011.

Eddison, E. R. *Egil's Saga: Done into English Out of the Icelandic with an Introduction, Notes, and an Essay on Some Principles of Translation.* Cambridge: Cambridge University Press Archive, 1970.

Eddy, Steve, and Claire Hamilton. *Understand Greek Mythology.* London: Hodder & Stoughton, 2012.

Edizioni, Enigma. *Vimanas and the Wars of the Gods: The Rediscovery of a Lost Civilization, of a Forgotten Science and of an Ancient Lore of India and Pakistan.* Firenze, Italy: Enigma Edizioni, 2016.

Edmison, John P. *Stories from the Norseland.* Philadelphia: Penn Publishing Company, 1909.

Edwards, Gillian Mary. *Hobgoblin and Sweet Puck: Fairy Names and Natures.* London: Geoffrey Bles, 1974.

Eickhoff, Randy Lee. *The Red Branch Tales.* New York: Tom Doherty Associates, 2003.

Eliasson, Stig, and Ernst H. Jahr, editors. *Language and Its Ecology: Essays in Memory of Einar Haugen.* Berlin: Walter de Gruyter, 1997.

Elliot, A. Marshall, editor. *Modern Language Notes.* Baltimore: Johns Hopkins Press, 1910.

Ellis, George. *Specimens of Early English Metrical Romances: Saxon Romances: Guy of Warwick. Sir Bevis of Hamptoun. Anglo-Norman Romance: Richard Cœur de Lion. Romances Relating to Charlemagne: Roland and Ferragus. Sir Otuel. Sir Ferumbras.* London: Longman, Hurst, Rees, Orme, and Brown, 1811.

Ellis, Peter. *The Mammoth Book of Celtic Myths and Legends.* London: Constable and Robinson, 1999.

Ellis, Peter Berresford. *A Brief History of the Druids.* New York: Running Press, 2002.

Ellis, Peter Berresford. *Celtic Women: Women in Celtic Society and Literature.* Grand Rapids, MI: William B. Eerdmans, 1996.

Ellis, Peter Berresford. *The Chronicles of the Celts: New Tellings of Their Myths and Legends.* London: Robinson, 1999.

Ellis, Peter Berresford. *The Druids.* Grand Rapids, MI: William B. Eerdmans, 1994.

Erskine, Thomas. *The Brazen Serpent, Or Life Coming through Death.* Edinburgh: Waugh & Innes, 1831.

Evangelista, Nick. *The Encyclopedia of the Sword.* Westport, CT: Greenwood Publishing Group, 1995.

Evans, Bergen. *Dictionary of Mythology.* New York: Dell Publishing, 1970.

Evan-Wentz, Walter Yeeling. *The Fairy Faith in Celtic Countries: The Classic Study of Leprechauns, Pixies, and Other Fairy Spirits.* New York: Citadel Press, 1994.

Evslin, Bernard. *Bernard Evslin's Greek Mythology.* New York: Open Road Media, 2017. Evslin, Bernard. *Gods, Demigods, and Demons: An Encyclopedia of Greek Mythology.* New York: Scholastic, 1975.

Falkayn, David, editor. *Russian Fairy Tales.* Doral: Minerva Group, 2004.

Farmer, John Stephen. *Slang and Its Analogues Past and Present: A Dictionary, Historical and Comparative, of Heterodox Speech of All Classes of Society for More than Three Hundred Years with Synonyms in English, French, German, Italian, Etc., Compiled by J.S. Farmer and W.E. Henley,* Volume 4. N.pag.: Harrison and Sons, 1896.

Faulkes, Anthony, translator. *Edda.* London: Viking Society for Northern Society for Research, 1985.

Faulkes, Anthony. *Snorri Sturluson. Edda. Prologue and Gylfaginning.* London: Viking Society for Northern Research, 1982.

Fedrick, Alan S. *The Romance of Tristan: The Tale of Tristan's Madness.* London: Penguin UK, 2005.

Fee, Christopher R. *Gods, Heroes, & Kings: The Battle for Mythic Britain.* Oxford: Oxford University Press, 2001.

Fee, Christopher R., and Jeffrey B. Webb. *American Myths, Legends, and Tall Tales: An Encyclopedia of American Folklore,* Volume 1. Santa Barbara, CA: ABC-CLIO, 2016.

Feller, Danielle. *Sanskrit Epics.* Delhi: Motilal Banarsidass, 2004.

Ferdowsi, Abolqasem. *Shahnameh: The Persian Book of Kings.* New York: Penguin, 2016.

Figulus, Benedictus. *Book of the Revelation of Hermes Interpreted by Theophrastus Paracelsus Concerning the Supreme Secret of the World.* Whitefish, MT: Kessinger, 2010.

Fiore, John. *Symbolic Mythology: Interpretations of the Myths of Ancient Greece and Rome.* San Jose, CA: Writers Club Press, 2001.

Fisher, Burton D. *Wagner's The Ring of the Nibelung: Opera Classics Library Series.* Miami: Opera Journeys Publishing, 2005.

Folkard, Richard. *Plant Lore, Legends, and Lyrics: Embracing the Myths, Traditions, Superstitions, and Folk-lore of the Plant Kingdom.* London: Sampson Low, Marston, Searle, and Rivington, 1884.

Folklore and Its Artistic Transposition: Proceedings of the Scientific Assembly. Belgrade: Faculty of Music Arts, 1989.

Forlong, James George Roche. *Faiths of Man: A Cyclopaedia of Religions,* Volume 2. London: Bernard Quaritch, 1906.

Foster, Michael Dylan. *The Book of Yokai: Mysterious Creatures of Japanese Folklore.* Oakland: University of California Press, 2015.

Foster, Michael Dylan. *Pandemonium and Parade: Japanese Monsters and the Culture of Yokai.* Berkeley: University of California Press, 2008.

Fox, Robin Lane. *Alexander the Great.* London: Penguin UK, 2004.

Frankel, Valerie Estelle. *From Girl to Goddess: The Heroine's Journey through Myth and Legend.* Jefferson, NC: McFarland, 2010.

Frazer, James George. *Folk-lore in the Old Testament: Studies in Comparative Religion, Legend, and Law,* Volume 2. London: Macmillan, 1919.

Frazer, James George. *The Golden Bough: A Study in Magic and Religion,* Volume 2. London: Macmillan, 1911.

Freedman, David Noel, editor. *Eerdmans Dictionary of the Bible.* Grand Rapids, MI: William B. Eerdmans, 2000.

Friberg, Eino, George C. Schoolfield, and Bjorn Landstrom, editors. *The Kalevala.* Helsinki: Otava, 1988.

Friedmann, Jonathan L. *Music in Biblical Life: The Roles of Song in Ancient Israel.* Jefferson, NC: McFarland, 2013.

Bibliography

Fries, Jan. *Cauldron of the Gods: A Manual of Celtic Magick*. Oxford: Mandrake, 2003.

Frog, Anna-Leena Siikala, and Eila Stepanova. *Mythic Discourses: Studies in Uralic Traditions*. Helsinki: Finnish Literature Society, 2012.

Froud, Brian, and Alan Lee. *Faeries*. New York: Harry N. Abrams, 1978.

Froude, James Anthony. "Mystic Trees and Flowers." *Fraser's Magazine* 12 (1870): 590–608.

Fulton, Helen, editor. *A Companion to Arthurian Literature*. West Sussex: John Wiley and Sons, 2011.

Gallusz, Laszlo. *The Throne Motif in the Book of Revelation*. London: Bloomsbury, 2013.

Gandhi, Maneka. *Penguin Book of Hindu Names for Boys*. New Delhi: Penguin Books, 2004.

Ganelin, Charles, and Howard Mancing, editors. *The Golden Age Comedia: Text, Theory, and Performance*. West Lafayette, IN: Purdue University Press, 1994.

Gantz, Jeffrey. *Early Irish Myths and Sagas*. Harmondsworth: Penguin, 1986.

Garbaty, Thomas Jay. "The Fallible Sword: Inception of a Motif." *Journal of American Folklore* 75 (1962): 58–59.

Garber, Marjorie B., and Nancy J. Vickers, editors. *The Medusa Reader*. New York: Routledge, 2003.

Garbini, Giovanni. *Myth and History in the Bible*. New York: Sheffield Academic Press, 2003.

Gardner, Gerald B. *Keris and Other Malay Weapons*. London: Orchid Press, 2009.

Gardner, John, editor. *Gilgamesh*. New York: Knopf Doubleday Publishing Group, 1984.

Garg, Gaga Ram. *Encyclopaedia of the Hindu World*, Volume 1. New Delhi: Concept Publishing Company, 1992.

Garmonsway, G. N., editor. *An Early Norse Reader*. Cambridge: Cambridge University Press, 1928.

Garrett, John. *A Classical Dictionary of India: Illustrative of the Mythology, Philosophy, Literature, Antiquities, Arts, Manners, Customs, Etc., of the Hindus*. Madras: Higginbotham and Company, 1871.

Garry, Jane, and Hasan El-Shammy, editors. *Archetypes and Motifs in Folklore and Literature*. Armonk, NY: M. E. Sharpe, 2005.

Gaynor, Frank. *Dictionary of Mysticism*. New York: Open Road Media, 2018.

George, Arthur, and Elena George. *The Mythology of Eden*. Lanham, MD: Rowman & Littlefield, 2014.

Gerald, John. *The Herball or Generall Historie of Plantes*. London: Norton, John, 1597.

Gerritsen, Willem Pieter, and Anthony G. Van Melle, editors. *A Dictionary of Medieval Heroes: Characters in Medieval Narrative Traditions and Their Afterlife in Literature, Theatre and the Visual Arts*. Woodbridge: Boydell & Brewer, 2000.

Gerwig, Henrietta. *Crowell's Handbook for Readers and Writers: A Dictionary of Famous Characters and Plots in Legend, Fiction, Drama, Opera, and Poetry, Together with Dates and Principal Works of Important Authors, Literary and Journalistic Terms, and Familiar Allusions*. New York: Thomas Y. Crowell Company, 1925.

Gibbon, Edward. *The History of the Decline and Fall of the Roman Empire*, Volume 4. London: J. Murray, 1887.

Gilbert, Henry. *King Arthur's Knights: The Tales Retold for Boys and Girls*. New York: Fredrick A. Stokes Company, 1911.

Gilhuly, Kate, and Nancy Worman, editors. *Space, Place, and Landscape in Ancient Greek Literature and Culture*. Cambridge: Cambridge University Press, 2014.

Gohdes, Clarence Louis Frank. *American Literature: A Journal of Literary History, Criticism and Bibliography*, Volume 13. Durham, NC: Duke University Press, 1942.

Goller, Karl Heinz, editor. *The Alliterative Morte Arthure: A Reassessment of the Poem*. Suffolk: Boydell and Brewer, 1981.

Gonda, Jan. *Aspects of Early Visnuism*. Delhi: Motilal Banarsidass, 1993.

Goss, Michael. *Lost at Sea: Ghost Ships and Other Mysteries*. Amhurst, NY: Prometheus, 1996.

Gowan, Donald E. *Theology in Exodus: Biblical Theology in the Form of a Commentary*. Louisville, KY: Westminster John Knox Press, 1994.

Granada, Miguel A., Patrick J. Boner, and Dario Tessicini. *Unifying Heaven and Earth: Essays in the History of Early Modern Cosmology*. Barcelona: University of Barcelona, 2016.

Granger, Frank. *The Worship of the Romans: Viewed in Relation to the Roman Temperament*. London: Methuen, 1895.

Grant, Michael, and John Hazel. *Who's Who in Classical Mythology*. New York: Routledge, 2004.

Graves, Robert. *Greek Gods and Heroes*. New York: Robert Graves Foundation, 2014.

Graves, Robert. *The Greek Myths*. New York: G. Braziller, 1957.

Gray, Douglas. *Later Medieval English Literature*. New York: Oxford University Press, 2008.

Gray, Louis Herbert, George Foot Moore, and John Arnott MacCulloch, editors. *The Mythology of All Races*, Volume 2. Boston: Marshall Jones, 1930.

Gray, Louis Herbert, George Foot Moore, and John Arnott MacCulloch, editors. *The Mythology of All Races*, Volume 3. Boston: Marshall Jones, 1918.

Green, Miranda Jane. *Celtic Myths*. Austin: University of Texas Press, 1993.

Green, Roger. *Myths of the Norsemen*. New York: Puffin Classics, 2017.

Greenslet, Ferris. *The Quest of the Holy Grail: An Interpretation and a Paraphrase of the Holy Legends*. Boston: Curtis & Cameron, 1902.

Greer, John Michael. *The Druid Magic Handbook: Ritual Magic Rooted in the Living Earth*. San Francisco: Weiser Books, 2008.

Greer, John Michael. *The Secret of the Temple: Earth Energies, Sacred Geometry, and the Lost Keys of Freemasonry*. St. Paul, MN: Llewellyn Worldwide, 2016.

Gregory, Augusta, editor. *Cuchulain of Muirthemne: The Story of the Men of the Red Branch of Ulster*. London: J. Murray, 1903.

Gregory, Augusta, and Finn MacCumhaill. *Gods and Fighting Men: The Story of Tuatha de Danann and of the Fianna of Ireland*. London: John Murray, 1905.

Gribble, Francis. "The Alpine Dragon." *Strand Mag-*

azine, Volume 31, Issue 186–Volume 32, Issue 191 (1906): 569–74.

Grimassi, Raven. *Encyclopedia of Wicca & Witchcraft.* St. Paul, MN: Llewellyn, 2003.

Grimes, Heilan Yvette. *The Norse Myths.* Boston: Hollow Earth, 2010.

Grimm, Jacob. *Teutonic Mythology,* Volume 1. London: W. Swan Sonnenschein and Allen, 1880.

Guerber, H. A. *Hammer of Thor.* El Paso, TX: Norte Press, 2010.

Guerber, H. A. *The Myths of Greece and Rome.* Mineola, NY: Courier, 2012.

Guerber, H. A. *Myths of the Norsemen: From the Eddas and Sagas.* Mineola, NY: Dover, 1992.

Guerber, Hélène Adeline. *The Book of the Epic: The World's Great Epics Told in Story.* Philadelphia: J. B. Lippincott, 1913.

Guerber, Hélène Adeline. *Legends of the Middle Ages.* New York: American Book Company, 1896.

Guerber, Hélène Adeline. *Myths of the Norsemen from the Eddas and Sagas.* London: George G. Harp and Company, 1908.

Guerin, M. Victoria. *The Fall of Kings and Princes: Structure and Destruction in Arthurian Tragedy.* Stanford, CA: Stanford University Press, 1995.

Guiley, Rosemary. *The Encyclopedia of Magic and Alchemy.* New York: Infobase Publishing, 2006.

Guirand, Félix. *The Larousse Encyclopedia of Mythology.* New York: Barnes and Noble, 1994.

Haas, Nibodhi. *Rudraksha: Seeds of Compassion.* Kerala: M. A. Center, 2013.

Haase, Donald. *The Greenwood Encyclopedia of Folktales and Fairy Tales,* 3 volumes. Westport, CT: Greenwood Publishing Group, 2007.

Haeffner, Mark. *Dictionary of Alchemy: From Maria Prophetessa to Isaac Newton.* Wellingborough: Aquarian Press, 1991.

Hall, Fitzedward, editor. *The Vishnu Purana: A System of Hindu Mythology and Tradition,* Volume 3. London: Trubner and Company, 1864.

Hall, Jennie, William Morris, Arthur Gilchrist Brodeur, J. Lesslie Hall, and Snorri Sturluson. *Saga Six Pack.* Los Angeles: Enhanced Media, 2016.

Halliwell-Phillipps, James Orchard. *Torrent of Portugal: An English Metrical Romance. Now First Published from an Unique Manuscript of the Fifteenth Century, Preserved in the Chetham Library at Manchester.* London: John Russel Smith, 1842.

Hamilton, Edith. *Mythology: Timeless Tales of Gods and Heroes, 75th Anniversary Illustrated.* New York: Running Press, 2017.

Hammer, Olav, and Mikael Rothstein, editors. *Handbook of the Theosophical Current.* Leiden, Netherlands: Brill, 2013.

Hande, H. V., and Kampar. *Kamba Rāmāyanam: An English Prose Rendering.* Mumbai: Bharatiya Vidya Bhavan, 1996.

Hansen, William F. *Ariadne's Thread: A Guide to International Tales Found in Classical Literature.* Ithaca, NY: Cornell University Press, 2002.

Hansen, William F. *Classical Mythology: A Guide to the Mythical World of the Greeks and Romans.* Oxford: Oxford University Press, 2004.

Hansen, William F. *Handbook of Classical Mythology.* Santa Barbara, CA: ABC-CLIO, 2004.

Hanson, Charles Henry. *Stories of the Days of King Arthur.* London: T. Nelson, 1882.

Hard, Robin. *The Routledge Handbook of Greek Mythology: Based on H.J. Rose's "Handbook of Greek Mythology."* London: Psychology Press, 2004.

Harlow, William Burt. *An Introduction to Early English Literature: From the Lay of Beowulf to Edmund Spenser.* Syracuse, NY: C. W. Bardeen, 1884.

Harney, Michael, translator. *The Epic of the Cid: With Related Texts.* Indianapolis: Hackett, 2011.

Hart, George. *A Dictionary of Egyptian Gods and Goddesses.* London: Routledge, 2006.

Hart, George. *The Routledge Dictionary of Egyptian Gods and Goddesses.* London: Routledge, 2005.

Hartmann, Franz. *The Life and the Doctrines of Philippus Theophrastus, Bombast of Hohenheim, Known by the Name of Paracelsus: Extracted and Translated from His Rare and Extensive Works and from Some Unpublished Manuscripts.* New York: John W. Lovell Company, 1998.

The Harvard Encyclopedia: A Dictionary of Language Arts, Sciences, and General Literature, Volume 3. New York: Harvard Publishing Company, 1890.

Haslam, William. *The Cross and the Serpent: A Brief History of the Triumph of the Cross, through a Long Series of Ages, in Prophecy, Types, and Fulfilment.* Oxford: John Henry Parker, 1849.

Hassig, Debra, editor. *The Mark of the Beast: The Medieval Bestiary in Art, Life, and Literature.* New York: Garland, 1999.

Hassrick, Royal B. *The Sioux: Life and Customs of a Warrior Society.* Norman: University of Oklahoma Press, 2012.

Hastings, James, John Alexander Selbie, and Louis Herbert Gray. *Encyclopædia of Religion and Ethics: Hymns–Liberty.* New York: Charles Scribner's Sons, 1915.

Hastings, James, John Alexander Selbie, and Louis Herbert Gray, editors. *Encyclopædia of Religion and Ethics: Picts–Sacraments.* Edinburgh: T. & T. Clark, 1919.

Hatto, Arthur Thomas. *The Nibelungenlied: A New Translation.* New York: Penguin Books, 1969.

Hauck, Dennis William. *The Complete Idiot's Guide to Alchemy.* New York: Penguin, 2008.

Hauck, Dennis William. *The Emerald Tablet: Alchemy of Personal Transformation.* New York: Penguin, 1999.

Hawthorne, Simon. *Vikings: Viking Mythology: The Complete Guide to Viking Mythology and the Myths of Thor, Odin, and Loki.* Raleigh: Lulu.com, 2017.

Hayes, Kevin J. *Folklore and Book Culture.* Knoxville: University of Tennessee Press, 1997.

Heinrichs, Ann. *Juan Ponce de Leon Searches for the Fountain of Youth.* Minneapolis: Capstone, 2002.

Hennig, Kaye D. *King Arthur: Lord of the Grail.* Friday Harbor, WA: DesignMagic Publishing, 2008.

Herbert, Jean. *Shinto: At the Fountainhead of Japan.* New York: George Allen and Unwin, 1967.

Herodotus. *The Histories Book 3: Thaleia.* New York: Simon & Schuster, 2015.

Bibliography

Hesiod. *Hesiod's Theogony.* Translated by Richard S. Caldwell. Cambridge, MA: Focus Information Group, 1987.

Hiltebeitel, Alf. *Mythologies: From Gingee to Kuruketra.* Chicago: University of Chicago Press, 1988.

Hockney, Mike. *World, Underworld, Overworld, Dreamworld.* Miami: HyperReality Books, 2013.

Hodgetts, J. Frederick. "On the Scandinavian Elements in the English Race." *The Antiquary* 13–14 (1886): 137–43.

Hollander, Lee Milton, translator. *Heimskringla: History of the Kings of Norway.* Austin: University of Texas Press, 2007.

Holtom, Daniel Clarence. *The Political Philosophy of Modern Shinto: A Study of the State Religion of Japan.* Chicago: University of Chicago, 1922.

Homer. *Homer: Iliad,* Book 22. Edited by Irene J. F. De Jong. Cambridge: Cambridge University Press, 2012.

Homer. *The Iliad.* Translated by E. V. Rieu. New York: Penguin Classics, 1950.

Homer. *The Odyssey: A Tom Doherty Associates Book.* Translated by R. L. Eickhoff. New York: Macmillan, 2001.

Hooke, Samuel Henry. *Middle Eastern Mythology.* Mineola, NY: Dover, 2004.

Hopkins, Edward Washburn. *The Social and Military Position of the Ruling Caste in Ancient India: As Represented by the Sanskrit Epic; with an Appendix on the Status of Woman.* New Haven, CT: Bharat-Bharati, 1889.

Houtsma, Martijn Theodoor, Thomas Walker Arnold, René Basset, Richard Hartmann, Arent Jan Wensinck, Willi Heffening, Évariste Lévi-Provencal, and Hamilton Alexander Rosskeen Gibb, editors. *The Encyclopaedia of Islam: A Dictionary of the Geography, Ethnography and Biography of the Muhammadan Peoples,* Volume 4. Leiden, Netherlands: E. J. Brill, 1934.

Howey, M. Oldfield. *The Horse in Magic and Myth.* London: William Rider and Son, 1923.

Hreik, Haret. *Hercules: Volume 8 of Young Reader's Classics.* Beirut: Dreamland, 2016.

Huang, Martin W., editor. *Snakes' Legs: Sequels, Continuations, Rewritings, and Chinese Fiction.* Honolulu: University of Hawaii Press, 2004.

Hubbs, Joanna. *Mother Russia: The Feminine Myth in Russian Culture.* Bloomington: Indiana University Press, 1993.

Huber, Michael. *Mythematics: Solving the Twelve Labors of Hercules.* Princeton, NJ: Princeton University Press, 2009.

Hudson, D. Dennis. *The Body of God: An Emperor's Palace for Krishna in Eighth-Century Kanchipuram.* Oxford: Oxford University Press, 2008.

Hughes, Thomas Patrick. *A Dictionary of Islam: Being a Cyclopoedia of the Doctrines, Rites, Ceremonies, and Customs, Together with the Technical and Theological Terms, of the Muhammadan Religion.* London: W. H. Allen and Company, 1896.

Humez, Alexander, and Nicholas Humez. *On the Dot: The Speck That Changed the World.* Oxford: Oxford University Press, 2008.

Hunger, Rosa. *The Magic of Amber.* Philadelphia: Chilton Book Company, 1979.

Hunter, R. L. *The Argonautica of Apollonius.* Cambridge: Cambridge University Press, 2005.

Hunter, Robert, editor. *The American Dictionary and Cyclopedia,* Volume 12. New York: Dictionary and Cyclopedia Company, 1900.

Hyamson, Albert Montefiore. *A Dictionary of English Phrases: Phraseological Allusions, Catchwords, Stereotyped Modes of Speech and Metaphors, Nicknames, Sobriquets, Derivations from Personal Names, Etc., with Explanations and Thousands of Exact References to Their Sources or Early Usage.* London: Routledge, 1922.

Illes, Judika. *Encyclopedia of Spirits: The Ultimate Guide to the Magic of Fairies, Genies, Demons, Ghosts, Gods, and Goddesses.* New York: HarperCollins, 2009.

Immerzeel, Jacques van der Vliet, and Maarten Kersten, editors. *Coptic Studies on the Threshold of a New Millennium: Proceedings of the Seventh International Congress of Coptic Studies, Leiden, August 27–September 2, 2000,* Issue 1. Leuven, Belgium: Peeters, 2004.

Indick, William. *Ancient Symbology in Fantasy Literature: A Psychological Study.* Jefferson, NC: McFarland, 2012.

Irving, Washington. *Works of Washington Irving,* Volume 9. New York: Peter Fenelon Colloer and Sons, 1897.

Irwin, Terence. *Plato's Ethics.* Oxford: Oxford University Press, 1995.

Isaacs, Ronald H. *Animals in Jewish Thought and Tradition.* Northvale, NJ: Jason Aronson, 2000.

Ish-Kishor, Sulamith. *The Carpet of Solomon: A Hebrew Legend.* New York: Pantheon Books, 1966.

Iyer, G.S. *Bhasa: Complete Works.* Kottayam: Wink, 2008.

Jacobs, Joseph. *English Fairy Tales.* New York: Crowell, 1978.

Jacobs, Joseph, Alfred Trubner Nutt, Arthur Robinson Wright, and William Crooke, editors. *Folk Lore,* Volume 4. London: David Nutt, 1893.

Jacobs, Joseph, Alfred Trubner Nutt, Arthur Robinson Wright, and William Crooke, editors. *Folk Lore,* Volume 10. London: David Nutt, 1899.

Jah, Muhammad Husain. *Hoshruba: The Land and the Tilism.* Brooklyn, NY: Urdu Project, 2009.

Jakobson, Roman. *Word and Language.* Boston: Walter de Gruyter/Mouton, 1971.

Jameson, Robert, editor. *Edinburgh New Philosophical Journal, October to April* 32 (1842).

Janik, Erika. *Apple: A Global History.* London: Reaktion Books, 2011.

Javeed, Alī Jāvīd, and Tabassum. *World Heritage Monuments and Related Edifices in India,* Volume 1. New York: Algora Publishing, 2008.

Jeffrey, David L. *A Dictionary of Biblical Tradition in English Literature.* Grand Rapids, MI: William B. Eerdmans, 1992.

Jennbert, Kristina. *Animals and Humans: Recurrent Symbiosis in Archaeology and Old Norse Religion.* Lund: Nordic Academic Press, 2011.

Jennings, Pete. *Pagan Portals—Blacksmith Gods: Myths, Magicians, & Folklore.* Alresford, UK: Moon books, 2014.

The Jewish Encyclopedia, Volume 2. New York: Funk and Wagnalls, 1925.

Jiriczek, Otto Luitpold. *Northern Hero Legends.* London: J. M. Dent, 1902.

Jobes, Gertrude. *Dictionary of Mythology, Folklore, and Symbols,* Part 1. Lanham, MD: Scarecrow Press, 1962.

Jobes, Gertrude. *Dictionary of Mythology, Folklore, and Symbols,* Part 2. Lanham, MD: Scarecrow Press, 1962.

Johns, Andreas. *Baba Yaga: The Ambiguous Mother and Witch of the Russian Folktale.* New York: Peter Lang, 2004.

Johnson, Buffie. *Lady of the Beasts: The Goddess and Her Sacred Animals.* Rochester, VT: Inner Traditions International, 1994.

Johnson, Samuel. *A Dictionary of the English Language: In Which the Words Are Deduced from Their Originals; and Illustrated in Their Different Significations, by Examples from the Best Writers: Together with a History of the Language, and an English Grammar,* Volume 2. London: Longman, Hurst, Rees, Orme, and Brown, 1818.

Jones, Charles W. *Medieval Literature in Translation.* Mineola, NY: Courier, 2016.

Jones, Steven Swann. *The New Comparative Method: Structural and Symbolic Analysis of the Allomotifs of "Snow White."* Helsinki, Finland: Suomalainen Tiedeakatemia, 1990.

Jones, T., and G. Jones. *The Mabinogion.* London: Dent, 1949.

Jones, William. *Finger-ring Lore: Historical, Legendary, & Anecdotal.* London: Chatto & Windus, 1898.

Jordanes. *The Origin and Deeds of the Goths: In English Version.* Princeton, NJ: Princeton University Press, 1908.

Journal of Indian History, Volumes 13–14. Department of Modern Indian History, 1935.

Joyce, Patrick Weston. *Old Celtic Romances.* London: C. Kegan Paul & Company, 1879.

Joyce, Patrick Weston. *A Smaller Social History of Ancient Ireland: Treating the Government, Military System and Law, Religion, Learning and Art, Trades, Industries and Commerce, Manners, Customs and Domestic Life of the Ancient Irish People.* London: Longmans, Green and Company, 1908.

Jung, Emma, and Marie-Luise von Franz. *The Grail Legend.* Princeton, NJ: Princeton University Press, 1998.

Kaldera, Raven. *The Pathwalker's Guide to the Nine Worlds.* Hubbardston, MA: Asphodel Press, 2013.

Kammer, Reinhard. *Zen and Confucius in the Art of Swordsmanship: The "Tengu-geijutsu-ron" of Chozan Shissai.* New York: Routledge, 2016.

Kane, Njord. *The Vikings: The Story of a People.* Yukon: Spangenhelm Publishing, 2015.

Karr, Phyllis Ann. *The Arthurian Companion.* Oakland, CA: Green Knight, 2001.

Kauffmann, Friedrich. *Northern Mythology.* London: Norwood Editions, 1903.

Kaur, Madanjit. *The Regime of Maharaja Ranjit Singh.* Chandigarh: Unistar Books, 2008.

Kay, Christian J., Carole A. Hough, and Irené Wotherspoon, editors. *New Perspectives on English Historical Linguistics: Selected Papers from 12 ICEHL, Glasgow, 21–26 August 2002. Volume II: Lexis and Transmission.* Amsterdam: John Benjamins Publishing Company, 2002.

Kayme, Sargent. *Anting-Anting Stories: And Other Strange Tales of the Filipinos.* North Charleston: CreateSpace Independent Publishing Platform, 2017.

Keary, Annie, and Eliza Keary. *Tales of the Norse Warrior Gods: The Heroes of Asgard.* Mineola, NY: Courier, 2012.

Keightley, Thomas. *The Fairy Mythology by Thomas Keightley.* London: H. G. Bohn, 1860.

Keightley, Thomas. *The Fairy Mythology Illustrative of the Romance and Superstition of Various Countries.* London: George Bell and Sons, 1905.

Keightley, Thomas. *The Mythology of Ancient Greece and Italy.* London: George Bell and Sons, 1877.

Keightley, Thomas. *The World Guide to Gnomes, Fairies, Elves, and Other Little People.* New York: Random House Value Publishing, 1878.

Kelly, Douglas. *The Romances of Chretien de Troyes: A Symposium.* Lexington, KY: French Forum Publishers, 1985.

Kelly, Tim. *The Magical Lamp of Aladdin.* Denver, CO: Pioneer Drama Service, 1993.

Kerenyi, Karl. *The Gods of the Greeks.* London: Thames and Hudson, 1951.

Kerven, Rosalind. *Viking Myths and Sagas: Retold from Ancient Norse Texts.* Morpeth, Northumberland: Talking Stone, 2015.

Keyser, Jacob Rudolph. *The Religion of the Northmen.* Translated by B. Pennock. London: Turbner and Company, 1854.

Khan, Nahar Akbar. *The Malay Ancient Kingdoms: My Journey to the Ancient World of Nusantara.* Singapore: Partridge Publishing, 2017.

Khan, Ruhail. *Who Killed Kasheer?* Chetpet Chennai: Notion Press, 2017.

Kibler, William W., and R. Barton Palmer, editors. *Medieval Arthurian Epic and Romance: Eight New Translations.* Jefferson, NC: McFarland, 2014.

Kimbrough, Keller, and Haruo Shirane, editors. *Monsters, Animals, and Other Worlds: A Collection of Short Medieval Japanese Tales.* New York: Columbia University Press, 2018.

Kinahan, Frank. *Yeats, Folklore, and Occultism: Contexts of the Early Work and Thought.* London: Unwin Hyman, 1988.

Kingshill, Sophia. *The Fabled Coast: Legends: Legends and Traditions from Around the Shores of Britain and Ireland.* New York: Random House, 2012.

Kinsella, Thomas, and Louis Le Brocquy, editors. *The Tain: From the Irish Epic Tain Bo Cualinge.* Oxford: Oxford University Press, 2002.

Kirk, Shoshanna. *Greek Myths: Tales of Passion, Heroism, and Betrayal.* San Francisco: Chronicle Books, 2012.

Kittredge, George Lyman, and the Bodleian Library. *Arthur and Gorlagon.* Boston: Ginn, 1903.

Knappert, Jan. *African Mythology: An Encyclopedia of Myth and Legend.* Berkeley, CA: Diamond Books, 1995.

Bibliography

Knappert, Jan. *Bantu Myths and Other Tales.* Leiden, Netherlands: Brill Archive, 1977.

Knappert, Jan. *Indian Mythology: An Encyclopedia of Myth and Legend.* Wellingborough: Aquarian Press, 1991.

Knappert, Jan. *Myths and Legends of the Congo.* London: Heinemann Educational Books, 1971.

Knappert, Jan. *Pacific Mythology: An Encyclopedia of Myth and Legend.* Wellingborough: Aquarian Press, 1992.

Knight, Gareth. *The Secret Tradition in Arthurian Legend.* Cheltenham: Skylight Press, 1983.

Knott, Eleanor, editor. *Togail Bruidne Da Derga.* Dublin: Institute for Advanced Studies, 1936.

Knowles, James. *The Legends of King Arthur and His Knights.* Munich: BookRix, 2018.

Koch, John T., editor. *Celtic Culture: A–Celti.* Santa Barbara, CA: ABC-CLIO, 2006.

Koch, John T., editor. *Celtic Culture: G–L.* Santa Barbara, CA: ABC-CLIO, 2006.

Koch, John T., and John Carey, editors. *The Celtic Heroic Age.* Andover: Celtic Studies Publications, 2000.

Koehler, Elisa. *A Dictionary for the Modern Trumpet Player.* Lanham, MD: Scarecrow Press, 2015.

Konstantinou, Ariadne. *Female Mobility and Gendered Space in Ancient Greek Myth.* London: Bloomsbury, 2018.

Koontz, Rex, Kathryn Reese-Taylor, and Annabeth Headrick. *Landscape and Power in Ancient Mesoamerica.* Boulder, CO: Westview Press, 2001.

Kosambi, Meera, editor. *Intersections: Socio-cultural Trends in Maharashtra.* Hyderabad: Orient Blackswan, 2000.

Kotru, Umesh, and Ashutosh Zutshi. *Karna: The Unsung Hero of the Mahabharata.* Mumbai: Leadstart Publishing, 2015.

Kozlowski, Frances, and Chris Jackson. *Driven by the Divine.* Bloomington, IN: Balboa Press, 2013.

Kozminsky, Isidore. *Crystals, Jewels, Stones: Magic & Science.* Lake Worth, FL: Ibis Press, 2012.

Kramer, Samuel N. *Sumerian Mythology: A Study of Spiritual and Literary Achievement in the Third Millennium B.C.* Philadelphia: University of Pennsylvania Press, 1972.

Kramrisch, Stella. *The Presence of Siva.* Delhi: Motilal Banarsidass, 1988.

Krishna, Nanditha. *The Book of Vishnu.* New York: Penguin Books India, 2010.

Krober, A. L. "Tales of the Smith Sound Eskimo." *Journal of American Folk-lore* 7 (1898): 166–82.

Kugler, Paul. *The Alchemy of Discourse: Image, Sound, and Psyche.* Einsiedeln, Switzerland: Daimon Verlag, 2002.

Kulkarni, Shripad Dattatraya. *The Epics: Ramayana and Mahabharata.* Bhishma: Shri Bhagavan Vedavyasa Itihasa Samsodhana Mandira, 1992.

Kumar, Bharat. *An Incredible War: IAF in Kashmir War, 1947–1948.* New Delhi: KW Publishers, 2013.

Kuntz, George F. *Rings for the Finger.* Mineola, NY: Dover, 1973.

Lacy, Norris J. *Lancelot-Grail: The Story of Merlin.* Cambridge: Boydell & Brewer, 2010.

Lacy, Norris J., and James J. Wilhelm, editors. *The Romance of Arthur: An Anthology of Medieval Texts in Translation.* London: Routledge, 2015.

Lacy, Norris J., Geoffrey Ashe, and Debra N. Mancoff. *The Arthurian Handbook,* 2nd edition. New York: Garland, 1997.

Lacy, Norris J., Geoffrey Ashe, Sandra Ness Ihle, Marianne E. Kalinke, and Raymond H. Thompson. *The New Arthurian Encyclopedia: New Edition.* New York: Routledge, 2013.

Lambdin, Laura C., and Robert T. Lambdin, editors. *Arthurian Writers: A Biographical Encyclopedia.* Westport, CT: Greenwood Press, 2008.

Lane, Edward William. *The Manners and Customs of the Modern Egyptians.* London: J. M. Dent, 1908.

Lane, Edward William, editor. *Selections from the Kur-án Commonly Called in England, the Koran, with an Interwoven Commentary; Translated from the Arabic, Methodically Arranged, and Illustrated by Notes, to Which Is Prefixed an Introduction Taken from Sale's Preliminary Discourse, with Corrections and Additions by Edward William Lane.* London: James Modden, 1843.

Lanfranchi, Edalfo. *Chintamani or Moldavite.* Berlin: Little French Ebooks, 2017.

Lang, Jeanie. *A Book of Myths.* N.pag.: Library of Alexandria, 1914.

Larrington, Carolyne, Judy Quinn, and Brittany Schorn, editors. *A Handbook to Eddic Poetry: Myths and Legends of Early Scandinavia.* Cambridge: Cambridge University Press, 2016.

Larson, Gerald James, C. Scott Littleton, and Jaan Puhvel, editors. *Myth in Indo-European Antiquity.* Berkeley: University of California Press, 1974.

Layman, Dale. *Medical Terminology Demystified.* New York: McGraw-Hill Professional, 2007.

Lecouteux, Claude. *The Return of the Dead: Ghosts, Ancestors, and the Transparent Veil of the Pagan Mind.* New York: Simon & Schuster, 2009.

Lee, Jonathan H. X., and Kathleen M. Nadeau, editors. *Encyclopedia of Asian American Folklore and Folklife,* Volume 1. Santa Barbara, CA: ABC-CLIO, 2009.

Leeming, David Adams, and Jake Page. *Goddess: Myths of the Female Divine.* New York: Oxford University Press, 1996.

Lehner, Ernst, and Johanna Lehner. *Folklore and Symbolism of Flowers, Plants and Trees.* New York: Tudor Publishing Company, 1960.

Lempriere, John. *Bibliotheca Classica: Or, A Dictionary of All the Principal Names and Terms Relating to the Geography, Topography, History, Literature, and Mythology of Antiquity and of the Ancients: With a Chronological Table.* Philadelphia: J. B. Lippincott, 1888.

Leodhas, Sorche Nic. *By Loch and by Lin: Tales from Scottish Ballads.* New York: Open Road Media, 2014.

Leonardus, Camillus. *The Mirror of Stones: In Which the Nature, Generation, Properties, Virtues and Various Species of More than 200 Different Jewels, Precious and Rare Stones, Are Distinctly Described. Also Certain and Infallible Rules to Know the Good from the Bad, How to Prove Their Genuineness, and to Distinguish the Real | From Counterfeits. Extracted from the Works of Aristotle, Pliny, Isiodorus, Diony-*

sius Alexandrinus, Albertus Magnus, &c. By Camillus Leonardus, M.D. A Treatise of Infinite Use, Not Only to Jewellers, Lapidaries, and Merchants Who Trade in Them, But to the Nobility and Gentry, Who Purchase Them Either for Curiosity, Use or Ornament. Dedicated by the Author to Caesar Borgia. London: Printed for J. Freeman, 1750.

L'Epine, Ernest Louis Victor Jules. The Days of Chivalry: The Legend of Croquemitaine. N.pag.: Library of Alexandria, 2014.

Leviton, Richard. The Gods in Their Cities: Geomantic Locales of the Ray Masters and Great White Brotherhood, and How to Interact with Them. Lincoln, NE: iUniverse, 2006.

Lewis, James R., and Evelyn Dorothy Oliver. The Dream Encyclopedia. Detroit, MI: Visible Ink Press, 2009.

Lewsey, Jonathan. Who's Who and What's What in Wagner. New York: Routledge, 2017.

Ley, Willy. Exotic Zoology. New York: Viking Press, 1959.

A Library of Famous Fiction Embracing the Nine Standard Masterpieces of Imaginative Literature (Unabridged). New York: J.B. Ford and Company, 1876.

Liddell, Mark Harvey. The Elizabethan Shakespeare: Tragedy of Macbeth. New York: Doubleday, Page, and Company, 1903.

Lightman, Alan. The Accidental Universe: The World You Thought You Knew. New York: Pantheon Books, 2014.

Lim, Johnson T. K. The Sin of Moses and the Staff of God: A Narrative Approach. Assen, Netherlands: Uitgeverij Van Gorcum, 1997.

Lindow, John. Handbook of Norse Mythology. Santa Barbara, CA: ABC-CLIO, 2001.

Lindow, John. Norse Mythology: A Guide to Gods, Heroes, Rituals, and Beliefs. Oxford: Oxford University Press, 2011.

Lindsay, Dennis. Giants, Fallen Angels, and the Return of the Nephilim: Ancient Secrets to Prepare for the Coming Days. Shippensburg, PA: Destiny Image Publishers, 2018.

Littleton, C. Scott, editor. Gods, Goddesses, and Mythology, Volume 4. New York: Marshall Cavendish, 2005.

Littleton, C. Scott, editor. Gods, Goddesses, and Mythology, Volume 8. New York: Marshall Cavendish, 2005.

Littleton, C. Scott, editor. Gods, Goddesses, and Mythology, Volume 11. New York: Marshall Cavendish, 2005.

Loar, Julie. Goddesses for Every Day: Exploring the Wisdom and Power of the Divine. Novato, CA: New World Library, 2010.

Lochtefeld, James G. The Illustrated Encyclopedia of Hinduism: A–M. New York: Rossen, 2002.

Lockyer, Herbert. All the Miracles of the Bible. Grand Rapids, MI: Zondervan, 1961.

Loh-Hagan, Virginia. Hades. Ann Arbor, MI: Cherry Lake, 2017.

Lomatuway'ma, Michael. Earth Fire: A Hopi Legend of the Sunset Crater Eruption. Walnut, CA: Northland Press, 1987.

London and Edinburgh Philosophical Magazine and Journal of Science, Volume V (July–December 1834).

Lonnrot. The Kalevala: The Epic Poem of Finland.

Translated by John Martin Crawford (1888). Woodstock: Devoted Publishing, 2016.

Loomis, Roger Sherman. Celtic Myth and Arthurian Romance. Chicago: Chicago Review Press, 2005.

Loomis, Roger Sherman. The Grail: From Celtic Myth to Christian Symbol. Princeton, NJ: Princeton University Press, 1963.

Loptson, Dagulf. Playing with Fire: An Exploration of Loki Laufeyjarson (Epub). Morrisville: Lulu Press, 2015.

Lucian (of Samosata). The Works of Lucian, Volume 2. London: T. Cadell, 1781.

Lurker, Manfred. Dictionary of Gods and Goddesses, Devils and Demons. London: Routledge Kegan and Paul, 1987.

Lutgendorf, Philip. Hanuman's Tale: The Messages of a Divine Monkey. Oxford: Oxford University Press, 2007.

Maberry, Jonathan, and David F. Kramer. They Bite: Endless Cravings of Supernatural Predators. New York: Citadel Press, 2009.

Mabie, Hamilton Wright, editor. Young Folks' Treasury: Myths and Legendary Heroes, Volume II. New York: University Society, 1909.

Macaulay, Thomas Babington. Miscellaneous Essays and Lays of Ancient Rome. New York: Cosimo, 2005.

Macbain, Alexander. Celtic Mythology and Religion. New York: Cosimo, 2005.

MacCulloch, John Arnott. Celtic Mythology. Mineola, NY: Courier, 2004.

MacCulloch, John Arnott. The Childhood of Fiction: A Study of Folk Tales and Primitive Thought. New York: E. P. Dutton, 1905.

MacCulloch, John Arnott, Jan Machal, and Louis Herbert Gray. Celtic Mythology, Volume 3. Boston: Marshall Jones Company, 1918.

Macdonald, Fiona. Heroes, Gods, and Monsters of Celtic Mythology. Brighton: Salariya Book Company, 2009.

Macdowall, M. W. Asgard and the Gods, Tales and Traditions of Our Northern Ancestors, Adapted from the Work of W. Wagner by M. W. Macdowall and edited by W. S. W. Anson. London: W. Swan Sonnenschein & Allen, 1884.

Macdowall, Maria Wilhelmina. Epics and Romances of the Middle Ages, Adapted from the Work of W. Wagner by M. W. Macdowall, edited by W. S. W. Anson. London: W. Swan Sonnenschein and Company, 1883.

Mack, Carol K., and Dinah Mack. A Field Guide to Demons, Fairies, Fallen Angels, and Other Subversive Spirits. New York: Henry Holt, 1998.

Mackenzie, Donald A. Teutonic Myth and Legend. London: Gresham Publishing Company, 1912.

Mackenzie, Donald Alexander. Myths from Melanesia and Indonesia. London: Gresham Publishing Company, 1930.

MacKillop, James. Dictionary of Celtic Mythology. London: Oxford University Press, 1998.

MacKillop, James. Myths and Legends of the Celts. London: Penguin, 2006.

Maginn, William. Miscellanies: Prose and Verse, Volume 2. London: S. Low, Marston, Searle, and Rivington, 1885.

Bibliography

Magnusen, Finn. "The Edda-Doctrine and Its Origin." *Foreign Quarterly Review* 2 (1828).

Mahusay, Nancy. *The History of Redemption*. Maitland, FL: Xulon Press, 2007.

Malinowski, Sharon. *The Gale Encyclopedia of Native American Tribes: Northeast, Southeast, Caribbean*, Volume 1. Detroit, MI: Gale, 1998.

Malory, Thomas. *La Mort D'Arthure: The History of King Arthur and the Knights of the Round Table*, Volume 1. London: John Russell Smith, 1865.

Malory, Thomas, and William Caxton. *Le Morte Darthur: Sir Thomas Malory's Book of King Arthur and of His Noble Knights of the Round Table. The Text of Caxton*. London: Macmillan, 1899.

Malotki, Ekkehart, and Ken Gary. *Hopi Stories of Witchcraft, Shamanism, and Magic*. Lincoln: University of Nebraska Press, 2001.

Mancing, Howard. *The Cervantes Encyclopedia: A–K*. Westport, CT: Greenwood Publishing Group, 2004.

Mandzuka, Zlatko. *Demystifying the Odyssey*. Bloomington, IN: Author-House, 2013.

Mani, Chandra Mauli. *Memorable Characters from the Ramayana and the Mahabharata*. New Delhi: Northern Book Centre, 2009.

Marballi, G. K. *Journey through the Bhagavad Gita—A Modern Commentary with Word-to-Word Sanskrit-English Translation*. Raleigh: Lulu.com, 2013.

March, Jennifer R. *Dictionary of Classical Mythology*. Oxford: Oxbow Books, 2014.

Martinez, Susan B. *The Lost History of the Little People: Their Spiritually Advanced Civilizations Around the World*. New York: Simon & Schuster, 2013.

Marzolph, Ulrich, editor. *The Arabian Nights in Transnational Perspective*. Detroit, MI: Wayne State University Press, 2007.

Mason, Andrew. *Rasa Shastra: The Hidden Art of Medical Alchemy*. London: Singing Dragon, 2014.

Mattfeld, Walter. *The Garden of Eden Myth: Its Pre-Biblical Origin in Mesopotamian Myths*. Raleigh: Lulu.com: 2010.

Matthews, John, and Caitlin Matthews. *The Complete King Arthur: Many Faces, One Hero*. New York: Simon & Schuster, 2017.

Matyszak, Philip. *The Greek and Roman Myths: A Guide to the Classical Stories*. London: Thames & Hudson, 2010.

Mayer, Fanny Hagin. *The Yanagita Kunio Guide to the Japanese Folk Tale*. Bloomington, IN: Indiana University Press, 1986.

McCasland, S. Vernon. "Gabriel's Trumpet." *Journal of Bible and Religion* 11–12 (1943): 159–61.

McClintock, John, and James Strong. *Cyclopedia of Biblical, Theological, and Ecclesiastical Literature: Supplement*, Volume 1. New York: Harper and Brothers, 1885.

McClintock, John, and James Strong. *Cyclopaedia of Biblical, Theological, and Ecclesiastical Literature*, Volume 9. New York: Harper and Brothers, 1891.

McColman, Carl. *The Complete Idiot's Guide to Celtic Wisdom*. Indianapolis: Alpha, 2003.

McConnell, Winder, Werner Wunderlich, Frank Gentry, and Ulrich Mueller, editors. *The Nibelungen Tradition: An Encyclopedia*. New York: Routledge, 2013.

McLellan, Alec. *The Secret of the Spear: The Mystery of the Spear of Longinus*. London: Souvenir Press, 1988.

McNamara, Kenneth J. *The Star-Crossed Stone: The Secret Life, Myths, and History of a Fascinating Fossil*. Chicago: University of Chicago Press, 2010.

Meltzer, Peter E. *The Thinker's Thesaurus: Sophisticated Alternatives to Common Words (Expanded Third Edition)*. New York: W. W. Norton, 2015.

Melville, Charles, and Gabrielle van den Berg, editors. *Shahnama Studies II: The Reception of Firdausi's Shahnama*. Leiden, Netherlands: Brill, 2013.

Menon, Ramesh. *The Mahabharata: A Modern Rendering*, Volume 1. New York: iUniverse, 2006.

Menon, Ramesh. *The Mahabharata: A Modern Rendering*, Volume 2. New York: iUniverse, 2006.

Menon, Ramesh. *The Ramayana: A Modern Retelling of the Great Indian Epic*. New York: North Point Press, 2004.

Menoni, Burton. *Kings of Greek Mythology*. Raleigh: Lulu.com, 2016.

Mercatante, Anthony S. *Who's Who in Egyptian Mythology*. New York: Barnes & Noble, 1995.

Mercer, Henry C. *Light and Fire Making*. Philadelphia: Press of MacCalla and Company, 1898.

Merrick, James Lyman, and Muḥammad Baqir ibn Muḥammad Taqi Majlisi. *Hayat al-qulub*. Boston: Phillips, Sampson, 1850.

Mettinger, Tryggve N. D. *The Eden Narrative: A Literary and Religio-historical Study of Genesis 2–3*. Winona Lake, IN: Eisenbrauns, 2007.

Metzner, Ralph. *Green Psychology: Transforming Our Relationship to the Earth*. New York: Simon & Schuster, 1999.

Meulenbeld, Gerrit Jan, and I. Julia Leslie, editors. *Medical Literature from India, Sri Lanka, and Tibet*. Leiden, Netherlands: Brill, 1991.

Meyer, Johann Jakob. *Sexual Life in Ancient India: A Study in the Comparative History of Indian Culture*. Delhi: Motilal Banarsidass, 1971.

Miller, Dean A. *The Epic Hero*. Baltimore: Johns Hopkins University Press, 2000.

Millingen, James. *Ancient Unedited Monuments Illustrated and Explained by James Millingen: Statues, Busts, Bas-Reliefs, and Other Remains of Grecian art, from Collections in Various Countries, Illustrated and Explained by James Millingen*, Volume 2. London: J. Millingen, 1826.

Minnis, Natalie. *Chile Insight Guide*. Maspeth, NY: Pangenscheidt Publishing Group, 2002.

Molnar, Adam. *Weather-Magic in Inner Asia*. Bloomington: Indiana University, Research Institute for Inner Asian Studies, 1994.

Monaghan, Patricia. *The Encyclopedia of Celtic Mythology and Folklore*. New York: Infobase Publishing, 2005.

Monger, George. *Marriage Customs of the World: From Henna to Honeymoons*. Santa Barbara, CA: ABC-CLIO, 2004.

Monod, G. H. *Women's Wiles: Cambodian Legends*. Holmes Beach, FL: DatAsia, 2013.

Moor, Edward. *The Hindu Pantheon*. London: Bensley, 1810.

Moorey, Teresa. *The Fairy Bible: The Definitive Guide to the World of Fairies*. New York: Sterling, 2008.

Morewedge, Rosmarie Thee, editor. *The Role of Woman in Middle Ages.* Albany: State University of New York Press, 1975.

Morford, Mark P. O., and Robert J. Lenardon. *Classical Mythology.* Oxford: Oxford University Press, 1999.

Morison, Samuel Eliot. *The European Discovery of America: The Southern Voyages 1492–1616.* New York: Oxford University Press, 1974.

Morris, Charles, editor. *New Universal Graphic Dictionary of the English Language, Self-pronouncing: Based on the Foundation Laid by Noah Webster and Other Lexicographers.* Chicago: John C. Winston Company, 1922.

Morris, Neil. *Moses: A Life in Pictures.* Brighton: Salariya Publishers, 2004.

Morris, William. *The Story of Sigurd the Volsung and the Fall of the Niblungs.* London: Ellis and White, 1877.

Morris, William, and Eirikr Magnusson. *The Saga Library: The Stories of the Kings of Norway Called the Round of the World (Heimskringla), by Snorri Sturluson,* Volume 2. London: B. Quaritch, 1895.

Morse, Ruth. *The Medieval Medea.* Cambridge: Boydell & Brewer, 1996.

Mountain, Harry. *The Celtic Encyclopedia,* Volume 2. Parkland, FL: Universal-Publishers, 1998.

Mountain, Harry. *The Celtic Encyclopedia,* Volume 3. Parkland, FL: Universal-Publishers, 1998.

Mountain, Harry. *The Celtic Encyclopedia,* Volume 4. Parkland, FL: Universal-Publishers, 1998.

Mountfort, Paul Rhys. *Ogam: The Celtic Oracle of the Trees: Understanding, Casting, and Interpreting the Ancient Druidic Alphabet.* Rochester, VT: Inner Traditions / Bear & Co., 2002.

Mouse, Anon E. *Ilmarinen Forges the Sampo—A Legend from Finland: Baba Indaba Children's Stories.* London: Abela Publishing, 2016.

Mouse, Anon E. *The Saga of Cormac the Skald—A Norse & Viking Saga.* London: Abela Publishing, 2019.

Mueller, Melissa. *Objects as Actors: Props and the Poetics of Performance in Greek Tragedy.* Chicago: University of Chicago Press, 2016.

Muljana, Slamet. *A Story of Majapahit.* Singapore: Singapore University Press, 1976.

Mullally, Erin. *Hrethel's Heirloom: Kinship, Succession, and Weaponry in Beowulf.* Newark: University of Delaware, 2005.

Murgatroyd, Paul. *Mythical Monsters in Classical Literature.* New York: Bloomsbury, 2013.

Murphy-Hiscock, Arin. *The Way of the Hedge Witch: Rituals and Spells for Hearth and Home.* New York: Simon & Schuster, 2009.

Murray, John. *Classical Manual: Or, A Mythological, Historical, and Geographical Commentary on Pope's Homer, and Dryden's Æneid of Virgil, with a Copious Index.* London: Longman, Rees, Orme, Brown, and Green, 1827.

Murty, Sudha. *The Serpent's Revenge: Unusual Tales from the Mahabharata.* London: Penguin, 2016.

Naddaf, Gerard. *The Greek Concept of Nature.* Albany: State University of New York Press, 2005.

Nagayama, Kokan. *The Connoisseur's Book of Japanese Swords.* Tokyo: Kodansha International, 1995.

Nahm, Oliver. *Dealing with Death: A Search for Cross-Cultural and Time-Transcending Similarities.* Zurich: LIT Verlag Münster, 2017.

Napier, Gordon. *Pocket A–Z of the Knights Templar: A Guide to Their History and Legacy.* Mt. Pleasant: The History Press, 2017.

Narasimhan, Chakravarthi V. *The Mahabharata: An English Version Based on Selected Verses.* Calcutta: Oxford Book, 1965.

Nardo, Don. *Greek and Roman Mythology.* Detroit, MI: Green Haven Press, 2009.

Narlikar, Amrita, and Aruna Narlikar. *Bargaining with a Rising India: Lessons from the Mahabharata.* Oxford: Oxford University Press, 2014.

Nath, Samir. *Encyclopaedic Dictionary of Buddhism,* Volume 3. New Delhi: Sarup & Sons, 1998.

Netton, Ian Richard, editor. *Encyclopedia of Islamic Civilization and Religion.* New York: Routledge, 2008.

New and Enlarged Dictionary of the English Language: The Pronunciation Marked and Modelled, with Important Variations, on the Plan of Walker. Preceded by a Complete Englisyh Grammar Stereo-type Edition. London: Isaac, Tuckey, and Company, 1863.

Newman, Jacqueline M. *Food Culture in China.* Westport, CT: Greenwood Publishing Group, 2004.

Newman, William R., and Lawrence M. Principe. *Alchemy Tried in the Fire: Starkey, Boyle, and the Fate of Helmontian Chymistry.* Chicago: University of Chicago Press, 2005.

Nielsen, Greg, and Joseph Polansky. *Pendulum Power: A Mystery You Can See, a Power You Can Feel.* Rochester, VT: Destiny Books, 1977.

Nigg, Joe. *A Guide to the Imaginary Birds of the World.* Cambridge, MA: Apple-wood Books, 1984.

Niles, Doug. *Dragons: The Myths, Legends, and Lore.* Avon, MA: Adams Media, 2013.

Nolan, Edward Peter. *Now through a Glass Darkly: Specular Images of Being and Knowing from Virgil to Chaucer.* Ann Arbor: University of Michigan Press, 1990.

Norroena Society. *The Asatru Edda: Sacred Lore of the North.* Bloomington, IN: iUniverse, 2009.

Norroena Society. *The Satr Edda: Sacred Lore of the North.* Bloomington, IN: iUniverse, 2009.

Nosselt, Friedrich August. *Mythology Greek and Roman, translated by Mrs. A. W. Hall.* London: Kerby and Endean, 1885.

Numismatic and Antiquarian Society of Philadelphia. *Proceedings of the Numismatic and Antiquarian Society of Philadelphia for the Years 1899–1901.* Philadelphia: The Society, 1902.

Nye. *Encyclopedia of Ancient and Forbidden Secrets.* Jakarta: Bukupedia, 2000.

O hOgain, Daithi. *Myth, Legend and Romance: An Encyclopaedia of the Irish Folk Tradition.* Upper Saddle River, NJ: Prentice Hall Press, 1991.

O'Bryan, John. *A History of Weapons: Crossbows, Caltrops, Catapults & Lots of Other Things That Can Seriously Mess You Up.* San Francisco: Chronicle Books, 2013.

Oehlenschlager, Adam. *Gods of the North.* London: William Pickering, 1845.

Bibliography

O'Farrell, Padraic. *Ancient Irish Legends: The Best-Loved and Most Famous Tales of Ancient Ireland.* Dublin: Gill & Macmillan, 2001.

O'Flaherty, Wendy Doniger. *Hindu Myths: A Sourcebook Translated from the Sanskrit.* New Delhi: Penguin Books India, 1994.

Ogden, Daniel. *Drakon: Dragon Myth and Serpent Cult in the Greek and Roman Worlds.* Oxford: Oxford University Press, 2013.

Olrik, Axel. *The Heroic Legends of Denmark,* Volume 4. New York: American Scandinavian Society, 1919.

Olsen, Karin E., and L. A. J. R. Houwen, editors. *Monsters and the Monstrous in Medieval Northwest Europe.* Leuven, Belgium: Peeters, 2001.

Olson, Oscar Ludvig. "The Relation of the Hrolfs Saga Fraka and the Bjarkarimur to Beowulf." *Scandinavian Studies* 3 (1916): 1–104.

Oppert, Gustav Salomon. *On the Weapons, Army Organisation, and Political Maxims of the Ancient Hindus.* London: Messrs, Trubner, and Company, 1880.

Orchard, Andy. *A Critical Companion to Beowulf.* Rochester, NY: Boydell & Brewer, 2003.

Orchard, Andy. *Dictionary of Norse Myth and Legend.* London: Cassell, 1997.

O'Reilly, John Boyle. *Ethics of Boxing and Manly Sport.* Boston: Ticknor and Company, 1888.

Orel, Harold, editor. *Irish History and Culture: Aspects of a People's Heritage.* Lawrence: University Press of Kansas, 1976.

Orme, Robert. *Historical Fragments of the Mogul Empire, of the Morattoes, and of the English Concerns in Indostan, from the year M,DC,LIX [by R. Orme]. [Enlarged]. To Which Is Prefixed an Account of the Life of the Author.* London: F. Wingrave, 1805.

Orr, Tamra. *Apollo.* Hockessin: Mitchell Lane Publishers, 2009.

Osborne, Mary Pope. *Tales from the Odyssey,* Part 1. Logan, IA: Perfection Learning, 2003.

Osborne, T., C. Hitch, L. Hawes, A. Miller, J. Rivington, S. Crowder, P. Davey, B. Law, T. Longman, C. Ware, and S. Bladen. *A Complete History of the Arabs: From the Birth of Mohammed to the Reduction of Baghdad; with the Life of Mohammed,* Volume 1. London: Osborne, Hitch, Hawes, Miller, Rivington, Crowder, Davey, Law, Longman, Ware, and Bladen, 1761.

O'Sheridan, Mary Grant. *Gaelic Folk Tales: A Supplementary Reader.* Chicago: William F. Roberts and Company, 1911.

Oswald, Eugene. *The Legend of Fair Helen as Told by Homer, Goethe, and Others: A Study,* Volume 10. London: John Murray, 1905.

Ovid. *The Essential Metamorphoses.* Translated by Stanley Lombardo. Indianapolis, IN: Hackett, 2011.

Owen, Michael. *The Maya Book of Life: Understanding the Xultun Tarot.* Tauranga: Kahurangi Press, 2011.

Padel, Oliver James. *Arthur in Medieval Welsh Literature.* Cardiff: University of Wales Press, 2013.

Palmatier, Robert Allen. *Food: A Dictionary of Literal and Nonliteral Terms.* Westport, CT: Greenwood Publishing Group, 2000.

Palmer, Robert Everett Allen. *Rome and Carthage at Peace.* Stuttgart: F. Steiner, 1997.

Palsson, Herman, and Paul Edwards, translators. *Seven Viking Romances.* London: Penguin UK, 1995.

Paracelsus. *Hermetic Medicine and Hermetic Philosophy,* Volume 2. Edited by Lauron William de Laurence. Chicago: De Laurence, Scott & Company, 1910.

Parada, Carlos. *Genealogic Guide to Greek Mythology,* Volume 107 of *Studies in Mediterranean Archaeology.* Uppsala: Astrom, 1993.

Parker, Janet. *Mythology: Myths, Legends and Fantasies.* Victoria, Australia: Global Book, 2003.

Parmeshwaranand. *Encyclopaedic Dictionary of Puranas.* New Delhi: Sarup & Sons, 2001.

Pate, Alan Scott. *Ningyo: The Art of the Japanese Doll.* North Clarendon, VT: Tuttle, 2013.

Patrick, David, editor. *Chamber's Encyclopædia: A Dictionary of Universal Knowledge,* Volume 10. London: William and Robert Chambers, 1892.

Patton, John-Paul. *The Poet's Ogam: A Living Magical Tradition.* Raleigh: Lulu.com, 2011.

Pauley, Daniel C. *Pauley's Guide: A Dictionary of Japanese Martial Arts and Culture.* Dolores, CO: Anaguma Seizan Publications, 2009.

Pausanias. *Pausanias's Description of Greece,* Volume 5. London: Macmillan and Company, 1898.

Peake, Arthur, editor. *A Commentary on the Bible.* New York: Thomas Neilson and Sons, 1919.

Penard, A. P., and T. G. Penard. "Surinam folk-Tales." *The Journal of American Folk-lore,* Volume 7 of *Bibliographical and special series of the American Folklore Society* edited by the American Folklore Society, 239–251. Lancaster: American Folk-lore Society, 1917.

Pendergrass, Rocky. *Mythological Swords.* Raleigh: Lulu.com, 2015.

Pentikainen, Juha. *Kalevala Mythology,* revised edition. Bloomington: Indiana University Press, 1999.

Peterson, Amy T., and David J. Dunworth. *Mythology in Our Midst: A Guide to Cultural References.* Westport, CT: Greenwood Publishing Group, 2004.

Peterson, Shelley Stagg, and Larry Swartz. *Good Books Matter: How to Choose and Use Children's Literature to Help Students Grow as Readers.* Markham, Ontario: Pembroke Publishers, 2008.

Petropoulos, John C. *Greek Magic: Ancient, Medieval and Modern.* New York: Routledge, 2008.

Pickens, Rupert T. *Perceval and Gawain in Dark Mirrors: Reflection and Reflexivity in Chretien del Graal.* Jefferson, NC: McFarland, 2014.

Pickering, William. *Beowulf: An Epic Poem Translated from the Anglo-Saxon into English Verse by Diedrich Wackerbarth.* London: William Pickering, 1849.

Pickover, Clifford A. *The Book of Black: Black Holes, Black Death, Black Forest Cake and Other Dark Sides of Life.* Mineola, NY: Calla, 2013.

Pinkham, Mark Amaru. *Guardians of the Holy Grail.* Kempton, IL: Adventures Unlimited Press, 2004.

Plato. *The Republic,* Volume 1. Introduction by David Arthur Rees. Cambridge: Cambridge University Press, 1963.

Polehampton, Edward. *The Gallery of Nature and Art; Or, a Tour through Creation and Science,* Volume 6. London: N. rose, 1821.

Pope, Paul Russel. *German Composition: With Notes*

and Vocabularies. New York: Henry Holt and Company, 1908.

Porteous, Alexander. *The Forest in Folklore and Mythology.* Mineola, NY: Dover, 2013.

Portnoy, Phyllis. *The Remnant: Essays on a Theme in Old English Verse.* London: Runetree, 2006.

Principe, Lawrence. *The Secrets of Alchemy.* Chicago: University of Chicago Press, 2013.

Principe, Lawrence M. *The Aspiring Adept: Robert Boyle and His Alchemical Quest.* Princeton, NJ: Princeton University Press, 2005.

Pritchard, James B., and Daniel E. Fleming, editors. *The Ancient Near East: An Anthology of Texts and Pictures.* Princeton, NJ: Princeton University Press, 2011.

Proceedings: Irish MSS. Series. Volume 1, Part 1 [only]. Dublin: M. H. Gill, 1870.

Puhvel, Martin. *Beowulf and the Celtic Tradition.* Waterloo, Ontario: Wilfrid Laurier University Press, 2010.

Pyle, Howard. *The Story of King Arthur and His Knights.* New York: Penguin, 2006.

Pyle, Howard. *The Story of Sir Launcelot and His Companions.* New York: Charles Scribner's Sons, 1907.

Quincy, John. *Lexicon Physico-medicum: Or, A New Medicinal Dictionary. Explaining the Difficult Terms Used in the Several Branches of the Profession and in Such Parts of Natural Philosophy Are the Introductory thereto with an Account of the Things Signified by Such Terms by the Author and Collected from the Most Eminent Author.* London: T. Longman, 1794.

Raff, Jeffrey. *The Wedding of Sophia: The Divine Feminine in Psychoidal Alchemy.* Berwick, ME: Nicolas-Hays, 2003.

Rajagopalachari, Chakravarti. *Mahabharata.* New Delhi: Diamond Pocket Books (P), 1972.

Ralston, William Ralston Shedden. *Russian Folk-Tales.* New York: R. Worthington, 1880.

Ralston, William Ralston Shedden. *Songs of the Russian People, as Illustrative of Slavonic Mythology and Rustic Social Life.* London: Ellis & Green, 1872.

Ramsey, Syed. *Tools of War: History of Weapons in Ancient Times.* New Delhi: Vij Books India, 2016.

Randolph, Joanne. *Norse Myths and Legends.* New York: Cavendish Square Publishing, 2017.

Rao, Shanta Rameshwar. *The Mahabharata* (Illustrated). Hyderabad: Orient Longman, 1985.

Rasums, Anderson Bjorn. *Norroena, the History and Romance of Northern Europe: A Library of Supreme Classics Printed in Complete Form,* Volume 12. London: Norroena Society, 1906.

Ravenscroft, Trevor. *Spear of Destiny.* Boston: Weiser Books, 1973.

Reddall, Henry Frederic. *Fact, Fancy, and Fable: A New Handbook for Ready Reference on Subjects Commonly Omitted from Cyclopaedias; Comprising Personal Sobriquets, Familiar Phrases, Popular Appellations, Geographical Nicknames, Literary Pseudonyms, Mythological Characters, Red-Letter Days, Political Slang, Contractions and Abbreviations, Technical Terms Foreign Words and Phrases, and Americanisms.* Chicago: A. C. McClurg, 1892.

Redfern, Nick, and Brad Steiger. *The Zombie Book: The Encyclopedia of the Living Dead.* Detroit, MI: Visible Ink Press, 2014.

Regardie, Israel. *Philosopher's Stone: Spiritual Alchemy, Psychology, and Ritual Magic.* St. Paul, MN: Llewellyn Worldwide, 2013.

Regula, DeTraci. *The Mysteries of Isis: Her Worship and Magick.* St. Paul, MN: Llewellyn Worldwide, 1995.

Remler, Pat. *Egyptian Mythology, A to Z.* New York: Infobase Publishing, 2010.

Renard, John. *Islam and the Heroic Image: Themes in Literature and the Visual Arts.* Macon: Mercer University Press, 1999.

Rengarajan, T. *Glossary of Hinduism.* New Delhi: Oxford and IBH Publishing Company, 1999.

Reno, Frank D. *Arthurian Figures of History and Legend: A Biographical Dictionary.* Jefferson, NC: McFarland, 2010.

Reuter, Thomas, editor. *Sharing the Earth, Dividing the Land: Land and Territory in the Austronesian World.* Canberra: Australian National University Press, 2006.

Rhys, Sir John. *Celtic Folklore: Welsh and Manx,* Volume 1. Charleston: Forgotten Books, 1983.

Rickert, Edith. *Early English Romances in Verse.* London: Chatto & Windus, 1908.

Ridpath, Ian. *Star Tales.* Cambridge: James Clarke & Company, 1988.

Rigoglioso, Marguerite. *The Cult of Divine Birth in Ancient Greece.* New York: Springer, 2009.

Rimer, J. Thomas. *Modern Japanese Fiction and Its Traditions: An Introduction.* Princeton, NJ: Princeton University Press, 2014.

Roberts, Helene E., editor. *Encyclopedia of Comparative Iconography: Themes Depicted in Works of Art.* Chicago: Routledge, 2013.

Roberts, Jeremy. *Japanese Mythology A to Z.* New York: Infobase Publishing, 2009.

Roberts, Morgan J. *Norse Gods and Heroes.* Dubuque, IA: Friedman Group, 1994.

Roberts, Wess. *Leadership Secrets of Attila the Hun.* New York: Warner Books, 2007.

Robinson, William. *The Life of Saint Dunstan.* London: G. Coventry, 1844.

Roe, Edward Thomas, Le Roy Hooker, and Thomas W. Handford, editors. *The New American Encyclopedic Dictionary: An Exhaustive Dictionary of the English Language, Practical and Comprehensive; Giving the Fullest Definition (Encyclopedic in Detail), the Origin, Pronunciation and Use of Words,* Volume 1. New York: J.A. Hill, 1907.

Roland, James. *Frightful Ghost Ships.* Minneapolis: Lerner, 2017.

Rolfe, William J., editor. *Tragedy of Macbeth.* New York: Harper and Brothers, 1892.

Rolleston, Thomas William. *Myths & Legends of the Celtic Race.* London: Constable, 1911.

Roman, Luke, and Monica Roman. *Encyclopedia of Greek and Roman Mythology.* New York: Infobase, 2010.

Room, Adrian. *Who's Who in Classical Mythology.* New York: Random House Value Publishing, 2003.

Rooth, Brigitta Anna. *Loki in Scandinavian Mythology.* Lund: C. W. K. Gleerup, 1961.

Bibliography

Rose, Carol. *Giants, Monsters, and Dragons: An Encyclopedia of Folklore, Legend, and Myth (in English)*. New York: W. W. Norton, 2001.

Rose, Carol. *Spirits, Fairies, Leprechauns, and Goblins: An Encyclopedia*. New York: W. W. Norton, 1996.

Rosen, Brenda. *The Mythical Creatures Bible: The Definitive Guide to Legendary Beings*. New York: Sterling Publishing Company, 2009.

Rosenberg, Donna. *World Mythology: An Anthology of the Great Myths and Epics*. Chicago: National Textbook Company, 1994.

Rosenberg, Marvin. *The Masks of Anthony and Cleopatra*. Newark: University of Delaware Press, 2006.

Ross, Margaret Clunies. *Prolonged Echoes: The Myths*. Odense: University Press of Southern Denmark, 1994.

Ross, Val. *You Can't Read This: Forbidden Books, Lost Writing, Mistranslations, and Codes*. Toronto: Tundra Books, 2009.

Rossel, Sven Hakon. *Hans Christian Andersen: Danish Writer and Citizen of the World*. Amsterdam: Rodopi, 1996.

Rossignol, Rosalyn. *Critical Companion to Chaucer: A Literary Reference to His Life and Work*. New York: Infobase, 2006.

Rough Guides. *The Rough Guide to Sri Lanka*. New York: Penguin, 2015.

Roy, Pratap Chandra. *The Mahabharata*, Volumes 8–11. Calcutta: Bharata Press, 1889.

Royal Society of Antiquaries of Ireland. *Journal of the Royal Society of Antiquaries of Ireland*, Volumes 72–73. Dublin, Ireland: The Society, 1942.

Ruland, Martin. *Lexicon Alchemiae*. Frankfurt: Johannem Andream and Wolfgangi, 1661.

Ryan, William Francis. *The Bathhouse at Midnight: An Historical Survey of Magic and Divination in Russia*. University Park: Pennsylvania State University Press, 1999.

Rydberg, Viktor. *Norroena: The History and Romance of Northern Europe*, Volume 3. London: Norroena Society, 1906.

Rydberg, Viktor. *Teutonic Mythology*, Volume 1 of 3: *Gods and Goddesses of the Northland*. N.pag.: Library of Alexandria, 1907.

Rydberg, Viktor. *Teutonic Mythology*. London: Swan Sonnenschein and Company, 1889.

Rydberg, Viktor, Rasmus Björn Anderson, and James William Buel. *Teutonic Mythology: Gods and Goddesses of the Northland*, Volume 2. London: Norroena Society, 1906.

Ryken, Leland, James C. Wilhoit, and Tremper Longman III, editors. *Dictionary of Biblical Imagery*. Downers Grove, IL: InterVarsity Press, 2010. St. John, Robert. *Through Malan's Africa*. Garden City, New York: Doubleday, 1954.

Sale, George, George Psalmanazar, Archibald Bower, George Shelvocke, John Campbell, and John Swinton. *An Universal History: From the Earliest Accounts to the Present Time, Part 2*, Volume 1. London: C. Bathurst, 1780.

Salisbury and South Wales Museum. *Some Account of the Blackmore Museum*. London: Bell and Daldey, 1868.

Salo, Unto. *Ukko: The God of Thunder of the Ancient Finns and His Indo-European Family*. Washington, DC: Institute for the Study of Man, 2006.

Salverte, Eusebe. *The Occult Sciences: The Philosophy of Magic, Prodigies and Apparent Miracles*, Volume 1. London: Richard Bentley, 1846.

Samad, Ahmad. *Sulalatus Salatin (Sejarah Melayu)*. Kuala Lumpur: Dewan Bahasa dan Pustaka, 1979.

Sample, Thomas Mitchell. *The Dragon's Teeth: A Mythological Prophesy*. New York: Broadway Publishing Company, 1911.

Samuelson, Pamela. *Baby Names for the New Century*. New York: HarperCollins, 1994.

Satish, V. *Tales of Gods in Hindu Mythology*. Singapore: Partridge Publishing Singapore, 2014.

Satow, Ernest Mason. *Ancient Japanese Rituals*. London: Routledge, 2002.

Satyamayananda, Swami. *Ancient Sages*. Uttarakhand: Advaita Ashrama, 2012.

Savill, Sheila, Mary Barker, and Chris Cook. *Pears Encyclopaedia of Myths and Legends: Chapter 1. The Ancient Near and Middle East. Chapter 2. Classical Greece and Rome*. London: Pelham, 1976.

Sayce, Olive. *Exemplary Comparison from Homer to Petrarch*. Cambridge: D. S. Brewer, 2008.

Sayers, Dorothy Leigh, translator. *The Song of Roland*. Middlesex: Penguin Books, 1957.

Scatcherd. *A Dictionary of Polite Literature, Or, Fabulous History of the Heathen Gods and Illustrious Heroes*, Volume 2. London: Scatcherd and Letterman, 1804.

Schein, Seth L. *Reading the Odyssey: Selected Interpretive Essays*. Princeton, NJ: Princeton University Press, 1996.

Schwartz, Howard. *Tree of Souls: The Mythology of Judaism*. Oxford: Oxford University Press, 2006.

Scobie, Alastair. *Murder for Magic: Witchcraft in Africa*. London: Cassell, 1965.

Scull, Sarah Amelia. *Greek Mythology Systematized*. Philadelphia: Porter & Coates, 1880.

Seal, Graham. *Encyclopedia of Folk Heroes*. Santa Barbara, CA: ABC-CLIO, 2001.

Sears, Kathleen. *Mythology 101: From Gods and Goddesses to Monsters and Mortals, Your Guide to Ancient Mythology*. New York: Simon & Schuster, 2013.

Sedgefield, W. J. *Beowulf*. Manchester: Manchester University Press, 1978.

See, Sally. *The Greek Myths*. N.pag.: S&T, 2014.

Segal, Alan. *Life after Death: A History of the Afterlife in Western Religion*. New York: Crown Publishing Group, 2010.

Seigneuret, Jean-Charles. *Dictionary of Literary Themes and Motifs*, Volume 1. Westport, CT: Greenwood Publishing Group, 1988.

Selbie, John Alexander, and Louis Herbert Gray. *Encyclopædia of Religion and Ethics*, Volume 12. Edinburgh: T. & T. Clark, 1917.

Sesko, Markus. *Encyclopedia of Japanese Swords*. Raleigh: Lulu.com, 2014.

Seyffert, Oskar. *A Dictionary of Classical Antiquities, Mythology, Religion, Literature and Art, from the German of Dr. Oskar Seyffert*. London: Swan Sonnenschein, 1891.

Seymour, Thomas Day. *Life in the Homeric Age*. New York: Macmillan, 1907.

Shahan, Thomas Joseph, editor. *Myths and Legends*. Boston: Hall and Locke Company, 1902.

Shakespeare, William. *The Tragedy of Anthony and Cleopatra*. Edited by Michael Neill. Oxford: Oxford University Press, 2000.

Shama, Mahesh, P. Balla, and Prasad Verna. *Tales from the Upanishads*. New Delhi: Diamond Pocket Books, 2005.

Sharma, Arvind, editor. *Essays on the Mahabharata*. Delhi: Motilal Banarsidass, 2007.

Shepard, Leslie, Nandor Fodor, and Lewis Spence. *Encyclopedia of Occultism and Parapsychology*. Detroit, MI: Gale Research Company, 1985.

Shepard, Odell. *Lore of the Unicorn*. N.pag.: Library of Alexandria, 1985.

Sherman, Aubrey. *Vampires: The Myths, Legends, and Lore*. Avon, MA: Adams Media, 2014.

Sherman, Joseph. *Storytelling: An Encyclopedia of Mythology and Folklore*. New York: Routledge, 2008.

Shirane, Haruo, editor. *Traditional Japanese Literature: An Anthology, Beginnings to 1600*. New York: Columbia University Press, 2012.

Shirazi, Saeed. *A Concise History of Iran: From the Early Period to the Present Time*. Los Angeles: Ketab, 2017.

Sibley, J.T. *The Divine Thunderbolt: Missile of the Gods*. Philadelphia: Xlibris, 2009.

Siculus, Diodorus. *Delphi Complete Works of Diodorus Siculus (Illustrated)*. East Sussex: Delphi Classics, 2014.

Sidgwick, Frank, editor. *Old Ballads*. Cambridge: Cambridge University Press, 1908.

Sierra, Judy. *The Gruesome Guide to World Monsters*. Cambridge, MA: Candlewick Press, 2005.

Sikes, Wirt. *British Goblins: Welsh Folk Lore, Fairy Mythology, Legends and Traditions*. Boston: James R. Osgood and Company, 1881.

Simek, Rudolf. *Dictionary of Northern Mythology*. Suffolk: D. S. Brewer, 2007.

Simpson, Jacqueline, and Stephen Roud. *A Dictionary of English Folklore*. Oxford: Oxford University Press, 2000.

Simpson, Phil. *Guidebook to the Constellations: Telescopic Sights, Tales, and Myths*. New York: Springer Science and Business Media, 2012.

Sims-Williams, Patrick. *Irish Influence on Medieval Welsh Literature*. Oxford: Oxford University Press, 2011.

Singer, Isidore, and Cyrus Adler, editors. *The Jewish Encyclopedia: Leon–Moravia*, Volume 8. New York: Funk & Wagnalls, 1904.

Singh, David Emmanuel. *Sainthood and Revelatory Discourse: An Examination of the Bases for the Authority of Bayān*. Delhi: Regnum International, 2003.

Sjoestedt, Marie-Louise. *Celtic Gods and Heroes*. Mineola, NY: Dover, 2000.

Sladen, Douglas Brooke Wheelton. *Frithjof and Ingebjorg, and Other Poems*. London: Kegan Paul, Trench, 1882.

Smedley, Edward, editor. *Encyclopædia Metropolitana; or, Universal Dictionary of Knowledge, ed. by E. Smedley, Hugh J. Rose and Henry J. Rose. [With] Plates*, Volume 14. London: B. Fellowes, 1845.

Smith, Bardwell L. *Hinduism: New Essays in the History of Religions*. Leiden, Netherlands: E. J. Brill, 1976.

Smith, Benjamin Eli. *The Century Cyclopedia of Names: A Pronouncing and Etymological Dictionary of Names in Geography, Biography, Mythology, History, Ethnology, Art, Archaeology, Fiction, Etc., Etc.*, Volume 6. New York: The Century Company, 1918.

Smith, Evans Lansing. *The Hero Journey in Literature: Parables of Poesis*. Lanham, MD: University Press of America, 1997.

Smith, Evans Lansing, and Nathan Robert Brown. *The Complete Idiot's Guide to World Mythology*. New York: Penguin, 2008.

Smith, Jerry E., and George Piccard. *Secrets of the Holy Lance: The Spear of Destiny in History and Legend*. Kempton, IL: Adventures Unlimited Press, 2005.

Smith, Mark S., editor. *The Ugaritic Baal Cycle*. Leiden, Netherlands: Brill, 1994.

Smith, William. *A Classical Dictionary of Greek and Roman Biography, Mythology and Geography*. London: J. Murray, 1904.

Smith, William. *Dictionary of Greek and Roman Biography and Mythology: Abaeus–Dysponteus*. Boston: Little, Brown, 1894.

Smith, William. *Dr. William Smith's Dictionary of the Bible: Comprising Its Antiquities, Biography, Geography, and Natural History*, Volume 4. Boston: Houghton, Mifflin, 1888.

Smith, William, editor. *A Smaller Classical Mythology: With Translations from the Ancient Poets, and Questions upon the Work*. London: John Murray, 1882.

Smithmark Publishing. *Robin Hood/King Arthur's Knights*. New York: Smithmark Publishers, 1996.

Smyth, Daragh. *A Guide to Irish Mythology*. Dublin: Irish Academic Press, 1988.

Snodgrass, Adrian. *The Symbolism of the Stupa*. Ithaca, NY: South East Asian Program, Cornell University, 1985.

Sommer, Heinrich Oskar, editor. *The Vulgate Version of the Arthurian Romances: Les aventures ou la queste del Saint Graal. La mort le roi Artus*. N.pag., 1913.

Soothill, William Edward, and Lewis Hodous, editors. *A Dictionary of Chinese Buddhist Terms: With Sanskrit and English Equivalents and a Sanskrit-Pali Index*. Delhi: Motilal Banarsidass, 1977.

Sorensen, Soren. *An Index to the Names in the Mahabharata: With Short Explanations and a Concordance to the Bombay and Calcutta Editions and P. C. Roy's Translation*, Volumes 1–7. London: Williams & Norgate, 1904.

Southey, Robert. *Southey's Common-place Book*, Volume 4. London: Longman, Brown, Green and Longmans, 1851.

Spence, Lewis. *A Dictionary of Medieval Romance and Romance Writers*. London: George Routledge & Sons, 1913.

Spence, Lewis. *Legends and Romances of Brittany*. Mineola, NY: Dover, 1997.

Spence, Lewis. *The Magic Arts in Celtic Britain*. Mineola, NY: Courier, 1999.

Bibliography

Spence, Lewis. *The Minor Traditions of British Mythology.* London: Rider and Company, 1948.

Squire, Charles. *Celtic Myth and Legend.* Mineola, NY: Dover, 2003.

Srivastava, Diwaker Ikshit. *Decoding the Metaphor Mahabharata.* Mumbai: Leadstart Publishing, 2017.

St. John, Robert. *Through Malan's Africa.* Garden City, NY: Doubleday, 1954.

Staver, Ruth Johnston. *A Companion to Beowulf.* Westport, CT: Greenwood Publishing Group, 2005.

Steiger, Brand, and Sherry Hansen Steiger. *The Gale Encyclopedia of the Unusual and Unexplained.* Detroit, MI: Thomson-Gale, 2003.

Stephens, Susan A., editor. *Callimachus: The Hymns.* Oxford: Oxford University Press, 2015.

Stephenson, Paul. *Constantine: Roman Emperor, Christian Victor.* New York: Overlook Press, 2010.

Stevens, Anthony. *Ariadne's Clue: A Guide to the Symbols of Humankind.* Princeton, NJ: Princeton University Press, 2001.

Stirling, Simon Andrew. *The Grail: Relic of an Ancient Religion.* Croydon, UK: Moon Books, 2015.

Stirling, Simon Andrew. *King Arthur Conspiracy: How a Scottish Prince Became a Mythical Hero.* Stroud, UK: History Press, 2012.

Stokes, Whitley, editor. *Three Irish Glossaries; Cormac's Glossary, Codex A (from a Manuscript in the Library of the Royal Irish Academy), O'Davoren's Glossary (from a Manuscript in the Library of the British Museum), and a Glossary to the Calendar of Oingus the Culdee (from a Manuscript in the Library of Trinity College, Dublin); With a Pref. and Index by W. S.* London: Williams and Norgate, 1862.

Stoneman, Richard, Kyle Erickson, and Ian Richard Netton, editors. *The Alexander Romance in Persia and the East.* Eelde, Netherlands: Barkhuis, 2012.

Stork, Mokhtar. *A–Z Guide to the Qur'an: A Must-have Reference to Understanding the Contents of the Islamic Holy Book.* Singapore: Times Books International, 2000.

Storl, Wolf D. *The Untold History of Healing: Plant Lore and Medicinal Magic from the Stone Age to Present.* Berkeley, CA: North Atlantic Books, 2017.

Stronge, Susan, and the Victoria and Albert Museum. *Tipu's Tigers.* London: V & A Publishing, 2009.

Stuart, Leonard. *New Century Reference Library of the World's Most Important Knowledge: Complete, Thorough, Practical,* Volume 3. Cleveland: Syndicate Publishing Company, 1909.

Sturluson, Snorri. *Heimskringla: History of the Kings of Norway.* Austin: University of Texas Press, 1964.

Sturluson, Snorri. *The Prose Edda—Tales from Norse Mythology.* Mineola, NY: Dover, 2013.

Sturluson, Snorri. *The Younger Edda, Also Called Snorre's Edda of the Prose Edda: An English Version of the Foreword; the Fooling of Gylfe, the Afterword; Brage's Talk, the Afterword to Brage's Talk, and the Important Passages in the Poetical Diction (Skaldskaparmal).* Chicago: S. C. Griggs, 1879.

Stuttard, David. *Greek Mythology: A Traveler's Guide.* London: Thames & Hudson, 2016.

Stuttard, David, editor. *Looking at Medea: Essays and a Translation of Euripides' Tragedy.* London: Bloomsbury, 2014.

Subramaniam, Kamala. *Ramayana.* Mumbai: Bharatiya Vidya Bhavan, 1981.

Subramaniam, Neela. *Mahabharata for Children.* Chennai: Sura Books, 2005.

Suckling, Nigel. *The Book of the Unicorn.* New York: Overlook Press, 1998.

Sundaram, P. S. *Kamba Ramayana.* London: Penguin UK, 2002.

Sutton, Nicholas. *Religious Doctrines in the Mahabharata.* Delhi: Motilal Banarsidass, 2000.

Tagore, Sourindro Mohun. *Mani-mala; or, A Treatise on Gems,* Volume 2. Calcutta: I. C. Bose and Company, 1881.

Taillieu, Dieter, and Mary Boyce. "Haoma." *Encyclopaedia Iranica.* New York: Mazda Publishing, 2002.

Takahashi, Seigo. *A Study of the Origin of the Japanese State.* New York: Columbia University, 1917.

Tangherlini, Timothy R. *Nordic Mythologies: Interpretations, Intersections, and Institutions.* Berkeley, CA: North Pinehurst Press, 2014.

Tapovanam, Sivananda. *Souvenir, Spiritual Refresher Course.* Sri Lanka: Sivananda Tapovanam, 1981.

Tatius, Achilles. *Achilles Tatius: With an English Translation by S. Gaselle.* London: William Heinemann, 1917.

Tatlock, Jessie May. *Greek and Roman Mythology.* New York: Century Company, 1917.

Taylor, John Edward. *The Fairy Ring: A Collection of Tales and Traditions, Translated from the German by Jacob and Wilhelm Grimm.* London: John Murray, 1857.

Taylor, Paul Beekman. *Chaucer Translator.* Lanham, MD: University Press of America, 1998.

Tegnér, Esaias. *Frithiof's Saga: Or The Legend of Frithiof.* Edited by William Edward Freye; translated by H. G. and R. C. Paris: A. H. Baily and Company, 1835.

Tegnér, Esaias, and Bernhard Henrik Crusell. *Frithiof's Saga: A Legend of Ancient Norway.* Chicago: The Translator, 1908.

Telesco, Patricia. *The Kitchen Witch Companion: Simple and Sublime Culinary Magic.* New York: Citadel Press, 2005.

Terry, Patricia Ann. *Poems of the Elder Edda: Edda Sigrdrifuma: Translated by Patricia Terry with an Introduction by Charles W. Dunn.* Philadelphia: University of Pennsylvania Press, 1990.

Thadani, N. V. *The Mystery of the Mahabharata,* Volume V: *The Explanation of the Epic Part II.* Karachi: India Research Press, 1935.

Thomas, Neil. *Diu Crône and the Medieval Arthurian Cycle.* Cambridge: D. S. Brewer, 2002.

Thorpe, Benjamin. *Northern Mythology, Comprising the Principal Popular Traditions and Superstitions of Scandinavia, North Germany, and the Netherlands.* London: Lumley, 1851.

Tibbits, Charles John. *Folk-lore and Legends: Scandinavian.* Philadelphia: J. B. Lippincott, 1891.

Titchenell, Elsa Brita. *The Masks of Odin: Wisdom of the Ancient Norse.* Pasadena, CA: Theosophical University Press, 1985.

Todd, Henry Alfred, and Raymond Weeks. "Sword of

Bridge of Chreitien de Troyes and its Celtic Origin: *The Romanic Review* 4, Issue 2, pages 166-190. (1913).

Tope, Lily Rose R., and Detch P. Nonan-Mercado. *Philippines*. Tarrytown: Marshall Cavendish, 2002.

Topsell, Edward. *The History of Four-footed Beasts and Serpents and Insects,* Volume 1. Boston: Da Capo Press, 1967.

Toune, Edward Cornelius, and Graeme Mercer Adam, editors. "Inquires Answered." *Modern Culture* 5 (April–September 1897): 552–62.

Trumbull, H. Clay. *The Threshold Covenant, or The Beginning of Religious Rites.* New York: Charles Scribner's Sons, 1906.

Trzaskoma, Stephen M., R. Scott Smith, Stephen Brunet, and Thomas G. Palaima. *Anthology of Classical Myth: Primary Sources in Translation.* Indianapolis: Hackett, 2004.

Tyeer, Sarah R. bin. *The Qur'an and the Aesthetics of Premodern Arabic Prose.* London: Springer Nature, 2016.

Tylor, Edward Burnett. *Researches into the Early History of Mankind and the Development of Civilization.* Boston: Estes and Lauriat, 1878.

Urdang, Laurence. *Three Toed Sloths and Seven League Boots: A Dictionary of Numerical Expressions.* New York: Barnes and Noble Books, 1992.

Urdang, Laurence, and Frederick G. Ruffner. *Allusions: Cultural, Literary, Biblical, and Historical: A Thematic Dictionary.* Farmington Hills: Gale Research Company, 1982.

Vaidya, Chintaman Vinayak. *The Mahabharata: A Criticism.* Bombay: A. J. Combridge and Company, 1905.

Valmiki. *The Ramayana of Valmiki: An Epic of Ancient India,* Volume 1: *Balakanda.* Delhi: Motilal Banarsidass, 2007.

Valmiki, Vyasa. *Delphi Collected Sanskrit Epics* (Illustrated). Hastings: Delphi Classics, 2018.

van der Toorn, Karel, Bob Becking, and Pieter Willem van der Horst. *Dictionary of Deities and Demons in the Bible.* Grand Rapids, MI: William B. Eerdmans, 1999.

Van Scott, Miriam. *The Encyclopedia of Hell: A Comprehensive Survey of the Underworld.* New York: Thomas Dunn Books, 2015.

Varadpande, M.L. *Ancient Indian and Indo-Greek Theatre.* New Delhi: Abhinav Publications, 1981.

Varadpande, Manohar Laxman. *Mythology of Vishnu and His Incarnations.* New Delhi: Gyan Publishing House, 2009.

Venkatesananda, Swami. *The Concise Ramayana of Valmiki.* Albany: State University of New York Press, 1988.

Venu, Ji. *The Language of Kathakali: Notations of 874 Hand Gestures.* Natana Kairali: Research and Performing Centre for Traditional Arts, 2000.

Vesce, Thomas E., translator. *The Knight of the Parrot.* New York: Garland, 1986.

Vigfússon, Gudbrandur, and Frederick York Powell, editors. *Court Poetry,* Volume 2 of *Corpus Poeticvm Boreale: The Poetry of the Old Northern Tongue, from the Earliest Times to the Thirteenth Century.* Oxford: Clarendon Press, 1883.

Viltanioti, Irini-Fotini, and Anna Marmodoro. *Divine Powers in Late Antiquity.* Oxford: Oxford University Press, 2017.

Virgil. *Aeneid 6.* Indianapolis: Hackett, 2012.

Vo, Nghia M. *Legends of Vietnam: An Analysis and Retelling of 88 Tales.* Jefferson, NC: McFarland, 2014.

Vogel, Jean Philippe. *Indian Serpent-lore: Or, the Nāgas in Hindu Legend and Art.* New Delhi: Asian Educational Services, 1926.

von Wildenbruch, Ernst. *Poet Lore,* Volume 3. Philadelphia: Writer's Center, 1891.

Wade, Stuart Charles. *The Wade Genealogy: Being Some Account of the Origin of the Name, and Genealogies of the Families of Wade of Massachusetts and New Jersey. [pt. 1–4] Comp. by Stuart Charles Wade.* New York: S. C. Wade, 1900.

Wagner, Donald B. *Iron and Steel in Ancient China.* Leiden, Netherlands: Brill, 1993.

Wagner, Wilhelm. *Great Norse, Celtic and Teutonic Legends.* Mineola, NY: Dover, 2004.

Waite, Arthur Edward. *The Holy Grail, Its Legends and Symbolism: An Explanatory Survey of Their Embodiment in Romance Literature and a Critical Study of the Interpretations Placed Thereon.* London: Rider and Company, 1933.

Waley, Arthur. *The Secret History of the Mongols and Other Pieces.* Cornwall: House of Stratus, 2008.

Walker, Barbara G. *The Woman's Dictionary of Symbols and Sacred Objects.* San Francisco: HarperCollins, 1988.

Walker, Benjamin. *Hindu World: An Encyclopedic Survey of Hinduism,* Volume 1. Sydney: Allen & Unwin, 1968.

Walker, James R. *Lakota Belief and Ritual.* Lincoln: University of Nebraska Press, 1980.

Wallace, Kathryn. *Folk-lore of Ireland: Legends, Myths and Fairy Tales.* Chicago: J. S. Hyland, 1910.

Walters, H. B. "The Trident of Poseidon." *Journal of Hellenic Studies* 13 (1893): 13–20.

Warner, Charles Dudley, Hamilton Wright Mabie, Lucia Isabella Gilbert Runkle, George Henry Warner, and Edward Cornelius Towne, editors. *Library of the World's Best Literature: A–Z.* New York: R. S. Peale and J. A. Hill, 1897.

Warner, Marina, and Felipe Fernández-Armesto, editors. *World of Myths,* Volume 2. Austin: University of Texas Press, 2004.

Warren, Michelle R. *History on the Edge: Excalibur and the Borders of Britain, 1100–1300.* Minneapolis: University of Minnesota Press, 2000.

Watson, J. Carmichael. *Mesca Ulad: Mediaeval and Modern Irish.* Series 13. Dublin: Stationery Office, 1941.

Wedeck, Harry E. *Dictionary of Magic.* New York: Open Road Media, 2015.

Welch, Lynda C. *Goddess of the North: A Comprehensive Exploration of the Norse Goddesses from Antiquity to the Modern Age.* York Beach, ME: Weiser Books, 2001.

Werner, Edward Theodore Chalmers. *Myths and Legends of China.* Peking: Prabhat Prakashan, 1922.

West, Martain L. *Hesiod: Theology.* Oxford: Clarendon Press, 1966.

Bibliography

Westervelt, W. D. *Legends of Ma-Ui—A Demi God of Polynesia and of His Mother Hina.* Honolulu: Hawaiian Gazette Company, 1910.

Westmoreland, Perry L. *Ancient Greek Beliefs.* San Ysidro, CA: Lee and Vance, 2007.

Weston, Jessie Laidlay. *The Legend of Sir Lancelot Du Lac: Studies upon Its Origin, Development, and Position in the Arthurian Romantic Cycle, Issue 12.* London: David Nutt, 1901.

Whatham, Arthure E. "The Magical Girdle of Aphrodite." *Journal of Religious Psychology: Including Its Anthropological and Sociological Aspects* 3 (1909): 336–77.

White, John. *The Ancient History of the Maori, His Mythology and Traditions.* Wellington: Government Printer, 1890.

Wikimedia Foundation. *Slavic Mythology.* Würzburg: eM Publications.

Wilde, Jane Francesca Elgee. *Ancient Legends, Mystic Charms, and Superstitions of Ireland: With Sketches of the Irish Past. To Which Is Appended a Chapter on "The Ancient Race of Ireland."* Boston: Ticknor and Company, 1888.

Wilde, Lyn Webster. *On the Trail of the Women Warriors: The Amazons in Myth and History.* New York: Thomas Dunne Books, 2000.

Wilk, Stephen R. *Medusa: Solving the Mystery of the Gorgon.* Oxford: Oxford University Press, 2000.

Wilkins, William Joseph. *Hindu Mythology, Vedic and Puranic.* Calcutta: Thacker, Spink and Company, 1882.

Wilkinson, James John Garth. *The Book of Edda Called Voluspa: A Study in Its Scriptural and Spiritual Correspondences.* London: J. Speirs, 1897.

Wilkinson, Philip. *Myths & Legends: An Illustrated Guide to their Origins and Meanings.* New York: DK Publishing, 2009.

Willford, Andrew C. *Cage of Freedom: Tamil Identity and the Ethnic Fetish in Malaysia.* Ann Arbor: University of Michigan Press, 2006.

Williams, George M. *Handbook of Hindu Mythology.* Oxford: Oxford University Press, 2003.

Williams, John D. *Chambers's New Handy Volume American Encyclopaedia,* Volume 7. New York: Arundel Print, 1885.

Williams, Mark. *Ireland's Immortals: A History of the Gods of Irish Myth.* Princeton, NJ: Princeton University Press, 2016.

Williams, Robert. *A Biographical Dictionary of Eminent Welshmen: From the Earliest Times to the Present, and Including Every Name Connected with the Ancient History of Wales.* London: William Rees, 1852.

Willis, Roy G., editor. *World Mythology.* New York: Macmillan, 1993.

Wilson, Daniel. *Prehistoric Annals of Scotland.* Cambridge: Cambridge University Press, 2013.

Winkler, Lawrence. *Samurai Road.* Raleigh: LuLu.com, 2016.

Winning, W. B. "On the Aegypto-Tuscan 'Daemonology.'" In *British Magazine and Monthly Register of Religious and Ecclesiastical Information, Parochial History, and Documents Respecting the State of the Poor, Progress of Education, Etc.,* Volume 17, edited by J. G. F. and J. Rivington, 646–50. London: J. G. F. and J. Rivington, 1840.

Wood, Alice. *Of Wings and Wheels: A Synthetic Study of the Biblical Cherubim.* Berlin: Walter de Gruyter, 2008.

Wood, Juliette M. *The Holy Grail: History and Legend.* Cardiff: University of Wales Press, 2012.

Woodard, Roger D., editor. *The Cambridge Companion to Greek Mythology.* New York: Cambridge University Press, 2017.

Woodard, Roger D. *Myth, Ritual, and the Warrior in Roman and Indo-European Antiquity.* Cambridge: Cambridge University Press, 2013.

Wright, E. W. *Rustic Speech and Folk-Lore.* London: H. Milford, 1913.

Wu, Cheng'en. *Journey to the West.* Chicago: University of Chicago Press, 1984.

Wu, Cheng'en. *Monkey King's Amazing Adventures: A Journey to the West in Search of Enlightenment.* Tokyo: Tuttle, 2012.

Wu, Cheng' en, and Anthony C. Yu. *The Journey to the West,* Volume 1. Chicago: University of Chicago Press, 2012.

Wu, Cheng'en, and Anthony C. Yu. *The Journey to the West, Revised Edition, III.* Chicago: University of Chicago Press, 2012.

Wyatt, Alfred John, and Raymond Wilson Chambers, editors. *Beowulf: With the Finnsburg Fragment.* Cambridge: Cambridge University Press, 1914.

Yarshater, Ehsan. editor. *The Cambridge History of Iran,* Volume 3, Issue 1. London: Cambridge University Press, 1983.

Yarshater, Ehsan. *Encyclopædia Iranica,* Volume 13. Abingdon: Routledge & Kegan Paul, 2004.

Yeats, William Butler. *Fairy and Folk Tales of the Irish Peasantry.* London: Walter Scott, 1888.

Young, Ella. *Celtic Wonder-Tales.* Mineola, NY: Dover, 1995.

Young, Francis. *A Medieval Book of Magical Stones: The Peterborough Lapidary.* Cambridge: Texts in Early Modern Magic, 2016.

Yousof, Ghulam-Sarwar. *One Hundred and One Things Malay.* Singapore: Partridge Publishing, 2015.

Yu, Anthony C. *Journey to the West.* Chicago: University of Chicago Press, 1984.

Zakroff, Laura Tempest. *The Witch's Cauldron: The Craft, Lore & Magick of Ritual Vessels.* Woodbury, MN: Llewellyn Worldwide, 2017.

Zell-Ravenheart, Oberon, and Ash Dekirk. *A Wizard's Bestiary: A Menagerie of Myth, Magic, and Mystery.* Franklin Lakes, NJ: New Page Books, 2007.

Zhirov, N. *Atlantis: Atlantology: Basic Problems.* Honolulu: University Press of the Pacific, 1970.

Index